I0816348

THE FATIMIDS

DYNASTIES

A series of substantial narrative histories that look at the genesis of dynasties, their dynamics and the derivation of power, demonstrating that history can be seen and reflected through the dynastic process and who or what ruling dynasties believed themselves to be. It seeks to put dynasties under discussion and reflection.

Already published:

Ashoka and the Maurya Dynasty: The History and Legacy of Ancient India's Greatest Empire
COLLEEN TAYLOR SEN

The Braganzas: The Rise and Fall of the Ruling Dynasties of Portugal and Brazil, 1640–1910
MALYN NEWITT

The Fatimids: Portrait of a Dynasty
DELIA CORTESE

The Ruling Families of Rus: Clan, Family and Kingdom
CHRISTIAN RAFFENSPERGER AND DONALD OSTROWSKI

THE FATIMIDS

Portrait of a Dynasty

DELIA CORTESE

REAKTION BOOKS

To the special 'you' in my life

Published by
Reaktion Books Ltd
Unit 32, Waterside
44–48 Wharf Road
London N1 7UX, UK

www.reaktionbooks.co.uk

First published 2025

EU GPSR Authorised Representative
Logos Europe, 9 rue Nicolas Poussin, 17000, La Rochelle, France
email: contact@logoseurope.eu

Printed and bound in India by Replika Press Pvt. Ltd

A catalogue record for this book is available from the British Library

ISBN 978 1 83639 019 0

Contents

Introduction: Writing a Portrait

In the middle period of Islamic history, when empires rivalled each other in splendour as much as in power, a dynasty stood out that shone with a brilliance all of its own: the Fatimids. Known by a name derived from Fatima – the daughter of the Prophet of Islam, Muhammad – from 909 for over two and a half centuries, this dynasty of imam-caliphs exercised direct and indirect control over a vast territory that stretched from the Mediterranean to the Arabian peninsula and Central Asia. The cultural and artistic legacy that the Fatimids left behind after their demise in 1171 endures to this day. For about 15 to 20 million Shi'a Nizari Isma'ili Muslims worldwide, the Fatimid dynasty forms the genealogical bridge that links their current spiritual leader, Prince Rahim al-Hussaini Aga Khan v, the fiftieth imam, to the Prophet Muhammad, the ancestor to whom they trace back his line of authority. Today the seat of the Nizari imamate, known as Diwan of the Ismaili Imamat, is in Lisbon, Portugal. Other Muslim minorities such as the the Shi'i Isma'ili Bohras, a mercantile community with a predominant presence in the Indian subcontinent, look at the Fatimids and the brand of Islam they shaped and promoted as foundational for their historical heritage, social lives and beliefs. The Druzes, a small socio-religious community with its main presence in the Middle East, have their roots in Fatimid history. Within academia dedicated to the study of Islamic history the Fatimid period represents a chapter that, to varying degrees, most scholars touch upon. To the cognoscenti, irrespective of areas of interest or expertise, 'Fatimid' is often a byword for the Golden Age of the Islamic cultural past. Art lovers might have come across the term 'Fatimid' when visiting museums around the world. Some will have encountered the name while on a guided tour of Cairo,

Rome
SARDINIA
UMAYYAD CALIPHATE
AL-ANDALUS
Palermo
Balarm
Seville
Cordoba
Tunis
Algiers
Ashir
Kairaouan/
Mansuriyya
Tahert
Mahdiyya
Fez
Tripoli
Tarāblus
Sijilmasa
FATIMID CALIPHAT

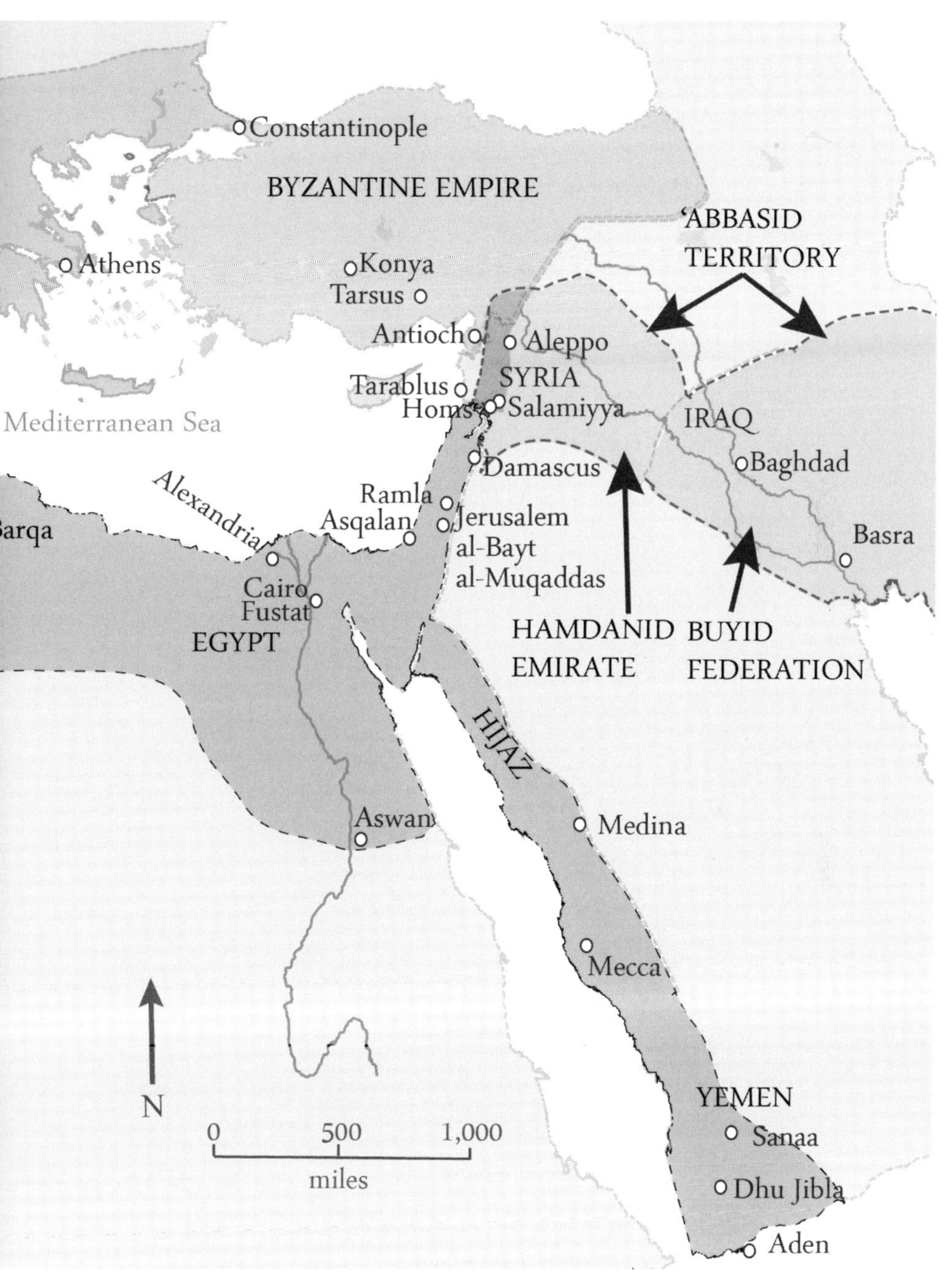

1 The Fatimid Empire, 909–1171.

the city the Fatimids founded in 969 as the capital of their empire. Others might have heard of them while spending a summer holiday in Tunisia, once part of the region where their dynastic history began. Beyond these realms, the name 'Fatimid' is unfamiliar to most or has been forgotten, having fallen off people's historical and cultural radar over time. And yet, this dynasty and its age have shaped the world in which we live in more significant and unexpected ways than we might realize. With this in mind, the aim of this book is to share with broader audiences the Fatimids' rich political, religious, social and cultural histories as well as explore the heritage they left behind.

This book is intended to be in many ways a written portrait of the Fatimids as a dynasty, the regime it headed, the religious and geopolitical climate it intersected with, the cultural environment it generated and its legacy. In general terms, a portrait is a representation of a particular person; here the sitter is instead a dynasty and its age. In this portrait the Fatimids occupy centre stage to reflect the integral role this dynasty played in events that took place from the tenth to the twelfth century in medieval Europe, the Mediterranean basin, the Middle East, Africa, Central Asia, the Indian Ocean region and beyond. This geographical expanse forms the symbolic canvas on which this portrait is painted. Placing the Fatimids at the heart of the picture serves to challenge the perception of a middle period of Islamic history in which observers have often conceived the role in it played by this dynasty to be an afterthought at the periphery of a medieval geopolitical map.

Since the seventh century, following the death of the Prophet Muhammad in 632, the expanding Islamic commonwealth came to be dominated by caliphal dynasties that endorsed the majority Sunni branch of Islam. Challenging this state of affairs, a religious-political revolutionary movement emerged known as Isma'ili, after Isma'il, the son of a Shi'i imam, whose leadership and cause they championed. It matured within the fold of the Shi'a branch of Islam. Motivated by messianic expectations, in time this group gave rise to the establishment of the Fatimids' counter-caliphate. This dynasty of Shi'i Isma'ili leaders became the only example of representatives of a Muslim minority who grew in power to the point of establishing an independent empire. For more than 250 years the Fatimid imam-caliphs – as their Isma'ili followers called their leaders – first from North Africa and later from Egypt, rivalled the Sunni 'Abbasid caliphs of Baghdad and the

Umayyads of Cordoba, as well as the Christian Byzantine emperors of Constantinople. Across its duration the Fatimid imperial power, whether exercised directly or indirectly, stretched from North Africa, Egypt, Sicily, Syria and Palestine to the Arabian peninsula and parts of Central and South Asia. By establishing Cairo as the empire's headquarters, Egypt was transformed from a provincial backwater of the 'Abbasid caliphate into the centre of Islamic and Mediterranean worlds, a position of political and cultural prominence that the country has held since. The Fatimids did not just sit at the table together with the powers of their time. For a period, albeit brief, they were the table.

How do we know about the Fatimids? When it comes to the question of gathering primary information about them the toolbox at our disposal is both half full and half empty depending on what we are looking for. It is half full because there are plenty of pre-modern historiographies, chronicles, travelogues and dictionaries that devote space, sometime entire works, to the Fatimids. Ever since the Shi'i Isma'ili Fatimids emerged as a force that posed an existential threat to the dominant Sunni and Christian empires of their time, the dynasty and its rule attracted plenty of attention among mainstream Muslim polemists and detractors. These – with some notable exceptions – reflected in their writings their own biased assessment of the period of Islamic history that saw this Isma'ili dynasty dominating the scene as a religious, political, economic and cultural player. The medieval and pre-modern authors whose works today represent the majority of historical primary sources on the Fatimids at our disposal looked back to describe the Fatimids and their age in a way that reflected the perspectives, standpoints and interests of the times in which they wrote. The esoteric character at the heart of Isma'ilism, that is, the brand of Islam the Fatimid dynasty embodied and promoted, meant the doctrinal departure from a solely literal reading of the Qur'an and the worldview that could be derived from it. The subversive character of the movement that brought the Fatimids into power meant that those operating for the cause of the Isma'ili imams had to fend off fierce persecution. This resulted in having to act under disguise and adopting subterfuge. Those who pledged allegiance to the propaganda that led to the rise of the the Fatimids as rightful leaders of the Muslim community operated in secret networks that could only be joined through a lengthy process of screening and the taking of an oath. All this mysteriousness and more fuelled the imagination of non-Isma'ili writers who, for centuries, often filled their narratives with fantasy at the expense of facts. As a result, in navigating through the accounts on the Fatimids at our disposal, we have to watch out for deliberate slander, accusations of heresy, outright lies, the occasional frenzy, entertaining exaggerations and bouts of paranoia. Some of the misconceptions that in the Middle Ages grew around the Fatimids continue to feed distorted information, within and outside the broader Muslim fold, about the Isma'ilis of today.

On several occasions, late medieval and pre-modern writers used documents written during the Fatimid period and for the dynasty. In this way they became by default repositories for extracts of material which might not have survived otherwise. These authors however took these sources out of their textual context, often in order to (mis)use them to validate their own agendas. With the boundary between fact and fiction often blurred in favour of the latter, to ignore the limitations embedded in these tools could mean risking losing sight of a more accurate historical portrait. Yet, though at second hand, repurposed and defective when taken at face value, scraps of extant original material quoted in later sources are vital in enabling us to add light to what would otherwise be a dull portrayal. Fragments of chronicles written at the time of the events they describe, letters and personal memoirs of royals or courtiers, transcribed chancery documents and archival records but also extracts of petitions submitted by ordinary people to the rulers and more – all contribute to sharpen our understanding of the character of the sitter in front of us. In this respect the most useful and authoritative informant on the Fatimids is the Egyptian historian of the Mamluk era Taqi al-Din al-Maqrizi (1364–1442). A prolific author, al-Maqrizi dedicated entire works to the Fatimid dynasty and its rule in Egypt, drawing from archival and library material at his disposal. Today the use of his texts, both as source and resource, is evident – to a varying extent – in the vast majority of academic studies on the Fatimids.

The sources toolbox is however half empty when it comes to the availability of relevant complete historiographical texts written under Fatimid rule by and for the dynasty. In the tenth century, as the dynasty's imperial ambitions grew in strength and territorial expansion, legitimization of its power took the form of a small number of written foundational narratives that together constituted the official record of the early history of the Fatimids as told from an insider's perspective. Over the years, some of these texts as well as extant Fatimid Isma'ili doctrinal literature (once preserved, surrounded by religious secrecy, in Isma'ili circles) have become accessible in print and manuscript forms. The bias that characterizes a limited number of Fatimid-produced historiographical works and the scarce historical information found in doctrinal literature makes these sources a type of colour that, if applied with rose-tinted glasses, risks resulting in the portrait being overworked. Fatimid historical works known to have existed in the eleventh and twelfth centuries would have complemented our understanding of the dynasty's self-perception across its era. These narratives however are lost, with many known only through fragmentary quotations or paraphrased in later sources by both Isma'ili and non-Isma'ili authors.

In general, extant original documents and archival texts going back to the Islamic middle period are scarce when compared with what is available for the study of medieval Europe. Archives did exist across the Islamic territories since all regimes, whatever the religious-political inclination, relied on administrative machines that generated documents in order to carry out the business of government. Irrespective of dynasty, the chancery was among the most important offices at the service of a Muslim ruler. Nevertheless, extant Islamic chancery records are rare and only a few original state documents from the Fatimid court have survived to this day.

However, in the face of this overall shortage of documentary material, in recent years the Fatimid period has emerged as distinctive for the relative abundance of a particular kind of record. At the end of the nineteenth century in the course of works in the Ben Ezra Synagogue in what is today a suburb of Cairo a room was uncovered that had been used as storage for all sorts of documents – from trade agreements and bills to personal letters, marriage contracts and petitions – many of which dated between the tenth and the thirteenth centuries. Comprising hundreds of thousands of pieces, ranging from stamp-size to whole letters, this corpus forms what is now known in academia as the Cairo Geniza Collection. Following Shelomo D. Goitein's (1900–1985) study of this material since the late 1940s, which culminated in his subsequent pioneering work in the field, research on this collection is still ongoing. While these documents record the life – both religious and secular – of the Jewish community of Egypt, they have nevertheless a relevance that stretches way beyond a narrow scope. This Jewish community did not live in isolation but interacted with the rest of the population, and the hoard also preserved documents concerning the everyday life of the Cairene population irrespective of religious affiliation. Beside Hebrew and other languages, most of the fragments are written both in Arabic and Arabic language in Hebrew script, thus reflecting mixed audiences.

Besides the Geniza find, recently another hoard of documents, written on papyrus, has come to light in the Egyptian central Fayyum region. It also contains contracts, letters and other items, some of which belong to the Fatimid period, with most of them relevant to the lives of Muslims. The contents of both the Geniza and Fayyum collections constitute as yet the most valuable resources for coeval information on ordinary people's everyday lives in Egypt under Fatimid rule and its immediate aftermath.

From the nineteenth century onwards, most of what became available from these two sets of primary and documentary sources has been used in combination to produce a body of outstanding specialized academic literature. These works represent the material needed to hold together this written portrait from its start all the way to its finish. These publications are intended for Islamic studies specialists and medievalists in general. Today's research on the Fatimids constitutes a field of academic study with contributors forming an international, inclusive community of Western, Middle Eastern, North African and Asian scholars. Their works on Fatimid history and society are the main building blocks on which the whole structure of this portrait stands.

The academic interest in the Fatimids in Europe developed in the nineteenth century within the context of a broader fascination with Egypt, shaped by factors as diverse as Western colonial interests, archaeological discoveries of its ancient past and changes to the geopolitical map like the opening of the Suez Canal. To some it became clear that there was more to the history of Egypt than Pharaohs and Saladin. Another contributing factor to a growing Western interest in the history of the Fatimids was the desire to unravel what came to be perceived as the mystery surrounding the brand of Islam they endorsed, Isma'ilism. Secrecy, esotericism, covenants, daring exploits carried out by activists in the name of occult leaders with a view to world domination, all of this and more fuelled the imagination of nineteenth-century writers as well as scholars of Islam. Narratives on the Fatimids became conflated with legends about the eleventh- and twelfth-century Isma'ilis of Iran and Syria. These gained fame in medieval Europe as Assassins as a result of stories that had reached the continent about their politically motivated murderous missions. A popular but not accredited etymology of the word 'assassin' – which has since entered the vocabulary of many European languages – is that it derives from hashish. It was believed that these Isma'ili militants, the *fida'i*s, took the drug in order to muster the courage to carry out their daring killing feats. As the proliferation of legends got out of hand, the lethal label stuck on the Isma'ilis for centuries. Fantasies grew around the lifestyle of their leaders and their followers that, depicted as extravagant and sexualized, were too titillating to be abandoned in the name of boring historical accuracy. Stories of the Order of the Assassins and the Old Man of the Mountain came to populate the literary pages, from the writings of the Venetian merchant and traveller Marco Polo (*c.* 1254–1324) all the way to those of the Beat generation author and artist William S. Burroughs (1914–1997) and more. In time, however the growing availability of primary written sources made possible an accurate and objective study of the Fatimids and Isma'ilism in general.

In 1881 Ferdinand Wüstenfeld (1808–1899) became the first author to publish, in German, a monograph devoted to the Fatimids. The earliest books in English covering the Fatimids tended to be histories of medieval and pre-modern Egypt, with the short history of the Fatimid caliphate by De Lacy Evans O'Leary (1872–1957), published in 1923, being the first main work in that language to focus on the dynasty. The first authoritative comprehensive book in Arabic on the dynasty was published in 1932 by the Egyptian scholar Hasan Ibrahim Hasan (1892–1968). From the 1940s onward, Islamic art historians pioneered the study of Fatimid artistic production, thus establishing its desirability among collectors and curators. Subsequent generations of scholars followed, resulting in the publication of monographs dedicated to Fatimid art.

Coins, textiles, artworks in a variety of media from ceramics to metalwork, archaeological finds, wall inscriptions, epigraphic plaques and architectural structures are among the source materials considered here. A look at some of the objects that have survived from the Fatimid era to this day will help to capture a glimpse of the spirit of the age through the eyes of those who – friends or foes of the Fatimids – witnessed it.

A once dominant voice at the heart of an interconnected world, the Fatimids became part of a collective narrative that transcended the boundaries of an Islamic realm. The Nobel Prize-winning economist and philosopher Amartya Sen stated that the hope for peace and harmony in the world rested in celebrating the plurality of identities as the best antidote against sharp divisions. The age of the Fatimids represents a time in history when notions of single identity and categorization could have no place. The story of the Fatimids reminds us of the challenges but also the opportunities that, in any given society at any given time, arise from transfer of know-how, mobility of human capital, shared experiences and inclusivity irrespective of geographical, gender and religious boundaries.

I

The Beginning of Shi'a Isma'ili Propaganda: From Covert Movement to the Unfolding of a Messianic Promise

He brushed his teeth, cried 'Nay, the most Exalted Companion is of Paradise' and then expired in the arms of his wife, 'A'isha.[1] These were the last moments of the Prophet Muhammad's extraordinary life as narrated by some of his early biographers and transmitters of *hadiths*, that is, accounts believed by Muslims to record the doings and sayings of the Prophet and his close companions. With his death in 632 in the Arabian city of Medina came to an end what, to his followers, was Muhammad's 22-year-long mission as messenger of God. To them he had been chosen in 610 to be the recipient of a sequence of divine revelations to humankind that once collected formed a holy book, the Qur'an. In the course of Muhammad's mandate those who accepted his prophetic role and the divine origin of the message he delivered had formed a community of believers. They recognized him as their leader and embraced the absolute monotheism that he preached. Its members became known as *muslims*, that is, those who committed themselves to *islam*, the unconditional submission to the will of the one and only God. By the time of Muhammad's death this group of followers had matured into a religious-political entity that, though left with the Qur'an as the pre-eminent spiritual and lifestyle guidance, felt the need nevertheless of human leadership. This was in order to ensure that no one in the community would stray from the injunction to worship one God and to implement His will on earth modelled on His messenger's example. With Muhammad – the last of God's prophets and an unparalleled model of virtue – gone, who could fulfil this daunting leadership role? The crisis that followed, due to disputes over issues of temporal and spiritual authority, in the making of such momentous decisions has been shaping the history of Islam and the lives of Muslims to this day. This is the context that gave origin to the devising of leadership figures like the *khalifa*, the caliph, at first intended as a temporal deputy of Muhammad, and the *imam*, a guide invested with spiritual charisma as well as political authority, to some, based on genealogical grounds as a descendant from the Prophet's close family. Others understood the ideal *imam* to be the one who proved to be the best and most pious Muslim. It is as a result of conflict over who would be best suited to lead Muslims and, one day the whole of humanity, that the community soon became divided into Sunnis, Shi'is and Kharijis, each splintering into subgroups over time. Within the Shi'a, one of such offshoots was the Isma'ilis or, as they called themselves, *ahl al-haqq*, the people of the truth or rightfulness. Within this group these antecedents became a brewing ground for the sequence of events that, shaped by propaganda informed by messianic beliefs, culminated in the rising of one figure to manifest himself as the awaited rightful ruler, bringer of ultimate peace and justice to Muslims and humanity. It was this man who would become the founder of a Shi'i Isma'ili dynasty: the Fatimids.

The Disputes Over Muhammad's Succession

Who should have the right to lead the Muslim community and on the basis of which authority? One group argued in favour of a leader chosen from among the Prophet's closest companions and belonging to his same powerful Arabian tribe from Mecca, the Quraysh, who would act as his deputy in managing the community. They saw their vision of leadership as the best to secure the following of Muhammad's model, *sunna*, in order to safeguard the practice of Islam. Another group instead grew around the idea that Muhammad's successor had to be chosen on the basis of the closest bloodline proximity to the Prophet, within his direct line of descent. On that basis the candidate had to belong not only to his tribe but to his clan, the Hashim, and his immediate family. Those who supported this claim formed a faction, *shi'a*, who championed the leadership of 'Ali who was a cousin of the Prophet and the husband of his daughter, Fatima. In time, with their two sons, al-Hasan and al-Husayn, the couple and Muhammad came to be revered as the people of the household, *ahl al-bayt*, in essence the holy family of Islam. According to Muslim historians, 'Ali and Muhammad had grown close to one another on account of the fact that 'Ali's father, Abu Talib, had raised Muhammad – an orphan – in his family. Looking back at many episodes that saw the two cousins together the *shi'a* of 'Ali claimed evidence that Muhammad had designated his cousin and son-in-law to be his successor.

The faction in support of 'Ali had emerged as an Arab political group motivated by legitimist aspirations. However, those who had wanted their champion to be appointed as the new leader saw their hopes dashed by their rivals' success in securing instead the nomination of Muhammad's closest companion and father-in-law Abu Bakr (d. 634) as the first caliph to govern the Muslim community. He died after two years in his role as the first *khalifa* and was succeeded by another prominent companion, 'Umar, also a father-in-law of Muhammad who, throughout his life, had had several wives. This caliph was responsible for the rapid expansion of Islam beyond the borders of the Arabian peninsula. After his murder in 644, 'Uthman became the third caliph. A son-in-law of Muhammad, he belonged to the Umayyad clan of the Quraysh tribe. He expanded the Islamic dominance further and Muslims credit him as the person behind the written codification of the Qur'an in the canonical version we know today. 'Uthman too was assassinated in 656 in Medina and only then the choice fell on 'Ali to become the fourth of what would become known as *al-khulafa' al-rashidun*, the rightly guided caliphs. 'Ali enjoyed great popularity among those who had converted to Islam in the acquired territories of the nascent Islamic empire, like Iraq where, in Kufa, he had a strong powerbase. This success set in motion a shift that in due course would turn the *shi'a* from being an Arab-centred faction into a broad-based religious-political movement. By contrast 'Ali was opposed by those who, among other things, blamed him for not having avenged the murder of his predecessor.

The Emergence of the Caliphate and the Imamate as Temporal and Spiritual Institutions

Prominent among the latter group was Mu'awiya (d. 680), who shared 'Uthman's Umayyad ancestry and had been appointed governor of Syria during his rule. The dispute between 'Ali and the governor escalated to the point of reaching full confrontation in Siffin, near Raqqa in present-day Syria. After a sequence of skirmishes, a stalemate followed that ended with 'Ali proposing an arbitration to his rival. The move, intended to avoid inter-Muslim bloodshed, was instead seen as a sign of weakness on ʻAli's part and a moral victory for Muʻawiya. ʻAli lost his authority over his troops and saw his suitability to be caliph thrown into doubt. A dissenting group quit (*kharaja*) ʻAli's fold to the point of formulating an altogether alternative vision of leadership. They became known as the Kharijis advocating that any man could head the community as long as he could prove himself to be the best Muslim of all in piety and rectitude. In 661 it was a Khariji who stabbed ʻAli to death while he was praying in the mosque of Kufa, south of Baghdad. In the immediate aftermath ʻAli's son, al-Hasan, was proclaimed caliph but, undermined from many fronts, he was forced to abdicate in favour of Muʻawiya. As Muʻawiya I he proclaimed Damascus the capital of the emerging Islamic empire and founded the first Muslim dynasty, the Umayyads, having introduced into Islamic statecraft a model of transmission of leadership based on a father–son hereditary principle. The Sunni Umayyads ruled over the Islamic empire until the year 750. By this time the Islamic domains stretched from Central Asia to North Africa all the way to the Atlantic coast, having replaced the rule of the Christian Byzantine empire in many territories in the west and that of the Zoroastrian Sasanian empire in the east. Today small and scattered Parsi communities are all that is left of the once mighty Zoroastrian past. Among other factors, the Byzantine empire from its capital, Constantinople, had been depleted of its former resilience by the plague that occurred between 541 and 549 under the rule of the emperor Justinian I. The effects of this pandemic were to be felt across the Mediterranean and affected regions as far away as Iraq, Syria and Egypt well into the mid-eighth century. Further bruised by the Muslims' advance, the Byzantines would nevertheless continue to command considerable political and economic power in the Mediterranean region for centuries to come. As for the Umayyads, under Caliph ʻAbd al-Malik (d. 705) an intensive process of Arabization and Islamization took place across the expanding empire. It became reflected among other spheres in the formulae on coinage and public signs of authority – the Arabic inscriptions on the Dome of the Rock, built in Jerusalem (Ar. al-Quds) during his reign, being a famous example. Urban landscapes were re-inscribed, a major example being what was once the Basilica of St John the Baptist in Damascus being transformed into the Umayyad Mosque. Most of what was inherited from the previous defeated regimes were rebranded with an Arabic-Islamic overcoat. Arabic replaced Greek as the language of the state administration.

In the meantime, rather than being deflated, 'Ali's supporters had become even more galvanized in wishing to overturn what they saw as an unforgivable usurpation perpetrated against their champion and the household of the Prophet. By now part of a fully fledged militant denomination of Islam, the Shi'is stood at this stage in political opposition to the Sunni majority. In addition to duping 'Ali first and al-Hasan later, the Umayyads were condemned for what Shi'is, up to this day, regard as the gravest act of injustice ever committed in the whole history of Islam. In 680 in Karbala, in today's Iraq, Mu'awiya's son and successor Yazid I (d. 683) led his large army against a small division headed by al-Husayn, son of 'Ali and grandson of Muhammad, who had challenged Yazid's right to the caliphate. In the course of the battle al-Husayn was killed, and his body decapitated. The abuse and martyrdom of Muhammad's flesh and blood was an unforgivable and unforgettable event that shaped the Shi'is' vision of history and their role in it. For generation after generation of Shi'is al-Husayn became the symbol of the oppressed and of those deprived of their God-given rights: the poster boy for militant action in the name of justice. Ever since, his martyrdom has played a profound role in Shi'i psyche. To this day across Shi'i communities and in particular in Iran, where Shi'i Islam has been the state religion since the sixteenth century, every year a month is dedicated to the mourning of al-Husayn. During the Islamic month of Muharram commemorative rituals and theatrical performances take place in which the battle in which al-Husayn died is re-enacted. Karbala is one of the most important Shi'i pilgrimage destinations.

With the loss of al-Hasan and al-Husayn as the ultimate blood descendants of the Prophet believed by Shi'is as having had the right to rule, some supporters of the descendants in 'Ali's line turned their hopes and aspirations for justice towards another man. This was Muhammad son of al-Hanafiyya, also an offspring of 'Ali but not Fatima. In 685, in the course of a revolt in Kufa, his followers proclaimed him to be the awaited *mahdi*, the guided one (by God). This episode constitutes one of the earliest appearances in Islam of a figure in whom belief in the context of growing religious-political rivalries would play a central role in the formation of Islamic messianism and the consequent rise of messianic movements. Though occupying large space in Islamic eschatological literature, the *mahdi* is not mentioned as such in the Qur'an but only alluded to. Instead, extensive information about this figure can be found in the *hadith*s corpuses, that is, systematic collections of Prophet Muhammad's traditions. In some corpuses collecting these narrations the Prophet was attributed the prediction that at the end of the world, God would send a member of his family bearing his name who would fill the world with justice and righteousness. Within two centuries from the advent of Islam the belief in the imminent coming of the *mahdi*, ushering in the ultimate triumph of Islam before the Last Judgement, had become well established.

Among most Muslims the following signs came to be seen as preceding the imminent eschaton: the sun rising from the west; the triple eclipse of the moon and other unusual astral phenomena; abundant smoke; the manifestation of Jesus in either Damascus or Jerusalem. The figures of Jesus and the *mahdi* are sometime conflated in Islamic eschatological literature, making it unclear whether one should consider their appearance as part of the same or separate events. Regardless, the role of Jesus or the *mahdi* would be to kill *al-dajjal*, the Islamic equivalent of the Antichrist, to break the cross and overcome all Christians and Jews. This sequence of episodes would inaugurate a period of peace and justice when the observation of the laws prescribed by the revealed religions would be lifted until the climax of the Last Judgement. Muslim exegetes offered varied opinions on the length of this phase, ranging from a few years to decades or more. In turn, the events marking the start of the Last Judgement would be inaugurated by the *qa'im*, he who will rise or appear, or the Resurrector when used in broad Shi'i context. Once again this was an eschatological figure whose role and characteristics have been often conflated with that of the *mahdi*.[2] It was against the backdrop of these and other eschatological expectations that one day the Fatimid dynasty would emerge and rise to power.

In 700, upon the demise of Muhammad, son of 'Ali and al-Hanafiyya, messianic beliefs grew around this man to the point that according to some he was not dead but had gone into hiding and would return one day to fill the world with justice and equity. It is at this junction that we witness the formulation of the messianic doctrine of occultation, *ghayba*, that is, the belief in the *imam* having shifted to living a metaphysical existence and in his return at an appointed time. The resorting to this doctrine became a core characteristic of all the Shi'i denominations that followed.[3] Alongside the supporters of al-Hanafiyya's son, there were those – the majority – who persevered in their allegiance to the Prophet's descendants in the line of Fatima by recognizing the authority of al-Husayn's progeny. Many other splinter groups formed during this time, so much so that a descendant of al-Hasan was also identified as the *mahdi* who, being in occultation, would one day return. In time most of these divided supporters regrouped by channelling their energies behind the partisans in favour of the line of the Prophet's daughter, Fatima.

The Shi'a never recognized the authority of the Umayyad caliphs as leaders of the Muslim community. Intent on restoring its guardianship into the hands of its rightful claimants, the now refocused Shi'is endorsed the leadership of 'Ali's and Fatima's blood descendants who, with the title of *imam*, followed one another in sequence for generations. To preserve the integrity and continuity of this transfer of authority a practice defining the mode of succession came into shape. Called *nass*, it meant that it was the incumbent imam who had the sole authority to appoint the leader who would come next after his death. On the strength of this method, after 'Ali, al-Hasan and al-Husayn, the allegiance to each imam continued until Zayn al-'Abidin (d. *c.* 713). After him, however, some believed that the appointed son was Zayd while others backed his brother, Muhammad al-Baqir. The majority remained loyal to the latter and then to his son, Ja'far al-Sadiq (d. 765). Those who endorsed Zayd and his descendants became known as Zaydis. This faction gathered a large following in the northern Iranian Caspian Sea region and in the Arabian peninsula. While the Iranian branch faded, over the centuries the Zaydis have maintained a powerful political presence in Yemen where today they are also known as Huthis.

During the imamate of Ja'far al-Sadiq the religious-political orientation of the Shi'a underwent a major transformation in response to an epochal geopolitical shift that changed the order of rule over and governance of the Islamic empire as a whole. By 748, the simmering opposition against the Umayyads had erupted into full confrontation. Seen as unjust and unworthy rulers, on account of what many perceived as questionable moral rectitude and poor administrative style, the Umayyads had managed to alienate the support of many Arab and non-Arab Muslims across the periphery of the empire. Upholding the Shi'is' ongoing calls for the restoration of Muslim rule to what they considered to be the intended leaders, rebels came forward to lead an anti-Umayyad revolution. Their leadership claimed to be from the Hashim clan on account of being blood descendants of ʿAbbas b. ʿAbd al-Muttalib, who was in turn related to Muhammad. Having secured a strong powerbase among Shiʿis and other discontented marginal groups, like the non-Arab Iranians, these rebels assembled a large army that scored a series of rapid victories under their trademark black flags. In 750 a group from among these revolutionaries unseated the Umayyad caliph Marwan II and replaced him with Abu'l-ʿAbbas al-Saffah (d. 754), a member of the Hashim clan. He inaugurated a new caliphal dynasty, the ʿAbbasids, that lasted until 1258, when it was swept away by the Mongols' invasion. As for the disbanded Umayyads, some members of the deposed royal family sought new territories in which to re-establish their rule. Since 711 the Muslim armies had advanced all the way to the territory today know as Gibraltar (from the Arabic *jabal Tariq*, the mountain of Tariq) and from there Umayyad forces had conquered large parts of Visigoth territories. The fugitive Umayyad royals resettled in the southern part of the Iberian peninsula that became the dominion of an independent Sunni Islamic dynasty: the Umayyads of al-Andalus. Muslim rule lasted, in various forms and to different extents, until the Catholic Reconquista of King Ferdinand and Queen Isabella of Spain in 1492.

Meanwhile the ʿAbbasids, from their new capital Baghdad (built on the ruins of the old Sasanian capital Ctesiphon) championed the Sunni vision of Islam. During the first decades of their rule, four canonical Sunni legal schools took shape. Named after their founders, the Maliki, Hanafi, Shafiʿi and Hanbali schools turned into jurisprudence the principles of divine guidance, *shariʿa*, they found to be embedded in the Qur'an and supported by the *hadith*s. In time these laws came to be collated in a number of authoritative written corpuses. In an about-face against the shared pro-ʿAlid revolutionary ideals, the ʿAbbasids became the staunchest opponents of the Shiʿa. From having been allies, the Shiʿis and their imams were now seen as posing an ideological, religious and political threat that the Sunni regime sought to suppress – with some exceptions – through persecutions.

The Shiʿis Fight Back

If the Umayyads had deserved the utmost contempt as usurpers and sacrilegious murderers, to the Shiʿis the ʿAbbasids deserved to be despised as the ultimate traitors. Betrayed in the expectation of seeing an 'Alid imam in Fatima's line in power, and subjected to suffering, the supporters of the Shi'a had found themselves in a position of military, economic and demographic disadvantage. The Shi'a leadership realized that, while playing the long game, the broadest possible grass-roots consensus had to be rallied to their cause. To increase its appeal, the 'Abbasids had to be proven to be not just inept rulers, but also unfit on genealogical and theological grounds, despite the ancestry they claimed to share with the Shi'a imams going back to the Prophet. In response to the need to reset the Shi'i cause, an intellectual development gained ground centred around the exegesis of written and oral records reflecting the teachings of past Shi'i imams. This exercise opened the way to the formulation of a divinely inspired religious-philosophical rationale to underpin the political claims of the Shi'i imamate. Leading this ideological warfare was Imam Ja'far al-Sadiq, an eminent scholar and erudite thinker who, among other things, would be credited in the Latin West with having passed his secret knowledge to the mysterious eighth-century alchemist Jabir b. Hayyan, known as Geber (illus. 2). Ja'far's ideas caused a shift in the Shi'i understanding of the status of the imam and the role of the imamate in this world in view of the next. 'Ali and the imams in his line of descent had not only inherited from the Prophet their right to political leadership but were exclusive recipients of his spiritual charisma. While the divine revelation had ended once and for all with Muhammad, 'Ali, as his legatee or executor, *wasi*, had been entrusted as the sole custodian of the esoteric knowledge,

2 Imam Ja'far al-Sadiq and the alchemist Jabir b. Hayyan, illustrated trade card, 1909.

batin, of the outer revelation, *zahir*. It was this exclusive transfer from one cousin to the other that made 'Ali's lineage via Fatima entitled to leadership above all others.

The empire, under the Shi'a imamate, was envisioned as rule founded on a school of jurisprudence rooted in Ja'far al-Sadiq's teachings and those of his predecessors in the imamate. The Shi'i Ja'fari school of law that emerged rivalled the four Sunni ones that were taking shape. In sum, from now on, as far as Shi'is were concerned, the authority of the imams and their right to lead the Muslim community rested not just on a political claim but on a religious one. It was on the strength of this argument that the movement dedicated itself to the fulfilment of a divine destiny via doctrinal, political and military means.

With the imamate now charged with such an imposing mandate, Shi'i adherents scrutinized the terms determining the succession of one imam instead of another. Although the *nass* system, in theory, left the incumbent imam with some room for manoeuvre in terms of choosing his successor, in practice, there was an expectation that the eldest son would be the one to take office after his father's death. But as the case of the split between those who supported Zayd against those who sided with Muhammad al-Baqir had demonstrated, the *nass* method could not guarantee that the transfer of power would be accepted by all. In the case of Ja'far al-Sadiq's succession a major division occurred once more. One group claimed that Ja'far had appointed his son Isma'il as the next imam. Another group sided with another son, Musa al-Kazim. Among the supporters of Isma'il, some claimed that he had died before his father while others maintained that he lived in occultation. In time, both these factions agreed that after Isma'il's death the imamate had been passed to his son Muhammad. Eventually these variant groups came to be known as the Isma'ilis.[4]

The Early Isma'ilis and Their Hidden Imams

According to Isma'ili belief, it was during the imamate of Muhammad b. Isma'il that the 'Abbasid oppression against the Shi'a intensified to the point that the life of the imam was in extreme danger. Also, the emergence of rival factions within the Shi'a fold was posing a significant threat to their champion. It was therefore for safety, they claimed, that Muhammad b. Isma'il had gone into hiding. Living, though not visible, he was believed to be still present among his community and in the fullness of time he would return to restore the peace and justice that, as promised, would one day prevail. Since the Isma'ilis believed that the imams were manifest in person up to the seventh in line, they also became known as Seveners. The Isma'ilis were also called Batinis because of their belief in the primacy of an esoteric (*batin*) counterpart to match every aspect of exoteric (*zahir*) life.

Parallel to this development, the majority of Shi'a had upheld the imamate of Ja'far's other son, Musa al-Kazim. While waiting for the appointed time for the Shi'i imamate to prevail, this group adopted a quietist stance as it continued to direct love and devotion – *walaya* – to each of the imams in the line of Musa. According to the supporters of this line, however, the twelfth to succeed – also called Muhammad – was exposed to mortal danger and he too went into hiding in 941. For these Shi'is this year marked the start of what came to be known as the great occultation, *al-ghayba al-kubra*. For this group, the line of manifest imams ended here. This belief earned them the name Twelvers, by which they became best known. The messianic Twelver Shi'i imam became Muhammad al-Mahdi, *al-muntazar*, the awaited one, a figure whose return the Shi'i world is still expecting. Today in his absence high-ranking scholars-cum-clerics, believed to have a metaphysical connection with him, function as spiritual and political guides on his behalf for the worldwide Twelver Shi'i community.

From a unified Shi'a in the name of 'Ali and his immediate descendants three lines of imams and concurrent visions of the imamate had evolved: the Zaydi, the Isma'ili and the Twelvers. The adherents of the last two, incensed by suffering the injustice and persecution that had culminated in the occultation of their respective imams, gave shape to their respective beliefs in the appearance of the salvific *mahdi* from the progeny of 'Ali and Fatima, though at different paces. In Shi'ism, contrary to Sunnism, the coming of the *mahdi* would become an article of faith. Over the course of history, the Zaydis, the Twelvers and the Isma'ilis, though all Shi'i, challenged each other's positions and in some regions even came into confrontation. Of these groups, it is the vicissitudes of Isma'ilis that we will follow from now on.

If, on the one hand, the 'Abbasid caliphate inaugurated an age of scholarship as well as cultural and architectural splendour, on the other, family intrigues and dynastic disputes in the ninth century soon marred the credibility of the Sunni caliphs of Baghdad in the eyes of many. The viziers, the highest-ranking officers in the administration of the regime, managed to position themselves as the truly powerful men of the empire, corruption prevailed and taxation was heavy. The 'Abbasids had transformed a dominion with its powerbase rooted in the agrarian and military classes into a commercial cosmopolitan empire. This shift generated changes that impacted on social-economic conditions. Against this background, general discontent with the 'Abbasid leadership and a widespread sense of injustice further fuelled messianic expectations that escalated to open unrest. Within decades of the start of 'Abbasid rule, the disintegration of the empire was already underway. Unlike the Umayyads, the 'Abbasids had adopted a decentralized approach to the management of their provinces by delegating the political and administrative control of the empire's territories to governors. Soon, however, these local rulers founded their own dynasties which, though recognizing the authority of the 'Abbasids and following their model in shaping their own institutions, in practice governed independently of Baghdad. The break-up of the empire ensued. In the mid-ninth century Yemen came to be ruled by a local Sunni dynasty, the Yu'firids; the Turkish governor of Egypt and Syria founded the Tulunid dynasty, and within fifty years of the 'Abbasids' enthronement, the Aghlabid *amir*s reigned in most of North Africa on their behalf. Shi'i and 'Alid dynasties also established themselves as rulers on behalf of Baghdad: the Hamdanids (*c*. 890–1004) governed over parts of Syria and northern Iraq; the Idrisids (788–974) controlled parts of Morocco, and the Zaydis established local dynasties in the Caspian region and Yemen. This trend culminated with the rise of the Shi'i Buyids (932–1055) who went on to rule from Baghdad over Iraq and part of Iran in the 'Abbasids' name.

Against this fragmented backdrop, the promise attributed to the Prophet Muhammad of the advent of a *mahdi* from his progeny, combined with Shi'i messianic propaganda, resulted in a plethora of claimants to the role, each attracting varied degrees of popular support. In response, in the middle of the ninth century the 'Abbasids intensified the repressions and persecution of the Shi'is, including those in Iraq and Iran. Caliph al-Mutawakkil (d. 861), and to an even greater extent his son and successor al-Muntasir (d. 862), carried out purges that forced scores of Shi'is to seek refuge in remote parts of the empire, where they lived undercover by practising religious dissimulation, *taqiyya*, and by adopting inconspicuous lifestyles as law-obeying citizens in the land they lived in.[5]

One such place of refuge was Salamiyya in Syria. This ancient desert town near Hama had fallen into ruin, but in the late eighth century the 'Abbasids had started redeveloping it as a trading post. At a later stage, around 870, settlers were recruited to repopulate the town. It might have been in the context of this demographic project that persecuted Isma'ilis found it convenient to relocate there.[6] Once settled, a group of them relaunched in secret their anti-'Abbasid activities under the guise of being wealthy merchants. They obtained a land grant on behalf of a figure whom they described as a merchant from the Iraqi city of Basra in the centre of Salamiyya, by the bazar, with a plan to build houses on it. Though engaged in commercial enterprises, these traders were in fact religious-political propagandists or callers, *da'is*, who had rallied around a leader who came to be known as 'Abd Allah the Elder. According to early Isma'ili historical accounts, this figure – ostensibly no more than a prosperous merchant – settled in Salamiyya in a compound formed of houses contained within towering walls.[7] Behind the commercial facade, the residence of 'Abd Allah the Elder and the colony that grew around it became the headquarters of Isma'ili propaganda, the *da'wa al-haqq*, the call to the truth on behalf of the hidden imam.

'Abd Allah the Elder: Isma'ili Propagandist or Hidden Imam?

The secretive nature of this Isma'ili operation meant that what is known about the activities of this period is based on sources in which events and personalities were described according to the retrospective biases and agendas of their authors. Detractors took advantage of this obscure period to fill it with genealogies aimed at exposing the falsehood of the 'Alid origins of the Isma'ili imamate. The ever popular 'Jewish conspiracy' found its way into this context too.[8] In contrast, Isma'ili insiders and supporters collected information on their hidden imams which, according to them, had been preserved within the early *da'wa*, to retrace the steps of the imams' ancestry. Many strands of Isma'ili knowledge, characterized by complex name camouflages, esoteric personas and cryptic alphabets, resulted in a more or less coherent narrative to illustrate this period. 'Abd Allah the Elder is described as having originated from a village near 'Askar Mukram in the province of Ahwaz, at the north end of the Persian Gulf. At the time, this was a thriving centre of textile manufacture and sugar production. There 'Abd Allah the Elder had become a wealthy merchant who owned two houses. It was in this region that for the first time he recruited propagandists to go out and spread the Isma'ili anti-'Abbasid cause in a systematic way. At first, he directed his mission towards the Caspian Sea region where, in Chalus, according to Isma'ili sources, he settled for some time, married an 'Alid woman and had his son, Ahmad.[9] The propaganda was then extended to the city of Rayy (today incorporated into Greater Tehran) where there was already a strong Shi'a presence, a factor that would have favoured the reception of his anti-'Abbasid campaign in the area. This region was also known for the production and trade of high-grade silk textiles. However, opponents of the Isma'ilis became aware of these subversive activities, forcing 'Abd Allah the Elder and his propagandists to hide, and then flee northern Iran. Having escaped from this region he took refuge with pro-'Alid families, at first in Basra, known for its maritime trade with the Indian Ocean regions. From this city, once again, he dispatched agents in various directions. In Iraq, around 875, he succeeded in establishing a secret cell in Hilla. One of his closest disciples was sent to what had become an Iraqi Shi'i hotbed, Kufa. The presence of this activist in Kufa would be linked in due course to the rise of another Shi'i movement, the Qarmatians, which recruited followers in Iraq and the Persian Gulf. From Iraq 'Abd Allah the Elder's emissaries ventured to remote destinations at the periphery of the 'Abbasid empire, such as Yemen. Meanwhile, forced out of Basra as well, 'Abd Allah the Elder reached Syria, where he took refuge at first in a Christian convent. It was there that 'Abd Allah the Elder's loyal supporters were able to rejoin him, also thanks to directions given to them by a local woman, before moving onwards to Salamiyya.[10]

Since in general they earned their living as merchants, tailors, cotton carders or date dealers, these *da'is* were active in markets. There they could gather intelligence on logistics and local news about the places where they operated. Selling textiles, spices, plants, mirrors and millinery products, they attracted female customers from whom useful practical information could be teased out. However, when it came for the *da'is* to share their secret knowledge with novices and sworn-in initiates, this happened in their homes or in secluded places where trusted doorkeepers ensured privacy. Early Isma'ili treatises on the characteristics of the ideal *da'i* advised on how members of the propagandist's household should serve as a model of zeal for the Isma'ili cause. Wives, daughters and female servants were called upon to validate, with their rectitude, the *da'i*'s trustworthiness to his guests. Participation in these covert gatherings was conditional on taking an oath of allegiance, whereby the aspiring adept swore to obey the hidden imam while complying with the tenets of Islam's prescribed laws. Bound to absolute secrecy to protect the *da'wa* activities, the initiate underwent a gradual induction into the meaning of Isma'ili esoteric knowledge. Once advanced in this learning process, the adherent became in turn a teacher, thus expanding the network under the same precautionary rules. From this time onward Isma'ilism and learning became intertwined and inseparable. In fact, at the heart of learning was the application of systematic decoding, *ta'wil*, to unlock the true meaning of the outer revelation.[11] While the masses only knew the outer, literal shell of the Qur'an, the Isma'ilis saw themselves as pre-eminent selected guardians of a salvific inner knowledge that from 'Ali onwards had been the ultimate preserve of their imams. Though persecuted, the Isma'ilis saw themselves as one day being vindicated when, with his advent, the *mahdi* would usher in the conditions for the revelation of the true meaning of religion, concealed by outer religions, and known to the selected few.

Based on his portrayal, one can infer how various beliefs grew around 'Abd Allah the Elder. In the past, as in the present, it was not untypical to use wealth as a way to measure an individual's worth. Rapid and mysterious acquisition of riches, in turn, could be construed as outer proof of divine reward for virtue as well as the possession of special charisma and supernatural powers. 'Abd Allah the Elder was described as a foreigner in Salamiyya, credited with sponsoring a campaign to spread a message calling for justice in an already heightened messianic-charged climate. There was another pulling power for prospective adherents to his cause: the allure of being offered the chance, once scrutinized, to share a secret, empowering and salvific esoteric knowledge while being granted membership of an exclusive network that also revolved around lucrative trade exchanges.

As far as his followers were concerned, they were the only ones to know 'Abd Allah the Elder's true identity and mission. To them he was an 'Alid with immaculate credentials, a descendant of a family within the Hashim clan that rivalled the one the 'Abbasids came from.[12] Additionally, or because of it, they believed him to be the deputy of the hidden imam, Muhammad b. Isma'il, delegated to prepare the Muslim community for his return as *mahdi*. This he would do by initiating people to his cause and collecting tithes in his name. To his followers

‘Abd Allah the Elder was therefore the proof, *hujja*, of the existence of the hidden *mahdi* with whom he was in exclusive, metaphysical contact. From Salamiyya this leader managed a web of recruiters who, camouflaged as merchants, were dispatched across all the Islamic territories to establish secret cells to attract further recruits. In some instances, Isma‘ili and Qarmatian propagandists succeeded in turning entire villages into fortified compounds in which Isma‘ili adherents could live as places of refuge. These types of locations became known as *dar al-hijra*, abode of migration, a form of shelter that came to be adopted in several regions where the Isma‘ili presence was under threat. The house of refuge modelled that of the earliest Muslim community which, led by Muhammad, escaped persecution in Mecca and took refuge in Medina in 622. In their writings, anti-Isma‘ili polemists focused on the communal living in these sheltered compounds to accuse the residents of sexual licentiousness, incest and turpitudes of all sorts. This slanderous reputation associated with the Isma‘ili *dar al-hijra* had enduring popularity and the authenticity of these fabrications remained unchallenged for a long time.

Moving from the fringes, the political goal of the campaign at the heart of Isma‘ili propaganda was to unseat what they considered to be the illegitimate caliphate of the ‘Abbasids. In time this network of *da‘is* brought into the cause more and more adherents who paid tributes to join this revolutionary plan. These fees were then dispatched in secret to Salamiyya. News exchanged via pigeon post and land couriers went back and forth between the regions where the cells had been established and the *da‘wa* headquarters. Besides vast amounts of money, from Yemen for example, textiles and precious goods ranging from musk to carnelian-decorated weapons were also dispatched. Dried myrobalan fruits, useful for their medicinal qualities but also for their dye extracts for fabrics, arrived in Salamiyya all the way from India. According to early Isma‘ili sources, in Salamiyya this growing treasure was secreted in a vault under the *da‘wa* headquarters, which was only accessible from a 19-kilometre-long (12 mi.) tunnel, the opening of which was on the side of a cliff. Camel caravans entered the tunnel at night and unloaded inside the house. At the start and finish of each delivery the entrance gate of this corridor was covered with earth so that the existence of this passage remained unknown to outsiders. Another safe place in which to hide money was described as a large tank filled with coins, dug under a basin containing water so that nobody would guess what was underneath it.

The Imamate from Hidden to Manifest: From One 'Abd Allah to Another

It is uncertain when 'Abd Allah the Elder was believed to have died. Today, in his memory, in the centre of Salamiyya there is a domed shrine housing a tomb surmounted by a canopy. The structure, called by the locals the abode of the imam, *maqam al-imam*, and dating back to the eleventh century, is believed to have replaced the original shrine marking 'Abd Allah the Elder's resting place (illus. 3).[13] Locals believe that the opening of the above-mentioned tunnel is located near this

3 *Maqam al-imam*, the 11th-century shrine of 'Abd Allah the Elder in Salamiyya, Syria.

shrine. The Isma'ili tradition has it that, after his demise, 'Abd Allah the Elder was succeeded by one of his two sons, Ahmad. This man, of whom Isma'ili sources say little, was said to have carried out his mission across Iraq and Iran disguised, as customary among covert Isma'ili activists, as a trader. It is perhaps because of the mystery surrounding this elusive figure that some have identified him as the commissioner or even the author of the compilation known as *The Epistles of the Brethren of Purity*. Reputed to be the first ever encyclopaedia, this work is structured in 52 epistles whose authorship is ascribed by most to the collective efforts of what has been typically described as a brotherhood based in Basra. The compilation was produced with didactic intent, aiming at covering all known aspects of physical and metaphysical knowledge as well as mundane and supernatural domains. Suffused throughout with a religious-political agenda, the tone of the treatises fluctuates between strong generic Shi'i leanings and Isma'ili-sounding inclinations. The work, which over time enjoyed great popularity in disparate learning circles including in Europe, is today available in various editions and translations. However, while studies and theories abound, the riddle of authorship, affiliation and dating of this important work has yet to be resolved once and for all.[14]

According to Isma'ili sources Ahmad had two sons: al-Husayn and Abu'l-Shalaghla. Continuing in the trading tradition of his father, sources depict al-Husayn as carrying out his propaganda among his female customers. Al-Husayn had married a woman of North African origins, Wasan or Wisan, who gave him a son and maybe two daughters. When al-Husayn died in Salamiyya, his brother Abu'l-Shalaghla took his son into his care, as well as the guardianship of the *da'wa* on this nephew's behalf. This child, born in 'Askar Mukram in Iran around 873 or 874, whose name was 'Abd Allah – but who was known as Sa'id to safeguard his identity – married Abu'l-Shalaghla's daughter. 'Abd Allah's chamberlain, the eunuch Ja'far, recorded in his memoir details of the wedding. He described it as a joyous occasion where he danced with unveiled women who were playing outside the nuptial bedroom to celebrate the consummation of the marriage.[15] From this union a son was born in 893, who became known as 'Abd al-Rahman. When his uncle and father-in-law died in 899, 'Abd Allah became the head of the *da'wa*, disclosing that his real name was not Sa'id, and that his son was called Abu'l-Qasim Muhammad, not 'Abd al-Rahman as had been thought up to that point. 'Abd Allah's choice of his son's name is emblematic in the way it capitalized on the Prophet's messianic promise of the return of a second Muhammad.[16] That year, although at first thought to be a cloth merchant who acted as proof of the hidden imam as his forefathers had done, 'Abd Allah began to circulate official correspondence to the scattered Isma'ili cells, suggesting that he would soon unveil himself as the actual imam. This announcement had major consequences. Though not openly stating it at this stage, by bringing the imamate out of temporary concealment, *satr*, 'Abd Allah implied he was the *mahdi* whose appearance had been awaited since the time of Muhammad b. Isma'il's occultation. In fact, it was claimed, the concealment by this imam had been a ruse to protect his line of succession which had continued in secret through his son, 'Abd Allah the Elder, Muhammad b. Isma'il's grandson Ahmad, and his great-grandson al-Husayn. Now, 'Abd Allah revealed his and his ancestors' real identity to his most trusted *da'is* as he saw that the time had come to make the imamate manifest once again to deliver its messianic promise.[17]

This extraordinary revelation was met with as much exhilaration as utter consternation among members of the *da'wa* in Syria, Iraq and beyond. Within the early Isma'ili fold a group had emerged, the Qarmatians, named after the founder, Hamdan Qarmat (d. *c.* 899). This figure, also known as Abu 'Ali, went from being an active recruiter of propagandists to becoming a staunch opponent of 'Abd Allah. From their base in Kufa, the Qarmatians had remained committed to awaiting the return of Muhammad b. Isma'il as the *mahdi*. Therefore, when 'Abd Allah challenged this core belief with his claim, they found it unacceptable and preposterous, and refused to recognize him as imam. As a result, a separate group emerged that, while continuing to challenge the 'Abbasids, would also stand in opposition to 'Abd Allah and his followers. In the same year in which 'Abd Allah announced his imamate, a Qarmatian activist, Abu Sa'id al-Jannabi (d. 913), who had entered the movement through his wife, began counter-missionary activity in regions along the Persian Gulf coast, disguised as a trader. The Qarmatians attracted followers in Syria, Iraq and Iran, but it was in Bahrain that they established their base. The *da'wa* in Iran, though not conflated with the Qarmatian movement, continued to uphold the belief in Muhammad b. Isma'il's return and therefore refused to recognize 'Abd Allah's imamate at this stage.[18]

Despite the setback caused by this dissenting group, by the year 900 'Abd Allah had the support of a strong network of agents, secret cells established in a range of regions, tithe-paying recruits and plenty of money acquired through followers' tributes, trading activities and other means. At the periphery of the 'Abbasid empire, from Yemen to North Africa, thousands of loyal supporters – be they merchants, urban elites, peasants, Bedouins, Arabs or Berbers – had been waiting for his appearance in full while preparing to fight for the fulfilment of the promise of the *mahdi*'s advent to lead the Muslim community to its universal victory.

Towards the Fulfilment of a Messianic Promise

In 902 'Abd Allah's cover in Salamiyya was blown by the careless actions of over-enthusiastic followers. Opposed by the Qarmatians and by the 'Abbasids, he had no other option but to leave. Tipped by *da'is* in Baghdad about the imminent dispatch of troops against him ordered by the 'Abbasids, 'Abd Allah left Syria at once, accompanied by a small retinue. Besides his son, this included the chief *da'i* Firuz, his chamberlain and milk-brother Ja'far and four Christian slaves who were his son's tutors. Care of his child was tasked to a woman, the housekeeper Umm 'Ali al-Qahramana, a Christian convert to Islam who had married one of 'Abd Allah's slaves. The hurried circumstances of 'Abd Allah's departure did not leave time to organize the decampment of his harem, which had to be left behind for the time being. At this stage the harem consisted of 'Abd Allah's mother, two daughters, two of his brother's daughters, Umm al-Qahramana and Umm Habib, a Greek/Byzantine slave who became his son's wife. Notably, the sources do not mention 'Abd Allah's wife, the implication being that she might have been dead by this time. At first 'Abd Allah headed for Ramla, a city with a strong Shi'a presence. They stopped in Damascus, where, one day, his son threw such a tantrum in public over a white dog he wanted that 'Abd Allah bought it for an exorbitant sum to quieten him, as the boy's cry would make them conspicuous among the crowds. With his son happy with his pet, the group had to move fast before their presence was reported to the 'Abbasid authorities. In Ramla, 'Abd Allah hid in the house of the local governor, an Isma'ili sympathizer, maybe even an initiate. In June or July of that year, one night he and his son went up to the roof to view an unusual spectacle in the sky. In early and medieval Islamic culture, the appearance of comets and unusual astral phenomena was interpreted as a portent with eschatological significance. The event 'Abd Allah and his son witnessed was an extraordinary meteor shower. A sign of his mission's success?[19] During the period of his residence in Ramla, 'Abd Allah bought several houses and moved from one to the next to avoid being tracked down by his enemies. Some supporters wanted to take him back to Salamiyya in triumph but he did not pursue this option. These followers settled in Homs and other towns in the Orontes region, where they gathered such momentum that, for the first time, the sermon accompanying the Friday congregational prayers – an Islamic ritual that also functioned as occasion for public announcements of political authority – was held in the name of 'Abd Allah, and coins were struck with his titles. This rudimental attempt at establishing a state for 'Abd Allah – to them the imam descendant of Muhammad b. Isma'il – was soon quashed by troops sent from Baghdad. Disenchanted by this outcome, these supporters turned against their champion.[20] The great Sunni historian al-Tabari (d. 923), in chronicling events which took place in ninth- to early tenth-century Syria, called the followers and *da'is* acting on behalf of 'Abd Allah *fatimiyyun*, fatimids, on account of their support for a leader claiming to be descended from Fatima's progeny. In his work, commonly known as *The History of al-Tabari*, completed in 915, though not referring to the dynasty, we find the first known instance of the use of *fatimiyyun* to designate Isma'ili activists.[21]

While 'Abd Allah was in Ramla, his closest associates looked after his properties and affairs in Salamiyya, dispatching parts of his wealth to his new abode. However, some of his disaffected *da'is* who had been caught by the 'Abbasids revealed the identity and whereabouts of 'Abd Allah, causing search warrants for him to reach Ramla. As his enemies approached, 'Abd Allah fled, leaving behind a trusted female servant, La'b. Interrogated under torture to reveal her master's whereabouts and the hiding place of his fortunes, she refused to betray him, paying with her and her children's lives the ultimate price for her loyalty.[22]

It was time to move again, and fast. Having left Ramla, 'Abd Allah and his group, in disguise, joined a caravan from Baghdad heading west towards Alexandria in Egypt. While travelling, the shipments of money and property from Salamiyya had to be suspended for the foreseeable future. 'Abd Allah's hagiographers praised his craftiness, recording his strategy to hide his treasure: he sent orders to his servants in Salamiyya to pretend to mount a revolt against him. They would use this pretext to destroy his house so that its rubble could bury the water basin under which his great-grandfather had hid a vast amount of money. To others, ʻAbd Allah's house was indeed destroyed, but by his opponents. Either way, by this time ʻAbd Allah had reached Egypt, where he was faced with a momentous decision for his future and that of the *daʻwa*: where to go next.

2

The Inauguration of the Fatimid Dynasty in North Africa

'Abd Allah's first instinct was to head for Yemen. However, news of a propagandist he had never met having rallied strong support to his cause elsewhere persuaded the imam to look at a new frontier to fulfil his destiny as universal leader. This *da'i*'s name was yet another 'Abd Allah: Abu 'Abd Allah al-Shi'i.

Abu 'Abd Allah al-Shi'i (d. 911) was an Iraqi from Kufa. Described as having been attracted to mysticism in his youth, he may have worked as a market inspector in Basra before embarking on a mission that would change his life, and history with it. Around 891, in Kufa, the Qarmatians' leader, Hamdan, had recruited him and his older brother, Abu'l-'Abbas, as agents for the Isma'ili *da'wa*. Having pledged allegiance to the imam via Firuz, his representative in Salamiyya, at first the brothers were dispatched to Egypt to carry out their secret mission from its ancient capital Fustat. From there Abu'l-'Abbas would act as a courier between Egypt and the *da'wa* headquarters in Syria. The *da'i* Abu 'Abd Allah al-Shi'i travelled to Yemen with a caravan of pilgrims on the way back from Mecca and Medina. Mecca, the Prophet Muhammad's birthplace, is the home of the holiest shrine in Islam, the Ka'ba housing the Black Stone. Medina is the second holiest city in Islam, the site of Muhammad's tomb and mosque. The pilgrimage to these sites, to be performed at least once in a lifetime, is one of five mandatory rituals in Islam.

In Yemen Abu 'Abd Allah al-Shi'i joined Ibn Hawshab (d. 914), known as Mansur al-Yaman, the conqueror of Yemen, thanks to his reputation as the most successful *da'i* of his time in that region. Ibn Hawshab – affiliated to the founders of the Qarmatian movement and also from the Kufa area – had arrived in Yemen in 881 disguised as a cotton merchant, linen weaver and exporter of cloth for turbans as well as a carpenter. He first ran a shop in Aden (Ar. 'Adan) and established with his associate 'Ali b. al-Fadl a local undercover propaganda network that had since increased its territorial expansion and human capital. Having also consolidated the bonds across *da'wa* members through intermarriages, Ibn Hawshab dispatched his wife's cousin to be a propagandist in Sindh, a region that had come under Muslim rule in the early eighth century. A cell was then established in Multan, in today's Pujab, which operated undercover for some eighty years. According to later Isma'ili literature, it was in this city and in Uch that Imam Isma'il, son of Ja'far al-Sadiq, had manifested himself and where he was believed to have performed miracles.[1]

Ibn Hawshab also sent propagandists to establish secret cells in parts of Arabia, Bahrain and other far-flung locations. In 892 he ordered Abu 'Abd Allah al-Shi'i to embark on a mission to conduct the *da'wa* in the name of the imam in a peripheral province of the 'Abbasid empire. The move set in motion a sequence of events that would result in the establishment of the Fatimid dynasty.

With other *da'is*, Abu 'Abd Allah al-Shi'i was once more in Mecca where he met a group of departing Kutama Berber pilgrims. Some of them, already pro-Shi'a, responded to his preaching. The encounter would be a turning point for the fortunes of the *da'wa*. Abu 'Abd Allah al-Shi'i had in fact intended to travel with them only as far as Egypt, where he would then settle. He knew the country already; his brother was there, and Egypt was a favourable trading post where, as an undercover *da'i*, he could conduct his mission camouflaged as a merchant while also supporting himself and his cause. This was not to be. Impressed by him, his Kutama followers persuaded him to join them all the way back to their homeland in North Africa so that Abu 'Abd Allah al-Shi'i could bring his message to their tribe as a whole. The Kutamas, divided into several clans each under the authority of a chief, lived in communities scattered across the Little Kabylie mountain range in today's northeastern Algeria, a region over which the Sunni Arab Aghlabid rulers (r. 800–909) had only nominal authority. Dissident religious groups were not uncommon among the Berbers. As a result, from their capital Qayrawan (also known as Kairouan, in today's Tunisia) the Aghlabid regime paid little attention to the Kutamas and the activities of the preacher they had welcomed to settle among them. The Aghlabids, *amirs* with roots in the military, had been ruling over the part of North Africa known in the middle period of Islamic history as Ifriqiya on behalf of the 'Abbasids in Baghdad.[2] Besides governing this region, in 827 the Aghlabids took parts of Sicily from the Byzantines. From there they went on to conquer towns on the island's northern coast, where they built naval bases that became launch pads for further incursions in the rest of the western Mediterranean. In the space of a few decades they had established a foothold on mainland southern Italy as well.

Under the Aghlabids, Ifriqiya had become an important centre of trade and cultural life. These rulers, who adhered to the Hanafi school of law, distinguished themselves as patrons of sumptuous mosques in cities like Qayrawan, Tunis, Sousse and Sfax. Qayrawan's Great Mosque became an important repository of Qur'anic manuscripts. Either produced or brought there, some of these artefacts and their fine bindings are extant to this day. Not having a royal pedigree and artistic terms of reference of their own to build on, the Aghlabids relied on builders, craftsmen and materials imported from across the 'Abbasid empire. Iraqi decorative tiles can still be seen inside Qayrawan's mosque. However, the Berbers, the autochthonous people of North Africa, as well as some Arab nobility with ancestry going back to the time of the Islamic conquest of Ifriqiya, resented this regime. The Kutamas, in particular, saw themselves as the true champions of Islamic values against the Aghlabid rulers whom they saw as arrogant and corrupt.

Against this background Abu 'Abd Allah al-Shi'i's promise of the advent among the Kutama of a messianic figure who would bring justice in this world and the next found fertile ground. This was also due to the Berbers' beliefs surrounding prophecy, something reflected in the rise over time of several so-called false prophets among them. The extent to which Abu 'Abd Allah al-Shi'i had prior information about the Kutamas and targeted his mission to them as part of a pre-planned strategy is hard to tell. The accounts of his encounter with them depict it as a fortuitous event and, likewise, his sudden change of mind about the final destination of his journey seem to exclude the hypothesis of a pre-conceived masterplan. At the same time hagiographical texts portraying his life among the Kutamas might have dwelled on the apparent randomness of events as a literary device to reinforce the predestined character of the *da'i*'s mission.

Abu 'Abd Allah al-Shi'i's character conformed to the ideals the Kutamas saw in a righteous religious-political leader. He imposed acts of worship on his followers, devised rules to curb offences, promoted pious deeds and applied justice. Unlike the frivolous Aghlabid royals, he was described as a single-minded man of firm character. Leaning towards asceticism, he ate the same food and wore the same modest clothes every day. He was a man of simple tastes they could relate to, all the way down to his occasional physical frailties. Trouble with his kidney stones almost gave him away: once the Aghlabids had got wind of his subversive activities, he came close to being arrested while he was at a spa to get treatment.[3] With such an intense life no wonder he needed occasional blood-letting to treat his high blood pressure. A simple diet of parboiled egg yolks would restore him to health.

Abu 'Abd Allah al-Shi'i was not an intellectual of the stature of his elder brother Abu'l-'Abbas but he was a formidable preacher nonetheless. He soon started a broad initiation process that concluded with an oath of allegiance. Referring to a tradition ascribed to the Prophet Muhammad, his claim that the *mahdi* would one day settle among a group whose name was associated with the word *kitman*, secret, must have made a strong impression on the Kutamas.[4] He preached in sessions, *majalis*, about the virtues of the family of the Prophet, the imams descending from it and Isma'ili doctrines. Shi'ism was already known in the region and this must have helped him spread his message. These lectures were attended by men and women who would engage in debates. One among them, Umm Musa, became, in early Isma'ili literature, an exemplary female figure at the service of the North African *da'wa*. Brought up as a Shi'i, when she joined the Isma'ili cause she not only participated in the *majalis* but contributed to the *da'wa* efforts by cooking for the militants. Upon becoming a widow, she was said to have bequeathed her inheritance to further propaganda in the name of the *mahdi*. Other women tended to the sick and offered other services.[5] While the visibility of ordinary women was rare in the Arab Islamic society of this time, this was not so among the Berbers, where women were known to occupy a prominent position. Irrespective of gender, the teaching sessions were reserved for Kutama initiates sworn to secrecy under oath. During their initiation ceremony Abu 'Abd Allah al-Shi'i would place his index finger on the mouth of each of them to signify silence, on account of the peril implicit in revealing the Isma'ili doctrines to outsiders. Abu 'Abd Allah al-Shi'i's success as a *da'i* in delivering a religious-political revolutionary message led him to acquire a loyal powerbase. Operating among the Berbers, for whom solidarity was a core value, his ability to harness their loyalty to its full potential would raise his status from that of campaigner to strategist and conqueror.

Emboldened by his following, Abu 'Abd Allah al-Shi'i set about reorganizing the Kutamas' political and administrative tribal organization. He turned clans into army divisions consisting of several regiments, each under their respective commanders. In turn the commanders were sided by *da'is* put in charge of each district. Commanders and *da'is* became therefore administrators of this nascent Isma'ili community, and were responsible for collecting revenues destined in part to the imam. However, the Kutamas' enthusiasm for Abu 'Abd Allah al-Shi'i was not shared by all the Berber tribes, with some forming coalitions against them and Abu 'Abd Allah al-Shi'i in particular, having joined the anti-Isma'ili Khariji cause. The Aghlabids were also waking up to the fact that Abu 'Abd Allah al-Shi'i's success was not a passing fad. Rather than being a deterrent, this opposition worked to the *da'i*'s advantage: his community of believers now had the means and ideological motivation to confront challengers and venture into territorial military expansion. After initial setbacks, success smiled on the Kutamas and their leader. As Kutama factions and other Berbers joined the cause, more victories followed. As enemies were defeated and booty was acquired, a community refuge, *dar al-hijra*, was established in Tazrut, in today's Algeria, that became the headquarters of the Kutama tribal confederation.[6] Above all, this headquarters represented the first actualization in North Africa of the promised righteous state founded on Isma'ili principles. This was no longer utopia: the Kutama families flocked there en masse. As a form of Isma'ili socio-territorial organization, the first *dar al-hijra* had been established in Yemen in 885 by Mansur al-Yaman, and others followed in Iraq and Bahrain, founded by the Qarmatians.

With the takeover of Tazrut, the Aghlabid regime at last reacted against Abu 'Abd Allah al-Shi'i and his supporters. At first it tried to corrupt the *da'i* with money, and when that failed it launched a major offensive to push him out of Tazrut. However, while military attacks succeeded in dislodging the Isma'ilis out of that town, it only led to the *da'i* and his community moving to Ikjan, a place understood to have been near Mila, where a new *da'wa* centre was established.[7] Abu 'Abd Allah al-Shi'i knew the area well, as he had tried to occupy it before while conducting his mission. It was also in this vicinity that he had made use of thermal baths to treat his kidney ailment. Within a short time, a fortress – described as impregnable by Isma'ili sources – was built there with amenities to serve the community. Taxes were abolished, which meant that more booty was needed to finance the enterprise. Following earlier successes, Ikjan became the base for raids and the successful acquisition of more territories. The ultimate aim of these campaigns was to reach the Aghlabid *amir*s' palace in Raqqada, founded as a royal residence in 876. Beside gardens and parks, the complex included several palaces, farm buildings, stables and cisterns, as well as artificial lakes as reservoirs for drinking water. What is left of it is an important archaeological site in today's Tunisia. Nearby Qayrawan was the religious and political administrative centre of government, with its mosque having become a centre of Maliki learning.

The Aghlabids' attempts to attack Ikjan in response to the Kutamas' threat came to nothing, due to confusion caused by internal disputes. Also, in 902 the *amir*s were more intent on trying to advance their control of Sicily and southern Italy at the Byzantines' expense. In October of that year the Aghlabid *amir* Ibrahim II died. A chronicler recording his death stated that on that night 'an infinite number of stars scattered themselves like rain to the right and left.' The year became known as the 'the year of the stars'.[8] As a portent, this extraordinary meteor shower foretold different destinies for its respective witnesses. As disruption reigned among the Aghlabids, in the year of the stars the Isma'ili imam 'Abd Allah had left Syria on his way to North Africa to fulfil his divine mandate: one astral event, two leaders set on a collision course. The accounts of this meteorite shower witnessed at the same time in Ifriqiya and in Ramla represent the earliest known records of a definite sighting of what is called a Leonid meteor storm.

More Aghlabid expeditions were turned back, thanks to Abu 'Abd Allah al-Shi'i's strategic skills and his ability to keep the Kutama cavalry's morale high with his participation in battle. This territorial expansion culminated in March 909 with the *da'i* leading the Kutama forces into the royal palace in Raqqada. Reinforced walls, military resources and anti-Isma'ili propaganda proved ineffectual in stopping their entrance. Against Abu 'Abd Allah al-Shi'i's orders, the Kutama started looting the palace, an act that prompted the *da'i* to assert his authority. He not only ordered the Kutamas to return the looted goods but punished them to deter any further acts of insubordination. After more military confrontations, the Aghlabid *amir* Ziadat Allah III

(d. *c.* 911–16) packed gold and other possessions on a caravan and fled towards Egypt. In response to these fast-evolving events the people of Qayrawan also looted the palace, taking what was left behind by the departed *amir*. Once again, Abu 'Abd Allah al-Shi'i had to intervene by dispatching a cavalry division to stop the pillaging and restore order. As spokesperson for the impending fulfilment of the promise to 'enjoin the right and forbid the wrong', a duty sanctioned in the Qur'an (31:17), the *da'i* had to act fast to assert his leadership credentials. Also, as the new occupant of Raqqada's royal residence, being only its caretaker on behalf of the imam, the *da'i* did not want its splendour to go to waste. Luxury artefacts imported from the eastern lands of the 'Abbasid empire and beyond were preserved. He ordered that the property of the old regime should be secured in Raqqada for safekeeping, including the concubines of the deposed royal masters who would be destined for the imam upon his arrival.

Having only ever led a large but nonetheless somewhat rustic bunch of tribesmen in some remote mountains, and with no personal experience of what living as an urban ruler might entail, Abu 'Abd Allah al-Shi'i was a parvenu when it came to the organization of court life. Yet he knew the importance of looking the part in the eyes of the urbanite Arabs of the capital. Having no precedent, he adopted the existing royal style of protocol while giving it an Isma'ili imprint. Faced with having to figure out the complexities of statecraft from scratch, Abu 'Abd Allah al-Shi'i availed himself of the experienced courtiers from the previous regime. At the same time, palace administrators, officers, cooks, gardeners and attendants had no other option but to serve the new masters to save their livelihood and, perhaps, their lives. Aftcr only a day, the court under new management was already operational, as Abu 'Abd Allah al-Shi'i met delegations of former Aghlabid Qayrawani high officers at the palace pleading for safe conduct. The *da'i* granted it to the population along with an invitation to members of the old regime to return – as long as they submitted to the new one. Within a short time, this first act of government was announced from the pulpits of all the mosques in Ifriqiya. Next, an edict was issued promising security and prosperity as well as military aid for Sicily against Byzantine incursions. He also sent another *da'i* and a new governor to Qayrawan, where a night curfew was imposed as well as the prohibition of alcohol consumption, a pursuit the Aghlabid elites were accused of indulging in. Soon visitors followed. These included ambitious *da'wa* adherents, such as the Qayrawani scholar Ibn al-Haytham, who went to Raqqada to engage in debates with the *da'i* Abu 'Abd Allah al-Shi'i. He belonged to a pro-Shi'a environment, embraced Isma'ilism and collected the debates he engaged in with the great *da'i* and his brother in a book that provides an insight into the inner working of the *da'wa* during this phase.[9] These encounters took place at Abu 'Abd Allah al-Shi'i's residence, which was located within the multi-complex city palace of Raqqada. The more luxurious quarters with a view over the artificial lake were destined for the imam. As for the rest of the Raqqada complex, other *da'is* and commanders occupied other buildings, while over time a vast number of Kutama troops settled around the palace area.

Abu 'Abd Allah al-Shi'i received visitors in a room guarded by fifty men. Repurposing former Aghlabid furniture, the hall was furnished with a couch covered by a saddle on which he sat. Kissing his hand, senior staff and general visitors would address him as *my lord*. Visitors included the leading physician of Qayrawan, called to treat his blood pressure problems. The *da'i* would get up to greet close associates and followers, ordering that washing water should be brought to them before meals. Fragrant roast poussins would be served on Chinese porcelain trays placed on tables made from scented wood. At the end of a convivial gathering with close associates, a gardener would bring fine censers crafted in the shape of a lion, surrounded by neatly arranged roses (illus. 4).

The incense-infused flowers would be then distributed among the attending believers as a sign of honour, to be reciprocated with a donation destined for the imam.[10] Drawing on a Byzantine-style way of dispensing blessings, and by reinventing the use of Aghlabid secular ornamental artefacts, Abu 'Abd Allah al-Shi'i devised a distinctive formula that made the imam's symbolic presence felt among his guests. Within weeks convivial yet sedate fundraising events to sponsor the imam's cause had replaced the exuberance of the Aghlabid *amir*'s palace parties. Though rumoured to have been raucous affairs – whoopee cushions and all – Aghlabid court life was in fact quite sophisticated, even enjoying for a while entertainment by the Iraqi celebrity musician of the time, Ziryab (d. 857).[11]

It had taken Abu 'Abd Allah al-Shi'i eighteen years of physical hardship and hard work to get to the point of establishing the territorial foundations for the manifestation of the universal reign of the imam. This was an extraordinary achievement for which he more than

4 Fatimid incense burner in the shape of a lion, Egypt, 11th–12th century, bronze. The lion, a worldwide recognized symbol of majesty, was adopted by the Fatimids too, who made the best use of its imagery on a range of luxury artefacts that became distinctive of the dynasty.

deserved the occasional indulgence. As he came under the Kutamas' pressure to have a female companion he relented, taking a slave girl for himself who gave him a son.

Outside the palace the new regime began its course by maintaining the administrative apparatus of the former government across its new domains. Faced with the lack of a systematic Isma'ili legal code – something he had no mandate or authority to devise – at this initial stage Abu 'Abd Allah al-Shi'i resorted to what he thought would work best: the broad application of Shi'i legal principles blended with local customary law. For example, in the administration of justice, he adopted the Berber practice of confinement or social isolation, where appropriate, as a form of punishment. Priority was given to making changes to the symbols of authority to make it clear to the subjects who the new rulers were, what they were about and that they were here to stay. A distinctive Shi'i formula defined the call to prayer; new coinage was introduced with Shi'i-specific legends; Sunni-specific prayers were abolished; the Friday sermon delivered in all mosques had to start with blessings on the Shi'i holy family: 'Ali, Fatima, al-Hasan and al-Husayn. At this stage, since the rule of the imam had yet to become manifest with his formal enthronment, reference to him was proclaimed only by implication. In the call to prayer, for example, this was done through invocation of his ancestry going back to the Prophet and, on coins, by reference to his title, *hujja*, proof of God rather than his name. In less than a week from the start of the new rule the Friday Isma'ili preaching seminars were up and running in Raqqada and Qayrawan, and people gathered almost every day to learn about new legal and ritual directives. Every item that had belonged to the old regime, from horse fittings to seals and banners, was rebranded with quotations of Qur'anic verses selected to suit a pro-Isma'ili propaganda.

Overnight a Sunni western province of the 'Abbasid empire, comprising today's Tunisia, Algeria, part of Libya and Sicily, had become Shi'i-ruled and independent of Baghdad. If, for the wider populace, the political changes the new Isma'ili regime brought were bearable, the religious and legal changes that came with them were harder to swallow. The cities of the now Isma'ili domains were dominated by Malikis and Hanafis, hostile to Shi'is to the point that even prior to the arrival of the Isma'ili regime, some Shi'is living in Qayrawan had to hide their faith out of fear. It is therefore no surprise that Abu 'Abd Allah al-Shi'i's appointment of the first pro-Shi'i judge in Qayrawan, tasked with ensuring rigour in adherence to Shi'i rituals and laws, caused uproar and resentment. Although Isma'ili practices and laws were implemented, conversion was not forced, and in fact joining the *da'wa* still required scrutiny. Apart from the Kutamas, the majority of subjects remained Sunni. Nevertheless, anti-Maliki and anti-Hanafi measures were set in place with judges belonging to those Sunni schools of law being prohibited to issue legal rulings. Books belonging to their schools of law were vilified by using their pages as wrapping paper for the sale of goods. Some volumes were exported to al-Andalus.[12] However, in spite of this repressive climate, the Sunni legal schools, Malikism in particular, continued to operate in practice, and even expanded somewhat, with wide networks of scholars gravitating to Qayrawan during this period and beyond.[13]

With a palace, a loyal army, a vast territory that was on the whole pacified and controlled, a *da'wa* that could at last operate in the open; all that was missing was the person in whose name all of this had been achieved: the imam. After about three months of palace life, in June 909 Abu 'Abd Allah al-Shi'i was ready for the most daring of all ventures

– to fetch the imam and bring him in triumph to Raqqada where the Prophet's messianic promise of the advent of the ultimate just universal rule would be fulfilled.

Abu 'Abd Allah al-Shi'i owed a lot of his success to his elder brother, Abu'l-'Abbas Muhammad. The two had conducted their propaganda activity together until they reached Egypt, where their service to the *da'wa* took them in different directions: Abu'l-'Abbas stayed in Egypt, while Abu 'Abd Allah al-Shi'i went to Yemen. Twenty years would pass before the brothers would be reunited for a lengthy period of time. During this phase, however, they had remained in constant touch, assisting each other in the realization of the imam's reign. In Fustat, at the time one of the most important commercial hubs of the 'Abbasid empire, Abu'l-'Abbas operated, like all other *da'is*, disguised as a merchant, moving as a courier between Fustat and the *da'wa* headquarters in Syria, still headed by Firuz. Abu'l-'Abbas would bring news of the progress achieved by the *da'wa* in North Africa and then, from Egypt, he dispatched updates to his brother regarding the situation in Salamiyya and the plans of the imam as they unfolded. It was around 899, in Salamiyya, that Abu'l-'Abbas persuaded Firuz to be taken into the imam's personal service by pledging directly to him. The imam accepted Abu'l-'Abbas' request from behind a curtain; once the pledge was completed the curtain was opened to reveal Imam 'Abd Allah together with his son.[14] The sight must have both amazed and perplexed Abu'l-'Abbas: the person in front of him was 'Abd Allah, not Muhammad b. Isma'il, whose messianic return the Isma'ilis had been promised. Also, the presence of his son at the ceremony indicated that the imam had in mind a dynastic programme even before his reign was established. Whether an example of the gift of foreknowledge granted to the imam or a long-term plan on his part, Abu'l-'Abbas was nonetheless convinced by what he saw. Overwhelmed, he had after all received the honour of being disclosed a secret: the physical identity of the imam of the time. After this brief encounter, Abu'l-'Abbas and the imam would be reunited in Fustat under different circumstances.

On the run from Syria, the imam 'Abd Allah arrived in Egypt. There he settled in Fustat where he reconnected with Abu'l-'Abbas. He lived there for a year, keeping a low profile, but 'Abbasid intelligence investigating the presencc of strangers in the territory closed on him, and Egypt's Tulunid ruler received orders from Baghdad to arrest him. Disguised as a trader, the imam fled, having dispatched his staff back to Salamiyya to retrieve the possessions and money left behind upon moving to Ramla. At first 'Abd Allah had considered heading for Yemen, but from there news had arrived that one of his most trusted *da'is*, 'Ali b. Fadl, had turned against him, claiming to be the awaited *mahdi*. Impressed by the news of Abu 'Abd Allah al-Shi'i's successful activities and territorial gains in Ifriqiya, the imam instead headed for Qayrawan, escorted by Abu'l-'Abbas and a few others. It is possible that 'Abd Allah's preference for North Africa as his destination might also have been influenced by the fact that his mother came from there, and therefore he might have been familiar with the region through her.[15] Among those accompanying 'Abd Allah to Egypt was Firuz who, however, on learning about his master's change of destination, defected to join the dissenting faction in Yemen.[16] From having been the flagship early *da'wa* hotspot, the imam saw his loyalty in Yemen reduced, with only one faction left there to support him. It would take about two centuries for Yemeni Isma'ili propaganda to be regalvanized, while the apostate branch of this group was quashed by the Sunni *amir* of Sanaa (Ar. San'a').

The imam 'Abd Allah, Abu'l-'Abbas and the others remaining left Fustat and were now on the way to Tripoli (Ar. Tarabulus al-gharb), on the North African coast, where the servants with the retrieved money from Salamiyya were expected to rejoin them. In Tripoli, the strangers' presence did not go unnoticed, and brigands attacked the group, leaving Abu'l-'Abbas with a broken nose. In a separate incident, 'Abd Allah had his books stolen, a loss he resented. That raiders were after books is not surprising, as these were a desirable commodity. This and other unsavoury episodes made it clear that this was no place to hang around while carrying great wealth. The obvious next port of call for 'Abd Allah would have been Ikjan, where Abu 'Abd Allah al-Shi'i had established the *dar al-hijra*. However, before embarking on the journey, the imam sent Abu'l-'Abbas ahead to investigate conditions in Qayrawan. Though disguised as a party of traders, Abu'l-'Abbas and his associates' presence in Qayrawan roused the Aghlabid regime's suspicion. The *amir* Ziadat Allah III had Abu'l-'Abbas arrested and tortured but never got him to admit the real purpose of his mission. He was freed during a revolt, but his arrest had been an eye-opener for the imam, who saw the region as an unsafe destination. Another change of direction ensued. This time the choice fell on Sijilmasa, an important centre for the trade of gold and slaves (among other goods).

For safety reasons, ʻAbd Allah planned to reach it via a less travelled route that passed through the interior of Ifriqiya. As soon as the money arrived from Salamiyya, hidden in bales of cotton, ʻAbd Allah departed from Tripoli, leaving behind Abu'l-ʻAbbas, who was charged with coordinating *daʻwa* covert operations there.

The journey proved to be not as relaxed as the travelling party had hoped. Mundane practicalities like finding a barber called for scrutiny and circumspection. Even allowing for the odd culinary indulgence could land the group in trouble. When the imam's servant ventured into a town market to buy aubergines his money was refused and he was beaten up. When he tried to buy a lamb to roast for ʻAbd Allah's table he had to flee, having been confronted by a vicious-looking dog owned by an even more ferocious-sounding master.[17] Trivial and other more serious accidents made ʻAbd Allah feel unsafe until at last he arrived in Sijilmasa in 905. There he rented a large house where his now expanding entourage joined him. The city was at the crossroads of three trans-Saharan trade routes, and was therefore an international wholesalers' hub. It was a place also marked by religious-political dissent, as the Khariji Berbers, who did not recognize the Baghdad caliphate or the Umayyad rulers of al-Andalus, also had a base there. Given the context, for some four years ʻAbd Allah's disguise as a rich merchant did not raise the suspicions of the locals. Having grown richer while there, ʻAbd Allah gained commercial prestige, and his reputation was such that the local governor bestowed favours on him. Behind this facade, the imam was in regular contact with Abu ʻAbd Allah al-Shiʻi, whose emissaries from Ikjan were sent to Sijilmasa disguised as poor vagrants, to deliver to ʻAbd Allah tributes collected from among his followers. Covert Ismaʻili delegations came to Sijilmasa to update the imam on the victories against the Aghlabids, and brought him booty collected in the process. They also brought gold coins that the *daʻi* Abu ʻAbd Allah al-Shiʻi had struck in the imam's honour in Raqqada. In turn ʻAbd Allah relied on trusted men to send confidential letters of instructions to Raqqada and Qayrawan. This arrangement worked until ʻAbd Allah started putting his new coins into circulation in town. Unusual in legend and of high-standard gold, the currency stood out in the markets even in a cosmopolitan centre like Sijilmasa, raising suspicions about ʻAbd Allah's real identity and the true nature of his residence in the city (illus. 5 and 6). The Aghlabid ruler realized that this wealthy gentleman might in fact be the master for whom Abu

'Abd Allah al-Shi'i had mounted his revolutionary campaign. When the governor of Sijilmasa put 'Abd Allah under house arrest, the risk of the imam's identity being unmasked became real. With his master in grave danger, Abu 'Abd Allah al-Shi'i saw that it was time to launch a rescue operation, and then to announce in public the actualization of the imam's awaited rule.

Before leaving Raqqada for the venture that would bring his quest to an end, Abu 'Abd Allah al-Shi'i had to ensure that the domain he had conquered in name of the Isma'ili cause would be in safe hands while he was in Sijilmasa. To him, the best person to manage affairs in Raqqada in his absence was his brother, Abu'l-'Abbas. Abu 'Abd Allah al-Shi'i sent letters to that effect to Tripoli and, when Abu'l-'Abbas agreed (after some convincing), a two-hundred-strong cavalry troop escorted him to Raqqada.

Abu'l-'Abbas became the de facto ruler of Isma'ili-conquered Ifriqiya, albeit only for about seven months. Like his brother, Abu'l-'Abbas was faced with a complex task, since he too had no previous experience of government at any level. He had close associates to help him and, aware of his caretaker role, took a low-key management approach in overseeing the affairs of the new regime. Described as reserved, erudite and witty, Abu'l-'Abbas differed from his more sanguine brother. Unlike Abu 'Abd Allah al-Shi'i, he refrained from holding audiences and from being seen in public at religious celebrations. While

5, 6 *Dinar* struck by Abu 'Abd Allah al-Shi'i, Qayrawan, dated 296 corresponding to the year 909.

Abu 'Abd Allah al-Shi'i had spent years in the wilderness, the urban lifestyle of Fustat and Tripoli must have influenced Abu'l-'Abbas's taste. Making use of what had been left behind from the previous regime, Abu'l-'Abbas's table exuded elegance on those rare occasions when he dispensed his encyclopaedic knowledge to eager *da'is*. Abu'l-'Abbas, like his brother, probably wrote at least a treatise in support of the imamate in the line of 'Ali and the *da'wa* in its cause. The Aghlabids had established a palace library in Raqqada that aspired to emulate the one of the famous House of Wisdom (*Bayt al-Hikma*) in 'Abbasid Baghdad. The new Isma'ili residents of the palace preserved the institution, and its books must have been available to Abu'l-'Abbas and other *da'is*. After discussing the finest points of Aristotelian philosophy, Abu'l-'Abbas would converse on botany and zoology. Having washed their hands in silver vessels, he and his guests would savour *faludhaj*, a nougat-like confection made of almonds, starch, honey and water. This, along with fruits, would be offered at the end of a meal served in gilded Chinese bowls, placed on gilded dining tables covered by bamboo mats. The gathering might end with discussions on the properties of certain herbs or foods, while sipping rose and violet essences mixed with scammony to help digestion, a potion that Abu'l-'Abbas would pour from a flask into engraved cups.[18]

Aside from personality and lifestyle, the most significant difference that set Abu'l-'Abbas and Abu 'Abd Allah al-Shi'i apart was that the former had established a close personal connection with the imam, while the latter had never met him.

The Proclamation of 'Abd Allah as the *Mahdi* and the Establishment of the Fatimid Dynasty and State

With Abu'l-'Abbas left in charge, in June 909 Abu 'Abd Allah al-Shi'i proceeded with the imam's rescue mission. The venture proved hazardous, with enemy factions launching fierce attacks against him and his contingent along the route to Sijilmasa. Once arrived in the city in August of that year, Abu 'Abd Allah al-Shi'i had an immediate practical problem to solve. Not having ever seen the imam before, he needed to find a person who knew him, so as not to risk freeing the wrong individual or being deceived by an impostor. He found this person in the son of one of 'Abd Allah's business associates.[19] Led by the boy, the group turned up at 'Abd Allah's house to rescue him. As it happened, the imam was caught by surprise, appearing in front of his rescuers in casual wear: a linen tunic, wrapped at the waist, a simple turban on his head and shoulders and plain sandals on his feet. It did not matter; scenes of jubilation followed, and the son of Imam ʻAbd Allah got lost in the commotion. Abu ʻAbd Allah al-Shiʻi genuflected in front of his master and broke down in tears. The Kutamas celebrated in their own way by going on a rampage, pillaging and looting houses across Sijilmasa.

Once ʻAbd Allah's possessions had been secured, his enthronement took place in a tent set up for him and his son. Dispatches were sent to Qayrawan and other territories announcing the unveiling of Imam ʻAbd Allah as the *mahdi*. He was announced as the caliph of God, imam, *amir al-mu'minin* – that is, commander of the faithful – whose mission was to conquer the world, East and West, from sinful rebels. The boy who had begun his life camouflaged as Saʻid in Iran, and who had revealed his identity as ʻAbd Allah in Syria, was now the imam unveiled in Ifriqiya as the messianic *mahdi*. To his supporters, the legitimate caliphal dynasty had made itself manifest in the person of ʻAbd Allah, who therefore was not just imam, but would be regarded as imam-caliph. At the ceremony the imam gathered his entourage and his rescuers, proceeding to bestow robes of honour. This was an ancient form of official investiture that had become the standard sign of royal favour in early and medieval Islamic courts. Abu ʻAbd Allah al-Shiʻi received a full set of clothes and the imam ʻAbd Allah in person took care of wrapping a turban around his head, as well as gifting him a sword. The *daʻi* could not have hoped for a greater honour. With his enthronement, the imam had shed domestic informality to assume the formal royal persona by donning luxury clothes prepared for the occasion. As a foreign-appointed ruler, representative of a minority obscure religious denomination, ʻAbd Allah showed awareness of the importance of projecting the right image to his new subjects from the outset. With no obvious statecraft pedigree or experience of royal protocol, he devised a performative vocabulary that could signal innovation, yet was rooted in tradition. Besides advertising and establishing hierarchies and ranks, while state protocol for the ʻAbbasids signified respect for the ruler, for the Fatimids it would become an expression of devotion to the imam.[20] Therefore, to shape from the outset the public perception and reception of the meaning of his rule, the imam gave orders that tents be raised, furnished with precious carpets. The next day, with the impromptu court now ready, he sat on a makeshift throne with his son to his right holding a sword, surrounded by his chamberlain Ja'far, his entourage and a page waving a fly-whisk over his head. Parades were organized so that the military and the civilian population could acknowledge him as the ruler. The people were introduced to him, organized in groups of various sizes based on rank and importance. Then *da'is* and commanders were given the chance to see him. The soldiers, in groups of ten, were instructed to introduce themselves to the imam's chamberlain at the entrance of the tent, go inside, follow what he told them to do and leave. As the proceedings continued, Abu 'Abd Allah al-Shi'i stood aside with 1,000 guards. 'Abd Allah sat in audience to greet the entire army for three more days.[21]

Abu 'Abd Allah al-Shi'i had reasons to keep in the background. If many must have been amazed by the parade, the Kutama forces were somewhat puzzled by this display of pomp. They expected a leader who would show his moral rectitude through modesty, just as Abu 'Abd Allah al-Shi'i had done. The *da'i* tried to advise the imam to tone down the style of the protocol in order to conform to the Kutamas' expectations, but 'Abd Allah had other ideas. After about two months of preparation the imam, his courtiers and his troops were ready to head to the seat of government. Against the astrologers' advice, on 12 October 909 'Abd Allah and his entourage set off eastwards on the way to Raqqada. After his departure, Sijilmasa remained for a short time under the Kutamas' control. Other territories conquered in the process of installing the imam also required Abu 'Abd Allah al-Shi'i's military intervention.

En route, the royal caravan stopped at Ikjan, an event that occasioned disappointment among the Kutama residents. First, they had believed that the imam would make Ikjan the capital of his reign; second, 'Abd Allah was a man in his mid-thirties, not the messianic youth of prophecy; third, the presentation of his son as heir apparent was confusing because nobody had mentioned eschaton having a dynastic character. The greatest setback, however, was when 'Abd Allah confiscated all the money and goods accumulated there, and ordered all the residents to decamp with him to Raqqada. As a city person, 'Abd Allah's self-image was that of an urban ruler who found Raqqada and Qayrawan more congenial headquarters than folksy, middle-of-nowhere Ikjan.[22]

The Fatimid Regime: The *Dawla*

Greeted by Abu'l-'Abbas outside Qayrawan, the imam made his triumphal entrance into Raqqada in January 910. Following his arrival he was announced for the first time as the new ruler with the royal title accompanying his full name. From this moment on he would be known as al-Mahdi. So that all bystanders could identify him during the parade, he wore a dark silk attire with a matching turban, and rode a chestnut horse. Behind him was his son and heir in a red silk robe and headdress on a dun-coloured horse. Both were preceded by Abu 'Abd Allah al-Shi'i wearing a mulberry garment surmounted by a white linen shawl, turban and kerchief, wiping sweat and dust from his face with a handkerchief while riding a bay horse. The timing had been planned to coincide with the most effective way to announce state news such as a regime change to the populace: the delivery of the sermon at the Friday congregational prayers in the main mosque. Once al-Mahdi and his heir had taken up residence in their respective palaces, sermons in Raqqada, Qayrawan and other cities also announced al-Mahdi's royal name and full titles – imam, *amir al-mu'minin* and caliph of God.

In a similar vein a manifesto was also read in public. It affirmed al-Mahdi's descent from Muhammad's family, and the promise of salvation for those who paid allegiance to him. It confirmed the safe conduct for all citizens accepting the new rule, as Abu 'Abd Allah al-Shi'i had already promised. It reiterated that, as ruler, his authority not only would apply to the Isma'ili faithful (*mu'minin*) but was extended to all *muslimin*, that is the Sunnis and other Shi'is, and non-Muslims too. It proclaimed the imam's mission of bringing universal peace and restoring justice in the name of Islam. The prophecy according to which a sign of the advent of the *mahdi* would be the sun rising from the west had been fulfilled: al-Mahdi, coming from the east and appearing in western lands as he had, was this sun. To the Isma'ilis these events marked the moment when al-Mahdi, as the first manifest imam-caliph, inaugurated the *dawlat al-haqq*, the regime of the truth, setting in motion the cycle of the rightful leadership of the ultimate legitimate regime. In this capacity this rightly guided state would supplant that of the 'Abbasid usurpers and grow into a universal empire. Sunnis and non-Isma'ilis in general called this regime and its rulers Fatimid, from Fatima, the daughter of the Prophet Muhammad, from whom the Isma'ili imams claimed descent. This made the Fatimids the first and, so far, only Islamic ruling dynasty to be known by a name derived from that of a woman. If intended to ridicule both claimants and supporters, the mockery backfired. Although the dynasty never called itself as such, Fatimid would become the name of choice by which the regime and its leaders would be known among sympathizers as well as detractors. The Fatimid dynasty and its era were born.

During the first months of rule delegations of local notables arrived to pay their respects. Al-Mahdi held assemblies and allowed followers as well as ordinary people to greet him. The physician of the former rulers would now attend to his wellbeing. In return for a generous allowance, a court poet under new patronage eulogized the son of Fatima being reunited with his harem upon its arrival from Salamiyya. Former Aghlabid concubines were added to al-Mahdi's female entourage, but most of them were allocated to the Kutamas. The Kutama regiments found themselves dispatched to garrisons across the Fatimid domains, while the administration and institutions of the state stayed in Arab hands in Qayrawan. As a sign of change, al-Mahdi reorganized the central government bureaux, appointing new staff from among his close associates to shadow the experienced officials of the old regime whose service he retained. The tax bureau, the post and the intelligence service needed to be managed by people who knew the land and its people well. To that effect he ordered the restoration of the land register that had been destroyed by the defeated Aghlabids. To strengthen his credentials as the just ruler, he made his moral stance visible by taking measures such as, for example, returning to the original owners illegally confiscated property. In taking ownership of what had belonged to the previous rulers al-Mahdi granted protection to their women, whom he had retained for his close entourage, by providing them with allowances. The superintendent of these women had requested on their behalf food, blankets and adequate shelter according to their status. They also demanded that wine and sex would be provided as they were used to.[23] Al-Mahdi only agreed to the second. He established a department of pensions, extended to include freed slaves. In contrast to the Aghlabids' extravagant personal use of state funds, he kept track of expenditures. Under new rule the landscape was re-inscribed accordingly: the name and titles of the imam replaced those of his predecessors on public buildings.

In the administration of the state, like the 'Abbasids and most other Islamic regimes, al-Mahdi relied on a system of bureaux, *diwan*s, with some adaptations. By far the most important *diwan* was the treasury. This department included the royal mint, the public treasury, the board of revenues that managed a convoluted tax system, the office of estates that had belonged to the Aghlabids and the board taking care of palace expenditures. Linked to the treasury was the royal textile factory, the *tiraz*. The fortunes of the Fatimids were interwoven with their mercantile dominance in the production and distribution of textiles. Leading to the rise of the dynasty, the trading of fabrics had provided safe mobility and regular cash flow to undercover *da'i*s and the hidden imams. One of the earliest known royal Islamic textiles to survive, dating back to the mid-eighth century, was made in Ifriqiya, thus testifying to state textile factories having been established in the region at an early date. These were then acquired by the Aghlabids and in turn by the Fatimids, who added their own factories, the products of which soon became a byword for superior quality and desirability.

Unlike other Islamic regimes, the new Fatimid administration had no vizier, no bureau for the military and no chancery office. The army was the imam's property and he ensured that its maintenance and equipment would be taken care of. He assigned to every Kutama contingent a district of Ifriqiya as more towns fell under his rule. The chiefs of each contingent would act as governors. Thanks to royal patronage, the Kutamas' possessions grew to include gifts and land grants, although this did not stop internal rivalries based on who was allocated what.

Once again, al-Mahdi took care to project a positive image of his regime: he ordered his high officers to ditch their rugged looks in favour of wearing the finest garments, and riding on exquisite saddles. As the Kutamas' status and roles diversified, the army was expanded to include Black slaves, and white slaves of Slav Christian origin who converted to Islam. The latter, known as the Saqaliba (sing. Saqlabi), acted in various capacities.[24] Originating from eastern Europe, they arrived in Ifriqiya via southern Italy, Sicily and the Iberian Peninsula. The Fatimids had inherited the practice of employing them from the Aghlabids, appointing Saqaliba eunuchs, for example, to tend to any requirements of al-Mahdi's harem that could not be addressed by a woman or a non-kin male. Al-Mahdi put some of them in charge of his private warehouses to facilitate the circulation of goods within his household. As customary, the imam-caliph distributed to them fine clothes to wear, such as multi-coloured garments in silk and thick stripy taffeta. Among these Slavs, one bright young eunuch, Jawdhar, caught the attention of al-Mahdi, who tasked him with serving his son and heir apparent. As a sign of favour, al-Mahdi had special clothes made for Jawdhar and granted him estates. In due course Jawdhar became a close advisor, a confidant and the highest-ranking officer of the state to serve the first four imam-caliphs.[25]

For chancery duties, al-Mahdi relied on an experienced secretary who had served the previous masters. Being a professional secretary, this officer was already familiar with the functioning of the administrative machine on which state management depended. Sitting with the imam-caliph, his role was to prepare documents and letters that were instruments of government. Due to the sensitive nature of the documents he handled, the secretary had oversight of the postal and intelligence services. The administration of justice was however a problem because, with the new regime being so young, as yet there was no codified Isma'ili legal system in place. Al-Mahdi therefore continued with the system adopted by Abu 'Abd Allah al-Shi'i of applying generic principles of Shi'i jurisprudence in Qayrawan. The imam however handled grievances in person. During his frequent outings or when holding audiences, people would hand to al-Mahdi petitions, *mazalim*, asking him to redress judges' verdicts considered unfair. Deemed infallible, according to Shi'i Isma'ili belief, the imam had the ultimate say in determining the correct application of the divine law.

A distinctive Isma'ili institution established by the Fatimids was the office in charge of propaganda, the *da'wa*. With the state apparatus, *dawla*, in place, Isma'ili propaganda now operated in full view in the territories under direct Fatimid rule. What had been, prior to 909, a covert network of *da'is* camouflaged as traders, the *da'wa* was now a systematic operation at the heart of the regime. The office coordinated learning sessions for Isma'ilis as well as generic ones for outsiders. In Raqqada, for palace purposes, trained Isma'ili Kutama Berbers were now trusted to hold formal learning sessions on doctrinal matters.

The sudden rise to power of an unknown newcomer destabilized the delicate religious-political balance of the western Mediterranean region, while putting rulers in the eastern 'Abbasid territories on alert. Challengers to al-Mahdi's regime soon mobilized to remove him, or at least limit his sphere of action. Within Ifriqiya opponents included pro-Maliki and pro-Khariji Berbers such as the Zanata, who stood in opposition to the pro-Fatimid Sanhajas and other tribes; the Idrisids, the first ‘Alid dynasty in Maghreb since 789, who claimed descent from ‘Ali b. Abi Talib’s son al-Hasan, unlike the Husaynid Fatimids; the Rustamids of Tahart; and Aghlabid resistance groups and various factions of Maliki Sunnis. External powers supported some of these groups: the Umayyads of al-Andalus backed the Zanatas in order to expand their own influence in North Africa. The ‘Abbasids supported, but without great conviction, the various Sunni uprisings. All saw the Christian Byzantines as the common enemy. The Byzantines, who by the tenth century had control of much of the northeastern Mediterranean, sought to take advantage of the Muslim rulers’ internal rivalries across the rest of the region. Within the Isma‘ili fold, the Qarmatians of Syria, Iraq and Bahrain continued to be the Fatimids’ greatest doctrinal and political opponents, by rejecting al-Mahdi’s claim to the imamate. Instead, they persisted in their belief in the return of Muhammad b. Isma‘il.

Standing up against internal threats and responding to external pressures reinforced al-Mahdi’s status as that of a ruler on a par with others, be they the ‘Abbasid caliph or the Byzantine emperor. Whether for defence or conquest or both, al-Mahdi’s *dawla* was indeed devised for war, and the conquest of Ifriqiya was only the beginning of an imperial project whose completion was intended to culminate with the conquest of Baghdad and Constantinople. However, in the immediate circumstances, if at one level al-Mahdi’s early reign had restored order where the Aghlabids had left a mess, it was nevertheless marked by regular outbursts of rebellion and conflict that needed addressing. But al-Mahdi was no combatant; in his daily life he had been a trader with no known military experience of any sort, and he never came close to engaging in battle. Instead, to fight on his behalf he had the Kutamas as well as his son and presumptive successor. This young prince was sent to lead campaigns to halt rivals’ expansionist ambitions, to quash revolts, to attempt to conquer new territories and to pacify subjects across the acquired domains.

But what of the brothers who had dedicated their lives to al-Mahdi’s cause? At the outset, al-Mahdi who, like Abu ‘Abd Allah al-Shi‘i and Abu’l-‘Abbas, had no prior experience of ruling over a territorial state, had confirmed the brothers’ policies and appointments. Abu ‘Abd Allah al-Shi‘i, helped by his brother, was in charge of the preaching sessions in Raqqada and was de facto the head of the *da‘wa*. However, in the space of just a year after taking power, al-Mahdi had marginalized the two men as the relationship between him and the brothers soured. Abu 'Abd Allah al-Shi'i had expected to occupy a power-sharing position in return for all his efforts. Abu'l-'Abbas and other *da'is* might have pushed him to argue his case with al-Mahdi, thus challenging the imam-caliph's absolute authority. Among the Kutamas, factions emerged that sided with Abu 'Abd Allah al-Shi'i out of solidarity, but they had other reasons to resent al-Mahdi. Ethnic rivalry played a part in this discontent. As Berbers, they accused the imam of neglecting their interests by favouring Arabs, since he re-employed officials of the previous regime in all the prominent government posts. Al-Mahdi's confiscations in Ikjan a few years before had not been forgotten either. The disappointment snowballed into doubt that led them to question al-Mahdi's imamate, with Kutama sceptics wanting to see miracles as proof. Sensing the mounting threat of large-scale rebellion, al-Mahdi's response was realpolitik. In 911 he ordered the execution of Abu 'Abd Allah al-Shi'i, Abu'l-'Abbas and a few other *da'is* on a charge of treason. The hero Abu'l-'Abbas was recast as the villain, mastermind of an anti-al-Mahdi conspiracy. Abu 'Abd Allah al-Shi'i was portrayed as the unwitting victim of his brother's plot. Because of this, al-Mahdi had him killed, but led his funeral prayer in recognition of his service. What drove apart these once close allies was the growing gap in their respective religious-political visions and aspirations. Only a few years before, the brothers had taken a leap of faith in abandoning their original belief in the return of Muhammad b. Isma'il to favour the cause of al-Mahdi. Abu 'Abd Allah al-Shi'i's idealism regarding the universal al-Mahdi's reign must have become, in practice, satisfaction with what had been achieved. Al-Mahdi instead thought big and continued to do so. Where the brothers could not see beyond Ifriqiya, for al-Mahdi its conquest was a cog in a much bigger wheel. In any event, al-Mahdi's purge of his once-closest associates backfired, because the Kutamas reacted to Abu 'Abd Allah al-Shi'i's death with anti-al-Mahdi unrest. Some even installed a little boy as the *mahdi* and organized a *da'wa* in his name in Ikjan; others believed that Abu 'Abd Allah al-Shi'i was still alive.[26]

In light of the presumed conspiracy, al-Mahdi set up a bureau of detection in an old fortress between Qayrawan and Raqqada. Then, to reassert his authority he began waging war against the rebels. However, since it was his son who would be sent out to lead the fight, al-Mahdi first granted him a formal status that would make his military leadership count. In 912 the imam proclaimed his son to be his nominated successor. Upon accession to the throne this heir apparent would become known by a royal name with strong messianic appeal, al-Qa'im bi-'Amr Allah, the One Who Arises at the command of God. On the strength of this sanctioned share of caliphal responsibilities, the prince was furnished with all the insignia of sovereignty, tasked with completing what al-Mahdi had started. Supported by loyal Kutama chieftains, al-Qa'im fought the dissenters off, crushed their revolts, denounced the rebels in ignominious parades and killed them in public executions to deter others. The split Kutama factions soon regrouped in support of the Fatimids. Meanwhile, al-Mahdi once more redistributed the Berber allies to distant provinces.

With conspiracies calmed, Kutama support reaffirmed and al-Qa'im's military abilities tested, there was scope for considering territorial expansion eastward, beyond Ifriqiya. To reach Baghdad it was essential to conquer Egypt, at that time ruled by the Sunni officers on behalf of the 'Abbasids. Between 914 and 915 the Fatimids launched a military and naval campaign aimed at conquering Alexandria, to then move inland towards Fustat. In order to advance east al-Mahdi's army took control of 'Abbasid garrison towns along what is today the Libyan coast, including the most strategic of them, Barqa. Following this success, al-Qa'im, with his palace affairs left in the eunuch Jawdhar's capable hands, was ordered by his father to lead the military expedition to Egypt. After initial success – in Alexandria al-Qa'im even delivered Friday sermons to promote the Fatimid cause – the advance was checked by the 'Abbasids. However, one outcome of this expedition, and a victory of sorts to al-Mahdi, was that somehow in the course of it al-Qa'im recovered the books that had been stolen from his father as he was escaping from Egypt towards Sijilmasa.[27] The Fatimid troops attacked Alexandria again in 919, and once more al-Qa'im was forced to retreat, with the added disaster of the Fatimid fleet having been destroyed at Rosetta. Al-Qa'im managed to retreat to Barqa, still under Fatimid control; it would take him three years before he would return, defeated, to his father in 921. Once back, he found that things had meanwhile changed.

The First Fatimid Capital: Al-Mahdiyya in Tunisia

While al-Qa'im was fighting for the Fatimid caliphate's life and the reputation of the imamate, al-Mahdi took to travelling along the Tunisian coast. Though opposition had been repressed with brutal force, the criticism he had received had not gone unheeded. While al-Mahdi could not conjure up miracles in the strict sense of the word, he could instead show that his reign was like no other; that his advent had ushered in a new era and that, as imam-caliph, his rule carried unprecedented religious-political meanings. The most effective way to signal to his subjects a break with the past (and to the world that as a ruler he was here to stay) was to build a capital city. Also, it had dawned on al-Mahdi that the conquest-of-Egypt strategy needed rethinking; al-Qa'im's campaigns had been expensive in human and material costs with no guarantee of success. To move the seat of power from inland to the coast would therefore tick many boxes. It would give the urban landscape a Fatimid imprint that signalled a definite break with the Aghlabid past, demoting the status of Qayrawan-based Arab Sunni elites while limiting the Kutamas' sphere of action (unfamiliar as they were with maritime life). It would also signal the caliphate's eastward geopolitical aspirations, advertising al-Mahdi as a serious contender in military, trading and diplomatic control of the Mediterranean.

Not a man of the sea himself, al-Mahdi, supported by a team of experts, carried out a logistic survey of the Tunisian coast before deciding on the perfect location for his new capital. The idea of moving out of Raqqada/Qayrawan had been conceived as early as 912, in the aftermath of the turmoil that followed the botched supposed conspiracy against him. It was however only around 915–16 that he found the perfect spot for his new capital: a mile-long rocky peninsula south of Sousse, jutting out into the Mediterranean. A finger of land pointing east and accessible only via a bottleneck isthmus, its topography was perfect for defence. Centuries earlier its strategic position had attracted the Phoenicians, who had built a harbour there. For al-Mahdi too the location made sense to assert his control of the Mediterranean, given that Sicily, Tripoli, Tunis and Barqa were already in Fatimid hands. Soon construction on the peninsula started, and in 921, with the palace not yet completed, al-Mahdi moved to his new capital, which he named al-Mahdiyya. It was there that al-Qa'im rejoined his father after years fighting in pursuit of conquering Egypt.

Built in stone by a cosmopolitan team of builders, the first construction to be raised was the entrance to the city-palace via a single gate at the neck of the peninsula. The gate was sided by round towers defended by four bastions, one part of which is still standing today. With its thick walls, the structure was like no other at the time. The gate door was made of iron plates with animal decorations, a technical marvel attributed to the genius of al-Mahdi himself. The tenth-century traveller and chronicler Ibn Hawqal, the earliest eyewitness whose description of the city has reached us, said, 'One can enter this city via two doors which surpass in form all those I had seen so far, except the two doors of Raqqa on which model these are made.'[28]

Through the gate, at the exit of a long corridor, the Great Mosque (construction begun *c.* 916) formed a huge bastion in the angle where the wall ran along the south side of the promontory. Similar to the Aghlabids' fortified mosques, it was rectangular with the prayer hall and courtyard facing south rather than towards Mecca. Unlike Qayrawan's mosque, the one in al-Mahdiyya was not open to the city's population but complemented the royal palace, for which it provided a monumental entry through the arched porch tower. This type of porch would become characteristic of subsequent Fatimid mosques. The architectural filtering of the palace entrance through the mosque symbolized the passage from an outer profane space into an inner sacred one with the imam at its centre. The portal on the mosque's facade was innovative, in that it looked like a Roman triumphal arch. It might have been meant to represent the first imam 'Ali who, according to some traditions, Muhammad had designated as the gate of knowledge. Today that portal is all that is left of the original building (illus. 15). Near the mosque was the mint. The earliest known evidence of coinage struck there in the name of al-Mahdi dates back to 928. Continuing along the south wall one would find the harbour, a walled rectangular basin dug out of the rock that could fit thirty ships. Its entrance was blocked by an iron chain stretched between two watch towers. Next to it was the arsenal, with two vaulted galleries to protect workers and with space for about two hundred hulls. Heading up from the harbour, on the highest hill, was al-Mahdi's palace facing west while, separated across a square, facing east was al-Qa'im's residence. From this position the ruler and his entourage, through the palace's gilded grilled windows, could get a bird's-eye view of the city while being isolated from his subjects. The central feature of the imam's palace (a multi-complex citadel) was the great hall, used for solemn occasions. Today parts of columns from the palace can still be seen used as masonry in old al-Mahdiyya houses.

In the royal city enclave lived the imam-caliph, his son, their respective families and their entourage. The household was extended to include clients of Iraqi and Andalusian origins. Aides and adjuncts had replaced the *da'i* Abu Abd Allah al-Shi'i and his staff at the head of the administration. Prominent among them were the Saqaliba, whose status rose in every aspect of court life, a deliberate policy to curb the power of the Kutamas, many of whom had by this time been relegated to dignitaries with ceremonial functions. The Kutamas however retained the headship of the *da'wa* and the judiciary in the person of Aflah al-Malusi (d. *c.* 922). A disciple of Abu 'Abd Allah al-Shi'i, al-Malusi first became a preacher and was later appointed judge, *qadi*, of Tripoli. He then became the supreme judge in Raqqada, and later in al-Mahdiyya. From the capital of the empire, he enjoyed a higher rank than that of the *qadi* of Qayrawan. In this capacity al-Malusi headed the *da'wa* affairs.[29] For the first time the two roles became fused under one headship, thus embodying the inseparable nature of the inner and outer aspects of the law. According to the Fatimid doctrine as sanctioned in the oath of allegiance, the Isma'ili initiates would have to follow both. Under the overall guidance of the imam-caliph al-Mahdi, and by his instruction, every week al-Malusi held learning sessions in al-Mahdiyya for those men and women who had pledged allegiance to the imam-caliph. His method of teaching women was notable, using metaphors that resonated with them to facilitate their grasp of Isma'ili doctrines. Female attendance at these sessions had become the norm, as women had been active participants at these events since Abu 'Abd Allah al-Shi'i's days. Al-Malusi applied the same method when he taught men, by using examples that related to their trade.[30] Under the imam-caliph's authority al-Malusi was the first scholar to write on principles of Isma'ili law. The progression of his career, and the beginning of a literary corpus of Isma'ili law taking shape in al-Mahdiyya with his contribution, indicate that the Isma'ili judiciary system was starting to become professionalized. The imam-caliph, believed to be infallible, was the ultimate judge and overseer. However while in Raqqada petitioners could hand their written complaints to al-Mahdi in person, in al-Mahdiyya this practice was no longer sustainable. Once transferred to his capital, al-Mahdi's books were accommodated in a designated new library, along with volumes that had belonged to the Aghlabids. In 925 a young man from Qayrawan, Abu Hanifa al-Nu'man, was appointed as the library's keeper. Known as al-Qadi al-Nu'man, the Judge al-Nu'man, he would become one of the greatest Muslim jurists of all time, and a key figure in Isma'ili history and thought.

Though serving the palace, most of the soldiers lived with their families in Zawila, an inland locality with a market, baths and other facilities. The suburb was named after its residents the Zawila, an army group of uncertain ethnic origin (maybe of Sudanese ancestry) made up of individuals acquired through the trans-Saharan slave trade. Today the Zawila area of al-Mahdiyya hosts a city market, has many cultural amenities and is a hub for city services. The space between Zawila and the palace walls was left clear for defensive purposes as well as for staging festivals and parades. This area stretched to the beach by the sea wall where open-air prayers were held during religious celebrations. The imam only left his palace on two occasions to officiate at the most important festivals in the Islamic calendar: the end of the fast of Ramadan, *'id al-fitr*, and that of sacrifice, *'id al-adha*. On these occasions he delivered the sermon, led the prayer and performed the sacrificial slaughter of a lamb with his own hands. The symbolic religious nature of these public rituals meant they had to be staged to the highest standards and with logistical care, as massive crowds converged.

Unlike other ethnic-based military groups, the army's Arab contingent had been banished to Qayrawan, and only occasionally were its officers admitted to al-Mahdiyya for audiences with the imam-caliph. As an Isma'ili imam-caliph, al-Mahdi would not risk having a Sunni army on his doorstep.

For all its strategic advantages, the peninsula had one major failing: it lacked water. This shortcoming was remedied by resorting to hydraulic interventions. Underground cisterns were installed, fed via some 360 gutters linked to the mosque towers. These in turn were fitted inside with vaulted reservoirs to collect rain water. A new cistern tower was added, connected to an aqueduct about 13 metres (43 ft) high above ground, from which water was conveyed to the palace via bucket wheels. Al-Mahdi however did not drink cistern water but fresh water delivered every day in casks carried by pack animals, from the mountain spring of Zaghouan about 150 kilometres (93 mi.) away.[31] The Romans had furnished this spring with an aqueduct which supplied water to Carthage. Today the area is part of one of Tunisia's National Parks.

With the building of al-Mahdiyya, in the eyes of the Isma'ili faithful al-Mahdi had delivered on the messianic prophecy that one day a white city would be built that would prove impossible for *al-dajjal*, an equivalent to the Antichrist according to Islamic tradition, to enter.

Conceived as a capital as well as *dar al-hijra*, the city was symbolic of al-Mahdi and his mission to the world.

The building of al-Mahdiyya put the Fatimids on the world map in more than one way. The city's inauguration amounted to a public declaration of aspirations to imperial expansion. As a capital with distinctive messianic allure embedded in its name, the city transformed the status of the territories under the imam-caliph's rule from a collection of dominions into a small empire. Across the Mediterranean and beyond, well-established powers that thus far had dominated the region unchallenged took notice. In the mid-seventh century the Byzantine empire had lost its North African provinces to the Arabs. By the tenth century the Byzantines had abandoned their claim to a universal empire in western Europe, but still rejected the papacy's counter-claim to a universal church in Rome. As a regional power in competition with Rome, Byzantium had brought the Balkans under its control and launched missions to the Slavs. Though still strong in Syria, the Byzantines saw their former domains in Sicily, southern Italy and Ifriqiya change hands from the Aghlabids to the Fatimids, with the difference that the latter had evident expansionist ambitions. Seeing al-Mahidyya's brand new port, a fleet and a well-equipped arsenal, the Byzantines followed Fatimid developments with apprehension. The potential to capitalize on the Fatimids' rise was not lost on one of Byzantium's Christian rivals, King Simeon I the Great of Bulgaria (d. 927). A major player in the control of the Slav regions, his imperial ambitions had been disrupted by Byzantium's interventions in the Slavic regions. Aiming at no less than conquering Constantinople, Simeon saw in al-Mahdi the perfect ally against a common enemy. From al-Mahdiyya, al-Mahdi could provide the Bulgarian king with what he needed: a fleet. In 922 Simeon I sent embassies to al-Mahdi to engage the Fatimids in his campaign against Byzantium. The imam-caliph agreed and in turn sent his own representatives back to the Bulgarian king to finalize the terms of the accord (illus. 18). The Fatimid envoys however never made it to Bulgaria, having been intercepted by Byzantine emissaries on the Calabrian coast. Byzantium came up with an enticing counter-offer for al-Mahdi, who in return dropped his plans to pursue the Bulgarian alliance.[32] The episode underlined al-Mahdi's status as an international power broker of influential standing: two seasoned Christian rulers had rivalled each other to court a Muslim newcomer. Byzantine territories came under threat elsewhere. In 928 the Fatimids raided Taranto and

Otranto in Apulia. In Campania they forced Salerno and Naples to pay a ransom in return for the Fatimid fleet's withdrawal from their shores. More tributes were paid to the Fatimids in 932 and 933 in exchange for the security of these southern Italian regions.[33] Striking the right balance between sharing trading activities, pursuing diplomatic avenues and resorting to confrontation became the dominant trait of Fatimid-Byzantine relations for decades to come.

From the west, the Umayyads of al-Andalus started to expand their naval defences in response to the Fatimid presence at sea. During Abu 'Abd Allah al-Shi'i's time anti-Umayyad Andalusians had established contacts with the *da'wa* headquarters in Raqqada and joined the Isma'ili cause. The *da'i* Ibn al-Haytham, trained by Abu 'Abd Allah al-Shi'i and his brother, went to al-Andalus to proselytize. Following the accession of al-Mahdi, Ibn al-Haytham and another *da'i* went as envoys to the Andalusian rebel Ibn Hafsun (d. 917) carrying robes of honour for him. In turn the Andalusian chief sent embassies to Raqqada/Qayrawan.[34] From his headquarters in the Bobastro fortress, in the northwest of the Malaga province, this rebel succeeded in bringing under his control a number of territories where the Friday sermon came to be delivered in al-Mahdi's name. Although the rebellion subsided and support switched back to the Sunni regime, the Umayyad *amir*s raised their game to check the Fatimids' religious, ideological, political and territorial threats. In 929 the *amir* of Cordoba 'Abd al-Rahman III (d. 961) took the bold step of proclaiming himself caliph and *amir al-mu'minin*, thus bringing to three the number of competing caliphates: the 'Abbasid in Baghdad, the Fatimid in al-Mahdiyya and the Umayyad in Cordoba. During the early decades of the Fatimids' rule direct confrontations between them and the Umayyads were rare. Instead, rivalries were played out in North Africa through proxy wars by setting rival Berber tribes like the Zanata and the Sanhaja against each other. This warfare would last for about a century and would define the boundary of the Fatimid western expansion. Having appointed himself as caliph, in 936 'Abd al-Rahman III built his own capital, also redolent of eschatological symbolism: Madinat al-Zahra' near Cordoba. As the first project of its kind in Muslim-ruled Iberian Peninsula, the Andalusian caliph also had to rely on the experience and expertise of foreign construction masters, be they from Baghdad or even Constantinople. Proud of their work, Nasr, Fahd and many other builders inscribed their names on their masterpieces. Today a UNESCO world heritage site, the city is said to have represented the model Islamic city of paradise, evoking it in several ways: its eight doors; the presence of a tank described as filled with mercury to reproduce the light effects of the celestial al-Kawthar river; upper and lower gardens as described in the Qur'an; ornaments that echoed paradisiac symbolism. 'Abd al-Rahman III conceived the city as his messianic architectural answer to al-Mahdiyya. For all the caliphal squaring up, Madinat al-Zahra' was constructed using materials that included masonry originating from Fatimid Tunisia, for example columns from the ruins of Carthage and pink marble from a derelict church in Sfax. No rivalries, ideological or otherwise, stood in the way of business, as commercial exchange between the two caliphates remained thriving on the whole.

In the meantime, the Qarmatians adopted a different strategy in asserting their messianic counter-claims: in 930 they stole the Black Stone from the Ka'ba in Mecca and took it back to Bahrain. During the raid they also took gold and silver artefacts housed in the shrine, including a giant pearl known as Yatima, the Orphan – a relic believed to have been an ear pendant that had belonged to Mary, the mother of Jesus – the horn of Abraham's ram and the staff of Moses. The Qarmatians had maintained peaceful relations with the 'Abbasids until 923, when they looted Basra and attacked pilgrims returning to Iraq from Mecca. Predicting the advent of the *mahdi* in 928, they set up a *dar al-hijra* in Bahrain, until matters escalated to their violation of the ultimate Islamic shrine. It is in the context of these events that in 931 the leadership of this group was handed over to a Persian boy of Zoroastrian background believed to be the awaited *mahdi*. This move was a disaster. A local woman denounced the boy as an impostor with the results that the Qarmatians lost credibility among other Isma'ili dissenters.[35] Some Qarmatians fell in line with the 'Abbasids, others aligned themselves with another Shi'i dynasty with roots in Iran and Iraq, the Buyids. Many persisted in their belief in the return of Muhammad b. Isma'il. Nonetheless, by their activities in Mecca the Qarmatians had made the pilgrimage route so dangerous that for years no 'Abbasid-sponsored official pilgrimage caravan from Iraq would depart. In 934 the 'Abbasid caliph al-Qahir negotiated with the Qarmatians a safe conduct for the pilgrims based on the agreement that the Black Stone would be returned to Mecca in exchange for tributes and other provisions paid to them. Effectively the Qarmatians secured a monopoly in the management of the pilgrimage caravans, and it was not until 950 that the Black Stone was returned. Throughout the initial phase of this crisis, al-Mahdi's intervention in the matter had been limited to urging the Qarmatian leader to return the Black Stone to its original location.

On the domestic front al-Mahdi faced more urgent challenges. In 921 some Isma'ili faithful took their belief in the fulfilment of prophecy to an extreme. With al-Mahdi's appearance, they proceeded to act in line with the messianic promise this event was believed to entail. According to Islamic belief, the advent of the *mahdi* as culmination of God's plan for humanity would make revealed religions redundant, thus bringing about the abrogation of all the outer ritual and moral obligations sanctioned by the Islamic revealed law. In light of this, these excited believers cast off all restraints, to the point of being accused by opponents to the Isma'ilis of praying in al-Mahdi's direction instead of Mecca, drinking wine and eating pork during Ramadan.[36] Al-Mahdi crushed this movement, thus dissociating himself from such antinomianism. From the outset the Isma'ili faithful were taught that the balance between outer law and its esoteric understanding had to be maintained; to delve into the inner knowledge of *shari'a* did not mean to drop its outer performance. Rituals had to be followed by all, Isma'ilis and other Muslims. All that was changed was the modality by which obligatory rituals were staged. In the case of prayer, for example, all had to adhere to the recitation of a new call formula; a variation in the performance of prostrations; changes in the forms of prayer; adding the cursing of the enemies of the imam. In fasting, the new method used astronomical calculation to determine the start and end of the month of Ramadan, instead of the Sunni practice of moon sighting. The Maliki jurists, seething at these Shi'i changes in rituals and resenting their exclusion from positions of influence in government, saw the rise of the extremists as an opportunity to oppose al-Mahdi by accusing him of licensing this behaviour. Al-Mahdi's reaction to the Malikis, according to their sources, was persecution and repression. Whether out of fear, conviction or calculation, some Maliki scholars went on to convert to Isma'ilism. Meanwhile, after the move to al-Mahdiyya, as heir apparent, al-Qa'im's enjoyment of palace life was short-lived, as he was sent to crush those who now opposed the *dawla* by turning against the *da'wa*.

While still in Raqqada, al-Mahdi had had other sons and daughters from some of the former Aghlabid concubines acquired as booty. For these women, giving a son to their master was their chance to become *umm al-walad*, mother of the son, a status that carried legal rights and social privileges. In the succession lottery, it meant the chance of becoming queen mother. One of these concubines, the mother of prince Abu'l-Hasan, had tried to promote her son, but he was blinded by smallpox, a disability that excluded him from succession. As for the other sons, an allegation was made that the incumbent heir apparent al-Qa'im had them killed. If true, one half-brother must have escaped the purge. In 928, when al-Qa'im was away suppressing yet another Berber revolt, he received a letter from his son, al-Qasim. In the letter the son alerted his father that al-Mahdi had shown signs of having a change of heart about al-Qa'im's succession as he had asked another son, Abu 'Ali Ahmad, to lead one of the great festivals. This was a sign of favour that could be construed as hinting at succession.[37] In response, al-Qa'im returned to al-Mahdiyya to assert himself as the designated heir. Accepting the allegation was true, al-Mahdi might have changed his mind out of disappointment at al-Qa'im's failure in his Egyptian campaigns. Or, with no news of his son from the battlefield, al-Mahdi might have feared him dead and therefore conceived an alternative succession plan. Although al-Qa'im's son al-Qasim disappeared from the scene (sources do not mention him again), the family rift over succession which he had sparked would last for generations to come. However, al-Mahdi's favour towards al-Qa'im and his line of descent is confirmed by many anecdotes pointing to him doting on al-Qa'im's grandson, the child who, in due course, would become the Imam-caliph al-Mu'izz. One day al-Mahdi was playing with the boy, hiding him under his coat while sitting him on his lap. Having invited him to eat fruits from a silver and gold bowl, al-Mahdi was taken aback when the child refused to eat. To persuade him to help himself, al-Mahdi suggested that if he ate all the fruit, he could then give the precious bowl to one of the girls in the household. At which point the little boy replied with a counter offer: he would keep the bowl and the girl could take the fruits. And so it was. The anecdote, retold decades later by al-Qadi al-Nu'man, was a premonition of great things to come from a clever little boy who outsmarted his great-grandfather.

Against a background of brewing family feuds, Kutama discontent and anti-regime sentiments simmering in Qayrawan, the concoctions prepared by the southern Italian Jewish court physician Musa could not cure al-Mahdi after days of illness. He died in March 934. Fearing the effects of instability on various fronts, al-Qa'im kept the death secret while preparing for transition to his own rule, only making it public two months later. Though it was a ritual discouraged on doctrinal grounds, public mourning was held in all the cities of the empire. To his followers al-Mahdi was the leader who, after a long time, had made the line of hidden Isma'ili imams visible again. To his Isma'ili followers as the *mahdi*, 'Abd Allah inaugurated a messianic era that his successor as the *qa'im* would bring to its climax. To the rest he was 'Ubayd Allah – his name turned into a diminutive – being a rich tradesman from Syria who, thanks to an astute, hidden propaganda on a manifesto promising justice, peace and prosperity, succeeded in becoming the head of an empire in North Africa.

The Succession of al-Qa'im

After de facto co-ruling with his father since 912, in 934, at the age of forty al-Qa'im began his reign. Al-Qa'im's life had been spent on the move and away at war. Now, as the imam-caliph, he was at last free to change all that. Early Isma'ili sources report that al-Qa'im grieved for his father all his life, and lived as a recluse in the palace. He delegated the management of the governmental offices to al-Mahdi's trusted assistants, many of them being manumitted slaves of Slav origin. Inherited from the Aghlabids, even when freed the Slavs maintained a client relation with their master. Employed as pages to start with, they reached positions of command in the military and other institutions. Among the Saqaliba operating in his entourage, al-Qa'im placed his trust in the eunuch Jawdhar. Years before, the young slave had impressed al-Mahdi and was appointed by him as al-Qa'im's personal assistant and palace superintendent. As the new imam-caliph, al-Qa'im nominated Jawdhar chief treasurer as well as overseer of the warehouse of cloths and garments. Al-Qa'im also made him the intermediary between himself, his followers and his slaves. Jawdhar epitomized the Saqaliba who had risen through the ranks to acquire wide-ranging powers and authority. Al-Malusi continued to head the *da'wa* and the judiciary, with an additional leadership role in the army. One *da'i* came all the way from Yemen to join al-Qa'im's court: Ja'far, son of Mansur al-Yaman, the figure who some fifty years before had launched far and wide from Aden the propaganda for 'Abd Allah. Forced to leave Yemen after being opposed by his brother among others, Ja'far arrived in al-Mahdiyya. With him he brought Isma'ili treatises written by his father and himself, something that in due course earned him a reputation as one of the most authoritative early writers of Isma'ili esoteric literature.

Beyond the palace, public works were carried out with the building of an aqueduct to serve Qayrawan. On the internal security front, for some time it was business as usual: bouts of rebellions to quash and the usual unrests to repress. After his father's death, false claimants to the *mahdi*-ship came forward. In Tripoli a Muhammad b. Talut claimed to be al-Mahdi's son and gathered some followers among some Berbers.[38] Rivalries between Fatimids and Umayyads resumed, played out again by pitching Sanhajas against Zanatas. Al-Qa'im sent money and supplies from al-Mahdiyya to the Sanhaja chief Ziri, who in 935–6 built a garrison city, Ashir, to protect the Fatimid borders. Remains of the Ashir palace erected around 947 are still extant in Algeria. A revolt also erupted in Sicily in 937. Arab military contingents of Sicily had attempted – without success – sea attacks against the Fatimids following their take over of the island in 910. At the time al-Mahdi had sent the prefect of Qayrawan, al-Hasan b. Abi Khinzir, an Isma'ili, to rule there on his behalf. After years of tensions and rebellions al-Mahdi sent Kutama forces that put Palermo under siege until it capitulated in 917. A new governor was then appointed, Ibn Abi Rashid, who lasted for twenty years. Now, al-Qa'im sent another new governor from Qayrawan, Khalil b. Ishaq, to the island to restore order after years of disruption blamed on the Kutama ruling elites. He proved unpopular, and calm was only restored in 941. However, it was during this period that the Fatimids added their imprint to Palermo's landscape. A new walled citadel with gates on three sides was built southwest of the harbour. Known as al-Khalisa (today Kalsa), it included administrative halls, the arsenal, army barracks, baths and the congregational mosque. Meanwhile, al-Qa'im's attempt at launching yet another campaign to take Alexandria failed once more. To al-Qa'im's relief, a truce agreed between al-Mahdi and the Byzantines continued to hold; the Byzantines paid the Fatimids tributes and, in return, the Fatimids would leave their southern Italian territories alone. Sicilian Muslims and Fatimid forces would have to make do with raids elsewhere instead. In 934–5 the Fatimids sacked Genoa and Pisa, bringing booty, and many women, back to the lands of the empire. They would return there several times. For brief periods, the Fatimids also occupied southern France, Sardinia and Corsica.

One threat, however, al-Qa'im did not see coming, a blunder that almost cost the whole Fatimid venture. The Kharijis and the Shi'is had been enemies since the days of 'Ali b. Abi Talib's caliphate. Supporting the principle of the equality of all Muslims, the Kharijis defended the right to depose any ruler who, in their eyes, had proved to be a bad Muslim and to replace him with a good one irrespective of status or rank. Their vision of the imamate stood in direct opposition to the idea of genealogically inherited charisma from the Prophet as the mandate for the leadership of the Muslim community. Kharijis saw it as a religious duty to fight against those who claimed leadership on such a basis. In time Kharijism took hold in North Africa among the Zanata Berbers. It is debatable whether, or to what extent, Kharijism formed the basis from which a brand of Islam known as *'ibadiyya* emerged. Today 'Ibadis, who refute the association with the Kharijis, can be found mainly in Algeria and the Sultanate of Oman, where, in the latter, this brand of Islam is the one endorsed by the state.

In the tenth century Khariji Tahart had come under Fatimid rule, thanks to the efforts of Abu 'Abd Allah al-Shi'i. In Ifriqiya, the Sunnis, also opposed to the Isma'ilis, found it convenient to overcome their own significant doctrinal differences with the Kharijis to join forces against a common enemy. In turn, the Umayyads of al-Andalus had their vested interest in seeking to overthrow the Fatimids and when the opportunity arose to intervene, they took it. Since 928 a Khariji Zanata Berber preacher named Abu Yazid had been gathering support to mount a revolt to remove the Fatimids. Jumping on the messianic bandwagon, Abu Yazid launched a campaign that capitalized on the Berbers' socio-economic grievances and tribal rivalries. The Sunnis supported his cause, seeing him as a useful tool to get rid of the Fatimid imam-caliph. He attracted the Umayyads' external sponsorship for the same reason. Over the decades Abu Yazid rose to the rank of imam, and in 944 he was ready to begin his offensive. With the Fatimids unprepared, within six months the rebels had conquered substantial Fatimid territory. They looted Qayrawan, and Raqqada was destroyed. From there the rebels advanced towards the sea but were met with resistance in Tunis. Here al-Hasan b. 'Ali al-Kalbi, an established figure in the Fatimid administration, managed to keep the coastal areas under Fatimid control. Undeterred, Abu Yazid, riding his trademark donkey that earned him the sobriquet *the man on the donkey*, continued his march towards al-Mahdiyya. Having set up camp outside it, in 945

Abu Yazid kept the capital under siege for nine months. Though under pressure to lead the Fatimid resistance, al-Qa'im dithered and refused to leave the palace to fight the enemy. Against all the odds the city, further defended by the addition of a ditch by its front gate, proved impregnable, thus validating al-Mahdi's strategic foresight. The Fatimids benefited from an unexpected breakthrough: Arab troops initially allied with Abu Yazid fell out with the Berber elements in his army and switched sides in favour of al-Qa'im. Abu Yazid's threat was far from over as he still had command of a large number of territories, but the Fatimids could breathe a sigh of relief.

With Abu Yazid's revolt still lingering, in May 946 al-Qa'im died. When it came to his succession, it fell to the imam's confidant, Jawdhar, to become in practice the kingmaker. He came forward to reveal a secret entrusted to him by al-Qa'im years before: during al-Mahdi's funeral al-Qa'im had revealed to him that his successor would be his son Isma'il who would take the dynastic name al-Mansur. Jawdhar had kept this revelation to himself; with family feuds still rumbling owing to al-Qasim's indiscretions regarding al-Mahdi having second thoughts on al-Qa'im's succession, Jawdhar bade his time to safeguard al-Mansur, to whom he had grown close. Besides his testimony, it is unclear whether al-Qa'im ever made a public announcement to confirm his choice, with some sources claiming that he did so before his death. As with al-Mahdi's death, al-Qa'im's demise was not announced immediately – this was in order to secure the smooth transition from one imam to the next while Abu Yazid was still in circulation and posing a danger to the regime. The child who, years before in Ramla, almost blew his father's cover to a man with a white dog, died as imam-caliph in al Mahdiyya after almost losing the empire his father had built to a man on a donkey.

3

New Imam-Caliph, New Capital, New Ventures

With his succession hanging on Jawdhar's word, ongoing family disputes over designations and the bitter end of Abu Yazid's revolt still posing a threat, al-Qa'im's son became imam-caliph with the name of al-Mansur bi'llah. Born in Raqqada in 914, from a slave woman called Karima, he was the first Fatimid Ifriqiya-born ruler. His mother and his wet nurse appear to have been influential at court in securing his succession. Before launching against the Khariji-led revolt, al-Mansur had to take care of matters in his household. With Jawdhar's help he had all his uncles and half-brothers placed under house arrest. Al-Mahdi had doted on al-Mansur since he was a baby, but some of his sons and those of al-Qa'im had refused to recognize al-Mansur's right to the imamate. To protect his master, who called these relatives 'the cursed tree in the Qur'an' (that is, the Zaqqum, tree of hell), Jawdhar kept them at bay.[1] As the defender of al-Mansur's succession and being as well his personal secretary, Jawdhar's position at court grew in importance. When al-Mansur left the palace to fight against Abu Yazid he delegated to Jawdhar the authority to oversee the royal court and the affairs of the regime.

In May 946 al-Mansur mobilized crowds and troops for a final push to drive Abu Yazid out of Qayrawan. The fighting dragged on for months until the end of that year, when the imam-caliph, assisted by Zirid commanders among others, led in person the decisive battle that crushed the rebellion. Abu Yazid's harem was brought to al-Mahdiyya, while his sons sought refuge at the Umayyads' court in al-Andalus. Before the final victory al-Mansur had appeared in public to celebrate the festival of sacrifice. Clad in a gold-embroidered red outfit, wearing a yellow turban with flowing train, he led the prayer under a yellow pavilion and slaughtered a she-camel with his own hands. On victory day al-Mansur raised the tone of the celebrations to convey more than just the military success. Wearing a gold-embroidered red tunic and a gilded red turban, he bore a gold and red round shield overlaid with brocade. Riding a horse and brandishing the sword Dhu'l-fiqar – believed to have belonged to the Prophet Muhammad and then passed to 'Ali – he announced Abu Yazid's death while formally disclosing himself as the new imam-caliph following his father's death. Letters to this effect were sent to all the cities of the empire to be read aloud from the mosque pulpits; in the mint at al-Mahdiyya the nomenclature on coins was changed and the royal textile factories were instructed to embroider or weave al-Mansur's name on artefacts. The triumph over Abu Yazid carried political and symbolical meanings. Recast as *al-dajjal*, his defeat revived the Fatimids' messianic credentials in the eyes of their supporters and subjects.

Although bouts of unrest across Ifriqiya continued for several years, the defeat of Abu Yazid had injected renewed optimism into the Fatimid leadership, and across their domains. At the end of 946, in this wave of enthusiasm, al-Mansur celebrated his victory by beginning to build a new capital. Established near Qayrawan, the city was called al-Sabra (city of endurance) al-Mansuriyya in the imam's honour. It was built with masonry salvaged from Raqqada's palace, destroyed by Abu Yazid. Based on a circular plan with the palace at the centre, its walls were made of pressed mud. They featured four gates furnished with iron doors, one on the south, the Zawila gate to the east, the Kutama gate to the north, and the triumphal gate to the west. Today the city no longer exists but recent archaeological excavations have brought to light parts of its walls, showing a layout that echoed Baghdad, founded by the 'Abbasid caliph called – as it happens – al-Mansur (d. 775). There have been suggestions that the choice of a circular design for this new capital on the part of the Fatimid imam-caliph whose royal name matched that of the founder of round Baghdad might have been deliberate as a sign of defiance aimed at the 'Abbasids. Following Abu Yazid's revolt, to move away from the coast by relocating near Qayrawan, hotbed of Maliki Sunnism, allowed the Fatimid imam-caliph to keep a closer eye on possible sources of dissent. The markets were moved from Qayrawan to al-Mansuriyya so that crowd control could be exercised on traders and the public forced to enter via obligatory passageways.

Al-Mansur had courtiers and soldiers as well as some 14,000 Kutama families transferred there. In January 948 the imam-caliph made a triumphal entrance into his new capital dressed in quince-yellow brocade for the occasion. Having defeated Abu Yazid's sons, al-Mansur returned victorious once more to al-Mansuriyya in March, this time wearing fine white clothing with wide bands and a red silk scarf. In building al-Mansuriyya, the imam-caliph showed understanding of the importance to the people of having both access to the ruler and a visual experience of his wealth as proof of his success. Secluded al-Mahdiyya was thus replaced with a city that served as stage for pageantry to promote the public image of the ruler.

Inside and outside the palace al-Mansur put his distinctive stamp on the life, style and activities of the court in a way that would shape the Fatimids' image for decades to come. Starting with his entourage, al-Mansur manumitted Jawdhar, who was granted the title of Client of the Commander of the Faithful to use in protocol and correspondence. Jawdhar – a man of discerning taste who liked to announce himself with wafts of fragrances – also received the privilege of having his name embroidered in gold thread on the bands of his clothes and on carpets made in al-Mahdiyya. Al-Mansur described as exquisite gardens the articles of unrivalled craftsmanship produced there by slave embroiderers and mat weavers. The imam-caliph ensured that his protégé would receive robes of honour and horses to ride. On occasions Jawdhar would have dinner with the imam. It was to Jawdhar that the imam-caliph gifted the first set of gold coins struck in the mint of al-Mansuriyya, established in 948 near the mosque. In practice the Slav slave had become the third most important person in the Fatimid state, after the imam-caliph and his heir apparent.

In keeping with the projected image of the just ruler but also to strengthen his powerbase at grass-roots level, al-Mansur determined that the inhabitants of the palace should receive salaries and allowances more generous than those allocated to his harem and his immediate entourage. He forbade genuflection in his presence. Like al-Mahdi before him, al-Mansur realized the importance of furnishing his court with the finest objects to impress his subjects and visitors. For example, he ordered for his troops expensive, engraved swords with baldrics, fitted with blades made in al-Mahdiyya rather than low-grade Frankish or Yemeni ones. Al-Mansur was the first Fatimid imam-caliph to adopt a systematic policy of royal gift-giving as a way to seal loyalty: money, gold, camels, curios, perfumes and other treasures were donated (and received).

Al-Mansur was a keen collector of treasures of all kinds but his greatest indulgence was books. Whether exoteric or esoteric, the pursuit of knowledge had been at the heart of Isma'ilism from the outset. Though in hiding and in danger, the *da'is* had persevered in the delivery of learning sessions far and wide among their followers. Books of the *da'wa* were written, circulated in secret, often lost and sometimes recovered. Al-Mahdi had brought with him books from Syria that, lost and found, came to be stored in the palace library at al-Mahdiyya. Raised in the cult of knowledge, al-Mansur had become the ultimate bookworm. By the time he became imam-caliph he had a large collection of books to immerse himself in. An author as well as a bibliophile, anecdotes describe him writing a book sitting under a tree on a hot summer day, sweating, with his shaved head uncovered. Unsolicited advice to move to a cooler place would be met with irritation at being interrupted and risking losing concentration. Even illness did not deter him from writing. In 947, in Tahart, though almost moribund, he was still trying to hold his pen, which fell out of his hand and stained his clothes with ink. Al-Mansur would annotate the margins of books of poetry by ancient Arab authors. At least one work on the necessity of the imamate attributed to him is still extant. Some books were sent to Jawdhar, then still in al-Mahdiyya, for safe-keeping and transcribing, but it was in al-Mansuriyya that a grand royal library was established. Having already served his grandfather in this capacity, it fell once again upon Abu Hanifa al-Nu'man to become the royal librarian. In time, if luxury textiles became the ultimate signifier of Fatimid commercial dominance in the Mediterranean, books and libraries would define the cultural image that the Fatimids projected of themselves.

Al-Nu'man was the son of an Arab Maliki scholar from Sousse who may have converted to Isma'ilism prior to the Fatimids' arrival and therefore raised his child in that denomination. After serving al-Mahdi towards the end of his life, al-Nu'man became a sort of news reporter to the recluse al-Qa'im. Under al-Mansur he was instructed to collect books and copy them. Emboldened by the air of optimism that pervaded al-Mansur's reign, al-Nu'man saw that the time was ripe for the production of a coherent Isma'ili literary canon to take shape. He set out to write his own works, including poetry, and to assemble the memoirs, letters and sermons of the imams. Al-Mansur then appointed him judge of Tripoli. As al-Qadi al-Nu'man he then took charge of the judiciary in al-Mansuriyya, where he was the first to hold the title of *qadi al-qudat*, that is, supreme judge among the judges of the empire. Alongside that role, thus reconciling the outer and inner aspects of Islamic law in his public persona, he took charge with the title of *da'i al-du'at* following the death of the Kutama al-Malusi. Like his predecessor he held learning sessions every week which he ran with the imam-caliph's approval. To make people aware of the imam's instructions relating to non-Isma'ilis, al-Qadi al-Nu'man held public teachings every Friday, after prayer, in Qayrawan's Great Mosque.

In al-Mansuriyya al-Qadi al-Nu'man was given free rein to give shape to an Isma'ili theological and theoretical framework that, when reflected in law, would assert the imam of the time as the ultimate authority, being the sole exponent of God's word and the Prophet's *sunna*. Spurred by the continued Maliki rejection of the Fatimid imams as the rightful leaders of the Muslim community, al-Qadi al-Nu'man set out in writing the definitive terms of a legal system resting on the doctrine of the Isma'ili imam as its sole authority on earth. Despite his prominent status, in al-Mansuriyya al-Qadi al-Nu'man conducted his business from a corridor leading to the palace, a dwelling he shared with his large family. Only at a later stage in his career, having complained about his living conditions becoming unsuitable, al-Qadi al-Nu'man was granted a more adequate residence.

With al-Qadi al-Nu'man in the capital, there was space to accommodate the wishes of the Sunnis by appointing a Maliki judge in nearby Qayrawan. As the Abu Yazid lesson had taught, the alienation of the Arab Malikis of Qayrawan had been counterproductive. If al-Mahdiyya had its commercial and strategic naval advantages, leaving Sunni-strong Qayrawan and its Arab army to its own devices had almost proved fatal for the regime. Now the new capital was back at the heart of the empire, with a Maliki jurist serving the Fatimid government by being in charge of the practical side of the administration of justice. With this move the regime sought to pacify the Malikis while broadening the base of the Fatimids' acceptance among the populace. The ruler facilitated this further by distributing among the poor of Qayrawan the booty taken from the defeated Abu Yazid. Al-Mansur also ensured that mosques had a special space reserved to auditors wishing to hear the imam's followers discuss Shi'i law.

Unlike his father, al-Mansur enjoyed relative calm in his empire that gave him the peace to join in public events and travel for leisure across his domains. At a time when ancient urban sites were used for salvage building materials, al-Mansur showed a genuine interest in the Roman ruins of Ifriqiya which he visited. With the son who would one day succeed him with the royal name of al-Mu'izz, al-Mansur visited the ancient sites of Carthage and Sbeitla, as well as the Roman aqueduct of Zaghouan. Thanks to his father, al-Mu'izz too developed an appreciation for ancient buildings, and the aqueduct he saw would later give him ideas on how to better use the water resources of that region. Al-Mansur had the Latin inscriptions found in Setif (in today's Algeria) translated, and even camped in the Roman theatre of the Tunisian town of Sousse.[2] Surviving fragments of mosaic floors made for Fatimid palaces belonging to the elite testify to the taste for styles and crafts echoing antiquity in North African history. In Iran at around the same period the Shi'i rival of the Fatimids, the Buyid ruler 'Adud al-Dawla (d. 983), was also taking an interest in antiquities in his area, having had the Achaemenid inscriptions in Persepolis translated for him while adding his own to the site. Another favourite spot of al-Mansur was Jalula (today 'Ayn Djelloula), not far from Qayrawan, where he gorged on the gigantic lemons that the local orchards were famous for. Though ill throughout most of his life al-Mansur nevertheless maintained a public presence until the end. He staged a great festival to celebrate the circumcision of five of his sons by having over 1,000 local youths also circumcised while bestowing on them clothes and money. In 953 a jaundiced al-Mansur still officiated at the festival of breaking the fast of Ramadan.

Festivals and outings were occasional respites from the more urgent and pressing job of running the empire. To rescue an economy marred by years of conflict al-Mansur tried to bring order into the finances of his empire to facilitate its economic recovery. The tributary system was complex to manage, with revenues reaching al-Mansuriyya from various sources ranging from import–export duties to taxes on crops paid in villages and levies on pastures. More money came from *da'is* delivering tributes to the imam paid by the faithful in the provinces of the empire, as well as dues collected in cells operating in secret outside Ifriqiya. The *da'wa* headquarters had maintained ongoing contact even with remote outposts such as Multan. Non-Muslims living in Fatimid domains paid the *jizya*, a special levy imposed in Muslim territories on Christians and Jews for the right to practice their faith. War booty was also a source of revenue, as well as tolls charged at ports or on trade caravans at border points and city gates; entering al-Mansuriyya's gates cost a silver *dirham* a day. Fines were imposed on rebellious cities. Money could be given to the imam as a gift, for example as Jawdhar did on several occasions. In practice however, the collection of tributes was disorganized. Governors delegated with collecting taxes did not always deliver the revenues, keeping what they saw as excess money. The nature and types of taxes imposed at times did not always comply with the principles of Islamic law, thus causing resentment among those expecting the implementation of a just Islamic governance. At the same time an Isma'ili legal code was not yet available to provide the rationale for a theological reformulation of taxation principles. The Kutamas, who had resented the Aghlabids over heavy tributes, discovered that under the Fatimids they were not tax-exempt after all. Fines were charged for delayed payment, but late payment was often due to late collection. In principle the revenues at the imam's disposal should have been huge; in practice the money that reached the state coffers was not as high as it could have been.

By this time, exports from the Fatimid empire included slaves, textiles, hides, silk from Qabis (Gabès in Tunisia), grain, figs, olive oil and corals. Dates were also exported, but those from Biskra were at the exclusive disposal of the imam-caliph. To this day the Biskra region, in Algeria, is famed for the quality of its Deglet Nour cultivar dates. Alum was dispatched to Europe for leather tanning, paper making and as a mordant to fix colours. Black slaves, gold and ivory from sub-Saharan Africa were traded in Fatimid Ifriqiya to reach other destinations across the Mediterranean.[3] In Sicily, the Fatimids expanded the sericulture industry to meet the ever-growing needs of their textile industry. There they also cultivated sugar cane to produce confectionery for use at court and during public festivals. Since the time when al-Mahdiyya had become the first purpose-built Fatimid capital, Sicily had supplied the Fatimids with fine wood for shipbuilding. Via Sicily, products reached Ifriqiya from other western Mediterranean ports. The Fatimids had a state monopoly over sectors including mining as well as the production of textiles and gilt saddles, products which could be bought in state storehouses. Most of the land in the empire, although not all, belonged to the state (that is, the imam-caliph, his entourage and his court). It was managed via trusted agents. Private ownership was rare but possible; on occasion the state sold plots to private individuals. In general, however, the state let land, thus gaining revenues from rentals. Like the crops used for textiles, grain-producing lands were owned by the imam and his close associates. Al-Mansur had formerly engaged in trading activities for his own personal gain, but upon coming to the throne he delegated his commercial affairs to Jawdhar. For example, al-Mansur's wholesale purchases might consist of gilded travel lamps or fine wood. However, even the imam-caliph was not exempt from experiencing his goods being lost; on one occasion a consignment of pottery and other goods sent from al-Mahdiyya to al-Mansur was pillaged on the way.[4]

Under al-Mansur diplomatic relationships with Byzantium strengthened. At the start of his reign Byzantine diplomats arrived at al-Mansur's field camp near Qayrawan in 946 to reach an agreement over the control of Sicily. Once the Abu Yazid revolt was over, in 948 a Byzantine embassy returned to al-Mansur's court. Like his grandfather, ever aware of branding the image of the dynasty through public display, the imam-caliph ordered Jawdhar to fetch the most outstanding presents in his custody to be given to the ambassador to take back to Constantinople. The message implicit in the Fatimids' politics of gift-giving was that they could outshine their rivals in splendour, display of nobility and generosity. In a climate of shifting alliances and tenuous truces, a special gift could make the difference between peace and war. The Byzantines were also entertaining diplomatic exchanges with the Umayyads of al-Andalus and al-Mansur knew it.

In attempting to expand the Fatimids' dominance of the Mediterranean, al-Mansur sought to increase his presence in Byzantine southern Italy. The move destabilized the region further since Sicily had already been the theatre of anti-Fatimid uprisings. In 947 al-Mansur had sent the former governor of Tunis, al-Hasan al-Kalbi, to stabilize the island and reassert the Fatimids' authority in this important outpost. Al-Kalbi had been a valiant supporter of both al-Qa'im and al-Mansur in the crushing of Abu Yazid, and being made governor of the island was his reward. There he founded a new Muslim dynasty: the Kalbids. Jawdhar built a close relationship with al-Kalbi through his trading activities with Sicily, a major source of his income. He even borrowed money from the treasury in Sicily for his business transactions. It was to Jawdhar in al-Mahdiyya that al-Kalbi – from Palermo – entrusted the care of his sons. It is not clear if the Kalbids were Isma'ilis or just Fatimid sympathizers as, in general, before and during their rule the Muslim population of Sicily remained Sunni. Ahmad, who succeeded his father al-Hasan, ruled until 969 and, with an intervening year, was succeeded by his brother 'Ali. This dynasty, as vassals of the Fatimids, defended the island against Byzantine-Umayyad attacks with al-Mansur's financial and military support, and later with that of his successor al-Mu'izz. Over time several members of this dynasty interacted with the Fatimid regime in defending their interests in Sicily as well as occupying high positions at the Fatimid headquarters in Ifriqiya. Notwithstanding long periods of engagement in warfare, the Kalbids remained in power until 1057 when, from Normandy in France, Count Roger I arrived in Italy. From there, Roger launched the conquest of the island, leading to the creation of the Norman Kingdom of Sicily and southern Italy. A few years later, a relative of Roger I left France to conquer England, where he would be crowned as William I. In Sicily, the French joined the island mix of Lombards, Greeks, Arabs, Berbers, Slavs, European Christians and non-Arab Muslims and Jews.

In March 953, al-Mansur died of dysentery attributed to fatty liver disease at the age of 39. During his short reign the self-assertiveness of the dynasty had become more visible and its hold on the empire more tangible. Unlike al-Mansur, his successor, the 21-year-old al-Mu'izz, inherited an empire in good enough shape for him to look to a bright future. The experience of Jawdhar, the sharp legal mind of al-Qadi al-Nu'man and the political talent of al-Mu'izz would prove to be a formidable combination of skills for the advancement of the Fatimids' ambitions. Such aspirations, however, might not have been realized if it had not been for the military acumen of a slave, Jawhar al-Siqilli or al-Saqlabi or al-Rumi, a man who had started his career at the Fatimid court serving al-Mansur as a scribe.

The Fatimids Expand Under al-Mu'izz

No formal public announcement is reported to have been made about al-Mu'izz's designation as successor. Many anecdotes point to the closeness between father and son, noting that al-Mansur consulted al-Mu'izz on *da'wa* matters. To the Isma'ilis this bond was by itself a proof of transference of *ta'yyid*, divine support, from father to son. However, al-Mansur seems to have shown occasional preference for the mothers of al-Mu'izz's half-brothers, to the point that al-Qa'im feared that his grandson might be overlooked. Beside al-Mu'izz's mother, Durrzade (d. 974), al-Mansur had at least two more concubines who gave him sons. One of these women, Qadib, appears to have been his favourite, gaining significant prominence at court. In a climate of shifting court politics and cryptic allusions regarding succession it is not surprising that a decision was left until the end. There is some evidence of a faction having supported the succession of a hidden son of al-Mansur.[5] However, there is also an indication that al-Mansur had set his mind on al-Mu'izz as his heir apparent a year or so before his death.

Like al-Mansur with al-Qa'im, al-Mu'izz kept his father's death secret for some time while he was away on a military campaign in the Aures mountains. Having entrusted the operations to a Zirid commander, he then returned to announce his father's demise and reveal himself as the new sovereign. Like his predecessors, he inherited the ongoing family rifts. Al-Mu'izz was already aware of his rival relatives before ascending the throne and, once imam-caliph, he kept them under house arrest in al-Mahdiyya. Much to his dismay al-Mu'izz discovered that trouble was brewing closer to home. In fact, Jawdhar had intercepted al-Mu'izz's eldest son, Tamim, exchanging secret correspondence with the troublemaking family members.[6] It is possible that this indiscretion cost Tamim the succession. Beyond the suspicion of intrigue, past and present historians have suggested that infertility might have been the reason behind him being ruled out of the imamate.[7] Marginalized either way, in time this prince would gain recognition as a talented poet.

During al-Mu'izz's rule al-Mansuriyya was expanded to fit a court in keeping with the Fatimid empire's geopolitical relevance as a regional force with international clout. A hall whose roof was supported by ancient columns originating from Sousse housed the throne. Fragments of these metre-wide columns can still be seen on the site today. The royal compound included stables, menageries of exotic animals including a lion kept in a cage, a recreation area, extensive gardens and imposing water features. Rooms had names such as the Camphor Hall, the Crown Room, the Myrtle Room and the Silver Hall. The magnificence of the complex inspired a court panegyrist, who described one of its courtyards: 'The secluded balconies around it were virgins wearing girdled gowns.'[8] The complex included a mosque named al-Azhar, the most resplendent (an epithet of Fatima), where learning sessions were held. In 960 al-Mu'izz extended to al-Mansuriyya an original aqueduct that al-Qa'im had used to serve Qayrawan. The lime and stone structure, remains of which are still visible near the Tunisian town of Haffouz, had ducts that fed three reservoirs. The Fatimid aqueduct had been built on top of an Aghlabid one which, in turn, surmounted the ruins of an ancient Roman structure. Al-Mu'izz's aqueduct became a model for others replicated across North Africa. To these water supplies the imam-caliph added artificial ponds and a lake palace called Dar or Qasr al-Bahr. More gardens and water features were built in the surrounding areas. The city featured a *suq*, a market, where vendors arrived in the morning and left in the evening.

In caliphal architectural rivalry, Fatimid al-Mansuriyya could now compete in splendour with Umayyad Madinat al-Zahra' and 'Abbasid Baghdad. From the centre of his circular city the imam could radiate his *baraka*, blessing, around 360 degrees. The mother of Sicily's Kalbid governor asked to be allowed to buy a house in al-Mansuriyya near the palace to benefit from it. Almost nothing is left today of the artefacts that must have graced the royal palace interior. One outstanding surviving piece that gives us a glimpse of al-Mu'izz's artistic patronage at his court is a large ivory casket with multi-coloured painted decorations that he commissioned from a craftsman of Iranian origins sometime after 953 (illus. 7). A similar casket can be found in Mantua, Italy.[9] Like most of those whose livelihoods depended on patronage, artisans followed the money. It is no surprise therefore that, irrespective of personal belief or political affiliation, the trend of attracting craftsmen from eastern 'Abbasid lands to Ifriqiya by lucrative rewards, already noted among the Aghlabids, continued with the Fatimids. Extant ceramics of this period are somewhat unsophisticated and might have been imported. As noted, al-Mansur had lost a cargo of pottery destined for al-Mansuriyya whose provenance was from overseas. From al-Mansuriyya, al-Mu'izz also oversaw changes to the urban plan of the empire's former capital al-Mahdiyya, where the Zawila area was walled and the Dar al-Bahr was repurposed as a prison.

In keeping with the architectural upgrade of al-Mansuriyya, al-Mu'izz sought to redefine the aesthetics of palace protocol. In addition to the throne, al-Mu'izz introduced the use of the crown by adding a diadem to the turban. When out on parade the canopy to shelter the imam-caliph was replaced by a *mizalla*, a parasol embellished with gold and precious stones carried by a horseman. This was an adaptation of

7 Ivory casket made for al-Mu'izz at al-Mansuriyya, *c.* 953–73.

the ceremonial umbrella already used by the 'Abbasids as symbol of authority, here invested with additional meaning. If the imamate was the fulfilment of the messianic promise of the sun rising from the west, a gleaming parasol that sparkled in the sunshine to shelter the imam conveyed that concept to an audience. In general, the symbolism of light, inspired by the esoteric interpretation of the Qur'anic 'light verse' (24:35), became the heart of Isma'ili spiritual identity. The imam was believed to be an emanation of divine light, a creed that was reflected in iconography through various media. It is not by chance that rock crystal, transparent and highly refractive, came to occupy a special place in Fatimid art.

Among the royal insignia, the legendary sword Dhu'l-fiqar – borne by al-Mansur on the day of his formal accession to the throne – became a powerful icon of the transmission of temporal and spiritual power in one line of authority. To the Isma'ilis, liberated from the 'Abbasids in Baghdad, the sword resurfaced among the Fatimid imams who passed it on from one generation to the next. To this day the sword holds legendary status in the Shi'a world, so much so that the bestowal of the Dhu'l-fiqar medal represents the highest military honour in Iran.

Under al-Mu'izz, Fatimid gold coinage became the most tangible conveyor of his caliphal authority. The *Mu'izzi dinar* became the most sought-after currency in circulation due to the outstanding quality of its gold. Its distinctive design and legend made it recognizable across the Mediterranean region and beyond. The success of this currency, however, came after an initial failure. Confident of the broad-based support he had secured among his subjects, al-Mu'izz issued his first coins using a formula that spelt out the imams' genealogy from Fatima. For the first time in Islamic numismatic history, a female name in the form of an epithet of the daughter of the Prophet appeared on a coin. However, the Sunni Maliki subjects took it as a provocation and rebelled; advertising Shi'i genealogy and a woman on one coin was a step too far. Al-Mu'izz relented and the Fatima *dinar* was withdrawn from circulation.[10] It would be centuries before another Islamic coin featuring a female name would be struck.

Al-Mu'izz adopted a hands-on management style in many aspects of palace and state administration, assisted as ever by Jawdhar, who had now been summoned to al-Mansuriyya from al-Mahdiyya. As a sign of the closeness between the two, the monarch lodged Jawdhar in the Dar al-Bahr palace which was close to his own. With al-Mu'izz's permission Jawdhar furnished his house with exquisite carpets. Always cautious not to rise above his station, the eunuch offered to pay for the carpets, a polite gesture that al-Mu'izz turned down. Under al-Mu'izz Jawdhar became chief administrator and advisor to the imam, charged also with the supervision of the navy and the organization of coastline defences. As confidant of the imam-caliph, Jawdhar conveyed people's letters and pleas to al-Mu'izz and delivered the imam's responses. He was also in charge of liaising with staff in al-Mahdiyya to update al-Mu'izz on matters there. As a mediator of written exchanges, Jawdhar would extract the main points raised in the letters received, and would then transcribe these extracts onto a scroll, spacing each item by leaving blank areas between them. The imam would then reply to each point by writing in the interlinear gaps. Issues submitted to his attention varied and might include defence and administrative matters such as progress on the expansion of the fleet and updates on Sicily. News about the behaviour of his annoying relatives remained a constant. Through Jawdhar's mediation the imam could be asked to adjudicate on land disputes, address complaints against officials, give guidance on punishment for drunkenness or the apostasy of slaves. Al-Mu'izz advised restraint, with recourse to robust actions as the last resort.

As proof of his zeal, rooted in the importance of making virtue visible, al-Mu'izz used to summon Kutama dignitaries to show them how even on a cold winter day he was busy working, reading and writing letters. However, granting people written access to the ruler meant that handling the correspondence became too much even for the most resilient of imam-caliphs. Letters would pile onto al-Mu'izz's desk, causing the imam significant stress. Jawdhar would send him gentle reminders, which al-Mu'izz would respond to with an apology and explanation for the delay. The imam-caliph explained to his confidant that at times the volume of work was too much and things would get on top of him. When that happened, he went out to wander around the garden, get some fresh air and clear his mind. Or he would sit in the *hammam*, a short ride away from his residential quarter. However, returning to his duty, he would feel more aggrieved at the time wasted. As a countermeasure, to get things done he would then avoid all distractions by secluding himself.

Adding to the work that came through Jawdhar, al-Mu'izz held audiences twice a day, sitting behind a veil held by a Saqlabi officer. Audiences tested the imam's knowledge and sharpness of mind, as questions on any subject would be presented to him. One person might seek theoretical elucidations on a legal matter, but the next would ask questions on Arabic grammar and semantics. As the imam was believed to be infallible and gifted with foreknowledge, al-Mu'izz – trained by his father in the art of debate – was expected to deliberate his ultimate and unquestionable judgement on the spot on anything that he was asked about.

Al-Mu'izz had revived al-Mahdi's practice of dealing with complaints in person. Audiences provided an opportunity to hand over petitions, but it was the imam's public appearances at festivals and public celebrations that offered the best opportunity to approach him. Al-Mu'izz led the congregational prayer, outdoors, every Friday during the month of Ramadan throughout his reign. He only missed it once because of extreme heat. Besides officiating during the month of ritual fast like his predecessors, he also celebrated the festival of sacrifice, dressed in red, by butchering a she-camel with his own hands. While these events were open to the general public, al-Mansuriyya palace staff were treated to a banquet laid on tables arranged in the palace courtyards. During these and other outings, people came close to the imam to pass him their petitions. Sometimes he was so besieged that, from his horse, he had to fend off people by poking the crowd with a lance.

Bound by the reciprocal obligations that royal patronage imposed whereby the ruler would take charge of all his staff's needs in return for their absolute loyalty, al-Mu'izz took good care of all his personnel irrespective of rank, ethnic background or race. Al-Mu'izz provided for everything including the welfare and education of his officers' children, who would serve him and his successors one day. He ensured that even adult sons of deceased high dignitaries would be put through an educational programme. Showing remarkable foresight into the therapeutic benefits of lifelong adult learning, al-Mu'izz was quoted as having said 'Education has an importance that has no equal for a mature man who has already had accidents and recovered from them.'[11]

Jawdhar took care of practicalities, as he managed the salaries and allowances of the palace inhabitants in general and the imam's entourage in particular. The eunuch himself was treated as family and granted open access to the imam. Once, having consulted his master about his poor health, al-Mu'izz gave him a silver phial containing a herbal decoction mixed with grape juice to be drunk diluted that the physician Musa had administered to him with great effect. On another occasion, the imam – as a way of *baraka* – sent to Jawdhar angora wool leggings that he and his father had worn. Al-Mu'izz lent Jawdhar his ships for trading in the Mediterranean. Once al-Mu'izz had to intervene with a money injection to rescue a *da'i* who had got himself into financial trouble. The Yemeni Ja'far b. Mansur al-Yaman, who had joined the court during al-Qa'im's reign, was a brilliant writer and thinker but poor at managing his finances. Having taken a loan, he offered his house as collateral but, unable to repay, he came close to being left homeless. The imam stepped in and bailed him out but made it clear that he deplored such foolishness. Though influential through his writings, Ja'far never had a formal career at the Fatimid court.

Besides grand gestures, al-Mu'izz's patronage could also be reflected in simple acts. Having received a consignment of apples dispatched to him from Salamiyya, he distributed the fruit among his close followers as a way of blessing and healing.[12]

Despite his busy life, al-Mu'izz found time to indulge in books and writing, a passion he inherited from his ancestors. He could spend hours in the palace library browsing through books. The collection was eclectic, covering subjects ranging from literature and poetry to science, grammar and ancient philosophy. When not sitting in the library until his legs hurt from cramps, al-Mu'izz would order books to be brought to him. He would read and write at night to combat insomnia. When asleep, hagiographic accounts tell us that ancient savants such as Ptolemy would appear to him in dreams to inspire him with their wisdom. Al-Mu'izz's all-encompassing knowledge was understood among Isma'ilis to be derived from divine inspiration, osmosis rooted in the nature of the imamate and book reading but also further expanded through oneiric means. Dreams, in Islam, were – and are – believed to be trustworthy sources of authority.

Al-Mu'izz's knowledge would have been at full display in audiences, letters and sermons, but also in his writings on various aspects of Isma'ili thought. Some works attributed to al-Mu'izz have been preserved to this day. In writing, this imam-caliph had mastered the art of calligraphy, having been trained by a Saqlabi eunuch. In 953 he refined this art by inventing a pen that would allow a scribe to write without having to dip it into an inkwell. According to his design, the ink would enter the pen itself until it filled and then emptied when the writer had finished with it. The writer could hold the tool as he pleased without the fear of staining or the ink dripping. Al-Mu'izz gave a craftsman precise instruction on how to turn his design into a prototype and after a few days a first golden pen filled with ink was presented to him. Al-Mu'izz suggested a few improvements so that the writing tool could be rotated and be inclined in all directions without ink loss.[13] The prototype of the modern fountain pen had been born. Given his and his ancestors' passion for books, it is no surprise that it is to the North African phase of his caliphate that one of the most celebrated Qur'anic manuscripts in the world has been attributed. Extant today in large portions of dispersed folios, it is known as the Blue Qur'an, a unique artefact featuring large indigo-dyed parchment leaves with text written in gold with silver decorative roundels. A luxury production, the manuscript might have served the Fatimid regime as a tool to project the dynasty's image as champion of Islam via artistic patronage. Parallels have been noted between the Blue Qur'an, which was a one-off as far as Islamic codicology is concerned, and Byzantine coloured-parchment book production (illus. 19).[14]

However his supreme authority had the most lasting impact through the imam's role as commissioner of, and overseer in the production of, Isma'ili legal literature. Already during the reign of al-Mansur, al-Qadi al-Nu'man had begun to collect a corpus of material reflecting the imams' authority that could serve as the ultimate basis for the devising of an Isma'ili legal system. This would be applied, in practice and in theory, to the inner and outer aspects of Islamic law. Following the consolidation achieved within his empire which galvanized expansionist plans to follow, al-Mu'izz gave impetus to the *qadi*'s initiative to establish an Isma'ili legal programme to be implemented by the Fatimid regime over the territories under its control. Having been confirmed as chief judge, and now housed in a comfortable purpose-built dedicated court, al-Qadi al-Nu'man set to work. Al-Mu'izz supervised and gave final approval to his many legal works, of which the mighty *Da'a'im al-Islam* (The Pillars of Islam) was his masterpiece. Completed around 960, with this work the judge systematized Fatimid jurisprudence, thus making it the official code of the state founded on principles derived from Isma'ili doctrine. He called it the law of the people of the Prophet's household as attested by the sayings of the imams. As a manual for statecraft, part of the *Da'a'im* served as a mirror for princes to portray the ideal ruler. In fact, it included a guide on governance claimed to have been authored by the first imam, 'Ali, outlining the principles behind ideal government and order in society. Advice ranged from how to relate to inferiors, to ensuring the satisfaction of ordinary people. The ruler's subjects were the source of state strength since the exercise of state authority depended on them, and so did its defence. Provision of justice was vital as the success of a regime depended on the welfare of its servants. Order could only be secured by peace and the protection of all. Governors should be selected based only on merit and competence.

On a more practical level, as the canon of a new school of law that differed from all others, the content of the *Da'a'im* was distinctive in aspects of ritual law which acquired a specific Isma'ili dimension. To the normative five obligatory rituals of Islam, al-Nu'man added ritual purity and *jihad*, effort in faith. Changes to the profession of faith to include the mention of the imam of the time became enshrined in law. The concept of faith, *iman*, was reformulated as *walaya*, devotion, to the imam of the time and obedience to his authority, *wilaya*. Those who recognized the imam were believers, *mu'min*s, while those Muslims who didn't were *muslim*s. As in other schools of law, the performance of the pilgrimage to Mecca was obligatory but, for the Isma'ilis, adherence to this ritual presented a practical problem. At this stage Mecca was in enemy hands. Nevertheless, Isma'ilis would head for the Holy City in state-sponsored caravans directed from al-Mahdiyya and al-Mansuriyya. The journey served other needs as well; disguised as pilgrims, *da'is* could also connect in secret with other Isma'ilis and collect tolls for the imams.

Apart from significant changes to acts of devotion, no major reformulations were applied to mundane aspects of the law that related to interpersonal affairs and civil transactions. In laws relating to diet, penal matters, or marriage and divorce, Isma'ili law remained similar to that of the four Sunni schools and, in some aspects, closer to the Twelver Shi'i one. Regarding marriage, however, al-Mu'izz, unlike all the other Islamic legal schools, forbade polygamy. Also, a significant difference from Shi'i marital law was that al-Mu'izz prohibited the contracting of temporary marriage. The practice, forbidden by Sunnis and since this imam's decree by Isma'ilis, is still legal today in Iran under Twelver Shi'i law. Since every Isma'ili imam had individual, absolute authority during his time of tenure, aspects of the law with effects on the judiciary could change from one imam to another. This subjectivity made it impossible, and presumptuous, for a jurist to formulate a universal code. Therefore, the guidance in the matter found in the *Da'a'im* was of a theoretical nature, an aid to jurisprudence but not a perpetually applicable tool for the judiciary. Al-Qadi al-Nu'man dedicated a separate work to the esoteric interpretation of the law called *Ta'wil al-da'a'im*. However, at no point did al-Qadi al-Nu'man mention dispensation for the Isma'ilis from adhering to the outer aspects of the law. Whether *muslims* or *mu'mins*, both had to follow the Islamic divinely sanctioned ritual prescriptions and rules, the *shari'a*.

As head of the *da'wa* the *qadi* continued to hold the learning sessions. Lessons on esoteric matters were delivered to initiates within the privacy of the palace, in a dedicated room. Al-Mu'izz would send the judge books on esoteric knowledge for him to read at these events. Lessons would be tailored to varied audiences. The sessions soon attracted large crowds, to the point that the audience spilled into the palace courtyard and those at the back could not hear what was said. Informed of the problem, a nonplussed al-Mu'izz discussed the issue with al-Qadi al-Nu'man while at the barber for a haircut.[15] Lectures to instruct the general public on laws relating to everyday life were held at al-Mansuriyya's al-Azhar Mosque. Al-Qadi al-Nu'man would go on to author some 62 tracts on law, traditions of the Shi'i imams up to Ja'far al-Sadiq, history and a compilation of al-Mu'izz's sermons as well as poetry. Al-Qadi al-Nu'man also oversaw the management of pious donations. Under al-Mu'izz, he reached the apex of his career and established a dynasty of jurists who were to monopolize the headship of the judiciary and the *da'wa* for subsequent generations.

During al-Mu'izz's reign the Fatimid empire enjoyed a period of stability that led to expansionist moves. This outcome was, however, achieved through ongoing hard work and continuous monitoring of internal and external factors that might be disruptive. Al-Mu'izz had to deal with the Byzantines and the Umayyads trying to destabilize the Fatimid domains. All the while the Fatimid fleet in al-Mahdiyya was on standby and ready for action. In the Mediterranean, the Fatimids and the Byzantines continued to compete for dominance between 955 and 965, and during this period naval confrontations alternated with fragile agreements. In 956–7 the Fatimids defeated the Byzantines in southern Italy in a naval war, forcing the Christian emperor to enter into negotiation with al-Mu'izz; Byzantium would pay tributes to the Fatimids in return for unlimited truce. Welcomed in the audience hall of the Fatimid palace, the Byzantine diplomatic mission brought gold and silver gem-encrusted vessels, brocade and silk, riding horses and Muslim captives released for the occasion. However, the terms of *jihad* meant that the Muslim ruler could only agree to a temporary truce. The parties settled for a five-year period. Nevertheless, the Byzantines broke the agreement, thus giving al-Mu'izz the perfect excuse to try to expand the Fatimids' hold on Sicily by annexing lands on the island that were still under Byzantine control. Al-Mansuriyya expected a retaliation from Constantinople, but following yet another defeat in Sicily the Byzantine emperor negotiated a new truce. While Sicily remained the barometer of Fatimid–Byzantine relations in the Mediterranean, in 970 the Byzantine naval force invaded Crete. Having asked in vain for help from the pro-'Abbasid Ikhshidids of Egypt, this island turned to the Fatimids for rescue. Al-Mu'izz responded by dispatching a fleet, manpower and money, but it took seven years before another truce was agreed on that front. In the meantime, in 962 the Kalbids had tried again to extend Muslim rule over all Sicily, capturing Taormina, which was renamed al-Mu'izziyya after the imam-caliph. More Fatimid victories on the island followed, to the extent that the Muslim ruler was able to impose the religious tax on Sicily's Christian inhabitants. The Fatimid victories were celebrated across all the Islamic territories where the Christian Byzantines were seen as the common enemy. However, another Byzantine–Fatimid alliance was soon agreed when a new potential mutual enemy appeared on the scene: the German Holy Roman Emperor Otto I (d. 973), who had advanced to southern Italy. During al-Mu'izz's reign Sicily enjoyed large investments. In 967 the imam-caliph commissioned major building projects in Palermo and across the island. New canals were dug so that more land could be cultivated. New fruits and plants were introduced, lemon being one. Plantations of mulberry trees and sericulture were expanded.

With the Umayyads there was no direct full-on confrontation, but skirmishes were a constant concern. Andalusian merchants crossed the sea to Fatimid lands, but in 955 an enemy boat intercepted a Fatimid carrier ship heading from Sicily to the empire's mainland. The governor of Sicily, al-Hasan al-Kalbi, intervened on behalf of the Fatimids, resulting in the Umayyad fleet and Almeria being burnt in retaliation. In the following years the Umayyads' influence became more pernicious in Fatimid inland territories. A plot was uncovered involving a man from al-Masila, in today's Algeria, who – in correspondence with the Umayyads – had attacked the authenticity of the Fatimid dynasty's genealogy. In 958 al-Mu'izz launched a campaign to retake Sijilmasa, which had switched allegiance in favour of the Sunni Andalusian rulers, and where a figure had come forward claiming the imamate for himself. The imam-caliph placed in charge of the mission Jawhar al-Siqilli, a former slave secretary freed by al-Mu'izz and nominated army general. Jawhar reasserted Fatimid control in the interior of the empire with the help of the Zirids and the Andalusian anti-Umayyad Hamdun family who had moved to Ifriqiya. He also conquered Fez and led his army up to what is today known as the Strait of Gibraltar. According to an anecdote, on his return from the victorious campaign in 960, as proof of his success, Jawhar brought back from the Atlantic coast for the imam in al-Mansuriyya tanks with live fish leaping in seawater. From Sijilmasa, where indirect Fatimid rule was imposed, he brought back rebels who were subjected to ignominious parades on a carousel contraption built according to al-Mu'izz's specification. From Fez Jawhar brought back the Idrisid rulers of the city who, claiming descent from 'Ali via his son al-Hasan's line, were treated as cousins and so sent back showered with presents. These exploits showcased Jawhar's extraordinary military talent, which, within the space of a few years, was to lead him to become one of the most heroic figures in Isma'ili history.

The solidity of the empire, the formulation of an official Isma'ili law to run it and the Fatimids' military successes against Christian and Sunni enemies further confirmed, in the eyes of the *da'is* in and outside the empire, the validity of the Fatimid imams' messianic claims. Al-Mu'izz reached out to remote Isma'ili propagandists, other Shi'i groups such as the Zaydis in the Caspian area and Yemen, and Twelver Shi'i dynasties like the Buyids. In Baghdad Fatimid agents were met with suspicion. A story circulated in the city according to which they were behind the theft of a silver lion attached to the stern of the Buyid Sultan 'Adud al-Dawla's barge that was never found again.[16] In time the Buyids' weariness of the Fatimids grew to the point that a network of spies was organized to report on their every move.

Al-Mu'izz realized that in order to fulfil the dynasty's universalistic aspiration, the broadest possible doctrinal and territorial consensus for his cause had to be secured first. From al-Mansuriyya *da'is* were sent to set up covert cells in hostile lands such as Iraq, Iran and Yemen. Pretending to be pilgrims travelling in caravans, propagandists returned from these places with religious dues, correspondence and reports to the capital, where they would receive legal and doctrinal instruction to take back to their communities. From 958 onwards al-Mu'izz revived the *da'wa* in the Indian subcontinent, with the cities of Multan and later Mansura coming under Fatimid control. In 965 al-Mu'izz sent a new *da'i* to Multan to replace one who had grown close to the local *amir* and had allowed Hindus who had converted to Islam to continue practices from their former faith. As a way to deter a return to polytheism al-Mu'izz instructed the new appointee to destroy the gigantic idol at the heart of a Hindu solar cult. The existence of the Sun Temple in the centre of the city, known to have attracted worshippers since ancient times, is well documented, with some ruins still extant. The number of pilgrims visiting the temple was so large that up until this point the Sunni Muslim *amirs* had granted these Hindus the status of *dhimmis*. Under Islamic law, non-Muslims living under Muslim rule were protected by the terms of a treaty, *dhimma*. As part of this contract, since the advent of Islam, Muslim rulers had imposed on non-Muslim subjects the payment of a poll tax, which granted them the right to worship according to their own faith. This arrangement was understood to apply to those who belonged to monotheistic faiths, that is, Christians and Jews. The extension of the law to include Hindus in Multan is the earliest and best-known episode of such status being granted to followers of a non-monotheistic faith.

Al-Mu'izz had other ideas. Once informed that the temple had been destroyed and the Hindu priests eliminated, the imam-caliph sent the *da'i* seven white banners with his name on them to congratulate him, but also to assert the imam's authority there. In the mosque, built on the ruins of the destroyed shrine, the sermon at the Friday communal prayer was now recited in name of the Fatimid imam. Al-Mu'izz might have prompted this particular expedition out of a desire to counter anti-Isma'ili propaganda, according to which the Fatimids worshipped an idol shaped as a giant head dispensing gold coins.[17] The traffic of *da'is* between al-Mansuriyya and Multan increased and correspondence was exchanged. Ibn Hani' al-Andalusi (d. *c.* 973), having fled Umayyad al-Andalus and joined al-Mu'izz's court as a panegyrist, sang that, faced with his masters, the Indian kings were losing their sleep and the elephants which symbolized their power were subdued and 'lowing like a young camel'.[18] In Multan his poetic fantasy became a reality. The Fatimid hold on that region lasted until 1005, when the Sunni Mahmud of Ghazna (d. 1030) invaded the area, destroyed the Fatimid mosque in Multan and massacred the Isma'ilis. Multan fell to the Ghaznavids in 1010 and Mansura in 1025. Some Isma'ili communities however survived, and even succeeded in establishing small local dynasties.

The *da'wa* expanded in the eastern territories of the 'Abbasid empire. Divisions had occurred between supporters of al-Mahdi's claims and his opponents, who clung to their belief in the return of Muhammad b. Isma'il. However, al-Mu'izz's successes led to a reconciliation with some of these factions, resulting in large numbers of eastern Isma'ilis responding to al-Mu'izz's call for unity in his name. Earlier the eastern *da'wa* had been conducted by great scholars who had spread Isma'ilism among notables in Rayy, Isfahan, Adharbayjan and Gorgan. Isma'ilism found favour among members of the Samanid dynasty, the rulers of Khurasan and Transoxiana. Among elite personalities in this region who came to adhere to the Fatimid cause, the father and brother of the polymath Ibn Sina (Avicenna) (d. 1037) are noteworthy. As stated in his autobiography, through his father, this scientist and philosopher learned about the Isma'ili doctrines, but there is no clear evidence to support the claim that he was or became an Isma'ili too.[19]

Forming a philosophical school that blended Isma'ili doctrines with metaphysics and Neoplatonism, these *da'is*-cum-scholars had distanced themselves from Fatimid Isma'ilism by withholding their allegiance to the Fatimid imam-caliphs. A *da'i* from that school however, Abu Ya'qub al-Sijistani (d. 971), broke ranks and accepted the Fatimids' claim to the imamate, thus bringing the eastern *da'wa* into the Fatimid fold. In his philosophy al-Sijistani aligned Neoplatonic cosmological hierarchies with metaphysical ranks that, arranged in descending order, demonstrated an unbroken link between the divine as emanative principle and the Fatimid imamate, as well as the *da'wa* as spiritual and temporal projection of divine authority. In the imam and his progeny, mediated by the *da'wa*, God's perfect unicity found its ongoing link to the imperfect multiplicity of creation. The return of Muhammad b. Isma'il was still awaited as the messianic Resurrector, *qa'im*, at the end of time, but the imams in his line, as his descendants, would rule on his behalf one after the other until the day of his reappearance. The Isma'ilis from Iran and parts of Central Asia followed suit. The Iranian *da'wa*'s endorsement of the Fatimids was a major political and intellectual achievement. Among the Qarmatians some now adhered to the Fatimid cause, while others in Bahrain continued to reject al-Mu'izz's imamate.

In 964 al-Mu'izz commissioned the manufacture of a large map of the known world of his time. At the cost of 22,000 *dinar*s, it was crafted as a wall-hanging made of blue embroidered silk featuring appliqués depicting regions, cities, mountains, seas and rivers as well as Mecca and Medina. An inscription on it recorded al-Mu'izz's longing for the Ka'ba in Mecca – which he would never visit – and his desire to celebrate the places linked to the Prophet Muhammad. Beyond the imam's devotional intentions, the map visualized al-Mu'izz's universalistic ambitions, which by 964 he saw to be within reach. Indeed, the imam-caliph had found in Jawhar al-Siqilli the military genius he needed to move into the next phase of Fatimid imperial expansion. After some ten years of careful preparation the time had come to succeed were his grandfather al-Qa'im had failed: the conquest of Egypt.

4

The Conquest of Egypt, Court Life and Imperial Expansion

As a province of the ‘Abbasid empire, since the mid-ninth century Egypt had been governed by local dynasties that, although vassals of the Sunni caliphs in Baghdad, became in practice independent of them. The first of these dynasties was the Tulunids. The Ibn Tulun mosque in Cairo, named after the dynasty's founder, is testimony to this period, with its spiral-shaped minaret being one of the most recognizable landmarks in the Egyptian capital. Failed expansion attempts and domestic mismanagement undermined the power of the Tulunids, whose grip on Egypt ended in 905 when the ‘Abbasids intervened to reassert themselves in the region. In 935 a new dynasty of Turkic extraction emerged, the Ikhshidids, whose recognition of the ‘Abbasids was also nominal. Though they controlled Egypt, parts of Syria and the the Hijaz region in the Arabian peninsula, natural disasters combined with poor state administration resulted in life in their domains becoming harsh. The mid-960s saw the flooding of the Nile, on which Egypt's agricultural economy depended, at one of its lowest levels on record. A combination of other adverse factors provoked widespread famine and disease.[1] With no crops to harvest, the state revenue system based on land tax was left in tatters. Internal succession disputes brought things to a head among the ruling class. At the death of the dynasty's founder, a Black eunuch, Kafur, became regent on the heir's behalf. The ‘Abbasids approved this arrangement but when Kafur died in 968 more confusion followed in deciding who the new governor should be and on what basis.

A vizier, Ja‘far b. al-Furat (d. 1001), was put in charge of the administration and the revenues while another high officer oversaw the military. When this power-sharing experiment failed, violence, famine and administrative paralysis ensued. Confronted with the spectre of total collapse, the Egyptian military and notables sought outside intervention. Beyond causing internal problems, the weakness of the Ikhshidid regime had exposed Egypt to what Muslims saw as the worst possible catastrophe: a Christian Byzantine conquest. The Byzantines had already advanced in northern Syria and were aiming for Egypt. The Qarmatians also showed signs of wanting to capitalize on the opportunity to expand their influence. In the end the Ikhshidid ruling elites considered the least worst of the options available to them to defend their domains and their interests. In the past the Ikhshidids had eyed an alliance with the Fatimids by proposing a marriage between the daughter of the Ikhshidid governor and a son of al-Qa'im. Then realpolitik made this arrangement unfeasible. Fast-forward twenty years and from the ancient capital, Fustat, the Ikhshidid ruling class, civilians and sections of the military pleaded for help from the Imam-caliph al-Mu'izz in al-Mansuriyya. And he responded.

The Reign of al-Mu'izz in Egypt

By the time al-Mu'izz received the invitation to intervene, the Fatimids' preparation for the conquest of Egypt had been some ten years in the making. A leading *da'i*, Abu Ja'far Ahmad b. Nasr, was one of several who had been operating in secret in Egypt during the early 960s, influencing the notables and the mercantile elite of Fustat.[2] The penetration of the Fatimid propaganda machine was such that coins in al-Mu'izz's name were already circulating in Egypt before the Fatimids' takeover. Likewise, textiles carrying al-Mu'izz's name were made in Egypt before his arrival. The lack of planning that had marred al-Qa'im's attempts to conquer Egypt had been a mistake that was not to going to be repeated.

News of the poor state of affairs in Egypt had reached al-Mansuriyya through Fatimid agents and reports from merchants operating in North Africa and the Mediterranean. Even before receiving the Ikhshidids' call, the Fatimids had sent their delegates to meet Kafur, proposing to fight together against the Byzantines, a plan that came to nothing. Propaganda activities had intensified in Egypt, trying to rally support in favour of the Isma'ili imamate among dignitaries and at grass-roots level. Isma'ili activists, for example, propagandized Isma'ilism in secluded settings such as shrines and cemeteries, where they found an audience among women who were the main frequenters of such sites, as well as at markets.[3]

By 966 systematic plans were already underway to launch the military operation that would enable the transfer of the whole Fatimid regime infrastructure from Ifriqiya to Egypt. Small palaces were built along the route to allow the caliph and his entourage to rest. Al-Mu'izz's son Tamim appears to have been put in charge of supervising these building works along the route to Egypt. Jawhar, who had already distinguished himself in several campaigns, was tasked with the military advance. The defection to the Fatimids of Ibn Killis, an Iraqi Jew who had converted to Islam, was crucial to the timing of the campaign. Having served the Ikhshidids as a high officer, Ibn Killis had fled to Ifriqiya, thus alerting al-Mu'izz to the favourable time for the conquest. In the meantime, the Qarmatians and the Byzantines continued to pose a threat; the Sunni 'Abbasids had grown ineffectual to the point of delegating to a Twelver Shi'i dynasty, the Buyids, the rule of Baghdad. As for the Umayyads in al-Andalus, after 'Abd al-Rahman III and his son al-Hakam II (d. 976), the threat to the Fatimids had subsided.

Jawhar had expanded the army to include (in addition to the Kutamas who were the bulk of the military force) Sicilians, Greeks, Saqaliba and African non-Berber elements. Having secured financial support for the troops' upkeep, he was ready to go. On 5 February 969 all gathered at Raqqada where al-Mu'izz oversaw the ceremony that celebrated Jawhar and his army's departure for Egypt. Al-Mu'izz bestowed on the commander his royal garments as a sign of honour and blessing, while attendants dismounted from their horses in a sign of respect. The army travelled 16 kilometres (10 mi.) a day, with Barqa being the last major stop for provisions before reaching Alexandria in mid-May. By then rumours of Jawhar's advance had reached Fustat, where it soon became clear that the Fatimids' response to a request for help was by way of a full invasion aimed at bringing regime change. The display of the Fatimids' military forces was said to have been the largest Egypt had seen since Alexander the Great's expedition. In early July, as the army closed in on Fustat, Jawhar's delegates went ahead to hand charity to the poor. At the same time, representatives went to greet the general stationed at the outskirts of the city to negotiate the terms of surrender. Heading the group were members of an aristocratic class known as the *ashraf* (sing. *sharif*). With the noblest among them, the *sayyid*s, they formed a distinctive social group that had emerged in the early Islamic middle period.

The *ashraf* of Egypt, like their counterparts elsewhere, claimed to be blood descendants of families that traced their ancestry back to the Prophet. These nobles occupied a position of prestige across the Islamic territories, having prominent status in Mecca and Medina. Among these, members of the Hasanid and Husaynid families, who claimed ancestry from ʻAli and Fatima's sons, had moved to Egypt from the eighth century to escape ʻAbbasid persecution. Descendants of Zaynab (d. 682), the eldest daughter of Fatima and ʻAli, came to be revered in Egypt to the point of generating strong popular devotion around this woman. One of Cairo's most important mosques is dedicated to her. Sayyida Nafisa (d. 824), reputed to have been the wife of a son of Jaʻfar al-Sadiq, also attracted strong sentiments of piety. She is described as belonging to the Hasanid line, and as a learned woman who won the esteem of al-Shafiʻi (d. 820), the founder of one of the four Sunni legal schools. After her death a shrine believed to house her relics, located in a mosque bearing her name, became a focus of popular devotion in the quest for her *baraka*. To this day Sayyida Nafisa's birthday is celebrated in Cairo with a festival. Several other ʻAlid women believed to have come to Egypt under similar circumstances became figures evoked by Ismaʻili propagandists. Undercover *daʻis*, operating prior to the Fatimids' arrival, gathered support for the Ismaʻili cause among women engaged with pro-ʻAlid piety. Female ʻAlid saints came to be honoured with burial sites and mosques, with many built or restored by the Fatimids.

In Egypt the *ashraf* were not powerful in a political sense but they were influential nonetheless in the affairs of the state on account of their nobility and wealth. Although most of these ʻAlids were Sunnis, they banked on their shared descent with the Fatimids in hoping for privileged treatment from the new regime. From the Fatimids' point of view the *ashraf*'s presence in Egypt was a double-edged sword. On the one hand they were a prominent group that would welcome Shiʻi Ismaʻili rulers on account of kinship. At the same time this common bond might undermine the exclusivity of the Fatimids' ruling rationale. On the whole realpolitik prevailed. In return for recognizing the new rulers, the *ashraf* named their demands: personal safety, preservation of their real estates and retention of fiscal privileges.[4]

Jawhar responded to these demands with an even more generous offer to the whole population in return for their surrender, in a proclamation of safety known as *aman*. This statement, the text of which was preserved in later sources, read as a God-given general amnesty, a Fatimid religious-political manifesto and a commitment to tolerance for all subjects irrespective of religious persuasion.[5] In delivering it, Jawhar explained the reason for the Fatimids' campaign in Egypt, to protect Muslims and the Islamic territories from the Byzantines. He offered reassurances regarding security, justice and religious freedom, as well as the revival of building projects. He promised a stable currency, together with safety for pilgrims. He reiterated that observation of religious duties was incumbent on all Muslims, whether Isma'ili or not. The rights of *dhimmi*s, that is, Christians and Jews, would also be respected. The proclamation reaffirmed to the people of Egypt the agreement that al-Mahdi, and the *da'i* Abu 'Abd Allah al-Shi'i before him, had already made with the people of Ifriqiya, by which the imam would be the only legitimate implementer of the covenant between God and humankind.[6] The terms of this pact became enshrined in law as a kind of Fatimid constitution in the compendium that would define al-Qadi al-Nu'man as one of the greatest legal minds in the history of Islamic thought. Although Isma'ilism would become the official brand of Islam endorsed by the regime, manifest in the external aspect of ritual, adherence to its doctrines would not be imposed. To proclaim an *aman* was a standard Islamic practice to guarantee people safe conduct when regime change by military conquest occurred. What made this one distinctive was the markedly tolerant tone of its message. In reality the Fatimids, foreign rulers representing a Muslim religious minority, had no option but to reach out to and find favour among their new subjects, mostly Sunnis and non-Muslim communities in which Christians formed the largest group.

At first, factions within the military that had belonged to the Ikhshidid regime tried to reject the *aman* and challenge the Fatimids' final push to Fustat, but Jawhar defeated them. His army was superior in size and his strategy proved effective, concentrating his efforts on conquering the capital. Before he entered Fustat, Fatimid supporters had already decked the city with the dynasty's trademark white flags. More amazement was caused when Jawhar, donning an embroidered silk robe and preceded by banners and drums, arrived carrying with him over a thousand coffers of money. On Friday 9 July the general led the congregational prayer in the ancient 'Amr Mosque in Fustat, but as he did not know by heart the new formula in the name of the new ruler, the imam-caliph al-Mu'izz, he had to read it from a piece of paper. He reiterated the Fatimid view of the Isma'ili imams whom God had designated to rule over the Muslim community as restorers of justice. The 'Abbasids' black was replaced by the Fatimids' white. Coins with al-Mu'izz's name soon became the official currency of the new regime. Rather than making Fustat his seat of power, Jawhar set up camp north of the city, in an agricultural area once occupied by a Coptic monastery, a small citadel and a zoo that had belonged to the Ikhshidids. Echoing the capital city of his masters in Ifriqiya, he called the settlement al-Mansuriyya. However, the new city that grew on that site was renamed al-Qahira, the victor, on the imam-caliph al-Mu'izz's instruction. Some have attributed the origin of the name to an epithet of the planet Mars, al-Qahir. According to legend Jawhar was waiting for the propitious moment to start the building of the city. He had planned to ring bells to signal to the workers the moment the walls' construction should begin. As he grasped the cord to ring the bells, a raven snatched the rope from Jawhar's hand, thus setting off the bells just as the planet Mars had reached its zenith. At the sound the workers began the construction. Beyond the legend, a suggested astrological link to the foundation and naming of the new city is implausible. The Fatimids were great sponsors of astronomy but opposed astrology, most of all al-Mu'izz who disliked the practice, as recorded by al-Qadi al-Nu'man. Also, an almost identical story had already circulated in tenth-century Egypt, before the Fatimids' arrival, about the circumstances of Alexander the Great's foundation of Alexandria. The megalopolis we know today – al-Qahira, or Cairo as the Italian traders who flocked to Egypt called it – was born.

Once settled, Jawhar started building the garrison town from which the dynasty's new capital would emerge. Situated north of the Ibn Tulun Mosque, at first the new city consisted of a 1 by 1-kilometre square citadel surrounded by a rectangular walled encampment, an innovation that Jawhar had imported into Egypt from North Africa. Access to the area was through eight entrances which consisted of arches rather than fortified gates, two for each side of the perimeter. In choosing the site Jawhar followed his instinct instead of al-Mu'izz's instructions. He went for a location where the first bulk of inhabitants, the military, would be able to defend the city while having Fustat within reach. The new residents of Jawhar's urban enterprise needed to have access to services and facilities that were not yet available in the new settlement, but which were provided in the ancient capital. Cairo only had a small market to meet the immediate needs of the population. Some fifty years or so after its foundation, many of its inhabitants still relied on Fustat for shopping. A cemetery for the new residents grew outside one of the gates. On a strategic level Cairo's orientation was determined on one side by its alignment with the *khalij*. This was a canal used for goods transportation that since ancient times had linked the stretch of the river Nile flowing in that area to the city of Qulzum on the Red Sea coast. Fallen into disuse, the second caliph 'Umar had reactivated the *khalij* around 642, following the Arab advance into Egypt. This canal existed until 1898, when it was filled in to make room for a tramway track. The Muqattam hills flanked the other side of the encampment. Another part looked towards Fustat and the fourth side was exposed to the plains that led to Palestine, Syria and Arabia. Army barracks were situated inside the encampment, with each regiment assigned its own area and thus giving the name to the quarter they occupied. Soon Jawhar established an enclosed prayer ground in the open air, a *musalla*, that would also function as a plaza for religious festivals, outside the city walls.[7] The space was made ready in time for the celebration of the feast at the end of Ramadan. It was here, on the occasion of this festival, that Jawhar gave the first indication to the Sunni subjects of a new procedure in the performance of ritual. In keeping with a practice that the Fatimids had introduced in North Africa, the start and end of the month of Ramadan was based on astronomical calculation. A Shi'i formula to call the faithful to prayer was imposed, together with changes to the Friday prayer and aspects of its performance. After a period of transition, in spite of remonstrations from Sunni judges and subjects, the adoption of these changes became mandatory across the capital and the territory under Fatimid control.

Less than a year after inaugurating the new city, construction started on the new capital's main mosque. Completed in 972, it was called the Mosque of Cairo, *jami' al-Qahira*, but was later renamed *al-Azhar*; the name by which the institution is famous to this day. This mosque evoked aspects of the Fatimids' North African past: the namesake mosque in al-Mansuriyya; similarities with the plan of the one in al-Mahdiyya; and some elements that echoed the mosque of Qayrawan. It was at first intended for royal use and only later opened to Isma'ili devotees. Reworked as a building over the centuries, al-Azhar is today one of the most famous Islamic places of worship in the world and the location of the most prestigious Sunni theological university (illus. 16). The original section of today's structure is the oldest surviving Fatimid building in Egypt. At its foundation al-Azhar consisted of a broad rectangle of which the prayer hall occupied one-third of the mosque. It featured aisles, with arcades decorated with vegetal motifs and propagandistic epigraphic panels displaying Qur'anic quotations in floriated Kufic font, an elaborate, ornamental type of Arabic script. The irregular columns were, and still are, topped with capitols that had been salvaged from ancient pre-Islamic buildings. A dome contained the inscription naming Jawhar as its founder. On the sides, halls were arranged around a courtyard. The walls were covered in plaster.[8] There is some debate as to whether al-Azhar Mosque was built with a minaret or not. While there is no architectural evidence to support the original existence of such a structure, textual references point to other Fatimid mosques built on the Azhar model after the dynasty's arrival in Cairo having this feature. A thirteenth-century text refers to the raising in height of an existing minaret in al-Azhar, implying that it dated to the Fatimid period. Its interiors might have been painted in many colours if we go by the example of at least one other mosque which was described as having had a polychrome interior and which was built not too long after al-Azhar in al-Qarafa area outside the city walls.

The 'Amr and Ibn Tulun mosques continued to be for Sunni use. As in al-Mahdiyya, although in different phases, two royal palaces were built facing each other. The central axis that divided the city into two parts, stretching between the Futuh and the Zuwayla gates, coincides with today's al-Mu'izz li-Din Allah al-Fatimi street in Old Cairo. Halfway along this street there is an opening known as Bayn al-Qasrayn that was originally the open space that separated the two palaces, the Eastern or Great Palace and the Western or Small Palace. The Great Palace, the first to be erected in Cairo, was built to al-Mu'izz's specification as a private residence and also as the official seat of the regime. It was used for ceremonials and consisted of a complex that included the departments serving the state, the treasury and the armouries. As for the Small Palace, its construction began under al-Mu'izz's successor. The area where it stood is now dominated by the Mamluk Qala'un complex, built in the thirteenth century with repurposed Fatimid-era columns and masonry.

At the end of a successful campaign in North Africa, Jawhar had charmed his master by bringing back to him tanks with live fish from the Atlantic to signify the territorial expansion achieved by the end of that military expedition. Now the general's presents dispatched to al-Mu'izz included hundreds of animals, among them dromedaries decked with gold brocade palanquins and stone-studded gold girdles, she-camels sporting Byzantine brocades and silver-decorated reins, and Arabian camels. In addition, there were beasts of burden, horses with decorated saddlecloths, saddles with gold or vermeil trappings, gold and silver bridles, two enormous pieces of aloe wood, caged birds and other rarities. The gifts were shipped via the Nile to Alexandria, loaded on a boat and then transferred to al-Mansuriyya.[9] In practice Jawhar had set in motion part of the transport system that would enable the Fatimid regime's apparatus to decamp to Egypt.

Across the country pockets of nostalgic Ikhshidids continued to mount resistance for some time, and it took four years before Jawhar could secure the functioning of the regime's infrastructures in readiness for the imam-caliph's instalment in his new domains. Following the model of Isma'ili governance in Ifriqiya, Jawhar ruled on al-Mu'izz's behalf, on the whole by diplomatic means. He dispensed with the Ikhshidid army but retained most of the experienced Egyptian administrators, pairing them with Kutamas and other North Africans from among his own staff as their supervisors. To avoid possible tensions between Sunnis and Isma'ilis over the introduction of new Isma'ili-based rituals, for a while different practices continued to be followed in different parts of the land. The recitation of the new Shi'i formula for the prayer call was adopted in some mosques but not others. Jawhar tackled impending financial collapse by creating a special *diwan* to manage the assets that had once belonged to the Ikhshidids. With grain being one of the main sources of state revenue, Jawhar dispatched the military to bring its trade under control and secure its distribution against robbers. It took Jawhar two years before economic stability and welfare could be restored. Paying the army continued to be a complex undertaking and it represented the largest expenditure the general had to address. Jawhar also presided over the petitions court.

The conquest of Egypt brought the Fatimids an additional sphere of influence that needed careful management and handling. They inherited the special relationship that the custodians of the holy cities of Mecca and Medina had already established with Egypt's former rulers. That part of Arabia depended on Egypt for financial aid and grain supplies to sustain the costs and logistical strain caused by the pilgrimage. The Sunni *sharifs*, custodians of the holiest sites in Islam, pledged allegiance to the Shi'i Isma'ili Fatimid imam-caliph in return for ongoing support. The arrangement added legitimacy to the Fatimids' claim as the only rightful caliphs, on the grounds of being recognized by the *sharifs* as the official patrons of the holy sites. This convenient trade-off would last almost until the end of the dynasty. Areas of Syria and Palestine were now part of the territorial legacy left behind by the Ikhshidids. For the Fatimids, full control of that region was a vital step to their ultimate goal: the conquest of Baghdad. After four months in Egypt, military operations eastward were undertaken to assert territorial control and to defend it from the Byzantine advance. When in 970 the Fatimids launched a campaign in Syria that, in time, brought Ramla, Tiberias and Damascus – albeit temporarily – under their control, Aleppo's pro-Shi'i Hamdanid rulers acknowledged the Cairo caliphate. The military advance into the region brought the Fatimids face to face with the Byzantines in the Antioch region. Fearing an attack against Egypt, Jawhar ordered the digging of a moat outside Cairo's walls that would cut across the plain stretching from the canal to the Muqattam hills to defend the vulnerable side of his garrison town. He had a bridge built over the canal to access the Maqs port that connected to the Nile,[10] since control of this port was imperative to secure supplies to the capital. Jawhar also had a gate built at the entrance to the bridge, furnished with massive iron portals that had once served as doors to an Ikhshidid polo ground. In 971 the feared attack came not from the Byzantines but from the Qarmatians, emboldened by having defeated the Fatimids in Damascus. Jawhar checked it, despite the assault having prompted the Delta towns of Tinnis and al-Farama to rebel in favour of the 'Abbasids.

Once the Cairo encampment had been secured, the traffic of people and trade as well as the commute to and from Fustat was made easier, with more gates added to the city walls. Despite Jawhar's efforts to deliver on his promise, it would take him three years before the organization of pilgrim caravans to Mecca could be resumed. However sufficient safety conditions had now been met to allow for the transfer of the Fatimid regime from Ifriqiya to its new seat of power. Cairo, the palace city, was ready to welcome the imam-caliph, his harem, his army and courtiers. In al-Mansuriyya the poet Ibn Hani' al-Andalusi celebrated the news of the Fatimid conquest of Egypt. Irrespective of affiliations, the quality of his poetry was such that it was read in the rival courts of Baghdad and Cordoba, something that turned his eulogies into a powerful Fatimid propaganda tool.

During the years Jawhar was asserting Fatimid rule in Egypt, in Ifriqiya preparation was underway for one of the most complex logistical operations ever undertaken in the middle period of Islamic history. The whole Fatimid ruling infrastructure, from the imam's household and the court to the administrative apparatus and the military all the way down to the first three caliphs' coffins, would leave al-Mansuriyya to relocate in Cairo. The transfer had been pre-planned and it was implemented in stages. First, wells and stopover stations had been built along the land route from al-Mansuriyya to Alexandria. Then the coordination of caravans carrying people and goods was organized, with departing groups being issued with passes. Jawdhar, in charge of the logistics as state secretary, informed al-Mu'izz of hiccups in the granting of these documents. At one point he was concerned that many men serving the state without travel passes had abandoned the idea of travelling. Also, he was aware that disputes could flare up between these dignitaries and the slaves who were in charge of checkpoints.[11]

Special licences were issued to officers authorizing them to collect money to pay for tolls charged on camels and beasts of burden entering the gates of city markets along the route. The treasuries of al-Mansuriyya and al-Mahdiyya had plenty of money but more was needed to pay for an enterprise of this size. Jawdhar was therefore given a free hand in the sale of precious objects from the state warehouse.[12] Unpaid taxes were collected and Jawdhar even contributed to financing the venture with his own money. From Sicily more wood arrived in al-Mahdiyya to expand the fleet that was to head for Alexandria, transporting more goods and supplies. In al-Mahdiyya houses served as depots for goods to dispatch. However, upon learning that traders had started using the city's mosques to store goods, al-Mu'izz forbade the practice.

The massive scale of the enterprise made it clear to those left behind in Ifriqiya that the Fatimids were leaving for good. However, the imam-caliph's transfer of the seat of power to Cairo did not mean the complete relinquishing of his authority over his North African subjects. Prior to his departure for Egypt al-Mu'izz had taken steps to seal a lasting bond between the populace and his dynasty, and also to secure the loyalty of Berber tribal leaders who would rule over Ifriqiya as his vassals. Since the early 960s al-Mu'izz had adopted a more assertive policy in imposing Shi'i Isma'ili formulae in the observance of rituals.

This extended, for example, to stopping women from wailing at funerals, a practice the Isma'ilis forbade. A more powerful symbol of the bond, guaranteed to leave an indelible mark, was to extend empire-wide the celebration of a ritual performed formerly by al-Mu'izz's father al-Mansur: the grand circumcision. For a month in 962 al-Mu'izz celebrated a successful military campaign by having his sons circumcised and ordering all the boys of right age in his empire to undergo the same procedure. The ritual took place in pavilions raised in the palace's great court where the circumcisers sat on stools with the boys sitting on the adults' laps. During the operation the boys were treated with blood coagulants, sprinkled with rose water and distracted by jesters. After it they were further entertained with music. With al-Mu'izz in attendance, tens of thousands of youths were circumcised. At considerable cost rewards and robes of honour were distributed to all the participants, depending on the parents' social rank. Money and outfits were also dispatched to Sicily where the same ritual took place. In Abraham-like fashion al-Mu'izz sought to establish an indissoluble covenant between himself and his subjects.[13]

As for securing lasting loyalty in Ifriqiya, al-Mu'izz could count on the Berber tribes that for generations had sided with the Fatimids. While most of the Kutama elites were to follow the imam-caliph to Egypt, al-Mu'izz could trust the Sanhajas to defend the North African provinces of his empire on his behalf. Upon Jawhar's leaving Ifriqiya in 969, the pro-Umayyad Zanatas resumed anti-Fatimid intertribal fighting. They were however defeated, and once their severed heads arrived in Cairo Jawhar paraded these in order to announce the Sanhajas' victory at the 'Amr Mosque. The Zanatas made one last attempt to prevail, which ended in defeat at the hands of the Sanhaja prince Buluggin b. Ziri. Having already fought on the Fatimids' side, with this success he became the pre-eminent Fatimid vassal ruler in Ifriqiya. In Sicily the Kalbids continued to govern on behalf of the imam-caliph, and several Kutama factions were left in control of Tripoli in his name.

During these preparations al-Mu'izz designated his son 'Abd Allah as his successor, having bypassed his eldest, Tamim. The latter became a respected poet whose verses, beside eulogies for his father and – later – his brother, were populated by sensual slave girls, female dancers and drink-pouring women. The themes of his verses contributed to the characterization of Tamim as a languid poet longing for the love of this lute playing or that singing slave girl. Al-Mu'izz confided his choice of 'Abd Allah as his heir apparent to Jawdhar, intending to keep the appointment secret for the time being. However, during a public ceremony Jawdhar, in a rare lapse of judgement, greeted 'Abd Allah in the typical way reserved to the nominated successor, thus giving the game away among those present. Family resentments soon surfaced and a mortified Jawdhar apologized to al-Mu'izz by letter. The imam-caliph comforted him but also rebuked him by reminding him of the right protocol to follow.[14] To break rules was not tolerated at any level and Jawdhar on this occasion could count himself lucky for getting away with it.

By all accounts Jawdhar's indiscretion could be forgiven, as the eunuch was old, frail and in poor health. On occasion al-Mu'izz had recommended to him potions that had been administered to him by his physician. The imam-caliph donated to Jawdhar clothes from his wardrobe as a way to convey his blessings to him. However, though plagued with swollen legs, Jawdhar was determined to follow his master all the way to his destiny. He sat in a litter mounted on a mule and joined the royal caravan on the gruelling journey westward.

In the late autumn of 972 al-Mu'izz and his caravan left for Egypt. A long convoy of tens of thousands of camels, horses and donkeys carried people, objects, textiles, armour, furniture and more. Ring-shaped gold and silver ingots dangled from the sides of animals of burden. The harem was on the move too, including the women of al-Mu'izz's household and female members of al-Mahdi's, al-Qa'im's and al-Mansur's respective families. The royal children sat on the camels carrying the carpets, among them a three-year-old granddaughter of the imam. As we will see, this girl grew up to become one of the most famous female figures in Islamic history, Sitt al-Mulk. The caravan's first stop was a day's travel away from Qayrawan, at the Jalula lemon grove that had been cherished by al-Mu'izz's father al-Mansur. Subsequent breaks took place at fortified stations built along the Libyan coast. In Ajdabiya the imam-caliph lodged in a marquee and was greeted by desert chiefs in a reception hall. In Barqa, al-Mu'izz staged his entrance into the city in a way that reflected the standing of the dynasty. The troops wore splendid armour and parade outfits. The time in Barqa was however spoilt by tragedy. First, the elderly secretary Jawdhar died. In recognition of his service to four imam-caliphs al-Mu'izz led the funeral prayer. Second, the court poet Ibn Hani' was murdered on a beach in the same locality. Archaeological evidence of the Fatimids' presence in

Libya has been found in Ajdabiya, consisting of a complex that once comprised a fortress with a mosque that the Fatimids built around 912.[15] Raided in 1051–2, the complex fell into prolonged decline, although some significant remains are still visible today. Not far from Ajdabiya are the ruins of a tenth-century mosque in the village of al-Sultan, believed to have served as a Fatimid army command base.[16] In the 1970s these areas were excavated by archaeologists who uncovered a rich selection of Islamic artefacts and coins, many from the Fatimid period. These and other objects, stored in the National Commercial Bank of Benghazi and other safekeeping locations, were looted in the 2010s during the civil war.

In the spring of 973 al-Mu'izz arrived in Alexandria, met by a delegation of notables and merchants. After a rest in a *hammam*, al-Mu'izz granted audiences at the famed city lighthouse where robes of honour were bestowed. Sitting on horseback and sheltered by a parasol held by a Saqaliba guard, al-Mu'izz also gave audience to a delegation of *ashraf* who acknowledged his descent from Fatima. The imam then joined the fleet that had by then reached Alexandria from al-Mahdiyya, and in June he arrived by ship in Cairo. In the mid-eleventh century visitors to Cairo could still see the royal ship that brought al-Mu'izz moored in the Nile port. Bypassing Fustat (which had been decorated for the occasion) the imam-caliph headed straight to his palace, followed by delegations and cortèges carrying his ancestors' coffins. The Kutamas, the Zawilas and the Saqaliba represented the largest groups accompanying al-Mu'izz into the new palace city. The prediction attributed to al-Mansur that one day his son al-Mu'izz would conquer Egypt had come true. As the imam-caliph installed himself in his royal residence, in al-Mansuriyya his Zirid vassals made the former Fatimid royal palace their new home.

With the arrival of the imam-caliph, Cairo became the administrative, military and cultural capital of the Fatimid regime as well as the headquarters of the Isma'ili propaganda network. The ancient city of Fustat flourished as the most important commercial metropolis across the region. Once in Egypt, al-Mu'izz had hoped to inaugurate his reign there with a diplomatic coup by rallying support from dissenting Isma'ili factions. Al-Mu'izz tried to persuade the Qarmatians of Syria to pledge allegiance to him, given the strategic importance of that region in the Fatimids' expansionist plans. They not only continued to oppose the Fatimid imamate but in 974 once again tried to invade Egypt, brandishing the 'Abbasids' black flags. Al-Mu'izz's heir apparent 'Abd Allah was sent to fight them off and succeeded in defeating them. The victory marked a major turning point for the Fatimids. It paved the way for their occupation of Damascus and, from there, parts of Syria and Palestine, at the time still under Byzantine threat. In Syria al-Mu'izz made clear the standard of conduct he expected. On one occasion, a governor from the region wrote to him, bypassing all the formal channels; the imam-caliph returned the letter unopened to its sender. Protocol, however, was not enough to secure the Fatimids' control of Damascus, which soon became precarious. Control was only reasserted after al-Mu'izz's death, under his successor.

In Egypt al-Mu'izz consolidated General Jawhar's adopted policies. He confirmed the terms of the *aman* by seeking cooperation between the regime and the notables in Fustat. Diplomatic relations grew stronger with the *ashraf* of Egypt and Arabia. While the *ashraf* of Syria remained opposed to the dynasty, those in the Hijaz had played an important role in securing the Fatimids' recognition as patrons of the holiest cities of Islam, with the Friday sermon being recited in the Cairo imam-caliph's name. In return for this formal acknowledgement of their authority the Fatimids pledged to secure the safety of pilgrims from Egypt, al-Andalus, North Africa, Sicily and Syria. They dealt with the maintenance of the wells along the pilgrimage routes, supplied food to the pilgrims and provided military escort against predatory Bedouins and the Qarmatians. The white, gold-embroidered mantle, *kiswa*, used to cover the Ka'ba in Mecca was sent from Egypt as a way to advertise Fatimid sovereignty and legitimacy to all Muslim pilgrims. In 973 on the festival day of 'Arafa, as part of the pilgrimage ritual celebrations, al-Mu'izz had a *shamsa* – a sun-shaped parasol-like ornament he had commissioned for the Ka'ba – displayed in his palace reception hall for all to see. It consisted of a red brocade embroidered with golden crescent moons, each containing a sphere enriched with pearls and multi-coloured stones. A Qur'anic verse on the pilgrimage, embroidered with emeralds and pearls, completed the look. The *shamsa* was perfumed with powdered musk. The parasol was destined for Mecca along with a prayer niche in gold and silver, with al-Mu'izz's name inscribed on it, intended to be placed inside the holy shrine. Other gifts ranging from grain to presents for the *sharifs* accompanied the white linen *kiswa* designed for the Ka'ba.[17] The Fatimid adornment for the shrine could not be more different from the black-and-gold one that today defines that site. The *sharifs* of Mecca and Medina, claiming descent from the Prophet and therefore seen as cousins by the Fatimid imam-caliphs, received rich pensions from the public treasury of the regime in Cairo. In the meantime, diplomatic missions were sent to the Christian king of Nubia to ensure that the payment of tributes (based on a pact negotiated centuries before at the time of the Arab conquest) was resumed, enforced and respected according to the agreed terms.[18]

Diplomacy extended to the country's religious policies, with a gradual imposition of Isma'ilism as the state doctrine in a Sunni-majority country. In Cairo al-Qadi al-Nu'man reached the apex of his career as the person in charge of Isma'ili jurisprudence and as head of the *da'wa*. His *Da'a'im al-Islam* became the canonical text of Isma'ili law in the empire.[19] The work deals with the seven obligations laid on the believer: loyalty to the imam (*walaya*), ritual purity (*tahara*), prayer (*salat*), paying alms (*zakat*), fasting (*sawm*), the pilgrimage to Mecca (*hajj*) and striving in faith (*jihad*). It contains regulations regarding the imamate and the believers' conduct in relation to it, as well as instructions on the acts of devotion to God, and reciprocal conduct between people. In writing this work, al-Qadi al-Nu'man relied on the authoritative sources shared by all jurists, such as the Qur'an and the prophetic traditions. He included principles derived from Shi'i law, but his innovation consisted in also basing his jurisprudence on the teachings on legal matters by the early imams, especially Ja'far al-Sadiq. To this day the *Da'a'im* represents a living code among the Bohras, the only community still practising Fatimid jurisprudence.[20] In al-Azhar, al-Qadi al-Nu'man delivered preaching that was specific to the Isma'ilis; also disseminated elsewhere were those principles of Isma'ili jurisprudence in his code that impacted on people's everyday lives. In Fustat, however, al-Mu'izz confirmed as *qadi* a prominent Maliki jurist with whom he maintained cordial relations.

As in Ifriqiya, Isma'ilism became evident in changes in ritual formulae and practices, as well as in all those contexts that called for Isma'ili symbols of authority to be proclaimed and to be made visible. In Egypt al-Mu'izz endorsed the performance of typical Shi'i festivals, such as those already celebrated in Baghdad under Shi'i Buyid rule. The festivals included the 'Ashura ceremonies to commemorate the martyrdom of al-Husayn and the feast of Ghadir, to celebrate an episode in 632 involving Muhammad and 'Ali at a place by this name where, according to Shi'i understanding, the Prophet designated his cousin as his successor in leading the Muslim community. Sunni festivals, however, continued to be celebrated, for example, in 973, the commemoration of a day when the Prophet Muhammad and his father-in-law Abu Bakr, later to become the first caliph for the Sunnis, took refuge in a cave on Mount Thawr, near Mecca, to escape from their enemies. On that occasion the streets were covered by canopies and lit by bonfires.

Outside Egypt the Isma'ili *da'wa* was further galvanized. Following al-Sijistani's philosophical reconciliation between eastern and Fatimid Isma'ilism, the once-reluctant eastern Isma'ili *da'i*s now came to Cairo, adding to the corpus of Isma'ili literature with their scholarship. At the same time some Isma'ilis arrived from Sicily, having left under persecution by Sunnis once the Fatimids had moved to Egypt.

The promise to restore financial stability was delivered with a massive injection of cash into the economy following the issuing of *dinar*s of the highest gold grade known to be in circulation at the time. The Fatimids must have brought the mint with them from Ifriqiya alongside the bullions of gold and silver in order to produce currency in their name soon after Jawhar's arrival. The *Mu'izzi dinar* featured the distinctive legend, consisting of the writing arranged in a sequence of concentric circles, already adopted in Ifriqiya. A distinctive feature of this coinage was a detail in its innermost circle: a central protruding dot that made his currency easy to recognize by sight and by touch in a Braille-like fashion. This currency became the dollar of its day, as it stabilized the exchange rates and its international circulation helped the growth of a market economy in Egypt. Confident and proud of his *dinar*s, it was quoted that al-Mu'izz, in response to some Egyptian notables who had questioned his pedigree, pulled his sword and said that this was his pedigree. Then he threw in front of the assembly a handful of his gold coins and proclaimed that this was his ancestry.[21]

Not all of those who contributed to the Fatimids' instalment in Egypt reaped the fruits of this achievement to the same extent. No sooner had al-Mu'izz arrived in his palace than the general Jawhar found himself relieved of his duties. He received a garment with a gold border, a red turban, a sword, 50,000 *dinar*s, 200,000 silver *dirham*s, items of clothing, and was forced into retirement. As Jawhar's star lost its shine a new one was rising: Ibn Killis, a former Ikhshidid high officer who climbed to the top of the Fatimid administration. Aided by an assistant, Ibn Killis was tasked with reorganizing the services of the regime, following an elaborate ceremony. Al-Qadi al-Nu'man died in 974, and he too was honoured by al-Mu'izz leading his funeral prayer.

Al-Mu'izz himself did not live long enough to bask in the glory of what had been achieved, dying at the age of 44. The imam-caliph was buried in the Turbat al-Safran, the mausoleum complex built near the palace as the resting place of his predecessors and members of the Fatimid royal family. In time, visiting this shrine became part of the formal ceremonial protocol at the end of royal processions. Al-Mu'izz's shrine was decorated with wall hangings including the fine blue silk map that he had brought from Ifriqiya featuring Mecca and Medina. Though a sponsor of the ritual, like his predecessors, al-Mu'izz never performed the pilgrimage to Mecca. He did not have to. According to Isma'ili interpretation, the esoteric meaning of the Ka'ba was that, as the house of God, it was the house of knowledge. Since the imam was the repository of all knowledge, in essence the Ka'ba was in fact the imamate. By being buried with this wall-hanging by his side al-Mu'izz was, in death as in life, at the centre of the universe of which, as far as his followers were concerned, he had been spiritual and political master.

Third Time Lucky: al-'Aziz and His Reign

Al-Mu'izz had designated 'Abd Allah as his successor. This son had distinguished himself in defeating a second attempted Qarmatian invasion of Egypt in 974. To celebrate the victory al-Mu'izz paraded him in public sheltered under the ceremonial parasol to mark him as his designated heir. However, 'Abd Allah died before his father in 975, and with Tamim already ruled out of the succession, the nomination as the next imam fell on Abu Mansur Nizar – the son that al-Mu'izz had with his consort Durzan (d. 995). He took the royal name of al-'Aziz. The appointment of a brother as replacement heir apparent for a dead sibling was somewhat at odds with Isma'ili precedent in matters of succession. Prior to this occasion, the only case of the imamate being transferred from brother to brother – one that the Isma'ilis considered to have been of a different nature anyway – was the one passed between 'Ali's sons, al-Hasan and al-Husayn. Under normal circumstances, in such cases the imamate would be expected to pass to 'Abd Allah's son rather than to his younger brother Nizar. Al-Mu'izz decided otherwise, on the basis of the Isma'ili belief in the infallibility that each incumbent imam could claim for himself. With no known public legitimization of his enthronement but on the strength of a deathbed appointment by his father, al-'Aziz became ruler. As was customary, the new imam-caliph kept the death of al-Mu'izz hidden from the general public for a period to allow the smooth transition of power from his predecessor to himself. When the time came, at a religious festival, he rode in procession under the ceremonial parasol to deliver a sermon in which he announced in public his rise to the throne. Back at the palace he received the oath of allegiance from members of royal family and courtiers. Thus a twist of fate had propelled Nizar to become al-'Aziz, the new monarch.

Destiny, and statecraft, did the rest. Under al-'Aziz's twenty-year-long reign the age of the Fatimids reached the zenith of its splendour. It was during his rule that Fatimid sovereignty reached its greatest territorial extension, whether by direct rule, through vassals, or nominal recognition of authority. Building on al-Mu'izz's legacy, it was under al-'Aziz that a combination of fortuitous circumstances, skilful administration and favourable geopolitical changes transformed Egypt into an international magnet for economic, social and cultural life. A number of core features defined al-'Aziz's reign: the development of court life to a level of splendour that upstaged Baghdad, Constantinople and Cordoba; the reform of the state administration with the institution of the vizirate; the ethnic diversification of the military and a more robust Fatimid presence in Syria and Palestine.

Al-'Aziz, the first imam-caliph whose reign started in Egypt, inaugurated his mandate by leaving a permanent imprint on the capital's landscape via his patronage. Perhaps at the instigation of Ibn Killis, he sought to project his image beyond the confines of the palace and reach out to a broader and mixed audience. The building programme started before the public announcement of al-Mu'izz's death and his formal accession to the throne, with al-'Aziz's mother, Durzan, named as the person behind several projects. Once enthroned in the Great Palace al-'Aziz added a Golden Gate to it, which was surmounted by a balcony from where he could deliver public addresses. From the gate a long portico led to the Golden Hall which functioned as a throne room for the hosting of audiences, official receptions and formal celebrations. The throne, made of gold encrusted with precious stones, covered in textiles and installed on a raised platform, was separated from the rest of the room by a curtain.

Al-ʻAziz also added to the palace a domed great *iwan*, a hall where Ismaʻili scholars and *daʻis* would gather to deliver sermons for the palace residents. The imam-caliph could follow proceedings from behind a grilled window looking into the room. Opposite the Great Palace, on the site of a former Ikhshidid garden, al-ʻAziz began the construction of the Western or Small Palace, also known as the Nile Palace because of its access to the river. A large part of the garden already existing was retained and served as leisure space for the royal family. To ensure that the royals could enjoy some privacy when moving around, underground tunnels were dug that linked the two palaces and pleasure gardens. These passages remained in use throughout the length of the dynasty. In due course al-ʻAziz assigned the Small Palace to his daughter Sitt al-Mulk. Both palaces consisted of compounds with several buildings, pavilions and courtyards, with the Great Palace being divided into two sections, one of which, the Emerald Palace, was the private quarters of the imam-caliph.

Al-ʻAziz had at least two consorts. The first, known as al-Sayyida al-ʻAziziyya, was a Melkite Christian, maybe of slave background. Al-ʻAziz appointed her brothers to be patriarchs of the Melkite churches: one in Fustat, then Alexandria, and the other in Jerusalem, while his father-in-law acted in a diplomatic capacity in Sicily.[22] This wife was the mother of al-ʻAziz's daughter Sitt al-Mulk. In 979 al-ʻAziz married again, this time to a high-status Egyptian woman or, according to some, a cousin. To strengthen his mass appeal, a public wedding procession was staged across the city which was accompanied by jubilant crowds to the sound of drums and trumpets. This woman, or another subsequent wife, may have been the mother of al-ʻAziz's son, who succeeded him with the dynastic name al-Hakim. In his private quarters al-ʻAziz hosted parties featuring music and dance that reflected the air of confidence and affluence that prevailed at court with the advent of his reign. An anecdote tells us that on one occasion al-ʻAziz's mother Durzan, his closest slave girls, the eunuchs and every woman musician in the palace gathered in the treasury hall. As partying, singing and the playing of musical instruments went on al-ʻAziz invited his female guests to help themselves to pearls scattered on a carpet that had been found in a casket that had belonged to al-Muʻizz but thought to have been lost.

Scenes of merriment and leisure became standard motifs in Fatimid decorative arts, appearing on lustreware ceramics, carved

8 Carved ivory panel from either Egypt or Sicily/Southern Italy, with hedonistic scenes, 12th century.

ivories and wood, reflecting scenes of a hedonistic life intended to project the prosperity the Fatimids brought to their domains (illus. 8). The realism of the scenes appearing on artefacts can be questioned, since standard decorative motifs were often shared across the courts of the Islamic middle period by craftsmen who moved from patron to patron. However, these objects can be seen nonetheless as useful illustrated catalogues of what was in fashion at the time: weaponry, musical instruments, textile design patterns and more. Al-'Aziz was often portrayed as a lover of beautiful things, with a penchant for curios as well as uncommon and extraordinary natural occurrences. When unusual phenomena were discovered across Egypt they would be reported to him. For example, he would be shown a woman with no arms who could write by holding a pen in her mouth, or a baby girl born with two heads.[23] Like his ancestors, al-'Aziz was also not immune to the book mania that had swept the lands of Islam since books (by this time mostly written on paper rather than parchment) had become more widely available. According to tales it was Chinese prisoners in 'Abbasid hands in mid-eighth-century Samarqand who had revealed the secrets of papermaking. By 993, al-'Aziz's library was known to contain, among thousands of books, thirty copies of a famous work on lexicography, one of which was an autograph; twenty copies of the world history by the tenth-century polymath al-Tabari, including an autograph; and one hundred copies of the Arabic dictionary by the Basran scholar Ibn Durayd (d. 933).

As for public works during al-'Aziz's reign, the first market in Cairo was established in 975–6, and within a few years the city was graced with bridges, gardens, bathhouses, caravanserais, fountains, pavilions, thousands of shops and buildings that were owned by the imam, his family and his close entourage and rented out. All of these provided eye-watering revenues for the royal family that, with other sources of income, were in turn used to sustain the expenses of the court's lifestyle. Many servants were employed to work in the royal kitchen, many of them women. Much later, in 990, al-'Aziz commissioned the construction of a major mosque, at that time outside Cairo's city walls, that was completed by his son and successor al-Hakim and bears his name. Today al-Hakim Mosque, with its two distinctive peppermill-shaped minarets, dominates the uppereast side of al-Mu'izz street, between the Futuh and the Nasr gates (illus. 9).

The capital served as a stage on which to advertise the dynasty, and for the public display of state power. Under al-'Aziz royal sponsorship of celebrations and religious festivals reached an unprecedented level of wealth, ostentation and generosity towards his subjects. Public celebrations were sumptuous and new occasions for public display of

9 Bab al-Futuh, Cairo.

authority were added to the customary religious ones. Outside Cairo open prayer spaces were renovated and upgraded. At court these events entailed banquets prepared by al-'Aziz's chefs, such as Abu Ayyub, the grandson of al-Qa'im's nurse, as well as the master chef of his time, 'Umar b. Sarraj (d. 989).[24] The feast extended to the general public, to whom vast quantities of food were distributed for free; al-'Aziz was the first ruler – at least in Egypt – to institutionalize the public distribution of sacrificial meat during Ramadan and the three-day feast at the end of the ritual fast. In 1047 the Persian Isma'ili propagandist, traveller and writer Nasir-i Khusraw (d. *c.* 1088) visited Cairo while on his way to Mecca, and found that the royal kitchen was staffed by fifty servants and located outside the palace, to which it was linked by an underground passage. This establishment was dedicated only to meat preparation and other savoury specialities. During the month of Ramadan every day 1,200 cauldrons of all sorts of meats would leave this kitchen to feed those who were entitled to have free meals, such as the military, the slaves and the poor. More were sent into the royal palace for the imam-caliph, his family and his dignitaries. The running costs were enormous. By the twelfth century the store stocked 5,000 lambs a day, not counting everything else. In Egypt al-'Aziz was also the first ruler to order the establishment, outside the palace and opposite one of the royal stables, of the *dar al-fitra*. This department was dedicated to the preparation of sweets to be distributed on the occasion of the *'id*. The annual budget needed to run it was phenomenal, with an average 20,000 *dinars* disbursed for making the sweets, not counting additional costs for firewood, lamp oil, musk, saffron, camphor and the bakers' salaries. Festive pastries were made with tons of flour, sugar, pistachio, walnuts, hazelnuts, dates, raisins, honey, sesame oil, sesame seeds and aniseed. To this day the confection popular at the time called *ka'k* or *kahk* remains a favourite Egyptian festive treat. An ancient type of cake consisting of stuffed pastry decorated with imprinted patterns on top, *kahk* was eaten by the Copts during their Easter celebrations. Prior to the Fatimids, the Tulunids and the Ikhshidids were also partial to it. With a dedicated *dar al-fitra* for its mass production the Fatimids raised the *kahk* to new heights. For example, at some stage the Fatimid regime had the cakes imprinted with thank-you formulae for the ruler and blessings for the hands of Hafiza, a woman tasked with their making. For the cakes to be ready by Ramadan, preparations had to start in the middle of the previous month. Some sixty varieties were prepared and distributed to the public on long tables. It also became traditional to insert gold coins into the pastries for random lucky consumers to find them. With the Fatimids, who from the outset understood the importance of public image through branding, the delicious *kahk* was turned into a most seductive propaganda tool for the populace to delight in.

On the occasion of the *'id* al-'Aziz would go by procession to attend the prayer and deliver the sermon at a dedicated public plaza outside Cairo. As was customary with his predecessors, such occasions provided people with the opportunity to hand petitions to the imam-caliph. Al-'Aziz then returned to the palace to share the celebratory meal with the ruling elites. Meanwhile the residents of Fustat were served festive meals at locations by the local police headquarters so that crowd control could be enforced. In addition to the festivals of 'Ashura and Ghadir which had been state-endorsed by his father, al-'Aziz joined in the celebrations of the middle of the Islamic months of Rajab and Shaban, staged near al-Azhar Mosque with a big display of lights and involving more food distribution, courtesy of the imam-caliph.

Royal funerals too became state-choreographed events. Although the Fatimids forbade women wailing at funerals and staying too long in cemeteries, the preparation of these solemn events and the staging of public mourning became elaborate affairs entailing the disbursement of huge amounts of money. The funeral of al-'Aziz's wife, al-'Aziziyya, was emblematic. According to the chronicler Ibn Muyassar (d. 1278), who described this event in his annals relating to the Fatimids, the women who washed her corpse, upon completing their task, took for themselves bedding and linen worth 6,000 *dinar*s. The deceased was wrapped in a shroud worth 10,000 *dinar*s. For seven days thousands of *dinar*s were given to the poor, the Qur'an reciters praying at her tomb and the poets for their elegies. Sitt al-Mulk sat at her mother's grave for a month and al-'Aziz visited almost every day. People gathered day and night by her grave sharing food and sweets.

The Vizirate and Ibn Killis

Many of the characteristics that defined al-'Aziz's reign can be credited to the ability of one man, Ya'qub b. Killis (d. 991). Born in Baghdad in 930, he moved to Palestine with his family, where he worked as a merchants' representative. Suspected of mismanagement, he fled to Egypt to join the Ikhshidid's administrative class. As the Ikhshidid rule descended into chaos, he defected to al-Mansuriyya to work as finance minister for al-Mu'izz. Having returned to Egypt with the Fatimid conquest, under al-'Aziz Ibn Killis at first held the role of *wasita*, middle man between the monarch and his subjects, a position that he shared with a financial assistant. In 977 al-'Aziz made him the first ever vizier to head the Fatimid administration, and in 979 he bestowed on him the title of most illustrious vizier. A Jew who had converted to Islam, he became the mastermind behind most of the ventures that characterized the period. Al-'Aziz's introduction of the vizirate in the Fatimid regime's administration marked an important shift in the imam-caliph's self-understanding of his role as a monarch. Al-'Aziz abandoned the personal, direct formula of family-run rule adopted by his forefathers, opting instead for an 'Abbasid-like model with the monarch leading a regime via a minister at the head of a team of functionaries. To their rivals and detractors, the Fatimids would now prove to be not just a small-time empire but one with ideological and organizational built-in infrastructures to replace the caliphs of Baghdad. Being an experienced 'man of the pen' in the previous regime, upon becoming the Fatimid vizier Ibn Killis could count on his former peers, many of whom looked to him for placements. During his vizirate they formed a new secretarial class that enabled him to keep the administration, finances and the military under control. To secure his staff's support, Ibn Killis gave pensions to those in his entourage. Marriage also played an important role as a way to forge or maintain a high position at court. Much to the mutual advantage of the respective fathers, the son of the last Ikhshidid vizier, who had played a pivotal role in the smooth transition from the old regime to the new, married the daughter of Ibn Killis.

With the disintegration of centralized power in Baghdad, there were plenty of talented easterners in search of work. As head of the *diwan al-majlis*, a central command office for the coordinated management of the *diwan*s system, Ibn Killis placed them in the departments he oversaw, including the *diwan al-insha'*, the state chancery, responsible for issuing decrees and letters; the *diwan al-jaysh* and *rawatib*, responsible for the army and its salaries, and the *diwan al-amwal*, the office dealing with properties. This was the most complex office, divided between the revenue and expenditure departments, with most income derived from land and commerce. Over time more *diwan*s were created with, for example, royal women having their own dedicated departments to manage their affairs. Other offices were established to administer specific concerns. In these departments, civilian and military officials were organized according to ranks that were signalled by different insignia, outfits, pay and positioning in the staging of ceremonials. On the whole, however, their salaries were inferior to those of their colleagues in Baghdad, although they were compensated with generous patronage in all sorts of other ways.

As vizier, Ibn Killis became the second most powerful man in the state, with privileges, wealth and lifestyle to match. His house consisted of a large complex from which he ran the affairs of state as well as private business. Ibn Killis became a wealthy man with revenues derived from extensive land grants, a handsome salary and lucrative trade. Like most Fatimid elites he was involved in the manufacture and sale of linen while managing the affairs of the state textile factories. At his death in 991 Ibn Killis was reported to have accumulated vast quantities of textile stock destined for wholesale trade. Medieval travellers' accounts of the Delta city of Tinnis, a major centre of textile production, depict Ibn Killis as a brutal administrator who imposed forced labour on the town's weavers as well as charging levies on those who entered and left the city.[25]

Ibn Killis spent his wealth enjoying the best life had to offer. It was alleged that he was a connoisseur of food, and that he had eight hundred women in his harem, many of whom had belonged to the deposed Ikhshidids. He was a sponsor of cultural activities as well as a patron of learned men. He endowed religious monuments, invested in commercial buildings and, by the time of his death, had assembled a personal militia of 4,000 men. Despite all his power and wealth Ibn Killis was nevertheless never exempt from the bouts of wrath that the imam-caliph could unleash on the staff who – irrespective of status – remained dependent on him. Like most, Ibn Killis incurred the occasional temporary dismissal followed by arrest and the confiscation of his property by al-'Aziz. In one instance, for example, Ibn Killis was accused of attempting to poison the Turkish commander Alptakin. Initially an enemy, once captured and brought to Cairo, this figure, as we will see, became instrumental in al-'Aziz's plan to diversify the ethnic composition of the Fatimid army.

In the time of Ibn Killis, from around 978, the boundaries between the spheres of activity of the vizier and the chief *qadi* became somewhat blurred, with the former eclipsing the latter in importance. After the death of al-Qadi al-Nu'man, his sons 'Ali and Muhammad had inherited their father's monopoly in the formulation, application and dissemination of Isma'ili jurisprudence as well as the headship of the *da'wa*. 'Ali was installed as chief of both offices in an elaborate ceremonial. When the letter of his appointment was read out in al-Azhar Mosque the reader made a sign to the audience to prostrate to the ground whenever the name of the imam-caliph was mentioned. 'Ali al-Nu'man was plenipotentiary in that he had responsibility for the whole of Egypt, with a Shafi'i jurist (a Sunni) as his deputy. His brother Muhammad was nominated judge for the Delta centres of Tinnis, Damietta and al-Farama as well as other coastal cities. Evidence that the old families in Fatimid service joined forces to defend each other's interests against newcomers advancing their positions at court is seen in family alliances forged through marriage. Muhammad al-Nu'man's son wed Jawhar's daughter, her dowry consisting of 3,000 *dinar*s and a monochrome robe. Jawhar's sister had married another of the Nu'man brothers. Similarly, bedroom politics saw another daughter of Ibn Killis marrying the Turk Yarukh, known as 'Alam al-Dawla, who became at some point governor of Syria during the caliphate of al-'Aziz's successor.

In Fustat 'Ali administered justice on Monday and Thursday in the 'Amr Mosque. He was at al-Azhar on Tuesday and Saturday, and also served in the caliphal palace. He kept records and documents at his residence, with handbooks and documents for pending cases secured in red boxes. Ibn Killis spared no effort in trying to dent the Nu'man family's control over Fatimid jurisprudence and the judiciary. While al-Qadi al-Nu'man's *Da'a'im al-Islam* remained the undisputed manual of Isma'ili law in the empire, Ibn Killis sought to rival the Nu'mans' reputation by promoting himself as an authoritative expert in Isma'ili law in his own right. He was the author of a book on Isma'ili jurisprudence in the form of a compendium of al-Mu'izz's and al-'Aziz's sayings, along with those of previous imams, to be used as reference for jurists. Having established a formal system to teach Isma'ili law, Ibn Killis also tried, but failed, to impose the use of his manual as a textbook in the Sunni 'Amr Mosque in Fustat. To signal the vizier's oversight over both *dawla* and *da'wa* Ibn Killis took the lead in turning al-Azhar into a centre for Isma'ili mission and training. He bought land and a house near the mosque from where he presided over debates between Muslim, Christian and Jewish men of learning. Documentary evidence shows Ibn Killis holding book club-like sessions. On one occasion the vizier was with the literati, philosophers and physicians who attended his court.

During the session he showed them the Arabic translation of a prayer book by the tenth-century Jewish author Saadia Gaon. Ibn Killis however ridiculed and scorned the book, much to the consternation of a Jewish savant who was present at the event and recorded the incident.[26]

Ibn Killis brought an 'Abbasid-style flair to the already rich intellectual life at the heart of Fatimid culture. Each Friday 35 jurists formed circles in the mosque upon receiving extra pay from Ibn Killis. At his instigation, at some festivals al-'Aziz gave them robes of honour as well as mules and made them part of his parade in the city. In the administration of justice Ibn Killis removed from the Nu'mans the control of the police and the handling of criminal cases, a jurisdiction that the chief *qadi* had exercised since the Ifriqiya days via the appointment of judges. The police were responsible for the application of penalties against criminals, a task that overlapped with that of the *qadi*. By granting the police a greater degree of autonomy from the judges Ibn Killis enhanced the importance of their role. In some high-profile criminal cases the judiciary was bypassed and the imam put the vizier in charge of investigations, for example when Ibn Killis was delegated to look into the murder of a foreign merchant. Ibn Killis also took away from the Nu'mans the management of petitions which up to this point had been heard by the monarch or his private secretary, or the *qadi*. With Ibn Killis claimants could go straight to the vizier's house rather than wait for the rare occasions when the imam-caliph could be accosted, or hand them to the *qadi*.

The Nu'mans only recovered full control of these activities after Ibn Killis's death. After that, 'Ali reaffirmed his position as chief *qadi*, as leader of the *da'wa* and as chief instructor in the sessions of wisdom. His jurisdiction was extended to all the Fatimid territories listed in the letter of his appointment. He shared judicial authority with additional responsibilities for the handling of petitions, the *hisba* or supervision of markets, the management of pious endowments, *waqf*s, oversight of the mint and custodianship of the estates of the deceased. Provincial judges had their own authority and their responsibilities reflected those of the chief *qadi*. In court, typical Shi'i Isma'ili formulae naming 'Ali al-Nu'man and the imam of the day were used.

Meanwhile intellectual life within the Isma'ili *da'wa* continued to flourish, attracting more and more scholars to Cairo from the eastern regions of the propaganda network. Among the most prominent *da'is* to arrive from Iran during al-'Aziz's reign was Ahmad al-Nishaburi

(d. early eleventh century). A prolific writer, his work became influential as part of the Fatimids' foundational narratives, as he disclosed details about the inner organization of the *da'wa* and what was expected of an ideal *da'i*. As a thinker he argued about the necessity of the imamate in this world. He wrote about the hidden imams and their circumstances as they were before the re-emergence of their line with the Fatimid dynasty. In so doing, with his work al-Nishaburi reflected an emboldened, affirmative Isma'ili propaganda that now could explain the past history of the *da'wa* to the Isma'ili believers in a systematic way. He also provided guidance about the correct way to conduct it.

In January 991 Ibn Killis fell ill. A story goes that, as his health deteriorated, so distraught was al-'Aziz at the prospect of losing him that he pledged to God that he would sacrifice everything – even his own son – if that would help save his vizier. In the end Ibn Killis died of natural causes and at the top of his career, an achievement in itself given the volatility of political lives in any court at the time. His funeral was a grand affair, staged with female slaves standing by his grave and the mourning crowd fed with silver spoons and cups. The following year also saw the death of the great general Jawhar, the man who had conquered for the Fatimids a territory from which their empire would expand further. However, on this occasion it was al-'Aziz's wife who sent the embalming and burial equipment for the funeral. Al-'Aziz and his son contributed too. Because of his presumed Christian Armenian ancestry, it is believed that he was buried in the cemetery by the St George Church, south of modern Cairo.[27] The contrast with Ibn Killis's final send-off could not be a more blatant indicator of the direction royal favouritism had taken.

For some time, Ibn Killis proved to be irreplaceable; after him, his position was taken by a number of acting viziers who were hired and fired in quick rotation. Ibn Killis left behind a legacy that in different ways impacted on the Fatimids well into the following century. With him diverse ethnic and religious representation in the highest offices of the state had become a characteristic that, though not exclusive to the Fatimids, made them stand out among contemporary Islamic regimes. During al-'Aziz's reign Christians were favoured for prominent positions and at times they also served as viziers. The Copts were valued because of their expertise in financial administration, with their centuries-long quasi-monopoly of the tax collection system in Egypt. Their knowledge of the country's complex land administration had been passed on within the same families for generations. Al-'Aziz's marriage to a Melkite might have played a part in his favouritism towards Christians in general. Jews were also appointed to high offices, though never to the vizirate unless they were converts to Islam.[28]

The system of *diwan*s that Ibn Killis left behind developed into an elaborate yet efficient secretarial and fiscal administrative machine which operated with some degree of autonomy. For a brief time, after Ibn Killis's death, the state administration was run by a consortium of Muslims, Christians and Jews supervised by Jawhar, who had been brought back for the task before his death. Eventually a Christian, 'Isa b. Nasturus (d. 1000), rose from being a financial administrator to becoming vizier in practice. A Jew, Manassa b. al-Qazzaz, became a caliphal military administrator and high-ranking officer in Syria and Palestine. Such was al-'Aziz's good disposition towards Christians and Jews that (according to a story circulating at the time) a Muslim poet sang in a tease 'Become Christian, for Christianity is the true religion! Our time proves it so. Worry not about anything else: Ya'qub, the Wazir, is the Father; 'Aziz, the Son, and Fadl, The Holy-Ghost.'[29] Upon hearing the verses the Muslims revolted, asking for the poet to be punished, but al-'Aziz interceded with Ibn Killis and the other high officer, Fadl, for the poet to be spared. Legends aside, the Sunnis of Egypt showed displeasure at the imam-caliph's openness towards Christians and Jews. Unrest followed and al-'Aziz had to resort to a reshuffling of appointments and the occasional volte-face to appease his Muslim subjects.

The most long-term consequence resulting from Ibn Killis's appointment as vizier was the rise of easterners, *mashariqa* – mostly Turks – as the dominant force in many aspects of Fatimid life. This destabilized the precarious ethnic balance at the heart of the regime. Much of the sovereign's preservation of power depended upon his success in securing the loyalty of chosen groups raised to elite status through his exclusive patronage of them. If he failed as a patron the same groups could seek protection elsewhere, thus empowering a more generous rival sponsor at the ruler's risk. In turn these elites were in constant fear of the withdrawal of the sovereign's patronage. A ruler could change his preferences due to political expediency, resulting in marginalization, a fall from grace and the loss of the privileges that came with it. Therefore, the elites returned the sovereign's loyalty so long as they remained his exclusive preference at the expense of others.[30]

The Kutama, the Saqaliba and Black people, typically described as Sudanese but of varied African provenance, formed the bulk of the westerners, *maghariba*. The Fatimids owed them so much and therefore they counted themselves as elites. Now, as a powerful new faction grew in influence and numbers, they saw their entitlement to preferential treatment eroded. The rivalry between *mashariqa* and *maghariba* in securing and preserving the ruler's favour generated disputes at all levels of Fatimid society which would eventually result in open conflict. The policy of ethnic diversification that Ibn Killis had encouraged, and the frictions that grew from it, became actualized in al-ʻAziz's systemic changes in the composition of the Fatimid army.

After a series of expensive yet unsatisfactory military campaigns in Syria, al-ʻAziz had realized that an overhaul of the army was needed to avoid a reoccurrence of past failures. What ensued was a reform that broke the westerners' monopoly as the dominant Fatimid army group. This had to do with the need to strengthen the army's capability by injecting new military skills as well as manpower. The Berbers had proven to be amazing fighters in cavalry and swordplay, while the Black *maghariba*, generically known as *ʻabid*, slaves, made a strong infantry corps and provided logistical support. These military abilities had worked well in Ifriqiya against enemies that used the same combat techniques but they were ineffective in fighting against armies that proved to be more efficient on account of being equipped with different skills suited to different territories and fighting strategies. Unlike their rivals from the eastern lands of the ʻAbbasid empire and the Byzantines, the Fatimids lacked archers in their ranks. It was therefore vital to absorb into the army soldiers from ethnic groups known for their dexterity in the use of the bow. Enter the Turks. In 978 the Fatimid army had defeated that of the Turkish governor in Damascus, Alptakin, following the latter's initial advantage against Jawhar's Fatimid troops which had intervened to quash Sunni-led anti-Fatimid agitations in the city. Rather than crushing the rebellious governor, al-ʻAziz went the extra mile to make him feel welcome: the imam-caliph let the defeated governor stay in his tent, gave him a horse, met all his needs, returned his insignia to him and let him socialize with other prisoners of war. According to an anecdote, taken aback by such magnanimity, Alptakin hesitated when the imam-caliph offered him a rose-flavoured drink. Al-ʻAziz, understanding that the governor feared he might be poisoned, drank first from the cup to reassure him. Indeed, to the imam-caliph

Alptakin was more useful alive than dead, and al-'Aziz jumped at the opportunity to incorporate him and his soldiers into the Fatimid army.

Excellent archers and horse riders – like groups of Daylami Persians who had defected from the Shi'i Buyids rulers – the Turks contributed distant-combat capability, speed and battle tactics, thus filling a major gap in Fatimid army operations. In theory, juxtaposing ethnic groups in the same army should have generated a healthy competition for bravery among rival contingents. In practice, the Kutamas, with their history embedded in that of the Fatimids and no alternative sources of patronage, found the Fatimid regime taking their loyalty for granted. Since the Turks were a new element, the imam-caliph had to double his efforts to earn their loyalty; if he failed, the Turks might defect to the 'Abbasids if that meant greater gain. Overnight the Kutamas saw themselves upstaged by the easterners as the imam-caliphs' darlings. Their response was to try to curb the Turks' ascent in every way possible, thus setting in motion what turned out to be an internecine tug-of-war that proved toxic for the Fatimids and Egypt.

With the transfer of the dynasty to Egypt, the imam-caliph's patronage of civil and military staff had expanded in size and quality. In addition to land grants and salaries, allocated according to rank, each individual serving the court received sets of clothes for each season, regular gifts and free food. With the military in particular the sovereign was responsible for supplying equipment and weaponry. In turn high officers of the state were responsible for their respective subordinates. As patron the ruler became a father-like figure, and this bond was nurtured with the military because of the mutual benefit each derived. Al-'Aziz's reform of the army's composition extended not just to ethnicity but to the social status of the soldiers. In Ifriqiya the Fatimids had made use of military slaves who had belonged to the Aghlabids. Under al-'Aziz, the incorporation of Turkish elements into the army also entailed the addition of Turkish military slaves, *ghilman* (sing. *ghulam*). These formed a distinctive class allocated to the cavalry corps and they gained a significance not found to the same extent in armies serving other Islamic regimes. The ruler took care of their training for seven years in archery and use of the lance, and was responsible for their lodgings in dedicated barracks. Al-Mu'izz had already implemented this type of youth training scheme soon after his arrival in Egypt. The imam-caliph had in fact ordered the governors of the provinces to recruit the fittest children from among the notable families and to lodge them in special hostels with a view to military training. For the first time Egyptians entered service in the Fatimid army. Al-'Aziz built on his father's programme and at some stage elevated a group of *ghilman* to be his own elite regiment, known as al-'Aziziyya. By contrast, among the military slaves, Black soldiers occupied the lower ranks. Al-'Aziz's expansion and diversification of the army had a major effect on the demographic profile of Egypt and the capital in particular. With their families in tow, the military contributed to the massive growth of ethnic diversity in the population.

It is self-evident that the army needed huge sums for its upkeep, access to which was a constant concern that impacted on political, economic and social life. For this reason, in Fatimid Egypt and the provinces of the empire, changes in society and in the military became from this time onwards more and more interconnected and interdependent.

Al-'Aziz in Syria and Palestine

Control of Syria was vital to the fulfilment of the Fatimids' ambitions to conquer Baghdad and dislodge the 'Abbasids from their leadership of the Muslim community. The Fatimids' attachment to Syria was emotive as well as strategic and ideological; it was the land where the Isma'ili imamate had resurfaced. Since the days of the hidden imams and al-Mahdi, Syria had suffered more political, religious and administrative fragmentation. In Egypt, a country used to central government, the ruler controlled his domains from the capital. Not so in Syria, where the conquest of Damascus in the south would have no bearings upon the control of Aleppo in the north. Since their move to Egypt, the Fatimids' ventures in Syria had involved confrontations with the Qarmatians who, though Shi'is, fought on the 'Abbasids' side. The other main regional rivals were the Byzantines, whose handling of the Fatimids continued to be shaped by alternating truces and wars. Under al-'Aziz it took over a decade before Damascus came under firmer Fatimid control. Expecting a major military confrontation caused by sedition, the Fatimids had deployed a vast army with Jawhar at its head. The general, however, could not work his magic on this occasion, instead running into serious trouble and facing an initial defeat at the hands of Alptakin. To remedy the situation al-'Aziz himself joined the campaign with a large army consisting mainly of Kutama cavalry and Black infantry. Al-'Aziz's intervention paid off and Damascus, which had come under firmer Fatimid control in 983, was at last brought under direct Fatimid administration in 988 with the instalment of Munir, who had served Ibn Killis, as the city's ruler. However, after the vizier's death this governor was caught conspiring against the Fatimids in favour of Baghdad. For all the effort spent on an ever-tenuous hold on Damascus, al-'Aziz's ultimate ambition had been to expand into northern Syria by taking Aleppo, the gateway to Baghdad. But Aleppo was also important to the Byzantines, whose advance into Syria had culminated in the capture of Antioch in 969. To defend the city against the Fatimids the Christians courted an alliance with Aleppo's ruler, the Hamdanid Sa'd al-Dawla.

Ibn Killis advised against the Fatimid conquest of Aleppo but the imam-caliph insisted since, beyond strategic reasons, to defeat the Byzantines there would be charged with symbolic power: it would be yet another proof of the dynasty's messianic mission. After a series of mixed results al-'Aziz's conquest of Aleppo came to nothing and Ibn Killis, proved right, had to intervene to reassert the Fatimids' position in Syria. The Byzantines asked for a truce and al-'Aziz accepted it, opening the way to convenient diplomatic arrangements for all involved in the region. In return for an end to Fatimid aggression on Aleppo, the Byzantines lifted anti-Fatimid commercial restrictions, released Muslim captives and in 988 agreed for the sermon delivered in conjunction with the Friday prayer to be recited in the Fatimids' name in Constantinople's mosque. This act represented an important turning point in the region's geopolitics: it signalled the Byzantines' formal acceptance of the Fatimids' claim over that of the 'Abbasids to lead the Muslim community. And although an attempted Fatimid–Buyid anti-Byzantine alliance had failed, diplomatic arrangements had been agreed with the Buyids too. At the same time an Aleppo tribal confederation offered alliance to the Fatimids, while Bedouin chiefs in Transjordan who controlled Palestine in Raqqa and Ramla maintained an ambivalent position towards the Cairo regime. Al-'Aziz obtained a nominal allegiance from the Qarmatians by paying them tributes in return for non-belligerence. The plans to conquer Aleppo were not abandoned but were hit by setbacks. In 995–6 the Fatimids had new ships built with Sicilian wood, ready in the Maqs river port of Cairo to be launched against the Byzantines. The fleet, however, was burned. People blamed Amalfitan traders housed by the *dar al-manak*, the toll station; they had been regular visitors to Fatimid shores since the North African days of the dynasty. Simmering anti-*dhimmi* sentiments erupted and there were riots against the Italians, and Christians in general. More than a hundred people were killed; the churches were pillaged and a bishop died. Merchandise belonging to the Italians worth 90,000 *dinar*s was looted. By the time calm was restored and the culprits punished the momentum to launch a naval expedition to conquer Aleppo had gone. To remedy the naval loss the vizier 'Isa b. Nasturus began building a new fleet. The materials needed were scavenged hastily around the capital to be repurposed for ship construction. The old wooden doors of the mint palace were reused and a hospice of the Tunlunid period was stripped of its wood. This new fleet was sent to Syria but once again adversity struck: as the ships approached Tartus they were dispersed by strong winds, and the crews were taken captive. In 996 an anti-Fatimid rebellion took place in Ramla led by a Shi'i of Meccan origin who came forward as a claimant to the caliphate. In spite of these troubling circumstances, in the summer of 996 al-'Aziz embarked on an anti-Byzantine campaign which, as it turned out, would change the course of Fatimid history in an unexpected way.

The concentration of military efforts in Syria and Palestine and the ongoing preoccupation with the consolidation of power in Egypt did not diminish the Fatimids' engagement with other regions. By the end of al-'Aziz's reign the Fatimid empire had reached its greatest extension. The dynasty exercised direct rule in Egypt, parts of Palestine and southern Syria. As for indirect control, its territorial possessions in North Africa had been entrusted to a vassal dynasty, the Sanhaja Zirids. Under al-'Aziz, Tripoli came to mark the border between the extent of Fatimid direct rule and that of Zirids. These North African rulers settled in the former Fatimid palace in al-Mansuriyya and gave rise to a dynasty that after 985 grew more and more independent of Cairo. Al-'Aziz nevertheless continued to maintain relations on a ceremonial and ritual basis. The oath of allegiance was still proclaimed in the name of the Fatimid imam-caliph. Embassies continued to be exchanged carrying gifts intended as symbols of their bond and loyalty. The Zirids in turn could show off in public functions the imam-caliphs' instruments of investiture that served to legitimize them as rulers to their subjects: decrees, banners, swords, robes and letters announcing Fatimid victories. In Sicily too, the Kalbids exchanged embassies with Egypt, bearing and collecting gifts. In 976, through military intervention, al-'Aziz had consolidated the Fatimids' indirect sovereignty over the Hijaz, Mecca and Medina by compelling the local rulers to pledge permanent submission to Cairo. From then on, Fatimid troops would escort the pilgrimage caravans every year and the *kiswa* cover for the Ka'ba continued to be sent from Cairo on a regular basis, circumstances allowing. In addition to the port of Qulzum, contacts with Arabia for dispatching grain and goods were also facilitated by the stationing of a Fatimid commercial fleet in Aydhab, a port on the Upper Egypt Red Sea coast. The Fatimids' expansion of infrastructures in that region favoured trade across the Indian Ocean coast to the mutual advantage of the Fatimids and local rulers.

In territories outside Fatimid control, al-'Aziz pursued diplomatic avenues in Iraq and Iran where, through the mediation of eastern Isma'ili propagandists, he sought to persuade princes and local elites to switch their allegiance to Cairo. In theory this region had become fertile territory for pro-Fatimid propaganda due to the Shi'i Buyids serving a Sunni caliphate. In practice the Buyids and their affiliates saw no advantage in changing a situation that had served them well. If anything, they saw the Fatimids as rivals in Syria, where they perceived them as conflicting with their own interests. Building on diplomatic relations already established by al-Mu'izz, embassies were also sent to Nubia. The Christian monarch of that region had resumed paying tributes to the Fatimids since the Coptic Patriarchate of Egypt, to which the monarch belonged, fell under the Fatimid *aman* arrangement. In 993 this tribute arrived in Cairo accompanied by an elephant and a giraffe as royal gifts.

'It's the economy, stupid'

What paid for it all? Fiscal and financial reforms, a coveted currency, political stability in Egypt matched by geopolitical changes elsewhere and a protracted absence of major natural disasters in the region, all contributed to a period of major economic growth in Egypt during the twenty years of al-'Aziz's reign. Ruling from the heart of a country at the crossroads of international trade between the Mediterranean, the Indian Ocean and the Red Sea, the Fatimids became import–export power brokers no one could afford to ignore. Cairo-Fustat became the new economic capital of a world in which Muslim, Christian and Jewish merchants all converged to dispatch Egyptian goods abroad, but also to trade in Asian and African goods destined for the European markets. In Egypt the production of sugar cane, flax, cotton and finished textiles expanded to meet foreign as well as internal demand. Flax became the main Egyptian industrial crop and a staple export in the Mediterranean. For example, Fatimid-exported flax came to be used in Naples to make linen cloth. After textile production, sugar was the second largest industry, with processing plants in Fustat. The growth of these state-owned industries provided employment for a growing urban population, even though, on average, wages remained low for ordinary workers.

To meet the high demand of a court with a sweet tooth the Fatimids expanded the cultivation of sugar cane in Sicily for export to Egypt. On the island this crop is attested as having been first introduced by the Arabs in Palermo around 930. Other imports from the Muslim west included iron, copper, lead, tin, silver, mercury and gold. Zirid Ifriqiya continued to supply coral, olive oil, soap, wax, honey, saffron and leather hides. Silk cocoons as well as finished silk textiles were imported from Tunisia, the Iberian Peninsula and Sicily to be processed or redistributed in Egypt. Sicily also became an important supplier of cotton. Imports from Italy ranged from wood to processed dairy goods, such as the *jibna rumi*, which is still a popular type of hard cheese sold in Egypt. From India, imported spices were redistributed across the Mediterranean. During al-'Aziz's reign, rock crystal arrived from islands in the Indian Ocean to be carved by Egypt-based craftsmen. The exceptional quality and mystique surrounding Fatimid craftsmanship in this field was not lost on European royalty and nobility of the time. A tenth-century Fatimid rock crystal ball carved with lions became – once encased in gold filigree – the head of the sceptre of the Holy Crown of Hungary. This object, dated around the turn of the first millennium, is the oldest piece among the Hungarian royal insignia to survive in its original form.[31] In eleventh-century Spain, Count Arnau and his wife Arsenda d'Àger entertained themselves with Fatimid-imported rock crystal chess pieces (illus. 10).[32] Today Fatimid-era carved rock crystal artefacts are among the most prized possessions in many Islamic art collections, whether private or public. From South Asia and Africa, the Fatimids imported ivory that was carved into luxury objects such as, for example, oliphants. These were mainly carved in Sicily and southern Italy, with most destined for export in Europe.

This system of exchange, matched by taxation favourable to trade, facilitated the expansion of an Egyptian middle class which, irrespective of religious persuasion, had a vested interest in preserving the Fatimid

10 Rock crystal Àger chessmen, Fatimid, 11th century, from the former Colegiata de Sant Pere de Àger.

regime. Farmers too did well out of a tax farm system that had been transformed from a fiscal instrument into a form of investment. The largest returns were of course for those in power: the royals, their families and their close servants, but also high dignitaries, ministers and army officers who came to be in charge of estates where taxes became, in practice, rents. Large sums of money were spent on consumption but also reinvested in industrial crops and manufactures as well as foreign trade. The men and women of the Fatimid royal family engaged themselves in wholesale trade, the women via prominent commercial brokers close to the regime.

Limited interference by the ruler in commerce carried on by his subjects, the rise of Europe as a trading partner, a dip in the economy of Iraq and the diversion of trade away from the Persian Gulf all added to an al-'Aziz-era economic boom. After years of penury and upheaval, al-'Aziz brought a prosperity and a lifestyle to Egypt that most of his subjects could not have dreamt of only a few decades earlier. Unlike his predecessors, al-'Aziz had time to enjoy the fruits of his success. Literally. According to a story reported by al-Maqrizi, fresh cherries were dispatched to him wrapped in silk sachets attached to the feet of carrier pigeons sent from Syria to Cairo. A recent test to verify the feasibility of such delivery having taken place in the way the sources describe it has established that some three hundred cherries might have arrived at their destination out of nine hundred sent by that method.

With success on several fronts, the conquest of northern Syria once and for all would have been for al-ʿAziz the proverbial cherry on his territorial cake. Al-ʿAziz decided to give it yet another push. In 996 the imam-caliph left Egypt at the head of his army for a military campaign which he expected to end in his favour. Indeed, as his father had done when moving for good from al-Mansuriyya to Egypt, al-ʿAziz took the coffins of his ancestors along with him. It was not to be. Al-ʿAziz fell ill on the way as a result of chronic colon disease and died in Bilbays, a locality on the eastern edge of the Nile Delta in Egypt.

The death of al-ʿAziz marked the culmination of almost a hundred years that had proved momentous in so many ways for the Fatimids. A venture that had started with an undercover Ismaʿili imam and a small group of followers on the run from Salamiyya had resulted in a dynasty of imam-caliphs that turned Cairo into the most magnificent imperial capital of the time, ruling over a vast empire. The Fatimids' fortunes had coincided with the disintegration of the ʿAbbasid empire, with the recognition of Baghdad's sovereignty across its territories having become only nominal. At the same time the Christian Byzantines showed renewed energy, posing an existential threat to Islamic rule in areas where the Fatimids nonetheless proved capable of checking them. In al-Andalus the Umayyads had raised their regime to the level of caliphate with Madinat al-Zahra' near Cordoba as a splendid capital to match, only to fade back to the regional power it had once been. As a centennial in the Islamic calendar was approaching – the year 400 – the Islamic messianic belief that God would send a renewer of religion every hundred years gathered momentum. In the Christian world millenarian expectation, with the imminent advent of the year 1000, triggered apocalyptic anxieties across medieval Europe. In Cairo the power of these beliefs propelled the Fatimids – a dynasty that had affirmed itself as the deliverer of a messianic promise – in surprising, new and uncharted directions.

5

The Imam-Caliph al-Hakim: Maverick or God Incarnate?

On an October day in 996 a boy was frolicking up a tree somewhere in the Nile Delta town of Bilbays. However, that carefree childhood play came to an abrupt end when the boy's minder and mentor, the eunuch Barjawan, rushed to summon him down. As the child descended, the eunuch bowed in from of him and addressed him with the regal title *amir al-mu'minin*. Al-'Aziz had just died, and the life of his child changed forever. The boy who had climbed up the tree as al-Mansur came down it as the new Imam-caliph al-Hakim. Aged eleven, he inaugurated a sequence of child rulers, a phenomenon that was to characterize the Fatimid leadership from this time onwards. Al-Hakim grew up to become one of the most enigmatic and divisive leaders in world history. Slanderous accusations by his detractors were counterbalanced by his apotheosis among his most ardent supporters. His reputation reached the West through stories about him that further fed the negative attitudes that medieval Christian Europe held against Islam. Stories about 'the mad caliph', from horror to dark comedy, have filled chronicles and fantasies ever since. Al-Hakim's reign was marked by great cultural achievements and visionary enterprises which came to be overshadowed by a spectacular mix of clumsy decisions, miscommunications, political upheavals, truculent deaths, adverse propaganda and a dose of bad luck. Whatever credit al-Hakim might have deserved was obliterated by the relentless vilification of his character in light of questionable decrees that he released throughout most of his reign.[1]

Al-Hakim: An Enigma

Following the death in 993 of al-ʿAziz's intended heir apparent, Muhammad, the imam appointed a younger son as his successor, following his father's precedent that landed al-ʿAziz himself with the imamate. During a religious festival al-ʿAziz had paraded this child under the royal ceremonial parasol, thus making the investiture public. Al-Hakim was the first imam-caliph born in Egypt and he was brought up in a court life dominated by rivalries for hegemony between *mashariqa* and *maghariba* factions. Once the future role of the boy had become known, representatives of those rival groups fought over the mentorship of the designated heir to mould his character and direct his patronage in favour of one group at the expense of the other. Growing up within the fold of the old North African elite families, al-Hakim found himself under the exclusive care of Barjawan, a slave eunuch of uncertain origins, described in some sources as one of the Saqaliba whom al-ʿAziz had made guardian of his harem and palaces.

Despite his young age al-Hakim's succession should have been a smooth affair on account of his father's public recognition. It was not. At the moment of al-ʿAziz's death al-Hakim was with his father, away from the caliphal palace in Cairo. Once back in the city the young imam was not met with the overall consensus of the court's civil and military administration. The *maghariba* saw the vacuum of power in the transition of authority from father to son as an opportunity to stage a *coup d'état* intended to restore their pre-eminence at the heart of the Fatimid regime. One faction supported the high-ranking officer al-Hasan b. ʿAmmar, a Kalbid Arab of North African ancestry, as the best candidate to take the reins of government. It was in the context of these days of confusion that Sitt al-Mulk, al-Hakim's half-sister, was propelled into a stardom that was uncommon for a woman in the middle period of Islamic history. Chroniclers contemporary to these events reported that, at night, Sitt al-Mulk marched to the royal palace escorted by the *qasriyya* cavalry, a military squadron assigned to her by her father. She sought to install on the Fatimid throne, instead of al-Hakim, a cousin, maybe the son of her deceased uncle ʿAbd Allah or a scion in al-Mahdi's line of descent. Some Sunni commentators on the events saw love as the motivation behind the princess's support for this man. Rather than romance, the manipulative force of court politics to secure patronage might have been the catalyst. Although, as events unfolded, the prince in whose name the coup was staged was not mentioned by name, narratives give details of the dignitaries who backed Sitt al-Mulk's plot: the *qadi* Muhammad b. al-Nu'man, Raydan the holder of the ceremonial parasol and Abu Sa'id Maymun the chief of police. She must have had also the tacit approval of al-Hasan b. 'Ammar who, though not mentioned at the scene, does not appear to have intervened to oppose her. These *maghariba* must have looked at Sitt al-Mulk and her cousin as congenial masters with whom to align themselves, since both belonged to the last surviving younger generation of North African-born royals living in Cairo. In the end, the coup failed when the Saqaliba Abu'l-Hasan Yanis, the dignitary left in charge of the palaces during al-'Aziz's absence, halted the princess and her entourage's irruption into the palace. Al-Hakim was rushed in while Barjawan placed Sitt al-Mulk under house arrest in the Western Palace – the residence that her father had assigned to her – guarded by 1,000 horsemen.[2] This deployment of armed force would not keep the princess out of action for long. In time Sitt al-Mulk would be at the centre of more exploits, real or imagined, that filled the chronicles reporting on al-Hakim's reign and that of his successor.

For the first four years, al-Hakim reigned as a nominal ruler. Being a young boy, Barjawan acted as his regent, thus in practice running the empire on the imam-caliph's behalf. In 997 the eunuch ousted al-Hasan b. 'Ammar, who had run the state as a *wasita*, a vizier-like position but less powerful, first by having him retired with a generous allowance and then killed. His record as state administrator had not been helped by the fact that under his watch Egypt had been hit by one of the recurrent famines, made more severe by the low flood of the Nile. This was made worse by mismanagement in the distribution of the grain reserves. With no immediate rivals left, Barjawan became the all-powerful chief executive of the regime. Assisted by a Christian secretary and with a strong powerbase among the eunuchs of the palace, no other eunuch in the service of the Fatimids would reach such a high status. On the whole Barjawan proved to be an efficient regent. He took care of handling the petitions to be signed off by al-Hakim; he led a strong anti-corruption campaign to protect inheritance rights; he created a network of personal ties in the administration of the state by appointing Saqaliba to high posts once occupied by Kutamas. One became head of the police in Cairo and Fustat and others headed the Fatimid navy in Tripoli (Ar. Tarabulus al-sharq), Gaza (Ar. Ghazza) and 'Asqalan (also Ascalon). He managed to reassert Fatimid control in Syria by crushing disorders and rebellions there, but he did not push to conquer Aleppo. Instead, he succeeded in negotiating a truce between the Fatimids and the Byzantines that would last ten years. In North Africa, however, he alienated the Zirids, thus further weakening their by now tenuous vassalage to the Fatimids.

Barjawan was an erudite patron of the arts and a shrewd investor. He lived in a residence so prestigious that the quarter of Cairo in which it was located was named after him. His house was a known gathering place where, to the accompaniment of male and female singers, parties lasted well into the night. Barjawan enjoyed singing along and it was said that on occasion he even cut his work short so that he could indulge in entertainment. The full extent of the wealth he had accumulated became apparent after his death. His estate included illustrated books and song treatises as well as tens of thousands of *dinar*s, with textiles making up the lion's share of his assets. At his death his possessions included thousands of coloured kerchiefs, trousers in linen voile and silk waistbands, as well as tailored garments of high quality.

As al-Hakim grew older, however, he became weary of the power Barjawan had accumulated and sought to reclaim full control of the empire. According to anecdotes, al-Hakim had long harboured deep resentment towards Barjawan, a disciplinarian mentor. Upon discovering that the eunuch had nicknamed him 'the little lizard', al-Hakim took offence and found the perfect excuse to exact his revenge and get rid of the powerful dignitary. The year 1000 saw Raydan, the parasol bearer, in action as the killer of Barjawan on the imam-caliph's order.[3]

'The little lizard has grown into a giant dragon'

Thus al-Hakim reportedly taunted Barjawan. The young imam-caliph had seen how his father's policy of delegating the management of the empire to civil administrators had yielded advantages but had also resulted in the creation of a parallel power structure within the regime. Before this trend could go further, al-Hakim put a stop to it by eliminating Barjawan. In restoring the primacy of the imam-caliph's rule he took full control of the regime at the expense of the Saqaliba network in the state administration, and he curbed the Kutamas' privileged position at court once and for all. High-ranking officers would be fired or liquidated in quick succession throughout his reign.

Al-Hakim's start of what amounted to direct rule coincided with a phase of profound societal transformation across the Islamic commonwealth that had broad repercussions. This was a time of renewed religious ferments, the rise of new forces on the military-political horizon and the recurrence of geoclimatic challenges. In Baghdad in 991 a new caliph, al-Qadir (d. 1031), had inaugurated his reign by injecting new vigour in championing Sunnism. Further east, in 997, with the title of sultan, Mahmud became the leader of what would become a Sunni Turkic dynasty, the Ghaznavids. Though de facto an independent ruler, he acknowledged the 'Abbasids' suzerainty and added his muscle to their Sunni cause. Under Mahmud's rule the Ghaznavids grew in power and territorial expansion, with their headquarters, Ghazni (today in central Afghanistan), becoming an important cultural and commercial centre. By the time of Mahmud's death in 1030, the Ghaznavid domains formed a military empire that extended from northern Iran to the Punjab. In the meantime, the West was in the grip of millenarian expectation with the approach of the year 1000 in the Christian calendar, while in the east, under Emperor Basil II (d. 1025), the Byzantines' revival of fortune was reaching its height. In Egypt, the year 999 saw a particularly meagre Nile flood, in a context of low levels on the whole, with severe consequences for an economy relying on agrarian production.[4] It is at least in part against this background that the policies which marked the first half of al-Hakim's reign should be appraised. The messianic mission that had brought the Fatimids to power meant that al-Hakim had to cultivate his image as a leader duty-bound to actualize the promises associated with the salvific role the dynasty had invested itself with. In Islamic apocalyptic literature it was prophesized that the fulfilment of the messianic era would be signalled by a time of high drama. Al-Hakim stuck to this script and, as far as embracing his messianic persona was concerned, his performance did not disappoint.

Al-Hakim signalled the start of his messianic mandate by seeking to reconfigure the gravitational centre towards which the Muslim community should orient itself. The complexities of controlling Syria and Palestine, and the consequent dwindling chances of conquering Baghdad, prompted a reassessment of the position the Fatimids held in relation to the 'Abbasids. If the Shi'i Isma'ili imamate had primacy over the Sunni caliphate, why waste energies on Baghdad when Cairo – the seat of the imam – should be the centre from which the Muslim community could be led? What if the 'Abbasid domains could be conceived as the periphery of the Fatimid empire rather than the other way around? Al-Hakim sought to transform Cairo into a religious and geopolitical heart which would pulsate its power throughout the Fatimid territories and sphere of influence. Al-Hakim channelled his vision into a recognizable rebranding of the dynasty through architectural projects, personal conduct, intellectual patronage and disruption of the established social order.

This geopolitical reconfiguration was, from an Isma'ili perspective, also validated in the spiritual sense. Since the first half of the tenth century Isma'ili thinkers had determined that the Ka'ba in Mecca, when seen from an esoteric perspective, should be understood to mean the abode of knowledge.[5] Since the repository of all knowledge was the imamate, the imam was in fact the Ka'ba and recognizing him was therefore the ultimate form of pilgrimage that the true believers should undertake. It might have been in light of this belief that al-Hakim sought to redirect the obligatory pilgrimage towards the abode of the imamate, Cairo. In 1000 al-Hakim ordered the construction of three shrines south of the capital to host the remains of the Prophet Muhammad and those of the first two caliphs. He instructed a covert mission to purloin the relics from Medina and bring them back to Egypt. If successful the stunt would have turned Cairo into a prime pilgrimage destination. Instead, the plan failed, although personal objects that had belonged to Imam Ja'far al-Sadiq were brought back: a copy of the Qur'an, weapons and Ja'far's prayer mat, which was later used by the imam-caliphs on public occasions.[6] The royal image was rebranded to better showcase al-Hakim's self-image as the leader at the heart of the Muslim universe. In 1001 al-Hakim received the envoy of the Byzantine emperor to seal a ten-year truce between the two empires. For the occasion two rows of soldiers stood in line to flank the emissary as he proceeded towards Bab al-Futuh. There, the Christian envoy dismounted and, kissing the ground at each step, he arrived at the imam-caliph's presence. For the occasion al-Hakim had ordered that the throne room be decorated with the most spectacular and exotic furnishings that could be found in the palace. His great-aunt, Princess Rashida, came to the rescue as she remembered that her father, al-Mu'izz, had brought to Egypt from Ifriqiya 21 bales of fine textiles in brocade and silk, made by servants in 942. These fabrics were hung on the walls of the room that glittered with gold. Displayed at the audience hall's entrance was a shield known as al-'Asjada, a symbol of Fatimid hegemony since the North African days. It was said that its gold and precious stones sparkled so much that the eyes could not stand the sight of it.[7]

In the space of a few years the capital's landscape was remodelled with imposing architectural works. A new gate was added to the city walls and beyond them al-Hakim resumed, at great expense, the construction of the mosque that had been started by al-'Aziz. In 1003 he ordered the addition to the complex of two distinctive carved stone minarets and a monumental entrance. The multiple minarets might have been intended to advertise a symbolic link between this Cairo mosque and those at significant sites displaying the similar feature, such as the mosque in Mecca, the one in Medina and those of Damascus and Jerusalem. Between 1010 and 1013 these minarets were fortified, with their bases encased in high bastions. One suggestion among many regarding the purpose of these added structures is that, based on the inscriptions featured at the site, the fortification amounted to an architectural proclamation of might and victory against rebels, with the bastions used as a canvas for Qur'anic verses celebrating triumph over unbelief.[8] While the precise reason behind the building of these bastions is still debated, there has been growing consensus in interpreting the minarets, the inscriptions they feature and their unusual encasements as architectural expressions of Isma'ili doctrinal symbolism and religious-political propaganda.[9] The mosque was completed in 1013, having been furnished at the cost of 5,000 *dinar*s. It is one of the most recognizable landmarks in Cairo, although the structure that we see today is the recent restoration of a rebuilding in 1304 in the aftermath of an earthquake.[10]

In 1003 al-Hakim had also ordered, again outside the walls, the building of a mosque by the Maqs port on the Nile. Besides serving the needs of the growing trading community that frequented the area, the imam-caliph was described as using a platform adjacent to the mosque to review the fleet. Around the same time, al-Hakim granted permission for monasteries to be restored in Fustat, yet he also ordered the demolition of the Jacobite Church of St Mark as well as Jewish and Christian cemeteries so that the Rashida Mosque could be built on the site. The destruction jarred with the Fatimid *aman* commitment towards *dhimmi*s which had been upheld up to that point. Past and present observers of al-Hakim's reign have regarded the order to demolish these Christian and Jewish places of worship as the first visible sign of the imam-caliph's perceived erratic behaviour. However, an examination of this action within the broader context of Muslim/non-Muslim relations of his time may shed a different light on the episode. Under al-Hakim's early reign, as under his father, Christians and Jews continued to enjoy protected status and many individuals reached positions of prestige in society and in government. Yet, Muslim resentment had already manifested itself during al-'Aziz's reign. Under al-Hakim this became even more evident, echoing anti-*dhimmi* sentiments across the Islamic territories that had been prompted by (among other factors) the 'Abbasid caliph al-Qadir's policies aimed at reviving Sunnism. Faced with the need to appease his Muslim subjects, but also to comply with his duty as the protector of tax-paying *dhimmi*s, al-Hakim resorted to religious separation by having the Christians and Jews living in the capital relocated to ghetto-like areas. As part of the programme, al-Hakim had many churches, houses and synagogues in these communities' former areas destroyed but, to ensure their access to facilities in their new locations, he had churches, synagogues and baths built so that interaction with Muslims would be limited. As for the destruction of the Church of St Mark on the site on which the Rashida Mosque was then built, it seems the church had been undergoing reconstruction without the obligatory state authorization required by Islamic law for *dhimmi*s. Al-Hakim therefore had the illegal construction pulled down and repurposed the site for Muslim use, but he also compensated the Christian community by allowing three new churches to be built elsewhere in Fustat.

11, 12 *Dinar* struck by Imam al-Hakim bi-Amr Allah, al-Qahira al-Mahrusa, dated 394 corresponding to the year 1003–4.

Al-Hakim assigned the administration of this mosque to a respected Sunni scholar, ʻAbd al-Ghani b. Saʻid. The Rashida Mosque was used as a congregational mosque until 1010–11 when it was pulled down, as it was apparently discovered that the prayer niche was not aligned correctly towards Mecca.[11] Orientation adjusted, the mosque was rebuilt three years later.

As part of al-Hakim's programme to showcase Cairo as the new centre of the Muslim universe, in 1003 *dinar*s (an effective means of advertising the dynasty and its authority) were struck featuring the legend al-Qahira al-Mahrusa, Cairo the Protected, as the place of issue (illus. 11 and 12). This is knowingly the first example of this legend; up to this point the Fatimids had continued the practice of inscribing coinage with Misr, a term referring to pre-Fatimid Fustat and/or Egypt in general. After al-Hakim, the dynasty's role as the city's founders continued to be proclaimed on coins through the use of al-Muʻizziyya or al-Muʻizziyya al-Qahira on the legend.[12]

The House of Knowledge

Al-Hakim gave impetus to turning the Fatimid capital into a cosmopolitan and inter-confessional centre of learning as well as an intellectual hub. Having overcome yet another year of Nile-related economic crisis, in 1005 al-Hakim founded the *dar al-ʻilm*, an academy open to scholars of different religious persuasions dedicated to the advancement of learning and science in a variety of subjects. Modelled on a similar institution already established by the Buyids around 991 near Baghdad, al-Hakim's *dar al-ʻilm* was housed in a section of the caliphal palace complex. No longer extant today, it stood opposite what later became the Fatimid al-Aqmar Mosque, the distinctive facade of which still adorns al-Muʻizz street in Old Cairo. The *dar al-ʻilm* was described as housing a library with more than 10,000 books that was open to visitors. Many volumes were transferred there from al-Hakim's private collection, including more than 1,000 Qur'anic manuscripts, many written in gold. The imam-caliph allocated a generous budget to this institution to cover the salaries of the scholars employed to run it, for its furnishing and utility bills, for the supply of stationery and funds for the restoration of books. While we have some information on individuals who worked in the academy, references to named users are rare, an indication that despite al-Hakim's ambition for it, the institution

13 Astronomer Ibn Yunus showing the *zij* to the Imam al-Hakim. From a copy of a Turkish translation of the compendium *Qanun al-dunya* by the 17th-century Egyptian scholar Ibn Zunbul.

may not have been frequented by the prestigious scholars of his time as much as he had hoped. Nevertheless, the foundation of the academy reflected the broader context of al-Hakim's extensive patronage of science. Only a few years before, Ibn Yunus (d. 1009), the greatest astronomer of the day, dedicated to the imam an astronomical handbook, *zij*, completed around 1000 and regarded to this day as one of the great scientific achievements in the field (illus. 5). Al-Hakim, however, wearied of his manners, so much so that Ibn Yunus collaborated with the Fatimids' scientific programme through the mediation of al-Hakim's court astronomer Abu'l-Hasan 'Ali al-Tabarani. According to one tale Ibn Yunus, while on the Muqattam hills to catch a sight of Venus, donned a woman's red garment, played a musical instrument and burned incense.[13] The arch-moralist al-Hakim, who had plans for the construction of an observatory there, on this occasion closed his eyes to the astronomer in drag. The observatory, however, was never built. Today a crater on the dark side of the moon is named after Ibn

Yunus. The polymath Ibn al-Haytham (d. 1040) conducted a feasibility study for al-Hakim on creating a hydraulic system that would regulate the waters of the Nile in Upper Egypt by diverting them in order to ensure regular land irrigation. However, on completion of the survey Ibn al-Haytham concluded that the project could not be carried out. According to an anecdote, in explaining his failure he commented – while admiring the pyramids of Giza – that surely had that feat of hydraulic engineering been possible, the Pharaohs would have realized it already. The excuse might not have convinced his master since, according to some, Ibn al-Haytham went into hiding to escape the rage of the disappointed al-Hakim. A prolific author, this scientist became famous in the Latin west as Alhazen for his work on optics.[14] On the whole the *dar al-'ilm* remained active – bar the occasional suspension of activities – until the end of al-Hakim's reign, when it closed, only resuming its full activities much later at another location in the capital.

The learning sessions that took place at the *dar al-'ilm* were kept separate from those intended for Isma'ilis. Under al-Hakim the practice of Isma'ili preaching was reorganized into dedicated lectures held within the palace for initiates, courtiers, royal women, high officials and palace staff. Ordinary Isma'ili believers congregated in al-Azhar Mosque which, since 1010, had received the imam-caliph's endowment for its upkeep, with funding for its staff but also for the purchase of silver lamps and their maintenance, as well as candles, incense, camphor and musk. The two carved wooden doors of Turkish pine that al-Hakim gifted to al-Azhar are still extant (illus. 14). In Cairo the teaching sessions had become an occasion for the collection of dues that were handed to the state treasury. Payments were made in silver and gold with a record kept of who paid what. For the *'id* at the end of Ramadan devotees contributed a special fee which the imam-caliph acknowledged with the distribution of sweets at the palace.

Besides the academy and Isma'ili-only venues, public lectures were also held in the other city mosques. Like most of the activities that defined al-Hakim's rule, the delivery of these learning sessions was discontinuous, as they were stopped and restarted via a succession of decrees. In addition to al-Azhar, al-Hakim was a great patron of other Islamic places of worship irrespective of denomination. In 1005 he sent to the 'Amr Mosque a gigantic new silver chandelier. Holding seven hundred glass lamps, it was so large that the mosque's doors had to be removed to get it inside. In 1013 al-Hakim at last inaugurated

14 Pair of wooden doors ordered by al-Hakim for al-Azhar mosque in 1010.

the mosque whose construction had been started by his father. In this mosque, as in others in the city, al-Hakim led prayers and held sermons during Ramadan in keeping with the tradition established by his ancestors. During his reign he ensured that hundreds of Qur'ans were gifted to the Ibn Tulun and 'Amr mosques. Some eight hundred mosques that had no revenues were allocated generous allowances.

Al-Hakim's Changes of Mood

So far so good. However, all these efforts and achievements were overshadowed by a series of decrees that al-Hakim issued over a decade from around 1004 that, taken at face value and out of context, are hard to make sense of. Ranging from the sublime to the ridiculous, his decrees sought to enforce state control over many aspects of public behaviour and security. In no particular order, these directives included a requirement for Christians and Jews to wear disproportionate identification signs, to ride only on mules harnessed with wooden saddles and not to have Muslim servants or be carried across the Nile by Muslim boatmen. He ordered the killing of all dogs. He prohibited the drinking of alcoholic honey wine and beer and forbade the consumption of a vegetable called *mulukhiyya* as well as other herbs and foods, and banned eating fish without scales. He restricted the frequentation of cemeteries, curtailed social gatherings in general and stopped lamentations in urban centres during the 'Ashura festival, but allowed this in the desert. He also prohibited chess playing, but most of all he became infamous for prohibiting women from going out of their homes. During his reign curses against the first three caliphs and the 'Abbasids were written in gold on public buildings, only for the practice to be revoked later. All these restrictions, while harsh, were temporary, imposed and lifted at regular intervals, limited in their geographical application and implemented with varying degrees of force. When contextualized however some of these whimsical ordinances appear to have been motivated by the need to respond to religious-political expectations, shifting popular attitudes towards morality and economic emergencies.[15]

For example, al-Hakim's public cursing of the first three caliphs was in keeping with *tabarra*, the ritual expression of disassociation from and disgust with those reputed to be adversaries of Islam. In Egypt, at the time of the first Islamic expansion into the region, the Sunni Umayyad caliphs imposed the cursing of 'Ali and his progeny on all Muslims in every mosque.[16] Later, in a role reversal, the practice became popular among Shi'is who saw it as a way to disavow themselves from those considered to be the enemies of the imams. Forbidding chess playing, like singing, was in keeping with the prevailing opinion against these pursuits within all Islamic legal schools. The decrees affecting Jews and Christians followed governance trends that other Islamic regimes had already applied with varied degrees of enforcement, following the caliph 'Umar's pact with these communities in the seventh century. While never condonable, al-Hakim's measures imposed on the Jews paled in comparison with the persecution they suffered at the hands of the Sunni Almohads of North Africa and al-Andalus. Likewise, al-Hakim was not the first or last Muslim ruler to impose restrictions on the mobility of women.

As for more inscrutable prohibitions, they might have been guided by hygiene or religious concerns, or practical considerations. For example, the booming export economy of the Fatimids needed a constant supply of jute to make sacks and cords for packaging goods destined for wholesale trade. Since the jute was made with the stalk of the mature *mulukhiyya* plant, forbidding the consumption of this vegetable might have been intended to safeguard the availability of primary material for industrial and commercial purposes. The cultivation of *mulukhiyya*, which required a lot of water, also occupied land that could have been better used for more valuable (and taxable) crops. Growing in dirty water, *mulukhiyya* was also a carrier of disease when consumed. Some saw religious-political propaganda behind this prohibition; according to anecdotes another forbidden vegetable – rocket (arugula) – was a favourite of 'A'isha, the wife of the Prophet, while the Umayyad caliph Mu'awiya loved *mulukhiyya*. Both these figures were reviled by all Shi'is for their opposition to 'Ali. Another prohibited herb was advised against by the Prophet Muhammad, according to al-Qadi al-Nu'man. As for forbidding the consumption of scale-less fish, this may have been dictated by such fish being considered unlawful, *haram*, in Islamic dietary law. Beyond being forbidden, fish without scales served a practical purpose. In Egypt land irrigation relied on the good maintenance of canals linked to the Nile. Shoals of scaleless fish that, being bottom dwellers, swam the rivers and canal beds were a good natural agent to prevent silt build-up with their movement to and fro. Besides a widespread canine aversion rooted in the Muslim mindset, dogs were perceived as carriers of disease. Culling them was a measure mistakenly adopted across the medieval world in trying to control the spread of plagues. Egypt was hit on a regular basis by epidemics, often in conjunction with bouts of famine, and al-Hakim's time was no exception. He, like his contemporaries, did not know that a major vector of a type of plague was a flea carried by the Nile rat. In the seventeenth century one of history's great scientists, Isaac Newton (d. 1727), believed that dried toad vomit was a sure remedy against the disease; the causes of the plague were only better understood in the nineteenth century.

Regarding banning the 'Ashura celebrations to the desert, there is some indication that in the city some people took advantage of the event to extort money from the participants. The prohibition on wine and beer was in keeping with Islamic dietary laws. Al-Hakim however allowed the use of wine on at least one occasion when his Christian physician Ibn Anastas prescribed it to him as a treatment. During al-Hakim's reign, a few episodes point to alcohol-induced sedition plots and scandals having matured among Fatimid royal family members and high-ranking men. A grandson of the imam-caliph al-Mansur who had been spied upon on al-Hakim's instruction was heard claiming the imamate for himself during a drunken party with his friends. On another occasion in 1007 a group among the highest dignitaries of the court gathered for a dinner party. At some point al-Hakim's Christian physician Ibn Anastas, a fine singer and lover of wine beyond its therapeutic qualities, joined in and things descended into chaos with most men ending up drunk. The physician, having left the house in a drunken stupor, fell into a lake and drowned. Al-Hakim not only lost his doctor but was embarrassed by the conduct of his senior aides. It has also been suggested that al-Hakim's prohibition against consuming honey wine, a drink sold by Jews, might have been linked to chiliastic expectations around the year 400 of the Islamic calendar. Beyond these motivations, the anecdotes tell us that the imam-caliph might have had prosaic, close-to-home reasons to want to enforce a ban on alcohol. There is no way to know for sure if any of these reasons or others informed al-Hakim's thinking but, as is often the case, the maxim that there are two sides to a story gives him the benefit of the doubt.

Al-Hakim's Reception

Though alien to us, the motives behind these measures must have been at least partly understood and perhaps even approved by a large proportion of al-Hakim's subjects. Some reacted to his rule with the occasional uprising, for example in 1012, when people revolted armed with knives and swords. There are anecdotes of women finding crafty ways to circumvent al-Hakim's restrictions in order to go out to meet their lovers, or others pinning insults against al-Hakim on puppets displayed in the street. Some women's attempts at rebelling against mobility restrictions were crushed. Yet al-Hakim remained on the whole a popular ruler among the people. At some point during his reign al-Hakim had abandoned the pomp of his predecessors in favour of a humble personal style. In the evening, he would sneak out of his palace to mix with people from all walks of life. He could often be seen touring the market alleys riding a donkey, dressed in simple clothes. He would try to overhear comments about his reign and rather than expecting people to prostrate themselves before him, he welcomed the handing in of petitions. In line with his messianic self-image as the bringer of justice al-Hakim was determined to actualize the Qur'anic command to uphold the right and forbid the wrong. From his perspective, it fell on the imam to fulfil this obligation and establish an upright society. In the name of fair judgement for all al-Hakim established practices such as having two witnesses in police headquarters to verify crimes. In times of economic crisis people called upon al-Hakim to save them. When in 1008 and 1009 the Nile failed to rise al-Hakim imposed strict control on the distribution of grain to prevent hoarding and consequent price speculation. As famine and disease increased among the masses the imam-caliph forced vendors to sell their stock to stop them hiking prices by withholding supply in response to high demand. Disaster was averted.[17] The use of wood to fire bakers' ovens was also monitored and dues on grain and rice were suspended. He abolished taxes not consistent with Islamic law. In times of scarcity, al-Hakim's ban on alcohol production might have been intended to prevent wheat, rice and barley from being used to make it.

Despite suffering sustained periods of repression during al-Hakim's reign, the Christians and Jews of Egypt fluctuated in their assessment of al-Hakim, from utter vilification of his character to praise. For example, in a document in Hebrew of 1012 al-Hakim is celebrated as a prince of justice. Elsewhere a Christian writer echoed the same sentiment. In a letter by a Jewish writer al-Hakim's name is accompanied by a well-wishing formula.[18] How can we explain polarized views? It is difficult to disentangle what people did to Christians and Jews in al-Hakim's name from what the imam-caliph decreed. It is similarly difficult to judge how far what he ordered matched what was put into practice, and how far actions imputed to al-Hakim were his doing, or the result of propaganda against him. Adding complexity to the evaluation of this aspect of al-Hakim's reign is how to reconcile his hiring (and firing) of Christians and Jews in high positions with the negative attitudes to *dhimmi*s ascribed to him in general. It is tempting to assume that the latter would have to exclude the former, but the pragmatism of finding skills wherever available meant that this was not the case. In turn Copts and Melkites with high positions in the service of al-Hakim benefited from their privileged status to the point of forming a well-to-do section of society that appears to have been unaffected by al-Hakim's decrees.

On the home front, after Sitt al-Mulk's failed coup, the relationship between al-Hakim and his half-sister remained patchy. Sitt al-Mulk sent him presents such as horses with gold and crystal stirrups, mules, eunuchs, fine clothes, a bejewelled crown, tons of spices and miniature trees in gold and silver with replica fruits made of precious stones. In return al-Hakim trusted her advice on governmental matters and uncovering fraudulent courtiers. In 1000 al-Hakim bestowed on her land grants that generated an income of 100,000 *dinar*s a year and more. At other times, however, he would purge high officers on account of being too close to her; he would accuse her of entertaining men in her palace and send nurses to check on her virginity; he confiscated her wealth as well as that of other female family members such as his mother and his daughter, Sitt Misr. The latter, whose personal fortune allowed her to afford as many as 8,000 slaves in her service, became known as a minor architectural patron. At her death her estate included 30,000 Chinese vases of musk, unique gems and precious stones as well as extensive land grants. Al-Hakim's confiscation took place in 1008, a year of major economic distress. In times of need it was not uncommon for Fatimid rulers to seek financial help from female members of the family. When this support was not forthcoming it was standard practice among Muslim rulers to help themselves to properties and money belonging to family members, high officers and other categories of people with wealth. Al-Hakim was no different and like others he took away but often also returned what he had subtracted. Sudden outbursts of political and economic insecurity, the capricious rules of patronage and the forging of relationships for mutual advantage that governed court life meant that no one could afford to let sentiments get in the way of pragmatism in decision making. Family relations were no exception.

In 1006 a spectacular phenomenon occurred. The year stands out in astronomical literature as one in which a supernova was observed. Not just a big, shiny star but what, to date, constitutes the brightest stellar event on record ever observed. Ibn Sina reported on this wonder of nature.[19] The phenomenon was experienced in Egypt and noted by a young man called 'Ali b. Ridwan (d. 1061). He grew up to become one of the greatest scientists of his time. Al-Hakim, like the imam-caliphs before him, was at best ambivalent to astrology when not opposed to it, having issued an edict against it in 1013. However, he cultivated astronomy, and the event must have made as strong an impression on him as on his contemporaries. In Islamic eschatology unusual cosmic events such as those associated with stars and comets were seen as signs of impending apocalypse. Since, according to traditions ascribed to the Prophet Muhammad, every one hundred years God would send a reviver of the faith (*mujaddid*) to his community, the supernova appearing in the year 396–7 of the Islamic calendar (1005–6 CE) as the fourth centenary was approaching must have been interpreted as a portent with messianic significance.

A year or so before this natural event, a Sunni rebel, Abu Rakwa, had staged the fiercest revolt the Fatimids had faced since the one carried out by Abu Yazid in North Africa during al-Qa'im's and al-Mansur's reigns. Abu Rakwa, who claimed ancestry from the Umayyads of al-Andalus, presented himself as a messianic figure by staging a Sunni rebellion against the Fatimids. He gathered consensus among various Berbers and, having laid siege to Barqa, he advanced to Alexandria intending to launch a final assault on Cairo. In the broader climate of a Sunni revival sponsored by the 'Abbasid caliph al-Qadir, Abu Rakwa's initial success followed in the footsteps of others who had advanced their pretences, for example one of the *sharif*s of Mecca who had attempted in 996 to have himself recognized as caliph.[20] However, Abu Rakwa's fortunes changed when at the eleventh hour the Fatimid army defeated him just outside the capital at Giza. In retreat Abu Rakwa fled to Upper Egypt where he was apprehended and brought back Cairo.

To mark the crushing of the rebellion, al-Hakim staged a triumphant and ignominious parade of Abu Rakwa. The rebel was made to sit on a camel and whipped by a monkey, a symbol charged with eschatological meaning in Islam, while the crowds lynched him. By the time Abu Rakwa arrived at the appointed place for his execution, the Tibr Mosque north of Cairo, he was already dead. His body was first impaled, then burned, and his detached head was put on display as a warning for all to see. In the context of al-Hakim's messianic self-narrative, the rebel matched the ultimate eschatological evil figure, *al-dajjal*. Abu Rakwa had come close to overthrowing al-Hakim and the people in the capital could have joined his revolt to topple the imam-caliph if they had wanted to . . . but they didn't. Yet al-Hakim saw the first major Sunni challenge to the Fatimid regime in a long while as a sign that it was time to change his attitude towards his Sunni subjects. In the aftermath of the Abu Rakwa episode al-Hakim not only had the anti-Sunni curses removed but punished those who continued with the invectives. He also sought a reconciliation with the Sunnis by allowing again practices he had once forbidden. In the *dar al-ʿilm* and other institutions Sunni scholars and jurists rose to prominence alongside Shiʿi Ismaʿili ones. In 1008 al-Hakim appointed Malik al-Fariqi, a man with knowledge of Fustat, to be head of the judiciary and the *daʿwa*, having assigned to him four judges representing the other legal schools. Members of the Fariqi family had been serving the Fatimid dynasty for some time and their rise broke the Nuʿmans' monopoly over the judiciary and the *daʿwa*. However, Malik was executed in 1014 by order of al-Hakim on suspicion, among other things, of colluding with Sitt al-Mulk against him. Nevertheless, members of subsequent generations of his family would continue to occupy high positions in the service of the Fatimid regime. During this period the Ismaʿili learning sessions were suspended. Besides a pragmatic desire not to antagonize a sector of society that could have turned against him, a universal community united in its devotion to God was part of what the *mahdi*'s era promised to bring about, and – as it seems – this is what al-Hakim was intent on delivering.

The Destruction of the Church of the Holy Sepulchre in Jerusalem

Of all the deeds that have contributed to al-Hakim's negative characterization, the one that perhaps more than most sealed his demonization in the eyes of some chroniclers of his time was his order to destroy the Church of the Holy Sepulchre in Jerusalem. The church had been erected in the fourth century by the Roman emperor Constantine (d. 337) over a site identified in the Christian tradition as the place of Jesus's crucifixion and subsequent burial. Prior to al-Hakim, the shrine had already been destroyed and rebuilt several times. As with most of al-Hakim's actions, here too there is no clear indication of the motives behind his order. Explanations range from wanting to please his Sunni subjects following Abu Rakwa's rebellion by staging an anti-Christian event, to dispelling an accusation that he himself was a Christian. This allegation circulated on the basis of the unsubstantiated belief that his mother was a Christian. The association might have arisen from confusion with al-'Aziz's first wife (not al-Hakim's mother) who was known to have belonged to the Melkite church. There is some evidence that when al-Hakim gave his orders the Church of the Holy Sepulchre had already been damaged by fire in 938 and pillaged in 966. The church however was razed to the ground and burnt, its contents looted or rescued in advance by the patriarch in charge of it at the time. Some pointed the finger at al-Hakim's appointed governor of Ramla as the actual culprit; a man who, from excess zeal but also to settle personal scores in the region, took things into his own hands. The destruction might have also been intended to counter rumours about a Christian messiah from the west appearing in Jerusalem in 1010. This belief may have gained further currency when Easter was celebrated at the Church of the Holy Sepulchre in defiance of al-Hakim's edict that had forbidden the festival in 1007 and 1009. According to a tale, al-Hakim stopped the Easter commemoration upon being informed about some Christians who took the festival as an opportunity to dupe the crowds. To him, these were tricksters who anointed a rod with oil, lowered it from the roof of the church down to the chapel of Jesus's sepulchre and, by setting fire to the rod, would make believe that a light had descended from heaven down to the tomb. This event had become very popular and Muslims were reported to attend it.[21]

When considered in the context of al-Hakim's self-image as a messianic leader the destruction of the Holy Sepulchre could be evaluated in yet another light. Most sources agree that the event took place on 28 September 1009, corresponding to 5 Safar 400, the second month of the Islamic calendar. The choice of timing for the deed in Jerusalem points to al-Hakim's intention to inaugurate the new Islamic centennial with an extraordinary act that would tally with his messianic persona. It is perhaps no coincidence that it was in this same year that, in Salamiyya, the shrine of the first of the hidden Isma'ili imams, 'Abd Allah the Elder, was re-erected. Today, *Maqam al-imam* is the only remaining major Fatimid purpose-built structure in Syria.

In Islamic eschatological literature the climax marking the advent of the *mahdi* is described as the moment when, after the killing of *al-dajjal*, the cross would be broken, all Christians and Jews and their places of worship would be subdued and a period of peace would prevail before the advent of the Day of Judgement. Having eliminated the Antichrist-like Abu Rakwa in the same year as an extraordinary astronomical event, what action would better enact the breaking of the cross and the subjugation of the Christians than the destruction of the site of the crucifixion? It seems that al-Hakim's order was to tear down only the shrine on the Golgotha section within the church, that is, the area commemorating the place where Jesus's cross stood. As it turned out the devastation was far more extensive. Out of Muslim respect for Jesus, regarded in Islam as one of the prophets sent by God, a mosque was built on the site. This destruction was not an isolated case, as in the same year in Egypt more churches were not so much destroyed as dismantled to be turned into mosques.

The act was intended to convey a strong symbolic message by taking aim at a physical space, but it was not matched by a spike in state-sponsored persecution of Christians. Although at times eyes were closed to Muslim mobs attacking Christians, during this period Christians continued to serve the Fatimid court. In fact, according to one story, it was a high-ranking Christian officer in the state chancery who countersigned the decree to destroy the Church of the Holy Sepulchre. Legend has it that he later regretted his role in the destruction of the church so much that he injured his own hand by inflicting damage on it every day for the rest of his life.[22] Towards the end of al-Hakim's reign those who had been forced to become Muslims were allowed to revert to their original faith and resettle in Byzantine lands, and goods confiscated from Christians and Jews in times of financial emergency were returned. If the acts of destruction were intended to please Muslims, they had the desired effect, as crowds expressed gratitude to the imam-caliph for this feat. However, whatever message the destruction of the Holy Sepulchre was meant to send to the Christians, it generated a mixed political reaction. The response of the Byzantines, the Fatimids' arch-rivals in Syria and Palestine, was astonishing: they did not retaliate. At least, they did not react as might have been expected to avenge the sacrilege. Instead of an all-out call to arms, the Byzantines' reaction to the Fatimids' blasphemous act was mild; the strongest action amounted to closing temporarily Constantinople's mosque where the Friday sermon had been in the Fatimids' name since al-'Aziz's days and had continued to be so with naming al-Hakim during his rule. That trade relations suffered somewhat and occasional naval confrontations occurred was not due to exceptional circumstances. These disruptions were commonplace and fitted within the pattern of relations between the two powers. The bottom line is that Byzantium adopted a passive stance when it came to confronting the Fatimids on the issue, preferring a pragmatic peace to warring over the destroyed shrine. Following the event, the ten-year truce between the Fatimids and Byzantines not only held but was renewed for another decade. In Egypt, on the whole, whether Copts, Melkites, Nestorians or Jacobites, the Christians expressed their consternation but in practice remained unmoved by al-Hakim's impious act.

By contrast it was in Catholic Europe, fervent with millenarian beliefs since the coming of the year 1000, that uproar was voiced in apocalyptic tones. In Limoges in France a young monk saw the destruction of the Church of the Holy Sepulchre as part of the coming Armageddon. He lamented: 'In these times there appeared signs in the stars, harmful droughts, excessive rains, great plagues, terrible famines and numerous eclipses of the sun and the moon, and the river Vienne dried up for two miles around Limoges for three nights.'[23] Beyond exaggerations, the narrative captured the prevailing mood in Europe upon receiving news of what had happened in Jerusalem. From 1009 onwards, people preoccupied themselves with accounts of rains of blood, the sun turning red and news of epidemics and death. The year 1010 was seen as a time of apocalyptic convulsion of major proportions, with al-Hakim matching the Christians' idea of the Antichrist. Trade relations between the Fatimids and Europe declined, anti-Muslim sentiments became heightened and conflated with antisemitism, resulting in widespread persecution of Jews across Europe. According to the Crusader chronicler William of Tyre (d. 1186) it was al-Hakim's destruction of the Holy Sepulchre that instilled in Europe the idea of launching a holy war to liberate the Holy Land from Muslim and Jewish infidels. Whether inspired by al-Hakim or not, in 1096 this idea was realized with the start of what became a series of Christian-led military campaigns which became known as the Crusades.

As well as political and commercial pragmatism, or fear of retaliation for those Christians who lived in Egypt, Syria and Palestine, the mixed reaction of the Christian communities to al-Hakim's act can also be explained by the fact that the Christian Church was divided. The Church of Rome and that of Constantinople fought for supremacy in theological and territorial terms. The Council of Chalcedon (October–November 451) had brought about a split, with the Melkites accepting its authority on the one hand and the Copts, Armenians and Jacobites on the other rejecting it by sticking to their belief in the one nature of Christ. Internal doctrinal rivalries meant that whatever action al-Hakim might have taken against one church was met with indifference at best by those who belonged to the rival denomination.

There are lesser-known instances of synagogues having been demolished. This might indicate that Jews complied more with Islamic law regarding *dhimmi*s on obtaining state authorization for any building or restoration works. In any event, in Egypt, towards the end of his reign al-Hakim granted permission for the reconstruction of many of the churches and synagogues whose destruction he had once ordered. Among the synagogues rebuilt in this period was the Ben Ezra Synagogue in Fustat. Over time this edifice became a site where a massive amount of written material, from letters to contracts, came to be deposited. Once discovered, this hoard of paper became famous among scholars as the Cairo Geniza documents.

The Baghdad Manifesto and the Fatimids' Reaction

Al-Hakim's charisma captured the imagination of people in other regions beyond his domains. During his reign the activities of the *da'wa* in Iraq and Iran saw great expansion under the leadership of the *da'i* and scholar Hamid al-Din al-Kirmani (d. *c.* 1021). Various social levels were targeted, with some local lords and rulers switching their support to the Fatimids against the 'Abbasids. In 1008 a Shi'i uprising in al-Hakim's favour took place in Baghdad. In 1010 the 'Uqaylid ruler of Mesopotamia pledged allegiance to al-Hakim, and for a brief time the Friday prayer was pronounced in his name in the Iraqi cities of Mosul, Kufa and al-Mada'in. This time the 'Abbasids reacted with a novel tactic that went beyond military interventions and localized persecutions. In Baghdad in 1011 the 'Abbasid caliph al-Qadir issued a manifesto, countersigned by many among the most

15 Great Mosque of al-Mahdiyya, Tunisia, 10th century.

16 Al-Azhar Mosque, Cairo, 10th century.

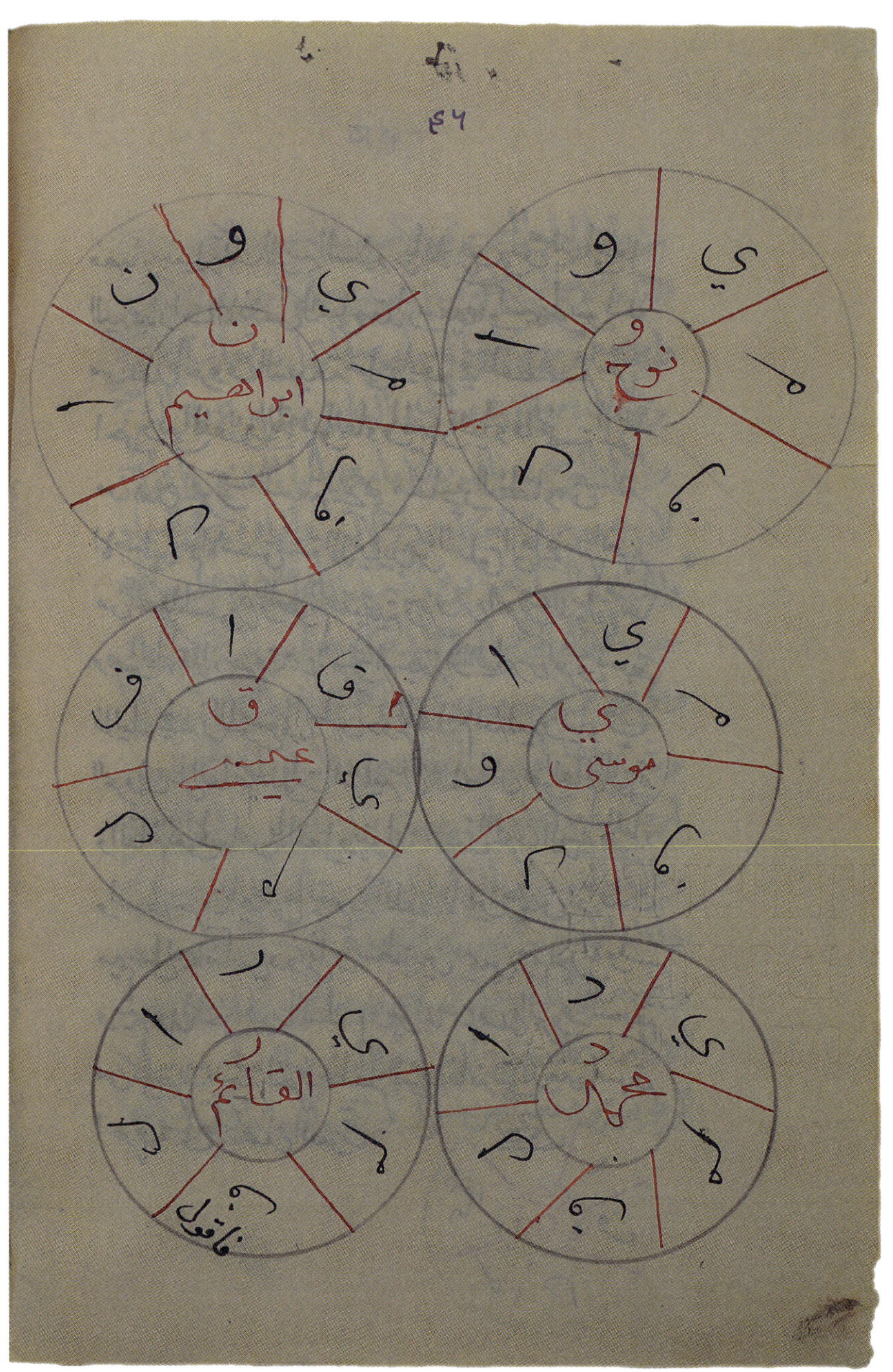

17 Diagrams on a page from a 14th-century Isma‘ili manuscript of *Kitab al-iftikhar* by Abu Ya‘qub al-Sijistani, 10th century.

18 King Simeon I's embassy to Imam al-Mahdi, illumination from a 12th-century Sicilian manuscript of John Skylitzes' Middle Byzantine chronicle, 11th century.

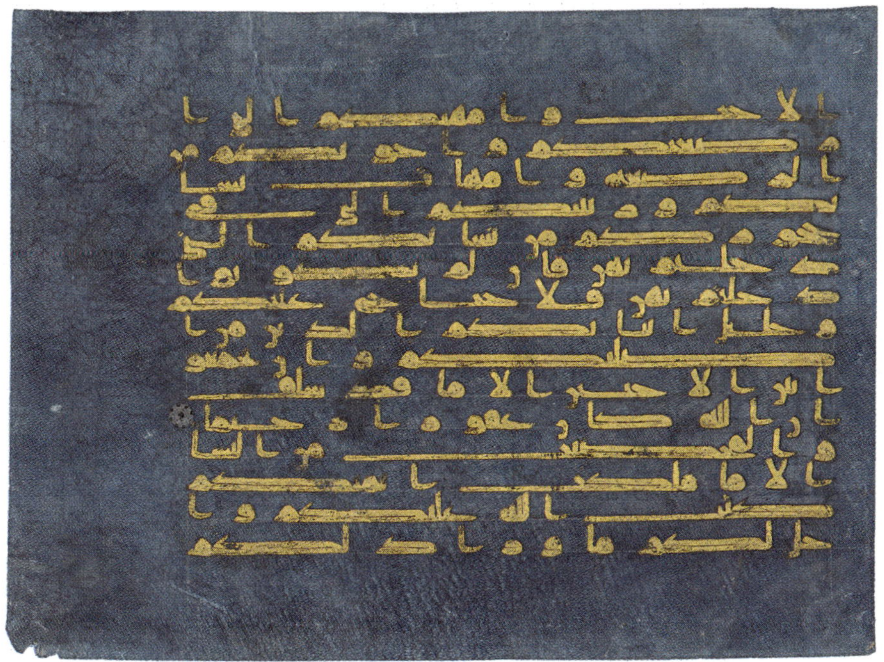

19 Page from the 10th-century Blue Qur'an, gold leaf, silver and ink on parchment coloured with indigo.

20 Carved ivory oliphant, Fatimid, 11th century.

21 Fatimid lustreware bowl with antelope, 11th century, earthenware.

22 European 14th-century reliquary made with 11th-century Fatimid half-moon rock crystal jewel inscribed with the imam al-Zahir's name.

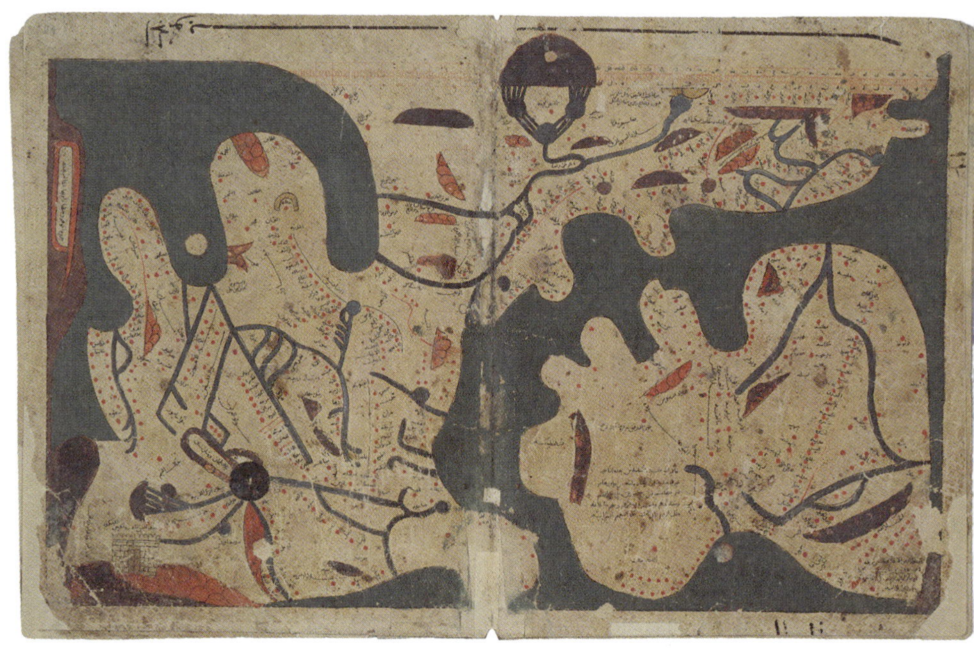

23 Map of the world from a *c.* 1190–1210 manuscript of the *Book of Curiosities*, a work originally written in the Fatimid period, *c.* 1020–50.

24 Map of Sicily from a *c.* 1190–1210 manuscript of the *Book of Curiosities*, a work originally written in the Fatimid period, 1020–50.

25 Drawing of a woman, Fustat (Old Cairo), 11th century, ink and watercolour on paper.

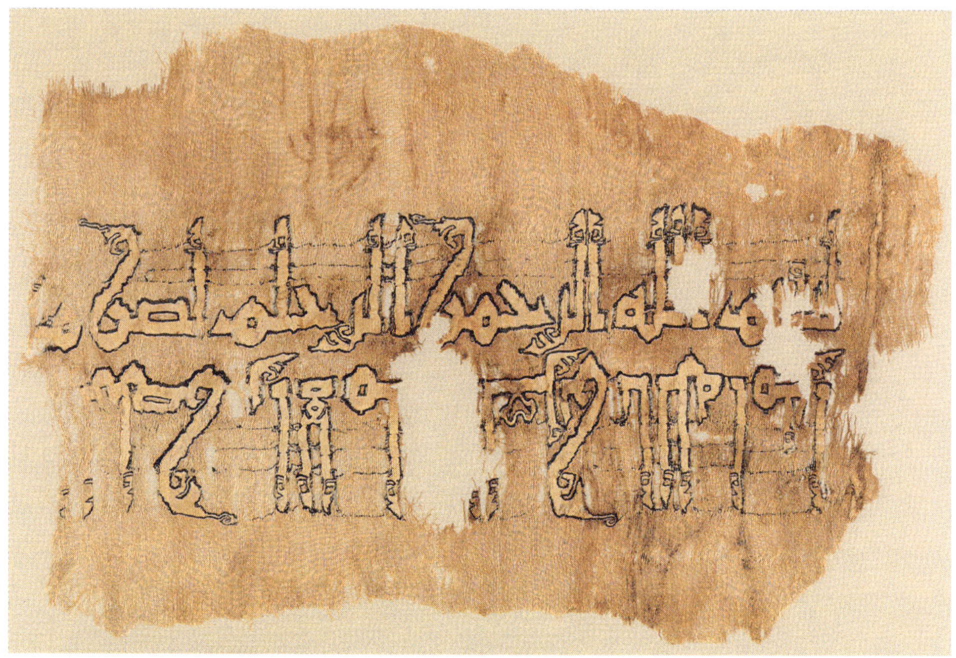

26 Fatimid *tiraz*, late 10th century. The tapestry-woven Arabic inscription in Kufic script reads, 'In the name of God, the Merciful, the Beneficent, Victory [is from God . . .] al-Mansur, the Imam al-'Aziz bi'llah, Commander [of the Faithful]'.

27 Detail of the *muqarnas* ceiling of Cappella Palatina, Palazzo dei Normanni, Palermo, 12th century.

prominent Sunni and Twelver Shi'i scholars as well as authoritative *ashraf* of the time, denouncing as false the Fatimid genealogical 'Alid claims. The manifesto was read out in mosques across the 'Abbasid domains, and al-Qadir also commissioned several theologians to write anti-Fatimid treatises. Centuries later the Sunni historian and polymath Ibn Khaldun (d. 1406), himself a supporter of the Fatimid claim of descent from Muhammad via 'Ali's line, critiqued this denunciation in retrospect as playing into the hands of the Fatimids. He reasoned that if the 'Abbasids believed the Fatimid claim to be false, why would they mobilize to such an extent to denounce it?[24]

However, on the Isma'ili part this theological challenge required a strong intellectual rebuff. At the Cairo *da'wa* headquarters the *da'i* al-Nishaburi, who had arrived in the city during the reign of al-'Aziz, set out to write a number of treatises aimed at counteracting the allegations.

The 'Abbasid attempt to undermine the credibility of the caliphs in Cairo did not dent the *da'wa*'s ambition to expand Fatimid influence in the east; if anything it emboldened it. Isma'ili envoys sent by al-Hakim even attempted to reach out to Mahmud of Ghazna, in spite of the fact that not long before he had massacred the Isma'ilis in Multan. Of what was left of the Qarmatians, some now embraced the Fatimid cause while the rest disintegrated, although some vestiges of Qarmatian rule in Bahrain were evident until the middle of the eleventh century. The *da'is* also resumed operations in Yemen, once at the forefront of the early *da'wa* activities but marginalized since al-Mahdi's imamate had been challenged there. In contrast the links between the Fatimids and their vassals in North Africa were showing signs of becoming loose. Nonetheless Fatimid diplomatic missions continued to be sent to Ifriqiya and Sicily with gifts intended to reaffirm the Zirids as vassals, as well as to confer titles on the Kalbids in Palermo. Barqa was also handed to the Zirids in order to strengthen relations between Ifriqyia and Egypt.

The Climax of al-Hakim's Messianic Mission

The completion of the year 400 in the Islamic calendar, corresponding to the year 1009–10, appears to have marked a turning point in al-Hakim's self-image as the ultimate messianic leader. The year came and went, but the mundane preoccupations of people's lives had not changed. A new register was therefore needed to keep the eschatological momentum alive. A temporary change in ritual occurred with the suspension of the Fatimids' pilgrimage caravans to Mecca in 1012 and 1013 due to adverse economic conditions. In 1012 al-Hakim began to show an inclination for funerary architecture, with building projects outside the royal city's al-Qarafa cemetery, an area declared an earthly paradise in Islamic eschatological lore. Works included a six-domed structure constructed over the graves of members of a prominent North African family that al-Hakim had had decapitated two years before. In the same cemetery, by the slopes of al-Muqattam hills, he also had a tower-shaped mosque built called Lu'lu'a in which he went to sit at night. Having become derelict, the mosque was rebuilt in the 1990s under the auspices of the Da'udi Bohras restoration project in Cairo.[25] From 1012 onwards, al-Hakim's programme for the implementation of an upright, just society gained futher impetus. Having shed the trappings of luxury that had marked his predecessors' image, al-Hakim extended his demure style to public protocol. In that year, at the parade celebrating the end of Ramadan, riding a horse, he wore a plain white garment and turban, under a white parasol surrounded by plain flags. No carpets lined the pulpit.

It was around these years, 1013 in particular, that women felt the full force of his prohibitions affecting their lives: whether singers, prostitutes or just women going about their business, most found themselves limited in pursuing their outdoor activities, until they were forbidden to go out of their homes altogether. Shopping was carried out through the mediation of door-to-door salesmen, and only when it was absolutely necessary were women allowed out upon obtaining a permit. Like the conduct of all his subjects, their behaviour was policed, with al-Hakim's spies (including women) instructed to report on misbehaviour. Those who tried to defy the rules did it at personal cost. Reports went as far as to say that large numbers of al-Hakim's concubines were thrown out of the palace, with some sealed in crates and drowned in the Nile. Aberrant and abhorrent as it was, al-Hakim's attitude to women reflected preconceptions about them that were in keeping with the socio-cultural context of his time. In the medieval mindset – Muslims included – a typical causational link was made between physical evil and moral evil, with women being regarded, because of their real or perceived misconduct, as the source of immorality that would result in the occurrence of natural disasters. In Islam, this view went further, with women given a damning eschatological role: according to traditions ascribed to the Prophet Muhammad the population of hell consisted of women. As a ruler bent on upholding the right and forbidding the wrong, the prohibition on women going out reads as the literal application of the Qur'anic injunction in 33:33, according to which women should stay in their homes. As stories of al-Hakim's gruesome repression of women entered into wide circulation, so al-Hakim's character assassination grew.

An act signalling a change of political and ideological direction in the imam-caliph's understanding of the function of the dynasty he represented was his appointment in 1013–14 of his cousin, ʻAbd al-Rahim b. Ilyas, as his heir apparent. ʻAbd al-Rahim became governor of Damascus in 1018–19. Although, based on the rules of *nass*, it was at the incumbent imam-caliph's discretion to appoint whomsoever he saw fit to succeed him, al-Hakim's choice to favour a cousin over his own son, ʻAli, was unusual. ʻAbd al-Rahim was nominated to be the next *amir al-muslimin* while, some time later, another relative was designated as the next *amir al-mu'minin*, a sign that al-Hakim had taken the unprecedented step of splitting the leadership into two spheres of concern: one intended for the Muslims' affairs and the other for the Ismaʻilis only. While the visibility of this latter figure faded, ʻAbd al-Rahim's acquired status was made public. After his designation al-Hakim delegated to him participation in most public functions, while he himself became more reclusive. Coins were minted featuring the name of this cousin along with that of al-Hakim, and banners as well as inscribed textiles carried his name. He became the public face of the regime, having been tasked with the addressing of petitions.[26] Like most of al-Hakim's decisions, conjecture and speculation abound as to why he overlooked his own son. A straightforward answer could be that seeing himself as the messianic new Muhammad whose advent had been promised by the Prophet, al-Hakim emulated him by appointing his cousin as his successor in the same way Muhammad did with ʻAli, according to Shiʻi belief. Another reason might have been that his son was a baby at the time and thus unsuited to the role. Not long before his cousin's nomination al-Hakim had lost another infant son, and perhaps feared the same fate for ʻAli. Having suffered as heir apparent because of Barjawan, he may have wanted to spare his own son the same misery at the hands of someone else. Maybe a political expedient was behind ʻAbd al-Rahim's nomination, intended to give him more authority in Syria in view of him becoming governor of Damascus. The region had been marred by anti-Fatimid revolts that had started at the end of al-'Aziz's reign and carried on under al-Hakim as a result of Jarrahid-led tribal alliance. In fact, in Syria al-Hakim had succeeded where his father had failed; for a brief period, he brought Aleppo under Fatimid control. Or were there doctrinal motivations behind his choice of 'Abd al-Rahim? If al-Hakim saw himself as the leader who brought to completion the Fatimids' messianic mandate, he might have regarded succession by direct genealogical descent as somewhat redundant after him. 'Abd al-Rahim was a cousin belonging to the dissenting branch of the family that had been a thorn in the Fatimid imams' side since al-Qa'im's days. Maybe al-Hakim, as the ultimate just ruler he wanted to be, sought to rectify what he might have recognized as an injustice perpetrated against his relatives?

Rather than settling the question of succession, the nomination of 'Abd al-Rahim prompted an immediate range of court countermeasures. For example, Sitt al-Mulk took under her protection al-Hakim's son 'Ali and his mother, sheltering them in her palace. 'Ali's mother and al-Hakim's consort was Amina (or Ruqayya), maybe a daughter of the late prince 'Abd Allah, son of al-Mu'izz.

Reflecting the saying 'be careful what you wish for', in building up his messianic aura al-Hakim got more than he had bargained for. Isma'ili activists from Iran arrived in Cairo and mounted an enthusiastic propaganda campaign in al-Hakim's favour. Their activities reached a climax in 1017 when its adherents declared al-Hakim's divinity. The faction that called itself Unitarian, *muwahhidun*, became better known as Druzes after Muhammad al-Darzi (d. 1018), one of the founders of the movement. They believed that al-Hakim had brought about the completion of the *mahdi*'s era, the advent of which was understood to render the observation of Islamic ritual law null and void. In their salutations the name of al-Hakim would precede that of Allah in benedictory formulae. Similar antinomian precedents had occurred in the Fatimid context when, in North Africa, al-Mahdi had crushed an extremist group that had been promoting similar beliefs. Al-Hakim, though he denied the idea of his apotheosis, did not repress it either. In Cairo the most outstanding intellectual mind of the time, the *da'i* Hamid al-Din al-Kirmani, who had arrived from Iraq, refuted the Druze doctrines and defended al-Hakim's imamate as well as the balance to be maintained between the *batin* and the *zahir*.[27] Beyond opposing the Druzes and extreme esotericism, in literary terms al-Kirmani was the author behind the most outstanding corpus of Isma'ili philosophical literature to prove the necessity of the imamate. In turn the Druzes produced a literary canon of their own consisting of a one-hundred-letter correspondence, claimed to have been exchanged from 1017 to 1020 between al-Hakim and Hamza b. 'Ali (d. 1021). This figure became the movement's leader after dissociating himself from his former companion al-Darzi.

The end of al-Hakim's reign was marked by a general state of socio-political confusion, economic uncertainty and the presence of religious agitators. To add to the chaos the army was further divided by internal rivalries. To break the *maghariba* versus *mashariqa* polarization al-Hakim had expanded the presence of Black troops, whom he put in charge of the Turks. As a result, Kutamas, Turks, other eastern elements of the army and sections of the population formed an alliance to combat the Black contingent. In 1019 the toxic mix of these factors resulted in riots, killings, looting and raping raging out of control. As Fustat burned, al-Hakim's detractors added a darker shade yet to his portrait: he became the Nero of Islam.

Calm was restored but the messianic dream of a harmonious life was over. After so much hope and expectation, for most the reality turned out to be nothing more than the usual mix of conflict, division and uncertainty. But al-Hakim had one more surprise in store. On the night of 13 February 1021 he left the palace for his usual ramble with two attendants but no military escort. On his grey donkey Moon, he headed towards the Muqattam hills. It is possible that he had intended to observe the planets, since according to some accounts he had had a copper astrolabe installed at the site, mounted between two towers. By the next morning, he had not returned to the palace, and search parties were dispatched to look for him. After days of search, all that was retrieved was his blood-stained tunic perforated by what looked like stabbings. His body was never found. To all intents and purposes all that could be said, as indeed the sources which reported on that eventful night state, is that he was lost, *faqada*.

The Druzes interpreted al-Hakim's mysterious disappearance as proof that, being God incarnate, he had reverted to his transcendental form, something that in their eyes proved his supernatural nature. Building on these beliefs, the Druze movement grew into a separate *da'wa* organization which took hold in Syria. Today there are about 1 million Druzes scattered across the Middle East as well as those who live in diaspora. Prominent Druzes include the Lebanese political leader Walid Jumblatt, the human rights lawyer Amal Alamuddin Clooney, the Arab diva Asmahan (d. 1944) and her brother, the musician, actor and poet Farid al-Atrash (d. 1974). A secretive community that does not allow conversion or apostasy, the Druzes await to this day the return of al-Hakim and that of their leader Hamza. The full content of their literary canon, its exegesis and the community's ritual practices are a guarded secret.

According to some, before the time of his disappearance al-Hakim had grown close to Christians and Jews, seeking to repair the damaged relations he had with them in previous years. In 1019 he had ordered the restoration of a Christian monastery in al-Qusayr on the Red Sea coast. Stories shared in Christian circles claimed that he had retreated to the desert where he lived as an eremite. Rumours circulated that he had spent time in the company of monks, whose secluded and simple life he longed for. Speculation arose that he had chosen to live a reclusive life in one of the monasteries on the Muqattam hills. Claims of sightings in disparate places were reported. However, as time passed a consensus was reached among most that al-Hakim had been killed. Over the centuries, the fate of al-Hakim has attracted attention as one of the great mysteries in Islamic history. Various medieval commentators came forward with their respective biased theories as to who might have carried out the killing. The Druzes were accused; so were high-ranking but disgruntled men at court. Culprits were looked for among renegades in the army, and his slaves and close servants became prime suspects. However, the majority of stories pointed the finger at his half-sister, Sitt al-Mulk, as the mastermind behind the demise of al-Hakim.

The tortuous way in which al-Hakim's rule has been described reflects his complex character, as far as one can infer from what was reported of him and his period. Did al-Hakim suffer from mental illness? Or has blaming insanity been a useful device to either dismiss his policies or find a rational answer for his most inscrutable actions? The most accredited advocate of al-Hakim's insanity theory was a physician and historian of his time who, as a Christian who had suffered at the hands of al-Hakim, might have been partial in his diagnosis of the imam-caliph's state of mind. The author of several works, among them annals covering the period between 938 and 1034, Yahya al-Antaki (d. 1066) described al-Hakim's condition as melancholia, advising a soak in a bath filled with violet oil to help his brain functions. For the same condition another Christian doctor prescribed him wine. That al-Hakim might have had health problems is also suggested by reports that on one occasion he gave a staggering 10,000 *dinar*s reward to his court physician for restoring him back to health. The vast majority of narratives portray al-Hakim wandering out at night, implying chronic insomnia. An anecdote adds an insight into his real or perceived state of health as a child. According to the historian of the Fatimid period, al-Musabbihi (d. 1029), in his youth al-Hakim had become ill to the point that his mother invoked the help of an imprisoned Sunni Andalusian legal scholar to pray for her son. He not only prayed but instructed that the entire Qur'an be written with ink made of musk and saffron on the inner surface of a bowl. He then advised washing the bowl with water from the Zamzam well in Mecca and administering the potion to the sick boy. Al-Hakim drank the mixture and lo and behold was healed. The scholar and his associates were released from jail in gratitude. To this day Muslim traditional healers recommend, among other methods, the writing with musk and saffron of chapter 26 of the Qur'an on a plate, to be washed with pure water to be administered to a patient as a generic treatment for all ailments.

The scanty records can at best point to some form of depression and anxiety but the nature of the sources makes a diagnosis inconclusive. The overall impression one gets is that of a man too eager to fulfil the messianic promises that came with his mandate. A leader who tried too hard to accommodate everyone in the face of changing moods, priorities and expectations. A ruler who, determined to restore power into the hands of the imam, paid the price of seeing his reputation in tatters by not availing himself of the managerial skills of an Ibn Killis, the expert communication of a Jawdhar and a scapegoat on whom to dump blame when things went wrong. A man whose intentions might have been good, but who found himself misunderstood.

An incarnate God? A misunderstood genius? A madman? Or just bad? Certainly, a man who did it his way. In recent times the figure of al-Hakim has been somewhat rehabilitated, thanks to a better understanding of the context in which he ruled and greater availability of primary sources, yet he remains an enigma. The centuries-long fascination with this imam-caliph has resulted in the production of a vast body of literature, covering genres from academic study to fiction. The mystery lives on.

Al-Zahir: The Light Comes Back On

Since the days of her failed attempted coup, Sitt al-Mulk had captured the imagination of those who chronicled or commented on the Fatimids. Her vicissitudes filled the pages of narrators more than those of any other woman in medieval Islamic history. Therefore, the awe that Sitt al-Mulk inspired made her the ideal figure to be evoked to add drama to the story of al-Hakim's disappearance. Ignored in Isma'ili sources, in anti-Fatimid chronicles she becomes a salvific figure, the scheming and fearless heroine who eliminated her brutal, mad half-brother. The exaltation of Sitt al-Mulk's character was as much a praise of her as a literary device to humiliate al-Hakim, whom *even* a woman could defeat in the eyes of the reader.

Irrespective of her involvement or not in al-Hakim's fate, it is beyond question that Sitt al-Mulk took control of events to fill the power vacuum that unfolded following the imam-caliph's disappearance. The belief that the imams entered periods of physical occultation was part and parcel of the Isma'ili cyclical vision of history. But al-Hakim's vanishing act was no supernatural disappearance; instead it was a missing person case devoid of spiritual meaning, except for the Druzes. Faced with a sudden leadership vacuum, most of the high-ranking men of the court accepted Sitt al-Mulk's overnight stepping into a leading role. She had personal charisma and was experienced in court politics after years of playing the rules of patronage to her advantage. Another contributing factor in the acceptance of her role might have been based on legal grounds. As the closest and most senior next of kin to a person categorized by law as *mafqud*, missing, she may have assumed the role of caretaker of al-Hakim's affairs and estate since the transmission of his inheritance was in limbo due to the uncertainty of his status. As one would expect, and in line with previous examples, Sitt al-Mulk took time before announcing to the public al-Hakim's disappearance and proclaiming his successor. During this short phase she became in essence the uncontested nominal ruler of the Fatimid empire, the first case of a woman reaching such a position in an Islamic dynasty. In that capacity she proceeded with a series of purges within the court to clear the way for her protégé nephew, 'Ali, to become the next imam-caliph. She summoned the heir apparent 'Abd al-Rahim from Syria to Egypt only to have him arrested and killed. Nothing more had been heard for quite some time of the other cousin that al-Hakim had appointed as *amir* of the Isma'ilis, so to still be regarded in the corridors of power as a figure of concern in rivalling Sitt al-Mulk's nephew's rise to the throne. Eventually, in 1024 a man was traced in Upper Egypt who confessed to the murder of al-Hakim and was sentenced to death. Meanwhile, she eliminated officers whom she accused of involvement in al-Hakim's demise.

Within a short time, the majority of the high dignitaries of the court pledged allegiance to her and accepted on her authority that 'Ali would become the next imam-caliph. There is no evidence that al-Hakim had ever rescinded his cousin's appointment as his heir apparent. In any case Isma'ili doctrine based on the precedent set by Imam Ja'far al-Sadiq did not allow for the incumbent imam to change his mind on the nomination of his successor, once this had been announced. Such reversal would be in flagrant contradiction to the principle of the imam's innate inerrancy. Therefore, on this occasion not only was *nass* overruled altogether to favour 'Ali's imamate, but the authority for his nomination was for the first time entrusted to a woman with no obvious mandate for it. In Islamic legal terms, however, this scenario might have been rendered possible on the grounds of Sitt al-Mulk's status as caretaker of al-Hakim's estate, which would have given her what we would call today power of attorney.

'Ali took the dynastic name al-Zahir and was about seventeen when he became imam. Given his youth Sitt al-Mulk acted as his regent during the initial phase of his reign. In that role she was assisted by 'Ali al-Jarjara'i (d. 1045), a former high officer in al-Hakim's service who had had his hands cut off by order of the imam-caliph for tampering with his confidential correspondence. Nevertheless, al-Jarjara'i rose through the ranks, having managed the bureau of expenditures and Sitt al-Mulk's private *diwan*. Al-Zahir's rule, whether direct or via his aunt, was to be marked by a policy of openness and détente to heal the empire after the tensions that had defined al-Hakim's period. During Sitt al-Mulk's regency and the first part of al-Zahir's reign state policies consisted of revising or sometimes confirming al-Hakim's decrees: land grants given by al-Hakim were annulled, properties confiscated by him were returned to the original owners. Taxes he had suspended were re-imposed and extra salaries he had paid were stopped. The restrictive policies al-Hakim had introduced, whether against women or *dhimmi*s, were relaxed, although during Sitt al-Mulk's regency limitations on women's movement and social gatherings were reintroduced for a short time. However, al-Zahir also confirmed by a decree dated 1024 privileges that al-Hakim and his predecessor had granted to the Coptic monks. He also ruled that rival Jewish sects should be allowed to follow their own customs, granting special protection for the Karahites, perhaps thanks to the intercession of Jews close to him who belonged to this group.[28] Court life and public pageantry recovered their splendour. In the short term, the measures paid off in restoring the economic fortunes of the state. In 1023 the Fatimids had appointed the Turkish Anushtakin al-Dizbiri (d. 1042) as military governor of Palestine. He had led successful military missions in Syria, and is described in positive terms in a variety of sources; thanks to him the Fatimids enjoyed, though briefly, their strongest ever control of this province.

Diplomatic relations with Byzantium were resumed with a return to the old terms and Constantinople's mosque reopened with the Fatimids acknowledged again at the Friday prayer. Muslim prisoners were released and commercial freedom of movement restored. In return al-Zahir granted permission for the Church of the Holy Sepulchre in Jerusalem to be repurposed back to its original Christian cult by allowing the emperor to finance its rebuilding and restoration following the destruction of the site by order of his father, al-Hakim. The permission was extended to many other churches of different denominations.[29] Many Christians who had been forced to convert to Islam were allowed to revert back to Christianity without fear of retaliation on the grounds of apostasy. Byzantium also asked the Fatimids to re-establish the patriarch in Jerusalem, to drop their interest in Aleppo and to abstain from helping the Muslim Sicilian rulers fighting against the Byzantines. Soon after the death of Sitt al-Mulk in 1023, al-Zahir's baptism of fire as ruler came in the year 1024–5 in the form of a severe famine that hit Egypt, made worse by market speculation on the price of grain. To no avail Baqi, one of the market inspectors of the capital, had tried to impose a fixed price on bread. Millers and bakers went on strike and the situation got worse until the order was partly lifted. Hungry people and unpaid soldiers rioted on and off for some time.

Meanwhile, in a matter of months, al-Hakim's hard work in keeping civil administrators at arm's length had been nullified. High dignitaries succeeded in relegating the inexperienced new imam-caliph to a ceremonial role. Al-Zahir took care of audiences, public appearances, diplomatic protocol and architectural patronage, while the civil administrators took executive control of the state. The most prominent of them was al-Jarjara'i. He was among the last of the generation of Iraqis who, since Ibn Killis's time, had moved to Egypt in search of work. After serving Sitt al-Mulk, he retained control of her estate after her death as well as heading other departments. In 1027 al-Jarjara'i was given the title of illustrious vizier by royal decree, with plenipotentiary responsibilities for the government on behalf of the imam-caliph, and he proved himself to be an able statesman. Following Ibn Killis's model, al-Jarjara'i operated via the *diwan* system, aided by a council formed of heads of departments. A distinctive administrative innovation for this period was the establishment of the *diwan al-Sham*, a department dedicated to Syria's affairs. Under al-Jarjara'i the taxation system became more efficient with (among other measures) dues imposed on Jews and Christians based on income at variable rates. This period saw an increase in the Jewish inhabitants, and the Copts still formed a large proportion of Egypt's residents. In general Fatimid Egypt enjoyed relative population growth, in contrast to an overall demographic decline across the Middle East.

Another figure who rose to power at this time was the Black eunuch Mi'dad, who had been employed by Sitt al-Mulk as al-Zahir's tutor. With his turban fastened under his chin, it was clear to all those who saw him that he belonged to the highest rank of the eunuchs' hierarchy. Mi'dad was wealthy and owned livestock that he kept in the Giza area. With al-Zahir as ruler, at first Mi'dad was appointed to manage the affairs of the soldiers and protection of the provinces. Then he rose to be head of the office of the Kutama, much to the latter's displeasure, and as leader of a coterie of high officers at the heart of government he rid himself of his direct rivals. During the famine riots of 1024 and in subsequent years Mi'dad took measures to protect the people of Fustat from soldiers on the rampage. It had been Mi'dad who, on the occasion of the festival to celebrate the end of Ramadan, had escorted al-Zahir to be presented to the dignitaries as successor to his father.[30]

As for the Nu'mans, they were back in charge of both the judiciary and the *da'wa*, a monopoly al-Hakim had curtailed. With the Nu'mans, the primacy of the Shi'i judiciary was re-established, with Maliki jurists expelled from Egypt in 1025. The *majalis al-hikma* intended for Isma'ilis that al-Hakim had suspended were resumed and the *da'wa* relaunched. In an edict of 1026, al-Zahir justified al-Hakim's closure of the learning sessions by explaining that his father had been forced to suspend them to eradicate supposed criminals. By these al-Zahir meant the Druzes, whom he would later persecute.[31] He reinvigorated the *da'wa* in Iraq and Iran with some success in Daylam. *Da'is* and sympathizers kept coming to Cairo from far and wide.

Relegated to a ceremonial role, al-Zahir made the most of making himself visible by treating his subjects to public festivals under any circumstances and on all occasions. Pomp had returned. Anecdotes circulated by detractors of the Fatimids tell us that he indulged in all that his father had prohibited: he drank wine and beer, enjoyed listening to singers and ate *mulukhiyya* and shellfish. The Golden Hall was refurbished with new gilt furnishings and brocades. Even the famine of 1024 did not prevent the court from staging a good show for the end of the fasting celebrations, to project a confident image of the regime even in the direst of circumstances. As famine raged, al-Jarjara'i had numerous sugar figurines and confectionery made in the shape of various palaces paraded to the sound of drums in the streets. Nasir-i Khusraw, who, 23 years later, witnessed in Cairo a similar show, described what he saw:

> They said that fifty thousand mounds of sugar were appropriated for this day ['*id*] for the sultan's feast. For decoration on the banquet table I saw a confection like an orange tree, every branch and leaf executed in sugar, and thousands of images and statuettes in sugar . . . Every day fourteen camel-loads of snow have to be provisioned for the use of the royal sherbet-kitchen.[32]

For the festival of sacrifice, al-Zahir performed the ritual prayer as was customary and delivered a sermon in the open air, but on this occasion the performance of the sacrifice took place inside the palace, followed by a lavish meal for the court. Under normal circumstances, the imam-caliph would sacrifice a camel at the open ground, and then return to the Great Palace escorted by high officers. There he would change into an outfit designed for the sacrifice celebration: a red robe with a special turban. He then would go out again, on three occasions, to a field north of the palace to officiate at the sacrifice of a large number of animals. In response to al-Zahir's change of protocol troops were called to defend the palace, but hungry rioters nevertheless made away with nine camels. Unlike al-Hakim who intervened to manage a grain crisis, there is no evidence that al-Zahir took direct action to alleviate the starvation of his subjects despite their cry for help. To be fair, sidelined as he already was by this stage, he might not have been in a position to intervene even if he had wanted to. However, al-Zahir did make himself visible by making allowances available for burials since, due to the famine, people who died by the score were left unburied and deprived of ritual washing. Also in 1024, for the festival of lights – a Shiʿi celebration in the middle of the Islamic month of Rajab that involved fasting and a ritual bath – al-Zahir had the palace as well as the mosques of Cairo, Fustat and al-Qarafa lit up and perfumed. He, his wives and entourage joined the crowds in the festivities. At festivals, everyone participated irrespective of religious denomination, although to avoid public disorder Muslims and Christians were kept separate. Christian processions were allowed and shared. The royal court took the opportunity at some of these celebrations to distribute garments and money among people serving the regime. On the occasion of the Coptic New Year feast, for example, state employees received garments and food.

In a typical parade al-Zahir rode a horse, wearing a fine linen shawl, sheltered by the customary golden ceremonial parasol and escorted by a lance-bearer, preceded by the army and unmounted horses bearing saddles studded with jewels and amber. On his head the imam-caliph sported a turban that on the occasion of the New Year festival procession was fitted with a special jewel. This adornment was described as being formed of a large central gem – a ruby, or a cluster of them – in the shape of a half-moon or a horseshoe, surrounded by a number of baguette-shaped emeralds. A similar jewel was apparently affixed to the forehead of his horse. Whether worn by himself or his horse, al-Zahir's insignia included one piece with a rock crystal core, inscribed with a benedictory formula that named him. This object functioned as an emblem of the imam: the transparency conveyed by his name, the esoteric meaning of light associated with the imamate and the crescent moon, a symbol associated with Islam. Whether combined or not, the use of rock crystal and crescent-inspired design became a dominant feature in the production of Fatimid ornamental artefacts, irrespective of context. Even caliphal boats used for leisure trips on the Nile featured crescent moons as decorative elements.[33]

By donning his special rock crystal jewel al-Zahir may have wanted to signal a symbolic parallel with the *qulayla*, a mysterious object believed to have been located in a niche in the Dome of the Rock in Jerusalem. The story goes that the *qulayla* ended up in the hands of the ʿAbbasid caliphs and got broken. Its myth, however, lived on. Described as a concave, bowl-shaped object made of rock crystal or ruby in which to nest a pearl, its light was described as so bright that it was impossible for people to look at it. The description of the object indicates that it was designed to tally with the Qur'anic verse of light, 'The example of His light is like a niche within which is a lamp, the lamp is within glass, the glass as if it were a pearly [white] star' (Q. 24:35). In Isma'ili and Shi'i gnostic literature the light in this verse is interpreted to mean Fatima and the lamp to be her son al-Husayn. Echoing this association is the epithet by which Fatima became best known, al-Zahra', the most radiant. Al-Zahir had established a profound association between himself and the Dome of the Rock as benefactor and patron of its restoration. Al-Zahir's rock crystal jewel may have been designed to echo the *qulayla* in order to advertise himself as an embodiment of the unbroken light that linked him to al-Zahra'. Similar to descriptions of the *qulayla*, the Fatimid jewel in the royal turban was believed to have held at some point the Orphan, the pearl earring of Mary, mother of Jesus, stolen from Mecca in 930 by the Qarmatians along with the Black Stone and other relics.[34]

In the processions with the imam-caliph were eunuchs and servants wearing gilded adornments and, behind, scores of high dignitaries in full regalia. A parade of old brocade banners and silver drums completed the spectacle. For the '*id* celebrations elephants and giraffes from the royal menageries were added to the procession. Echoing the Fatimid court taste for exoticism, images of giraffes and other wild beasts became a recognizable Fatimid decorative motif applied to a variety of artefacts, in particular lustreware ceramics.

Hunting was a pursuit cultivated by the Fatimid royals, and scenes of animals being chased was a common decorative element on Fatimid artworks. Images of cheetahs held on a leash appear on late tenth-century Fatimid rock crystal jugs. Al-'Aziz had a hunting manual written for him and al-Zahir indulged in the practice. He also enjoyed leisure trips. He took his harem and entourage to the Nile resort of al-Mushtaha, on Rawda island, and to Rumayla, an ancient Roman site. Al-Mushtaha is to this day an upmarket area of Cairo. Rumayla has been turned into a square, now renamed Maydan Salah al-Din and dominated by an early twentieth-century monumental mosque in neo-Mamluk style. Outside Cairo, al-Zahir undertook trips to 'Ayn Shams and the Tibr Mosque by the canal.[35] In 1024 this site was the destination of an innovative procession introduced by al-Zahir – that of the first day of Ramadan – when, with gold-threaded robe, turban and parasol, he paraded escorted by his army. The Tibr Mosque, built around 762–3 to house the shrine of an 'Alid martyr, was named after Tibr, an Ikhshidid commander who suppressed a rebellion in the area. Al-Hakim used the mosque as Abu Rakwa's place of public execution. It was at this site that Hamza preached al-Hakim's divinity. These events point to this mosque as having been a site associated with the spirit of rebellion. Al-Zahir's regular visits might have been motivated by wanting to affirm the presence of the regime in a volatile area.

Al-Zahir's reign was marked by a significant programme of architectural and artistic patronage. Rather than in the Cairo landscape, where his main contribution was an extension of al-Hakim mosque's ablution hall, al-Zahir's patronage became visible in Jerusalem. Al-Zahir was the first Fatimid imam-caliph to engage in major acts of patronage in that city. Besides supporting the reconstruction of the Church of the Holy Sepulchre, al-Zahir sponsored the repair of the Dome of the Rock, the Aqsa Mosque and other parts of the Temple Mount or al-Haram al-Sharif, which in 1016 and between 1033 and 1035 had been damaged by earthquakes (illus. 28). The Aqsa Mosque was further adorned with an elaborate mosaic design, and al-Zahir donated silver lamps to the Dome. Some ten years after the repairs had been carried out, inscriptions with the names and titles of the Fatimid caliphs could be seen over the monumental gates to the site.[36] Al-Zahir also had the city walls rebuilt where the Romans had raised them, corresponding more or less to where they are now. By imprinting his name on Jerusalem's landscape, al-Zahir sought to defy all other claimants to the site, reinforcing Fatimid ownership of the second holiest city in Islam and countering Sunni predominance there. Jerusalem was believed to have been the destination of Muhammad's miraculous night journey from Mecca, described in chapter 17 of the Qur'an. Al-Zahir's inscription on the Aqsa Mosque was the first to publicly advertise the area as the farthest mosque *al-masjid al-aqsa* (also known as *al-bayt al-muqaddas*), indicated in the Qur'an as the landing spot.[37] In light of these associations, the Fatimids' investment in Jerusalem was also motivated by wanting to promote it as a destination for Muslims on pilgrimage. To go to Jerusalem would do for those who, for whatever reason, could not reach Mecca.[38] This programme of restoration works impacted on Ramla as well.

28 Part of a letter recovered from the Cairo Geniza, dated December 1033, sent by a Jewish resident of Ramla to a person in Fustat describing in detail the terrible effects of the earthquake that hit his city and its inhabitants.

In 1027 a provisional agreement was reached with the Byzantine emperor that built on negotiations already begun by Sitt al-Mulk before her death. Crucial to the agreement was al-Zahir's permission to rebuild the Church of the Holy Sepulchre in Jerusalem in exchange for the sermon at the Friday prayer in Constantinople's mosque to be recited in his name. Restoration works on the church were completed in 1048. Notwithstanding the goodwill years of cordial antagonism, Fatimid–Byzantine relations became tense around 1030 when the Byzantines resumed their expansionist plans in northern Syria. This venture threatened the ever-tenuous hold that the Fatimids had in the region, with local rulers in Palestine and Syria tempted to form alliances in support of the Byzantines for their own advantage. The Fatimids had responded to these threats and managed to reassert their control, thanks to the efforts of Anushtakin al-Dizbiri who had governed Syria and Palestine until al-Jarjara'i put a drastic end to his career. At the same time, despite these tensions, a Fatimid–Byzantine entente continued to be pursued. In 1032 the Fatimids and Byzantines entered into a coalition to launch an attack in Jabal Summaq against the Druzes, who were thus driven into hiding. Massacres took place in Antioch and Aleppo. As a result of this persecution the Druzes were forced to conceal their faith, only resuming open profession in 1038, after al-Zahir's death. The terms of a Fatimid–Byzantine treaty were finalized in 1034. A clause in the treaty stipulated a pledge of mutual assistance in the event of famine, whereby the better-off regime would be bound by the agreement to send grain to the needy one. Trade exchanges between the two empires continued irrespective of military friction. Evidence of these transactions can be seen, for example, in the exceptional hoard that emerged from the 1977–9 shipwreck excavation of a Byzantine ship that sank around 1030 in Serçe Limani, near the island of Rhodes. The findings show that the ship carried a cargo of tens of thousands of Fatimid Syrian glass pieces, glazed pottery and other artefacts, including tons of shredded glassware for recycling, destined for the Constantinople market. The size of the hoard typifies the large quantity of Fatimid glass artefacts produced for average everyday use that were in circulation, fine examples of which have survived to this day (illus. 29).

Lavish gifts were exchanged between al-Zahir and the governors of the Egyptian provinces. In North Africa, diplomatic missions between the Fatimids and the Zirids continued.[39] Occasionally al-Zahir

29 Fatimid ornate glass jug with handle, Egypt, 10th–11th century.

received slave women adorned with silver lockets on their breasts. He reciprocated by sending female slaves who were singers and dancers, along with exotic textiles, precious stones and a saddled giraffe. Umm Mallal (d. 1023), who acted as regent for the future Zirid ruler, her nephew al-Mu'izz b. Badis (d. 1062), carried on a correspondence with Cairo and sent presents to Sitt al-Mulk. In al-Mahdiyya Umm Mallal, along with other noblewomen at the Zirid court, had grown to great prominence and, at her death, she was honoured with the most lavish funeral known to have been staged at the time. Part of a splendid Qur'an manuscript she commissioned for the Great Mosque of Qayrawan is still extant. Despite all these efforts to secure their loyalty, from the 1030s the Zirids showed further signs of distancing themselves from Cairo. They experienced internal family disputes, with some factions siding with the ʿAbbasids. Once the succession of al-Muʿizz b. Badis had been legitimized, he was faced with growing Maliki opposition to the Fatimids, which he did not challenge, with the result that Ismaʿilis in Qayrawan and al-Mansuriyya were massacred. In Sicily the Kalbids also began to distance themselves from the Fatimids, although on the island generally and in Palermo in particular, coins continued to be minted in the name of al-Zahir and his successor.[40]

During this period grain continued to be sent to the Hijaz to feed the annual pilgrims and to ensure that the *sharif*s, who controlled the holy places, continued to pledge allegiance to the imam-caliph in Cairo. Meantime, in the east, the apogee that the Shiʿa had reached thanks to the Buyids was coming to an end. In 1031, al-Qadir was succeeded by al-Qa'im (d. 1075), a caliph who adopted a messianic name that challenged the Fatimids in their ideological territory. Further east, Mahmud of Ghazna and his successors were supplanted by a rising new Turkish confederation of families from Central Asia: the Seljuqs. Their leader, Tughril Beg (d. 1063), having defeated the Ghaznavids, made the Seljuqs the new champions of Sunnism in the ʿAbbasids' eyes, with their plan to rid them of both the Buyids and the Fatimids.

Of the women in Zahir's life, one in particular stole his heart. She was Rasad, a slave of either Abyssinian, Sudanese or Nubian origins whom the imam-caliph had bought from a Jewish dealer in jewels, Abu Saʿd al-Tustari. Rasad bore a son to al-Zahir who would become his successor with the name of al-Mustansir, and at least two daughters. One of them, a three-year-old child, died of disease on the night of the Epiphany celebration of 1024. The girl's funeral prayer was led by the chief *qadi* and she was buried in the royal Saffron mausoleum. As for Rasad, she became the most powerful woman of her time during the reign of her son.

In 1035 Egypt suffered a massive rat infestation which destroyed a large quantity of crops. Famine followed, and a year later in 1036 the plague struck the country again. A half-moon-shaped rock crystal segment, maybe part of al-Zahir's turban *jawhar*, featured an inscription that read 'The religion is for Allah, ʿAli al-Zahir li-Iʿzaz Allah, God will prolong his life'. This well-wishing statement, however, did not produce the desired effect of securing longevity for the imam-caliph.

Al-Zahir died of plague in a garden resort by the arsenal on the Nile. If its protective powers had failed the imam-caliph, the rock crystal component of al-Zahir's jewel, which resurfaced in fourteenth-century Venice, became a source of solace to Christian devotees in the Latin west, where the exotic object was venerated as part of a gold-embellished reliquary (illus. 22). Though a somewhat marginalized ruler, al-Zahir nonetheless (with al-Jarjara'i's help) left behind a state that was characterized by relative stability and, as indeed his name promised, transparency. Like their carved rock crystals, during the reigns of al-Mu'izz and al-'Aziz the Fatimids had projected their multicoloured prismatic lights in all directions. Then clouds had descended on court life under al-Hakim's rule. Under his successor al-Zahir, as a Melkite poet said of his reign, 'The People awake on a new morning after the fear.'[41] Of this 'new morning' the seven-year-old boy who succeeded al-Zahir was now the new master.

6

The Fatimids and the World as They Saw It in the Eleventh Century

A seven-year-old child now ascended the Fatimid throne with the royal name of al-Mustansir. Before following this imam-caliph in the vicissitudes that marked his reign, we take a pause to look at the state the Fatimid domains were in at this juncture. Two main sources give us an insight into life under the Fatimids in Egypt, and into the rest of the world as the Fatimids saw it in the middle of the eleventh century. One is the eyewitness account by Nasir-i Khusraw recorded in his travelogue *Safarnama*. The other is an Arabic text known as the *Book of Curiosities* which belongs to the wonders genre of Islamic literature that flourished between the ninth and eleventh centuries.[1] It was written by an anonymous author for a Fatimid royal or a member of the court. In both works, enthusiasm and a desire to amaze as well as amuse on the part of two ardent servants of the regime blur the realism of what is described. Nevertheless, complemented by fragmentary texts, artefacts and documents, a reasonably balanced perspective can be attained in painting the landscape that formed the background in which to place our sitter.

Living in Cairo and Fustat

What did Cairo look like by the mid-eleventh century? The Persian Isma'ili propagandist, thinker and writer Nasir-i Khusraw, a staunch pro-Fatimid voice and one prone to embellishing his account, was most impressed by Cairo's urban layout, lifestyle and architecture. Besides describing the royal palace, he wrote on the houses, the gardens and the markets of the royal city.

> The city of New Cairo has five gates, Bab al-Nasr, Bab al-Futuh, Bab al-Qantara, Bab al-Zuwayla and Bab al-Khalij. There is no wall but the buildings are even stronger and higher than ramparts, and every house and building is itself a fortress. Most of the buildings are five storeys tall, although some are six. Drinking water is from the Nile, and water carriers transport water by camel. The closer the well is to the river, the sweeter the water; it becomes more brackish the further you get from the Nile. Old and New Cairo are said to have fifty thousand camels belonging to water carriers. The water carriers who port water on their backs are separate: they have brass cups and jugs and go into the narrow lanes where a camel cannot pass. In the midst of the houses in the city are gardens and orchards watered by wells. In the sultan's harem are the most beautiful gardens imaginable. Waterwheels have been constructed to irrigate them. There are trees planted and pleasure parks built even on the roof . . . These houses are so magnificent and fine that you would think they were made of jewels, not of plaster, tile, and stone! All the houses of Cairo are built separate one from another, so that no one's trees or outbuildings are against anyone else's walls . . . Going west outside the city, you find a large canal called Khalij, which was built by the father of the present sultan [al-Mustansir], who has three hundred villages on his private property along the canal. The canal was cut from Old to New Cairo, where it turns and runs past the sultan's palace. Two kiosks are built at the head of the canal, one called Lulu (Pearl) and the other Jawhara (Jewel). Cairo has four congregational mosques where men pray on Fridays. One of these is called al-Azhar, another al-Nur, another the Mosque of al-Hakim, and the fourth the Mosque of al-Mu'izz. This last mosque is outside the city on the banks of the Nile.[2]

The Persian visitor estimated that some 30,000 people lived in houses he described in his travelogue. According to him, most properties belonged to the ruler, meaning the ruling class which, besides the royal family, included high officers and the closest members of the royal entourage. This real estate consisted also of some 20,000 shops as well as caravanserais and bathhouses that the ruler let at two or ten *dinar*s per month. However, Nasir pointed out that rentals on some residential and commercial properties like shops, oil presses, wedding halls and mills were reduced during the month of Ramadan to account for the slowing in productivity in that period. Countrywide, the revenues for the ruler and his court from properties had seen a substantial incremental growth by this stage. The geographer and historian al-Muqaddasi (d. 991) claimed that a few decades before the arrival of the Fatimids, the revenue derived from property in Egypt was 2.5 million *dinars*. Within a year of the Fatimid commander Jawhar's taking over the administration of Egypt, the annual revenues had risen to 3.5 million *dinars*. In addition to real estate, the imam and his family owned agricultural properties extending along the Cairo canal, and in the countryside outside the capital. Some of these properties, in Egypt but also in Syria and Palestine, were allocated to men and women of the court through a land grant system.

Beyond housing, Cairo lacked main facilities for a long time. A small market had existed not long after the city's foundation, but it burned down in 976. The first bathhouses were established by al-'Aziz and his daughter Sitt al-Mulk. Cairo residents went to Fustat for these services. Nasir enthused about Fustat's vibrant life. Built on a hill, the city he described as looking like a mountain, with its houses between seven and fourteen storeys high. To his amazement he learned that on top of one such house a tenant kept a calf that he used to turn a waterwheel to lift water from below to irrigate orange and banana trees, flowers and herbs planted on the roof. Fustat's market made a big impression on him, especially the alley of the lamps by the 'Amr Mosque near the book *suq* that was lit day and night. He saw some two hundred warehouses selling works of art from all over the world: inlaid artefacts, carved rock crystal, dainty pottery, transparent green glass, elephant tusks and exotic birds, not to mention fruits, vegetables, sugar and honey. Traders sold at fixed prices and moved around on rented donkeys.

Nasir's observations on the capital's housing style have not been corroborated by archaeological evidence. The Persian traveller's rose-tinted description is indeed contradicted by what reads as a more realistic assessment by the Egyptian Ibn Ridwan, who worked at the court of al-Zahir's successor, al-Mustansir. From humble beginnings the self-taught Ibn Ridwan grew up to become an accomplished physician and, though a divisive figure, he was nonetheless acknowledged by many as one of the most brilliant minds of his time. An environmentalist and climatologist *ante litteram*, Ibn Ridwan offered a more objective assessment of living conditions in Fustat, Cairo and the Qarafa district. Fustat was the most crowded part of the capital and, in his view, the worst area to live in. The quality of its air was poor and stagnant, trapped as it was in narrow lanes flanked by high-storey buildings. The fumes and steam coming from multiple burners used in the city's many bathhouses made the air worse. The area around the 'Amr Mosque was bad, being further contaminated by the rotting carcasses of animals and rubbish dumped in the street. During their respective reigns al-'Aziz and al-Hakim ordered that large water containers be put outside the shops of the capital to ensure the cleanliness of the streets, but also to function as fire extinguishers if needed. Order was given that when carried by camel or mule these containers had to be covered by lids to ensure that spillage would not drench people.[3] Suppressing the stench that prevailed in the streets was a constant concern at a time when it was believed that miasmas were a cause of epidemics.

With Fustat being situated close to the Nile, its inhabitants relied on the river for their water supply. This water, however, was polluted owing to people throwing garbage and animal faeces in it to such an extent that the build-up could block the flow of the river. One line of defence that people adopted against this filth when drinking the water consisted of sieve-like pottery water filters that, when inserted in the neck of a jug, would prevent the larger pieces of rubbish and insects seeping through. Often decorated with animal figures or geometric patterns, these humble everyday utensils have today become collectable artefacts and are counted among the most recognizable examples of Fatimid art (illus. 30). The throwing of rubbish into the water escalated to the point that in the early twelfth century boats had difficulty in entering the clogged *khalij* canal. To remedy this situation an officer was put in charge of ensuring that no one dumped garbage in its water.[4]

As for Cairo, Ibn Ridwan considered it more pleasant because its buildings were not so high, and its lanes were broader and less littered with rubbish. Cairo was also somewhat distant from the main course of the Nile which meant that its inhabitants drank well water, which was cleaner than that of the river. Nasir-i Khusraw observed how fetching it had generated a sideline business in the rental of jugs. He learnt that a woman had invested in the purchase of 5,000 metal pitchers that she then leased to customers for a *dirham* each, with rentals to be renewed every month on condition of returning the jug in good shape at the end of the lease.[5]

Al-Qarafa, once a quarter outside the city walls between Cairo and Fustat, is today known for its vast cemetery, but it has also been an inhabited space for the living since ancient times. During the Fatimid period the population of al-Qarafa was served by a congregational mosque whose imam, in 973, was a certain Muhammad b. 'Abd al-Sami'. In that same year the *maghariba* moved into areas of al-Qarafa and al-Ma'afir and settled there by expropriating the houses of local residents and deporting them elsewhere. In time, al-Mu'izz recalled the *maghariba*, ordering them to settle in Cairo. The consort of al-Mu'izz, Durzan, became associated with al-Qarafa as a patron of imposing architectural structures. We have references to everyday services and facilities supplied to its residents during the reign of al-'Aziz: garden maintenance, mills, *hammams* and ovens. The traveller al-Muqaddasi, who referred to the inhabitants of the area as the *qarafiyya*, spoke of its

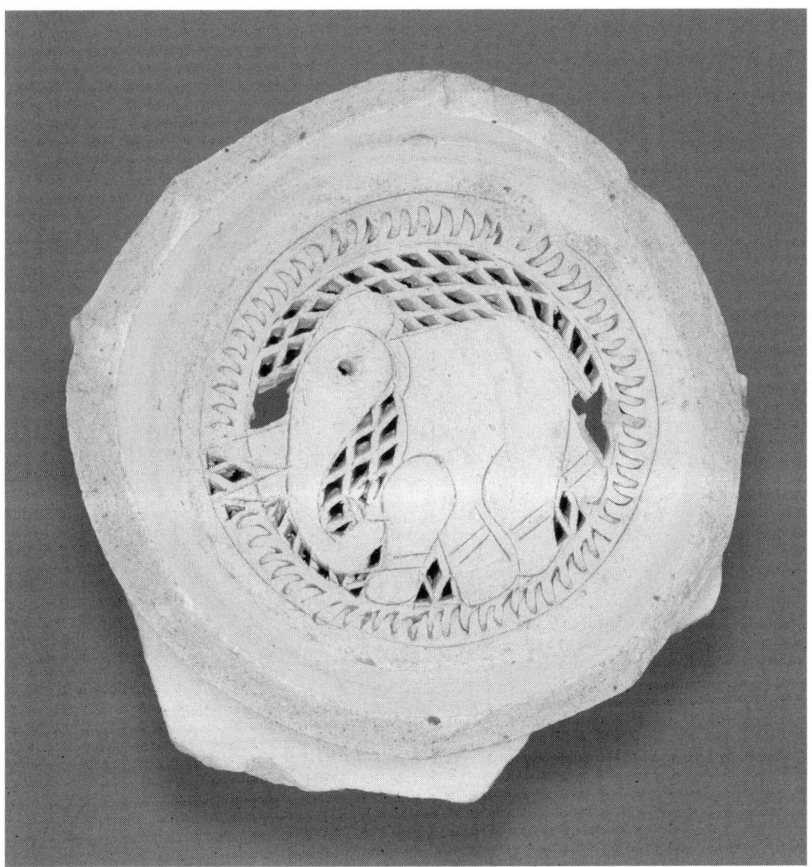

30 Water filter with an elephant figure, Fatimid, 11th–12th century, earthenware.

rapid urban expansion, describing the quarter as being characterized by a dusty colour, in contrast to the whiteness of its cemeteries. Ibn Ridwan proclaimed al-Qarafa to be one of the best residential areas of the capital (he lived there), due to the good quality of its air. It also had water, supplied by aqueduct since Tulunid times. Al-Qarafa became a favourite place for the non-resident palace staff to live in. Today al-Qarafa, where the living and the dead still share the same space, is known as the City of the Dead, and is one of the most crowded areas in Cairo.

The capital had two grain ports, one which served Cairo and the regime, Maqs, and another that served Fustat. In this port there were separate docks for uploading grain shipped from Tinnis, Lower Egypt and Upper Egypt. A special dock was devoted to the shipping of barley. In Cairo in the late Fatimid period there were three storehouses to which the grain belonging to the imam was shipped via the Maqs. Revenues from this stock amounted to millions of *dinars*.

In terms of living standards and arrangements within the home in the capital and other cities, valuable information can be found in the letters of merchants preserved in the Cairo Geniza, in which incidental references are made to the domestic surroundings in which people lived and met. The typical house of a well-to-do person had a court with a fountain or a well in the middle. The idea of reflecting the sky in a water basin is an ancient one, rich with symbolism. Here, however, the presence of the fountain would transform the courtyard into a temperature regulator whereby the cooled air trapped in it would flow into the surrounding rooms.[6] These consisted of at least one large social room on the ground or upper floors, and numerous smaller rooms. Most houses had kitchens, a few had bathing facilities and almost none had a fixed bedroom, as sleeping arrangements changed according to the season. Some houses had a secret door opening into a back alley through which women could come and go unobserved. Both men and women owned houses, or shares in them, with real estate being a popular form of female investment.

Today, the palace in Palermo that was once named al-'Aziz but that has since become famous as the Zisa can give us an idea of what a complete provincial palace of the period looked like, notwithstanding the presence of decorative and functional details not known to have defined Fatimid architecture. The castle, which retains many of its original features, was built in the twelfth century under Norman rule by Muslim craftsmen who brought to Sicily skills and motifs which were shared across the Islamic territories at the time. Its style echoes structures in the citadel that the Zirids (still vassals of the Fatimids at the time) founded in 1007 known as Qal'a Bani Hammad; this complex is now one of Algeria's UNESCO world heritage sites. The Zisa palace, which served the Norman kings as a hunting lodge, is surrounded by the Genoardo (from the Arabic *jannat al-ard*, paradise on earth) garden. There are fountains (those outside were undergoing restoration at the time of writing, in spring 2023) and, inside, there is an ingenious system of shafts that channels the cooled air from floor to floor.

Ibn Ridwan formulated what today we might call a public health policy, outlining the ideal housekeeping rules that people should aspire to on the basis of their level of affluence. Houses should be spacious, sunlit and well ventilated. The floors should be tiled with marble or either paved or plastered with gypsum. They should be cleaned often, and kept covered with straw mats in hot weather, or with carpets, felts, silk brocade and wool when it was cold. Those who could not afford expensive furnishings could use instead tatted mats and sheepskins. In hot weather the house should be sprinkled with water. Fountains and pools should be filled with skin water containers, and water-filled silver, lead, ceramic or earthenware containers should be put in the corners of rooms. The survival of many exquisite examples of Fatimid carved marble water jar stands, *kilgas*, testifies to the importance affluent

31 Fatimid marble *kilga* (water container stand), 11th–12th century.

people gave to having decorative water jars around the house (illus. 31). Indoor fans and awnings outside the house should be installed to keep it cool. The living room should face north, and furnishings should include potpourris of cooling aromatic plants such as violet, rose, narcissus, wild thyme and mandrake. It was recommended for the private rooms to be perfumed with camphor, rose water, sandalwood and rose oils. In cold weather, rooms should be equipped with stoves and furnished with branches of warm flowers, which might include citron, camomile, lily of the valley and jasmine. The most appropriate home deodorants were ambergris, aloe wood, cardamom, frankincense and mastic. In keeping with the science of his time, Ibn Ridwan relied on hygiene rules that had been formulated in ancient Greece.[7] Nasir-i Khusraw's observations point to a health service system having been in place within the royal city: 'if people of the city make requests on behalf of the suffering, they are given something. Whatever potion or medication is needed in the city is given out from the harem, and there is also no problem in the distribution of other ointments such as balsam.'[8]

In the capital and elsewhere, gardens featured as part of the real estate that belonged to the imam-caliph, his family and his entourage. In one sense garden meant large orchards where fruit and vegetables were grown that would generate revenues for the regime. Once in Egypt the Fatimids took over Kafur's gardens, as well as two large orchards. In time the royal family extended the ownership of gardens across their domains as far as Syria. Orchards feature among the properties of Sitt al-Mulk. The Fatimid royals also owned pleasure gardens and retreats. Nasir-i Khusraw reported that

> The sultan [al-Mustansir] also has a garden called Heliopolis . . . outside the city . . . There is a balsam tree in the garden, and it is said that the ancestors of the present sultan brought the seeds of this tree from the Maghreb . . . The tree itself looks like a myrtle tree. When it reaches maturity, the branches are scored, and cups are attached to catch the sap-like oil that comes out . . . It has a thick bark that . . . tastes like almond.[9]

The Persian visitor also described the gardens of the royal palace as consisting of twelve pavilions, terraces with planted trees and small courts turned into small gardens thanks to hydraulic devices.[10] Besides three city gates, by the end of the nineteenth century all that was left of

Fatimid-era buildings (or parts of them) were the mosques of al-Azhar, al-Hakim, al-Aqmar, al-Fakahani and al-Salih al-Tala'i'. Remaining structures also dating back to that period include a mausoleum and part of a tower.[11]

Looking Out of the Capital: The Fatimids and the World Around Them

Taking the city as a 360-degree viewpoint and looking into the far distance, how did the Fatimids see the world around them? From their geographical, religious, political and commercial positions, what was out there that mattered the most to the Fatimids in terms of their interests, be they of a pragmatic or intellectual nature? An answer to these questions is provided in the text, illustrations and maps contained in *The Book of Curiosities*. The work's earliest known extant manuscript, dating back to the early thirteenth century, is today among the most prized treasures of the Bodleian Libraries, University of Oxford. *The Book of Curiosities*, written in Egypt between 1020 and 1050, was authored by a thus far unnamed Isma'ili supporter or strong sympathizer of the Fatimid regime, for an unidentified patron who belonged either to the Fatimid high-ranking members of court or to the social elite. The vizier Abu Muhammad al-Yazuri (d. 1058) who, as we will see, served al-Mustansir, is described as a collector of illustrated books. Could he have been the person behind the commissioning of this work? Gazing at the book's splendid astral charts, maps of seas, rivers and distant lands, as well as representations of mythical animals and wondrous creatures, we enter the celestial and terrestrial worlds as the Fatimids saw them or imagined them. The work is the result of a blend of knowledge drawn from a mixture of ancient Greek, Coptic and Hindu sciences as well as Islamic intellectual traditions. Descriptions are often based on accounts left by previous Muslim travellers and observers, but always with the addition of an extra twist that contributes to the uniqueness of this book. Its author is an exemplar of the erudite class of his time.

Unlike the land-oriented Islamic dynasties, the Fatimids sought to assert themselves – and to be recognized as such by their rivals – as an important military and commercial maritime power. A browse through the maps in the *Book of Curiosities* confirms the Fatimids' pre-eminent interest in the sea and navigable water networks. The maps are often unusual in layout. There is a wealth of information in the captions which corresponds to the topography of regions along the Mediterranean, the Aegean, the East African coasts and the Indian Ocean. There are maritime diagrams, town plans and portolan charts, all reflecting the historical, commercial and strategic interests of the Fatimid regime (illus. 23). In the process of depicting and describing this world we find the earliest extant map of Sicily; here Zanzibar is first mentioned in an Arabic text. The island of Pemba is indicated where, in 1984, archaeologists unearthed Fatimid gold coins. The word *Inqiltira* makes its earliest known appearance on a map of this kind to designate England.

Reflecting the Fatimids' preoccupations of the day, we find topographical information on locations that might have been useful to seafarers navigating in areas under Byzantine control. In regions of predominant Fatimid commercial interest, priority is given to details on the size of the ports and access to supplies such as fresh water. Reading at times as a nautical guide for mariners, parts of the *Book of Curiosities* are based on accounts and reports by crews working on vessels out at sea, or so its author claimed.

Of all the seas described, it is to the Mediterranean that the largest section of the book is dedicated.[12] This is not surprising given the special significance that this sea occupied in the Fatimid history and mindset: it was on its shores that the imam became manifest again; it was across its waters that the Fatimids built their empire; it was across its ports that the Fatimids established their commercial dominance. In dealing with this basin, two places stand out in the *Book of Curiosities* as symbolic of what the Fatimids considered an inalienable and integral part of their narrative: al-Mahdiyya and Sicily. The earliest known map of the Fatimids' first capital in the book testifies to how, even after the Fatimids had settled in Egypt, the memory of the city of al-Mahdi still carried symbolic and emotional weight. Though under Zirid rule by the time the book was written, at least on paper al-Mahdiyya was still – and for the Fatimids would always be – the city of the imams. The centrepiece of this unique map is a depiction of three complexes: the wall, the harbour and the twin royal compounds labelled as the palace of the imams. The images were intended to convey a message of impregnability and of Fatimid dominion across the Mediterranean, which encircled the city (illus. 32).

Northwest of al-Mahdiyya is Sicily. The author declares that 'The island of Sicily is the largest of the Islamic islands and the most

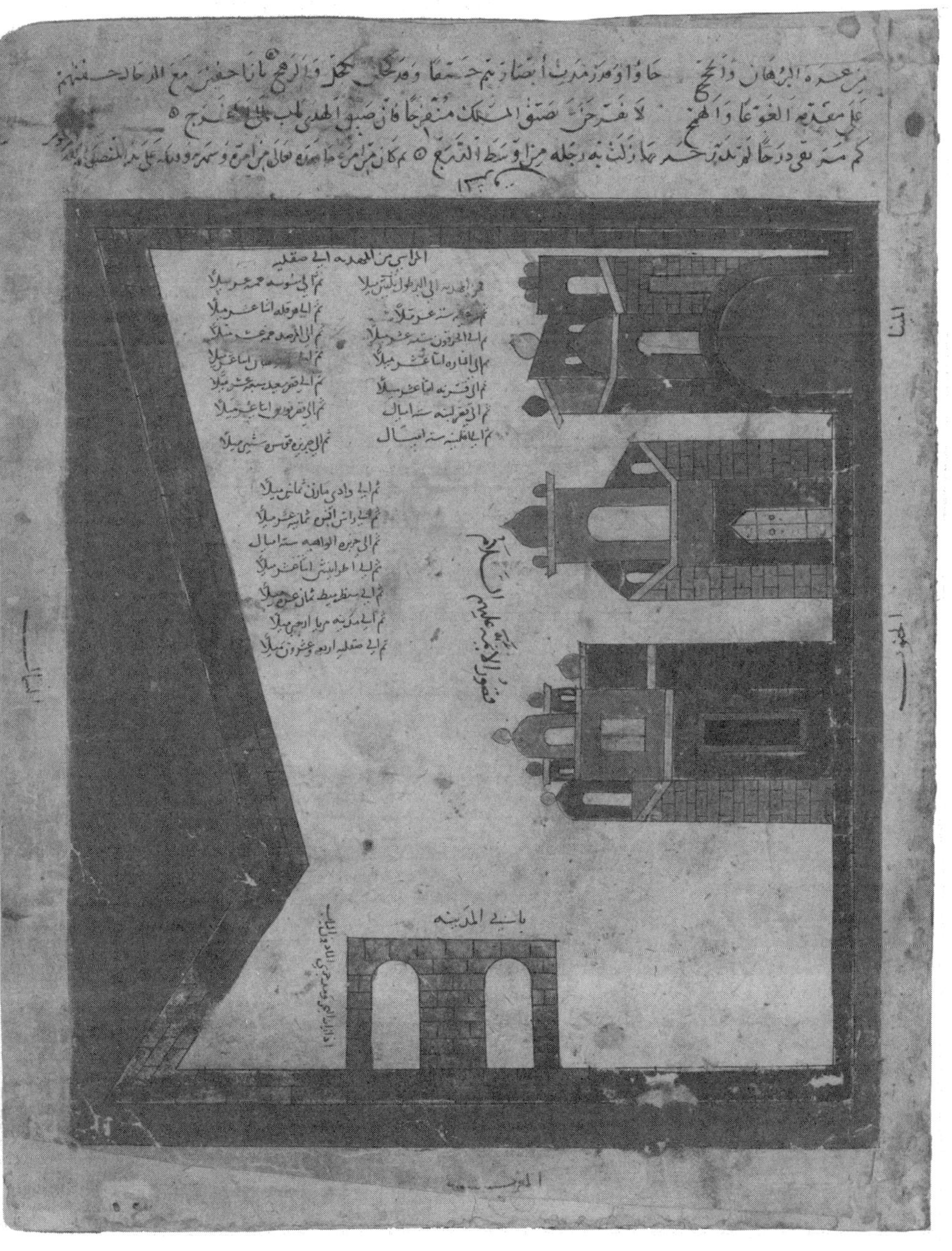

32 Plan of al-Mahdiyya from a *c.* 1190–1210 manuscript of the *Book of Curiosities*, a work originally written in the Fatimid period, *c.* 1020–50.

honourable on account of its continuous military expeditions against the enemy [the Byzantines].'[13] The map of Sicily shows the island as a flattened oval shape, with only the port of Palermo highlighted along the coast by a circular enclosure in red, showing its gates, that the author glorifies as tall and impregnable. A map of Palermo depicts the city as walled, with the harbour and the arsenal next to it. Al-Khalisa is represented as a domed structure labelled as the Ruler's Palace, the citadel established in 937–8 to house the Fatimid ruling administration. This quarter is not described in great detail in the text and its overall representation does not appear to be realistic. The suburban quarters of the city that are labelled and described include, for example, the Saqaliba as well as the Ja'fariyya with their 10,000 houses and freshwater provisions. As for Palermo's markets, butchers and grain merchants operated outside the city, while vendors of fruit and vegetables traded within the walls. Outside Palermo, mills, orchards, gardens and aristocratic villas adorned the countryside. One of the Kalbid rulers, Ja'far, had a hunting lodge built near Erice. The site is still extant and maintains its original leisure purpose to this day, with the lodge having been transformed into a luxury holiday rental property. Of note on the map is the representation of Mount Etna, highlighted with a red cap (illus. 24).

Looking further west, the Iberian peninsula is just about outlined. The Umayyad of al-Andalus, once the Fatimids' Muslim rivals in the Mediterranean, were a spent force by the time the *Book of Curiosities* was compiled. In contrast, looking east, the Byzantine coasts of Anatolia, the Aegean Sea and its islands, as well as Cyprus, are described in more detail than the Egyptian or indeed the Syrian–Palestinian shorelines, which at the time were still under nominal Fatimid control.

Turning towards the Egyptian Mediterranean coastline and moving inland, the areas that are given most space are the port city of Tinnis and the Nile, which appears in four maps, including one dedicated solely to this river. That Tinnis received so much attention should not surprise. Part of a maritime triangle with al-Mahdiyya and Sicily, Tinnis – a stopover for traders between Egypt and Syria–Palestine – had been a powerhouse for the production of textiles. Under the Fatimids Tinnis's importance grew even more, as the regime founded most of its economic fortunes on its industrial and agricultural might. With Tinnis having been destroyed in 1227 by the Ayyubid sultan al-Kamil to prevent it from falling into the hands of future Crusaders, its map in the *Book of Curiosities* constitutes the earliest known to exist for this period. On it, the city is shown as an island, encircled by sea and the Delta's Manzala lake, surrounded by gated walls and with two ports. In the *Book* the textual description of Tinnis appears to be based on the accounts of an earlier local historian. Access to the city and its ports was through gates furnished with copper and iron fixtures. In it there were 55,000 weaving looms, and services included a congregational mosque, the arsenal, the governor's palace, public prayer grounds, fishermen's storehouses and more than fifty merchant inns, of which six had been built during al-Hakim's reign in 1014–15.

There are no references to churches, despite the city having had a strong Christian presence and most of the textile workforce having consisted of Copts. The 50,000 inhabitants (a nominal figure) are described as people full of joy and happiness, indulging in life's pleasures such as music and rest. However, this idealized portrayal of Tinnis's lifestyle is not matched by what was reported in other medieval sources. Before the advent of the Fatimids, the Syrian Jacobite Patriarch Dionysius Telmaharensis (d. 845), who visited the area circa 815, reported having found Tinnis populous and with numerous churches, but lamented the harshness of living and working, for both men and women, in private workshops in the city. A worker who acted as an informant to the patriarch lamented:

> Our trade is exclusively that of linen which our women spin and we weave. We get from the dealers half-a-dirham per day. Although our earning is not sufficient to feed our dogs we yet have to pay 5 dinars a head in taxes. They beat us, imprison us, and compel us to give our sons and daughters as securities. For every dinar they have to work two years as slaves.[14]

In the tenth century the severe treatment of the Tinnis workers was imputed to the vizier Ibn Killis. Nasir-i Khusraw observed that working conditions had changed for the better, although he noted that the city was hot and riddled with disease which affected the local women in particular. He heard that they suffered from the 'Tinnis convulsion', a condition that made them howl like cats and then faint. The poor living standards of Tinnis did not escape the attention of Ibn Ridawn, who commented on the impact of the air's excessive humidity on the virility of the city's male population.[15] Others lamented how Tinnisi people did not engage in exercise and indulged in excessive consumption of cheese, fish and cow's milk. Leaving aside exaggerations and tropes, the geographical position of Tinnis was such that the city did suffer from a lack of good quality drinking water. The huge amount of waste from the intensive industrial textile production, discharged into the water that surrounded the city, must also have caused severe pollution that impacted on the population's health. Fatimid-era anecdotes featuring people with disabilities tend to identify them as originating from Tinnis. Despite the predicaments afflicting its inhabitants, a century later the city still retained its fame as a centre of excellence for the production of the finest textile manufactures; it was there that a force of 150 workers was employed to make a royal tent that took nine years to complete.

Fatimid Alexandria

Considering the centrality given to the sea in the *Book of Curiosities*, it is surprising to find that not much space in it is dedicated to Alexandria, despite the city's place in Egyptian history since antiquity. Alexandria had been the first major target of the earliest Fatimid attempts at conquering Egypt. It was there that al-Mu'izz, on his way to Cairo, entered his acquired domains and announced to local notables his intentions as ruler. Yet the Fatimids maintained an ambivalent relationship with the city. Alexandria was cherished for its strategic position as Egypt's main gateway to the Mediterranean, placed as it was near the Nile's commercial riverine highways. At the same time, it was a source of anxiety because of its exposure to external enemy forces. In the Fatimid period Alexandria became a distant neighbourhood of Fustat, thus occupying a secondary role in relation to the capital.

Information about the city in the Fatimid period that is missing in the *Book of Curiosities* can be retrieved instead from remarks found in the Cairo Geniza documents, complemented by literary and material sources. Medieval Alexandria was contained within walls with five gates that preserved some Roman and Byzantine elements, although the area they enclosed was smaller than what it had been in antiquity. The outskirts of the city consisted of agricultural lands and gardens which also served as recreational parks. The city dwellers appreciated in particular the nearby area by the shores of Lake Mariut, famous for its fruit gardens and for fishing. A certain type of reed growing in that region was praised for making quality pens. This area was so beautiful that, according to some narratives, the Crusaders, though they ransacked it during their attack on Alexandria in 1167, lamented its destruction and pillage.

During this period Alexandrians got their water through a double system: rainwater that was gathered in cisterns, and Nile water that, from the Ptolemaic period, had been channelled to the houses. The river was connected to an urban supply system that received its water via underground pipes leading to wells. Not unlike Cairo, Alexandria was linked to the Nile's fluvial highway via an artificial canal that had existed since the Hellenistic period. The canal needed constant maintenance and repair since it silted, and when it clogged during periods of low Nile it brought chaos to the city's water supply system. Besides providing water for human consumption and irrigation, the canal was an important transportation artery that linked Alexandria to the Fatimid capital and the villages along the Nile valley in between. The entrance and exit of the canal were official passage stations, where passengers were charged a special customs duty, the amount of which depended on the value of the merchandise transported, or on the whim of the customs officer. The canal was open only during the flood season and was closed off during the long periods of low water. Its opening and closing dictated the city's life cycles and the trading calendar. An overall precariousness of water supply rendered Alexandria dependent on a delicate balance in the deployment of a range of natural and technological strategies in order to function as a city.

As a transport route, the life of the canal was linked to that of the port of Alexandria, which was divided into two sections. One was the eastern port that, difficult to navigate due to its narrow entrance, was meant for Christian and other non-Muslim boats only. The other, the western port, protected by iron chains, was intended for Muslim ships alone. The entrance to the port area as a whole was through the Sea Gate which, closed during the night, was manned by an appointed officer. This person, who could be a non-Muslim, was responsible for issuing obligatory passes to those entering or leaving the port. He was assisted by a secretary in charge of writing down the many documents needed at the gate. The port area was dominated by the famous lighthouse of Alexandria, which the Fatimids had reconstructed and which continued to attract the admiration of historians, geographers and travellers. The lighthouse was a point of reference in the city: sailors offloaded merchandise from their boats onto others waiting to collect the goods by sailing close by to the lighthouse. Ships waiting to depart also anchored at this point between the port and the sea. The port was active during the sailing seasons, which excluded winter, a time of year when ships were dragged onto land for maintenance.

Inside its walls, Alexandria preserved the layout of the Hellenistic city it once was. Long, straight, broad avenues lined by stone buildings preserved from ancient times characterized the city and impressed its medieval visitors. The sunlight reflecting off these buildings was so bright that travellers said that it shone even at night, or that they had to cover their eyes to protect them from the extreme glare. Columned avenues criss-crossed the city from one gate to another. The main market area was located in the centre, with shops and stalls situated along the city's central axes that sprawled into a network of lanes. The bazar was divided based on the traders: the goldsmiths, the cobblers, the money changers, the perfume sellers, to name a few. The shops, at street level, had storerooms located in their basements where the packing and weighing was done. Trade was also conducted in houses comprising a complex of buildings, which functioned as a mini-bazar with activities ranging from commerce and money changing to running the shop's administrative office. The various houses were named after the main merchandise that was traded: the house of flax, of precious stones, or of almonds, and so on. The commercial centre of the Qalus served wholesalers of flax and other bulky goods. Unlike other cities across Islamic territories Alexandria had no dedicated industrial quarter, with manufacturing activities being conducted in private houses. Also, unlike other Islamic cities, Alexandria did not have one city centre, but two: the commercial and the religious-political. The latter was created after the Muslim conquest and developed in the western part of the city.

Information regarding the Fatimids' involvement in the construction or sponsorship of public buildings in Alexandria is limited, and tainted by anti-Fatimid bias, since Sunni authors who wrote on the city were concerned only with buildings linked to Sunni institutions. However, the absence of curiosity about Alexandria shown in the *Book of Curiosities* may also betray an attitude the Fatimids held towards the city, with the regime not too keen on investing many resources in it. Was there a deliberate policy in not making Alexandria too prominent, thus avoiding the risk of emboldening it as a rival to Cairo? Two mosques are known to have been built inside the city near the commercial area. One was Masjid al-Mu'tamin, built by the city governor, and the other was Jami' al-'Attarin or Jadid. Once the fourth-century Byzantine church of St Athanasius, this building was turned into a mosque soon after the Arab conquest in the seventh century. It was then rebuilt in 1084 by Badr al-Jamali (d. 1094), the Armenian commander who, as we will see, was summoned to Cairo by the imam-caliph al-Mustansir at a time of crisis. This mosque, featuring a North African style with an ornamental garden in its courtyard, is the only one in Alexandria known to have been designated at some point for Isma'ili rituals. The Fatimids used it for propaganda, since the Friday sermon endorsing the regime was delivered there. The mosque was repurposed for Sunni use in the aftermath of the fall of the Fatimid regime.

Between the eleventh and thirteenth centuries there were at least two adjacent synagogues. Churches such as St John the Baptist and St Mary were left to decay, although others survived. The Melkite churches served not only the local Christian population, but the European Catholic merchants who frequented the city. The Church of St Nicholas, for example, was used by Pisan traders, and the Church of St Mary was shared with the Venetians. Sitt al-Mulk donated to one of the city's Melkite churches the ritual paraphernalia that had belonged to her uncle, who had been patriarch of Alexandria. About five Coptic churches and two monasteries were still functioning at this time, most of them outside the confines of the city.

In Alexandria the wealth that the religious and commercial elites accumulated during the Fatimid period was displayed in their private houses through elegance, size, height, fountains and gardens. Famous private palaces came to be immortalized in poems and accounts, to the point that the Alexandrian style became a byword for fine housing. A typical Alexandrian villa belonging to this period was described as having a big guest hall, which could be closed by folding doors, with narrow closed chambers connected to it. At the front of the house there was a ventilation system, which included a wind tower that caused the air to flow from the roof through the whole house. The entrance was through a large open space in which two parallel stone benches were placed on either side. Adjacent to the house there was a small shed made of light materials. At the front there were large windows that looked over the gardens. According to a description of a four-storey house, on the ground floor was the women's apartment and another large room. Above it there were another three residential storeys. On the top floor there was a secret door. A kitchen was also mentioned. In addition, houses such as this might feature an extra room, a cistern, a well and a garden. Of course, there were also houses that were modest and simple. Renting houses in Alexandria was common, likewise for shops and storerooms, which foreign merchants needed to store their merchandise and to lodge in during long months spent in the city.

Until the end of the eleventh century, the city was still divided along ethnic lines. Members of specific Arab tribes occupied entire areas. In 1051, for instance, the Banu Qurra tribe, whose members had settled in one of the new quarters of Alexandria during the Islamic advance in the region, caused serious riots and even took over the city for a while until expelled by the Fatimid vizier al-Yazuri. The mention in the *Book of Curiosities* of this tribe as being present in Alexandria provides us with a clue to the date of the book's completion. While getting rid of the Bani Qurra, the Fatimids, in keeping with their policy of tribal redistribution, replaced them with the more loyal Bani Sunbus. Other areas were inhabited by immigrants grouped together according to their region of origin, although it seems that this division was not so clear-cut by the end of the eleventh century. As in the capital, Cairo, Alexandria also had its al-Qarafa quarter, an area of ancient tombs outside the city walls that became a residential area.[16]

As a gateway city during the Fatimid rule, Alexandria was both a blessing and a curse to the regime. It helped to secure control of international trade, but it also served as a platform for trouble and sedition. During the last quarter of the eleventh century Alexandria became a hub for anti-Fatimid rebellions of various kinds. Alleged agitators, suspected of spying and plotting on behalf of Sunni regimes, were detected passing through the city, and were detained there. The commander Badr al-Jamali crushed all attempts, real or perceived, including one mounted by one of his sons against him. In 1121 Badr's other son and successor, al-Afdal, pushed back Lawata Berbers who had reached the city. In the late eleventh century the city became an important intellectual outpost of Sunni scholarship. Under the Fatimids from the tenth century, Sunni learning in Egypt had remained a constant in the religious and juridical life of the country, thriving in important commercial cities such as Fustat and Tinnis. However, from the late eleventh century onwards, with the onset of the gradual decline of the Fatimid regime in Cairo, and the consequent loss of Tinnis's mercantile prestige, Sunni intellectual elites found Alexandria a more congenial place to live and work in. Two figures dominated the Sunni cultural scene of the city from the eleventh to the twelfth century, the Maliki Andalusian Abu Bakr al-Tartushi (d. 1126) and the Shafi'i Abu Tahir al-Silafi (d. 1180), both of whom contributed to the introduction of the *madrasa* in Egypt. Well established elsewhere in the Islamic territories, in Cairo this Sunni model of theological college was only established in the late twelfth century, after the fall of the Fatimids.

After travelling to Baghdad, Basra, Syria, Jerusalem and more, al-Tartushi arrived in Alexandria at a time when key positions in the city administration were in Sunni hands. These included the local chief judge, a Maliki of Andalusian origins, who invited him to settle there. Around 1125 this judge assigned him a mosque that stood outside the city walls near the Sea Gate. Al-Tartushi himself explained his residence in Alexandria by saying that it was his way to spread correct belief, mingling with the people in order to guide those who had gone astray. Besides refuting Isma'ilism, and challenging the Fatimid administration in Cairo, he authored ardent essays prohibiting the purchase of any merchandise from Christians or Jews. Al-Tartushi, suspicious of foreigners, was active in the port area where he confronted sailors, visitors and customs officers about their morals.

The large presence in Alexandria of traders from Amalfi, Venice, Pisa and Genoa is documented from around the middle of the eleventh century, and seems to have been somewhat encouraged by Muslim rulers over the following decades. They must have appreciated the gains to be made from the goods and money, including tax revenues, that foreign merchants brought. In Alexandria the Venetians are attested from at least 1039, with a steady increase of trade contacts up to the end of the dynasty. As for the Amalfitans, the Fatimid regime put at their disposal a hostel for traders visiting the city and their goods, an indication that the troubles the Amalfitans had suffered in Cairo during the reign of al-'Aziz had been forgotten in the name of commerce. From 1070 onwards, there is evidence that the Muslim authorities granted charters of protection for merchants which became more formalized over time. Italian interest seems to have grown in proportion; a cartulary of a Genoese notary covering the years 1156 to 1164 indicates that most of his clients were interested in Alexandria as much as in the

Frankish East. With the growth in foreign visitors came a growth in the number of trade hostelries which in Alexandria, as in other cities, were located in the port area. Pisan traders, for example, are known to have used one of the hostels in and around 1153. These inns served as depots and lodgings but also as brothels, something that must have troubled the moralist al-Tartushi a great deal.

Having tutored hundreds of students in the house that his wife adapted to school use for him, al-Tartushi was credited with having revived Malikism in Egypt. One of his disciples, Sadr al-Din b. ʿAwf, became the most prominent Maliki teacher of his age. In 1138 Ridwan b. al-Walakhshi (d. 1148), a Sunni who would become a Fatimid vizier, put Ibn ʿAwf in charge of the first fully purpose-built *madrasa* in Egypt. This *madrasa* was on Alexandria's main avenue, by the marketplace. Ibn ʿAwf taught in the city until his death in 1185.[17] Throughout this formative period of *madrasa*-led Sunni learning in Egypt, the houses of reputable *shaykh*s continued to be the preferred gathering places. Ibn ʿAwf's residence was a well-known intellectual centre where jurists used to gather in groups of seven at a time. In Alexandria, in 1149, the Shafiʿi al-ʿAdil b. Sallar, a city governor who became vizier to one of the last Fatimid caliphs, ordered the building of a *madrasa* for Abu Tahir al-Silafi. Of Iranian origin, in Egypt al-Silafi gained a reputation as one of the greatest Sunni scholars of his day. His was the second *madrasa* to be built in Egypt, and the first Shafiʿi one.[18]

Though not immune from bloody rebellions, Alexandria was on the whole less affected by the major upheavals that hit the Fatimid capital hard, and by the vicissitudes that affected the Fatimid regime in consequence. Other factors contributed to turning Alexandria into a destination of choice for Sunnis. One was the long-established presence of Malikis resulting from its proximity to the western stretch of the North African coast. The second was the settlement there of Muslims from al-Andalus who had been driven to the city by the Christian advance southwards in the Iberian Peninsula. Also, Shafiʿi Sunnis from the eastern lands of the Muslim world came to Alexandria for trade and while on pilgrimage. Alexandria also became a refuge for people forced to escape from Cairo. The city enjoyed a favourable strategic position as a stopping place on the international trade route between East and West. From the late eleventh century onwards, at Alexandria one could come and go by sea with relative ease and, if through circumstance one was stuck there, the place itself was not disagreeable.

Up the Nile

The waterways branching off Lake Manzala connected Tinnis to the Nile and all the way to Upper Egypt and the Red Sea. A canal linking the Nile to the Red Sea port of Qulzum had been opened by the Greeks and Romans and re-excavated during the Arab conquests. The *khalij*, as it became known, was then blocked by order of the 'Abbasid caliph al-Mansur (d. 775) but was opened again by the Fatimids, who had founded Cairo near the point of its confluence with the Nile.

Since time immemorial the life of Egypt had depended on and revolved around the flood cycles of the Nile. For the Fatimids success or failure in managing the Nile would also play a part in determining the fate of their rule. It is therefore understandable why in the *Book of Curiosities* much space is given to descriptions of the river, and the largest map in the book is dedicated to it. In this work, the Nile's origin is traced back to the mythical Mountains of the Moon, represented in the shape of what looks like an open parachute. The textual description of the river also mentions another mountain, again in connection to its source, this time located in the middle of a lake. According to Coptic belief it was the amount of snow melting from this mountain that would determine the level of the Nile's water rise. As for forecasting its abundance, the author of the *Book of Curiosities* drew – as elsewhere in his work – on the interrelation between the celestial and the terrestrial realms, advising that speed in the motion of the planet Mars should be observed to determine it in advance.

The period between the years 935 and 1094 was, with a few intervals, one of the driest periods on record in the history of the Nile. The reasons for this phenomenon have been assessed in the context of a global warming phase that affected most of the known world between the eleventh and thirteenth centuries. In addition to the idealized representation in the *Book of Curiosities*, information on the geography of the Nile and the customs that developed around it during the Fatimid period can be derived from the accounts of travellers who journeyed through Egypt at the time. The fascination with the river is also reflected in literature dedicated to the virtues of Egypt, many featuring traditions about the Nile and information about land, taxation, measurements and distances relating to the river. Not unlike the *Book of Curiosities*, compendia of this kind produced during the Fatimid period testify to some of the beliefs surrounding the river's supernatural qualities, its mysterious origins and the Nile's relevance to Islamic sacred history. Many of these contributions touch on environment-related matters. Concerns included the role of the river in the economic and everyday life of communities under Fatimid rule, the Nile as stage and space for ritual, pageantry and public displays of power in Cairo, modes of navigation on the river, its role in shaping the commercial and administrative policies of the dynasty in Upper Egypt, and the challenges the Nile posed to the Fatimids because of periodic wheat penury linked to poor flooding.[19]

The severe low flood of the Nile that afflicted Egypt in the decades prior to 969 had contributed to the collapse of the Ikhshidid rule. While this state of affairs had opened the way to the Fatimids' conquest of Egypt, famines and plagues related to the low river reoccurred with alarming regularity in the decades that followed. Soon after its establishment in Egypt, the Fatimid regime appears to have become aware of the strategic possibilities the Nile offered as the highway to control Upper Egypt and beyond. One of General Jawhar's earliest diplomatic moves was to send envoys to renew the pact with the Christian king of the Nubians, according to which the monarch would pay the Fatimid regime an annual tribute. As a result of this mission a report was compiled containing the earliest known Fatimid survey on the source of the Nile, its rise, its tributaries and cataracts. The Fatimids also sent embassies to Abyssinia, for example during the reign of al-Mustansir (1036–94). These missions took place in the context of competing interests in the region that saw the Fatimids and their respective Abyssinian and Nubian counterparts each seeking to take advantage of the others by exploiting mutual rivalries. The Fatimids have been regarded as among the earliest rulers of Egypt who tried to extend their reach to the lands in the uppermost part of the river. The missions were linked to the fact that the Abyssinian emperors had threatened – as al-Hakim had tried to do before them – to divert the course of the Nile, thus risking the water supply along the whole valley.[20] Tensions between Egypt and Ethiopia over the control of the water of the Nile have continued to this day.

In 973, the imam-caliph al-Mu'izz and his entourage had arrived in the new capital on seven large boats upstream from the Delta. Al-Mu'izz's scenic entrance into his new domains marked the beginning of the Fatimids' long-standing tradition of using the river as a stage for public displays of authority. Once in Cairo al-Mu'izz issued one of the most important early decrees of his rule: he forbade the public announcement of data relating to the rising of the Nile until it reached optimal level. Only he and a specially appointed officer were to be informed in writing about these measurements, and only when the river reached the level of 16 cubits was a public announcement made. Prior to this decree, the unpredictability of the river's rise had meant that people panicked for their livelihoods when early public release of data indicated that the Nile might be low. In response, people hoarded foodstuffs, causing shortages that drove prices up, thus triggering famine.

Al-Mu'izz's decree elevated the rank of the officer in charge of observing the water levels during the rising phase of the river. The official reading of the gradual rise of the Nile took place at the Nilometer on the island of Rawda, although other Nilometers stood along the river. Today the Rawda Nilometer is one of Cairo's most popular tourist sites. The original structure in Rawda, consisting of a well fitted with a pole with measuring tacks that featured monumental Qur'anic epigraphic panels, underwent major additions in the Fatimid era. With the arrival of the Fatimids, during the period of rising water – about forty days – the official in charge would report every day to the imam-caliph. This person received gifts such as riding animals, robes of honour and extra titles in the years when the Nile reached the optimum level of around 18 cubits. According to Nasir-i Khusraw this officer was paid 1,000 *dinar*s a year. When the water reached 18 cubits, drums would be played in towns as a sign of joy. If the rise stalled instead, it could be a sign of insufficient inundation, in which case charity was distributed and sombreness prevailed. In 1008, a poor Nile performance was imputed to moral decline, and al-Hakim issued decrees prohibiting singing by the river and drinking alcohol when sailing its waters.

The Nilometer acquired a sacred-like status, so much so that the site became a catalyst for popular devotion and propitiation rituals. In the years 1008, 1023 and 1085, when the Nile stopped rising, mass prayers took place on the Muqattam hills overlooking Cairo. A public observatory was built for paying spectators to watch the rising of the river. In the twelfth century, this platform collapsed due to overcrowding, causing many deaths. Another viewpoint was built in 1124–5, to replace a precarious wooden one. This structure was destroyed by fire in 1163. In 1092, al-Mustansir built a mosque on the west side of the Nilometer for propitiation purposes. It is however in the twelfth century that we find reference to an elaborate ceremonial that saw the caliph leading a ritual aimed at transforming the status of the Nilometer itself from a profane to a sacred space. At its climax, the ceremony consisted of the perfuming of the Nilometer, celebrated on the Nile reaching the promising 16-cubit level. Unlike other festivals, participation in this ceremony was restricted to the caliph and his closest entourage. On these occasions the caliph and the vizier rode to the Nilometer, where the caliph made a perfume, mixing saffron and musk for the measuring officer. The latter would then jump into the well still dressed, where he would cling to the column with his left arm and anoint it with his right hand while the Qur'an was recited.

Every year, the rising of the water to the highest level marked the most important moment in the Fatimid economic calendar. It signalled the start of the agricultural cycle and, with it, the land tax year. The start of the Fatimids' fiscal year was aligned with the Coptic calendar, which fell between mid-September and early October in the Christian one. The land tax was due after the harvest and its full payment was required before the next seed time could start. The Fatimids adopted a land tax calculation based on the farmers' declaration of intention in using the land. Farmers benefited from this system as they were granted estates and other properties with or without tax liabilities. The Copts benefited too as, even under the Fatimids, the land tax calculation continued to be estimated by them, as they held the monopoly of this occupation. However, it was the ruler (who along with his family and close entourage was a major owner) who granted permission to the peasants to cultivate it. The ruler could not impose tax on arable land until the Nile reached plenitude. After the water receded, an agent surveyed the territory, distinguishing between cultivable land and non-cultivable, and indicated the extent and type of cultivation that was feasible according to the flood level. Where the Nile's rise was insufficient, the ruler did not charge the land tax on the farmers. At harvesting time, the treasurer and secretary serving the regime went out to determine the proportion of crop to be paid as land tax, leaving the remaining harvest to the peasants. These arrangements regarding the payment of land tax were deemed to be based on the unpredictable performance of the Nile along the whole valley. The imposition of a fixed land tax risked creating unfairness, since in that case those who were affected by a low Nile would pay the same as those who were not. Though not conditioned by the Nile floods, the application of the land tax system was extended to the Fatimid domains in Syria and Palestine, much to the displeasure of the governor of Tripoli, today in Lebanon, then in Greater Syria, who in 1032 defected in protest to the Byzantines.[21]

The Fatimid regime relied on an elaborate management system to exploit the Nile's water. Foremost among the government responsibilities was the maintenance of irrigation canals. From the Nile, canals irrigated villages and, if necessary, water could be raised via hydraulic pumps. Villages were built above the river level and during the inundation period they were linked by boat service. A land track along the river served as a road and, according to Nasir-i Khusraw, the treasury paid an officer 10,000 *dinars* for its maintenance. Egypt possessed an unmatched system of waterways and its economic ascendance over its neighbours rested in part on this advantage. But despite the effort the Fatimids put into maintaining their canal networks, diversification in the adoption of irrigation policies across their domains meant that operations were not equally distributed across Egypt. This resulted in the central Fayyum region suffering a sharp decline in the second half of the eleventh century that lasted for over a hundred years. Before this crisis, thanks to a state-regulated water supply, the area had been an important centre for the cultivation of flax intended for the textile industry and international trade, as well as the cultivation of wheat, rice and barley.[22]

In keeping with an ancient system, the canals were closed by dirt dams which were opened when the water reached the appropriate level. The opening of the canals' major dams occurred in the context of ceremonies which the Fatimids transformed into elaborate rituals. In 973, al-Mu'izz rode to the dam at the mouth of the canal that served the capital, at the time outside Cairo, in a grand procession escorted by the dignitaries of the regime. Nasir-i Khusraw gives a detailed description of this ceremony as it took place during the reign of al-Mustansir. At the climax of the event:

> The sultan proceeds to the head of the canal . . . and remains mounted beneath the pavilion for a time. He is then handed a spear, which he throws at the dam. Men quickly set to work with picks and shovels to demolish the dam, and the water that has built up on the other side breaks through and floods the canal . . . The first ship that sails into the canal is filled with deaf-mutes, whom they must consider auspicious. On that day the sultan distributes alms to these people.[23]

The celebration coincided with the Coptic feast of the Holy Cross (27–29 September) and was attended en masse by Muslims and Christians. After the opening of the dams, the Nile flooded the whole valley and it took some forty days for the water to recede before the farmers could start seeding.

Often the Nile underperformed, with disastrous consequences for the population at large and for the fortunes of the dynasty. On these occasions, famine, plagues, price inflation and widespread death occurred. This devastation was, however, due to the regime's economic miscalculation as much as natural disaster. To supply raw material for their lucrative textile industry, the Fatimids limited the growth of wheat in favour of flax crops. While domestic wheat cultivation did not stop, extensive land once used for grain came to be destined to farm flax and other industrial crops like sugar cane. In theory, this policy freed the regime's agricultural programme from its dependency on the river's unpredictability, and on revenues based on perishable goods and consequent market instability as the supplier of the main staple food. Industrial, non-perishable crops could guarantee a regular flow of money to the regime, some of which the ruler could use to import extra wheat, if needed, from North Africa, Sicily, Syria and – thanks to the agreement of mutual support in times of crisis – from Byzantium. Privileging industrial crops favoured farmers while procuring the regime revenues from land tax, retailing of crops and exports of finished products. In practice, however, it also meant that when the Nile flood was low and the arable land at disposal was limited, famine erupted because insufficient space was available for growing wheat. Miscalculation and mismanagement of the state grain reserves to be used in times of penury added to the strain. Fewer crops also meant insufficient fodder for farm animals. Husbandry was caught in a vicious cycle. High human mortality meant that even when the land became available, there was an insufficient workforce to farm it. When low Nile phases coincided, variously, with poor state planning and distribution of wheat reserves, the need to dispatch grain to the *sharif*s of Mecca and Medina to secure their allegiance, adverse geoclimatic conditions across the eastern Mediterranean regions, and volatility in relations between the Fatimids and rival dynasties preventing grain imports, the consequences for the people of Egypt were catastrophic. To some extent these crises were preventable; the regime decided in advance what, where and how much to grow. Giving precedence to industrial crops that were not perishable, thus securing regular cash flow, put public welfare at risk. In the end the regime's self-interest and short termism added long-term damage to that caused by the river's poor performance. That trading interest prevailed over public welfare is indicated by evidence that in the aftermath of bad years the production and trading of flax and its finished products, as well as other industrial crops, was apparently unaffected.

Informed by the scientific knowledge of his time, Ibn Ridwan provided his analysis of the sequence of events leading to famines and epidemics: when pests affect plants, crops fail, prices rise and people are forced to change their eating habits. As large numbers of people increase consumption of particular foods at the same time, dyspepsia increases and illness occurs. This happened at festivals, when crowding and high consumption of food converged. According to Ibn Ridwan, epidemics also happened as a result of people living in fear of the ruler. They felt stressed and lost sleep due to worry for their safety. Under such pressures people became violent, and if a sense of impending famine was looming, they panicked and hoarded food.[24] It seems that he was referring to the time of al-Hakim's rule. On Abu Rakwa's crisis during his reign Ibn Ridwan remarked that the extent of decaying bodies was such that both water and air were polluted. The coinciding of this event with a poor Nile performance led to a catastrophic famine and epidemic.

To the Fatimids, the Nile was not only the bread basket of Egypt but the north–south highway that allowed them to be strong international commercial players. As the implicit message in the maps of the *Book of Curiosities* conveyed, the Fatimids were suppliers of desirable goods and monopoly holders on trade transiting between the Indian Ocean ports, East African trading posts and the Mediterranean regions. Archaeological evidence shows, for example, that direct and regular trade occurred between Fatimid and Swahili traders during the tenth and eleventh centuries. Fatimid merchants were interested in these commercial partners' supply of gold, ivory and rock crystal, the latter originating from islands today known as the Comoros, Madagascar and Mayotte.[25] The Fatimids' access to ivory contributed to a flourishing of Egyptian ivory-carving craftsmanship, and to a similar blossoming in Byzantium, Norman Sicily and al-Andalus. From Cairo tusks reached Europe, where medieval French artists turned them into Christian sacred scenes as well as statuettes of saints and Madonnas.

In 977 a massive earthquake had destroyed the port of Siraf on the Iranian coast of the Persian Gulf, an event that had diverted to the Fatimids' shores a significant volume of trade once under 'Abbasid control. This and other factors all contributed to the Fatimid regime coming to control a vast international commercial network. The Fatimid capital became the nerve centre of a trading exchange whereby goods would transit back and forth between the Mediterranean, via Alexandria, and the river harbours of Fustat and Cairo. From there goods travelled to the Nile's commercial terminals in Upper Egypt, Aswan first and, later, Qus. From these hubs, the network branched off, from ports such as 'Aydhab (and later al-Qusayr), to Yemen, India and East Africa. The Fatimids' efforts to secure administrative and military control of these trading stations reflected the strategic role that Upper Egypt acquired in the eleventh century.

The Fatimids in Upper Egypt

The earliest association of Upper Egypt with the 'Alids goes back to the time of the Islamic conquests. The town of Qift was given as a land grant to 'Alid families in the caliphate of 'Ali b. Abi Talib in the seventh century.[26] Tombstones from the necropolis in Aswan dating from the middle of the third Islamic century onwards point to the presence of 'Alids in that city. Today this site is known as the Fatimid cemetery due to the relative abundance of funerary stelae dating back to that period. There is evidence that the Fatimids pursued a deliberate policy of 'Alidization of the region, by displacing tribes that had inhabited the area long before their arrival, to replace them with 'Alid clans of the Quraysh.[27] The measure was intended to secure the Fatimids' control over Aswan and the towns along the upper Nile valley, as these places gained increasing commercial and administrative strategic importance for the life of the regime. In addition to the region being rich in gold and precious stone mines – emeralds in particular – its cities became entrepôts for the traffic of trade coming into Egypt from the Arabian peninsula, India and East Africa. It is perhaps because of the strong 'Alid association with the region that, on the basis of local legends, the belief grew that illustrious 'Alid descendants of the Prophet Muhammad, such as his grandchildren al-Hasan and al-Husayn, but also distant family members like Sayyida Nafisa and the Shi'i imam Zayn al-'Abidin, were buried in Aswan's necropolis (illus. 33).[28] An eighteenth- or

33 'Fatimid' cemetery, Aswan.

nineteenth-century carved graffito inside one of its mausolea goes as far as claiming the site to be the holy resting place of Fatima, the daughter of Muhammad, although the same burial place has also been associated with the Prophet's granddaughter, Umm Kulthum.[29]

After his arrival in Egypt, General Jawhar had placed Upper Egypt under the control of a commander who was a member of the local Bani Kilab tribe. In 973 this commander defected in favour of the 'Abbasids. To repress what degenerated into a mass uprising Jawhar sent men and weapons on forty ships down the Nile as well as a massive land army. The operation succeeded, with Upper Egypt brought back under control. The rebels' possessions were confiscated and the dissenters' heads paraded across Egypt. In Upper Egypt the Fatimids also had to contend for decades with the presence there of Qarmatians. They were active in the vicinity of Asyut and Akhmim, accused of ransacking properties, killing people and attacking groups of North African origins whom the Fatimids had installed as part of their demographic reworking of the region. The Qarmatians were quashed in 975. During the reign of the imam-caliph al-'Aziz, Jawhar had to crush another defection in Aswan, this time led by a Kutama jurist who, having governed the town, tried to assert his autonomy from his Cairo masters.

The implementation of a pro-Shi'i tribal policy in Upper Egypt had proved providential in the defeat of Abu Rakwa's revolt during the reign of al-Hakim. Defeated in Cairo, Abu Rakwa took refuge in Upper Egypt, where he gained a following. However, he was overcome by the ruler of Aswan, a member of the Bani Rabi'a. The Fatimids had consolidated this tribe's control over the mines in the southeastern Wadi 'Allaqi desert region to protect the area from rival hostile groups. In return for the loyalty shown to the dynasty in the Abu Rakwa affair, al-Hakim bestowed the title of *kanz al-dawla*, treasure of the regime, on the family, an honour that became hereditary and the name by which this local dynasty came to be known. In the year 1023 a large army was sent from Cairo to Upper Egypt to support the local governor in suppressing a revolt mounted by a Khariji activist who had rallied support from tribes such as the Juhayna who were hostile to the Fatimids. When more sedition erupted in that same year, the governor of the region demonstrated loyalty to the Cairo regime by capturing an insurgent from the Bani Husayn tribe who was then charged with al-Hakim's murder. Of all the Arabian tribes who had settled in Upper Egypt, none had its destiny more intertwined with the history of the Fatimids than the Bani Hilal. In the course of Islamic history, a branch of this tribe had relocated, together with the Bani Sulaym, from Arabia to the Delta region. From there, after forming a pro-Qarmatian alliance that the Fatimids defeated, they were forcibly moved to Upper Egypt by the imam-caliph al-'Aziz. In the middle of the eleventh century the Banu Hilal were mobilized by the Cairo regime to march all the way to Ifriqiya to punish the Zirids following their shift of allegiance in favour of the 'Abbasids. Their invasion of North Africa changed the landscape as well as the demography of that region, as the Banu Hilal influenced and shaped the rise of new ruling dynasties. Often described as unsophisticated, the Banu Hilal had in fact developed their own narrative and proud sense of history, expressed through an oral epic poem that chanted their vicissitudes from their ancestry in Arabia to their venture in North Africa. Following a classic canon passed on since the fourteenth century from generation to generation but adapted to fit the times, the poem known as *al-Sira al-Hilaliyya* is still performed in song and music by families of storytellers in the streets of Egypt. A professional performer can undergo up to ten years of training, starting at the age of five. In a twist of fate, it was the rustic Banu Hilal who, in the end, produced one of the most sophisticated Egyptian cultural artefacts. A major example of the Arab folk tradition, this epic is today the only one still performed in its entirety in its musical form. In 2008 the poem's performance was added to the UNESCO Representative List of the Intangible Cultural Heritage of Humanity.

Although these tribal policies strengthened the Arab element in cities like Aswan, not all the inhabitants of the region were of Arab descent. Many were converts to Islam of various ethnic extraction, and there were Jews as well as Nubians. Members of both these groups came to settle in Aswan as traders. The agreement sealed between the Fatimid regime and the king of Nubia secured, beyond the payment of tributes, the commercial flow between the two domains. Fortresses and warehouses were established where traders from whatever denomination could exchange goods. Slaves and also ivory and ostrich feathers arrived from Nubia to the markets of Aswan to be distributed to other destinations. The Copts formed an important part of the population, as demonstrated by the fact that many financed the building of churches well into the eleventh and twelfth centuries. Some of them were turned into mosques during al-Hakim's reign.

By the mid-eleventh century, diplomatic, administrative and commercial relations between the regime in Cairo and Upper Egypt appear to have strengthened. For example, a wealthy dignitary from al-Muhadditha, a town near Aswan, travelled by boat up the Nile to ingratiate himself with the imam-caliph al-Zahir by presenting him with a gift that included horses, a number of male and female Black slaves, a cheetah, Nubian sheep, birds, monkeys and elephant tusks. Officers from Upper Egypt took charge of the *diwan* of the Kutama, among them the Jewish merchant Sadaqa b. Yusuf al-Fallahi. This individual had arrived in Cairo from an earlier posting in Upper Egypt, only to be met with the wrath of al-Zahir's wife, the mother of al-Mustansir, who was to become one of the most influential women in the history of the dynasty. In the early 1050s Nasir-i Khusraw described his encounter in Aswan with a local savant-cum-merchant. The account of the meeting is illustrative of the type of financial transactions that might take place in such a bustling trading hub: this man gave Nasir-i Khusraw a promissory note to hand to one of his agents in the port of 'Aydhab should Nasir need money (he did). Nasir-i Khusraw claimed that when he arrived in 'Aydhab, from where he set sail three months later to reach the Arabian coast, the people asked him to deliver the Friday sermon.

By the time of Nasir-i Khusraw's journey through Upper Egypt, and in the decade that followed, Qulzum had long been abandoned as the port of choice to cross the Red Sea in favour of the ʿAydhab-Aswan or ʿAydhab-Qus routes. Qus grew so much in strategic importance that by the second half of the eleventh century the city governor had become the second most important administrative figure in Egypt, after the vizier in Cairo. He was responsible for the Fatimid mercantile fleet in the Red Sea. The privileging of these routes grew with the establishment of the Sulayhids and other sub-groups as vassal dynasties of the Fatimids in Yemen. With their military and commercial prominence in the Mediterranean challenged by old rivals and the rise of new political adversaries, the Fatimids redirected *daʿwa* and trading activities southwards, with Yemen having been resurrected as a vital outpost through which commercial exchange with the Indian Ocean ports could be increased. Control of these routes made it imperative to secure the flow of the *daʿwa* and commercial traffic between Egypt and Yemen. As a result, the strategic importance of Upper Egypt as a distribution centre for the Fatimids increased further. All the stakeholders in the region benefited from the Fatimids' control of this network. The Christian Nubians had their own vested interest in the Fatimid commitment to keep safe and manned the desert route from Aswan to ʿAydhab that, across the Red Sea, took them to the Arabian coast.

With the rise of Upper Egypt's importance in serving the interests of the regime, however, so also grew the potential for interested parties in the region to hold the Cairo court to ransom. Indeed, Aswan was the theatre for an episode that saw Turk and Black army contingents fighting over the delivery to al-Mustansir of a gift sent from Yemen. The importance to both the Fatimids and the Sulayhids of ensuring stability in Upper Egypt for mutual benefit is reflected in letters sent by al-Mustansir to the Sulayhid sovereign of Yemen, reassuring him about the pacification of that region and about new efforts to maintain order there. Eventually several long-standing local supporters of the Fatimid regime tried to assert themselves as autonomous rulers. In 1076 a member of the Kanz al-Dawla revolted in Aswan; near Akhmim local tribes formed an anti-Fatimid coalition; Black troops pushed to Upper Egypt by rival Turks continued to cause havoc. Eventually these seditions were quashed and the region was brought back under Fatimid authority.

In the early twelfth century a Fatimid expedition was sent from Qus to help restore order in the Sulayhid domains. The relevance that

Upper Egypt had gained for the Fatimids influenced in turn the circumstances of other Yemeni Shiʿi dynasties, such as the Zurayʿids in Aden (1080–1173). Once sub-vassals of the Sulayhids, they had adopted the title of *daʿis* as propagators of ʿAlid doctrines, and recognized the legitimacy and authority of the Cairo regime. This local dynasty had prospered from the trade between Fatimid Egypt and India that passed through the Red Sea. Despite the frequent pacifications, however, Upper Egypt would again become a theatre for extensive internal turmoil and acts of dissent during the rule of the last Fatimid caliphs.[30]

The World Beyond Egypt

By the mid-eleventh century the Fatimids had come to terms with envisioning a reconfigured Cairo as the heart of the universal Islamic empire that one day the dynasty expected to rule. Though still part of the rhetorical repertoire, the conquest of Baghdad was no longer a feature of the Fatimid political narrative. That Baghdad had become irrelevant is evident by the fact that the city receives no attention in the *Book of Curiosities*. Also noteworthy is the lack of references to Jerusalem in the text. The Fatimids' hold on Syria and Palestine had been patchy and tenuous, being threatened by regular conflicts with the Byzantines, confrontations with the Qarmatians and the shifting loyalties of local tribes. From the second half of the eleventh century onwards Tripoli and other coastal towns that had prospered as hubs of Fatimid trade became semi-independent city-states governed by local dynasties of Twelver Shiʿi judges.

The fragile presence of the Fatimids in Syria meant that there was never enough continuity of rule to enable them to leave a strong visible mark on the land through extensive construction works. Apart from the shrine dedicated to the hidden imam ʿAbd Allah the Elder built in Salamiyya during al-Hakim's caliphate, the other significant appearance of the Fatimids on the Syro-Palestinian urban landscape was limited to restoration works, the most significant of which were carried out during al-Zahir's reign. To these his successor al-Mustansir added a monastery, a church, a hospital and two hostels which he had allowed the Amalfitan traders to build near the site of the Holy Sepulchre.[31] Many of al-Zahir's building projects in the region took place in response to earthquakes that hit the Jordan valley in the first half of the eleventh century, which caused widespread destruction and death. Beyond architecture, outside Damascus, Aleppo and Jerusalem, other locations in the region with a Fatimid association include Alexandretta (today Iskenderun in Turkey) and Apamea by the Orontes river. These were the theatre for crucial battles between the Fatimids and the Byzantines at the end of the tenth century. Besides 'Asqalan, Tripoli on the then Syrian coast remained a valued hub which served the Fatimids' interests in the eastern Mediterranean throughout the history of their empire.

In the *Book of Curiosities* Mecca and Medina are represented on account of the sacredness of these cities, but also because at the time their *sharif*s still recognized Fatimid suzerainty in return for receiving financial sponsorship. In practice, the Sunni revival in the eastern lands of the 'Abbasid empire had forced the Fatimids to turn their gaze in other directions. India, China, Central Asia, East Africa as well as the coasts around the Indian Ocean now captured Cairo's attention. Even the Philippines might not have been out of bounds. The revival of the Isma'ili penetration of Yemen injected new enthusiasm for a region that had long been forgotten. The memory of the Fatimids' hold on Sindh looms large in the maps of the *Book of Curiosities*. The tracing of routes that put that region (where some Isma'ilis had survived the Ghaznavid onslaught) at the junction of trade towards China and India betrays the Fatimids' desire to reclaim the memory of a once-important *da'wa* outpost. The maps of the *Book of Curiosities* reflect this reorientation of the Fatimids' priorities in terms of untapped opportunities for commerce as well as Isma'ili propaganda. In this respect parts of the *Book of Curiosities* could be read as a *Lonely Planet Guide* for *da'is* to travel by sea or land – for real or in imagination or via carriers – to the most remote regions of the world to promote the Cairo imams' cause.

For two centuries the Fatimids had been able to capitalize on the synergies that this multifaceted landscape generated. Notwithstanding occasional yet brutal crises, the empire enjoyed an overall buoyant economy that found its expression in a vibrant cultural climate and in the output of a kaleidoscopic array of artefacts for all to see, enjoy, envy and imitate. But how was the empire managed in order to make all of this happen?

7

From Propaganda Ideals to Managing the State Administration

When seen from the Isma'ilis' perspective, the advent of the Fatimids conformed to the fulfilment of expectations based on what had developed into their distinctive cyclical vision of history. According to this vision, the manifestation of the imamate that the dynasty embodied was not an accidental event shaped by temporal contingencies. It was instead the ultimate fulfilment on earth of a God-preordained plan for humankind, the physical manifestation of an archetypal spiritual order. The imam, as material hypostasis resulting from an emanative process that originated in the universal intellect – that is, the first principle from which God caused the creation to be – was the proof of this plan. In Islamic belief, in keeping with a covenantal vision of sacred history, from the moment of creation God sent a sequence of prophets to each community, starting with Adam, to command humanity's obedience and to warn of the consequences of failing to be so. Among many, these prophets included (besides Adam) Noah, Abraham, Moses and Jesus, with the last of them all being Muhammad who, according to Islamic dogma, is the final God-sent messenger to humanity. As such, for Muslims Muhammad came with a universal mandate: to affirm once and for all the ultimate true religion – at its core the return to the absolute obedience to one God – as first intended at the moment of creation.

The Isma'ilis call the prophets sent by God *natiq*s, that is, speaking, since they consider them bringers of an outward, 'spoken', literal divine revelation. With it each prophet communicates to the community of his cycle of prophethood a set of divine instructions for it to abide by. The Isma'ilis came to believe that in each of such prophetic cycles God assigned to each of his envoys a silent counterpart, a legatee or *wasi*, as the receiver of the divine message's esoteric meaning. With regard to Muhammad's time they identify the foundation, *asas*, of divine esoteric wisdom in his cousin and son-in-law, 'Ali. As Muslims, the Isma'ilis believe that Muhammad's outer revelation is the final one but they also assert that God would never leave people without guidance towards fulfilling the true meaning of the revelation, that is, its esoteric significance. The full realization of this inner dimension would occur at the Resurrection, when the performance of the outer obligatory divine instructions would be lifted for the true believers.

In keeping with this belief, 'Ali, the repository of this enabling divine knowledge during Muhammad's cycle of revelation, was the first of a sequence of guides, *imams*, in his line of descent. These were entrusted with the preservation and perpetuation of this wisdom. Throughout its history the imamate underwent alternating cycles of manifestation and occultation due to safety concerns in the face of oppression. With the Fatimids, the imamate was made present and visible on earth, tasked with performing its salvific messianic mission until the Day of Judgement. In this light, the eschatological function was no longer to be understood as pertaining to an individual imam expected to manifest himself at an imminent apocalyptic time. Instead, the role of this figure was to be performed by the dynasty as a whole until the future eschaton, the Last Days culminating in the final Resurrection. But how could a metaphysical theocratic idea of state be translated into an ever-sustainable temporal governance? Neoplatonic cosmology and Aristotelian philosophy provided Isma'ili thinkers with an interpretative key to rationalize the overcoming of the gap separating the realm of the transcendent from that of the immanent world. Isma'ili thought as formulated in the tenth century and elaborated further explained how the terrestrial microcosm was the reflection of a celestial macrocosm, how the order of the universe arranged along hierarchies and spheres had its corresponding parallels in the imam and the spiritual ranks below him; how the imamate was the bridge that linked the metaphysical and the physical worlds. The imam was the medium through whom metaphysical esoteric wisdom entered the realm of materiality. In the world, the implementation of God's divine plan that the Fatimid imams had made tangible with their presence became operational with the implementation of the *dawla*. This was the state apparatus run through a government machine consisting of religious and secular institutions (the boundary that exists between the two being often blurred), offices and administrative departments.[1]

The Religious Institutions

Upon unveiling himself as the ultimate manifest religious-political agent tasked to lead the universal Muslim community, the Fatimid imam became to his followers and his subjects not only imam but caliph. He was caliph of God in his role as divine spiritual vicar on earth and caliph of the Prophet in his capacity as the exclusive executive leader of the Muslim community. This was on the basis of genealogical descent from Muhammad and ʻAli, respective embodiments of the literal and esoteric contents of God's last revelation. The imam-caliph was *amir*, commander, at once supreme spiritual and temporal leader of the Ismaʻili *mu'mins* and head of the ultimate office governing the affairs of all *muslims*. As supreme master of *daʻwa* and *dawla*, for the Ismaʻilis the imam's authority rested on him being recognized as the infallible and sole repository of the totality of the eternal truths, *haqa'iq*, concealed behind every manifest aspect of life. By virtue of their ownership of this knowledge the Fatimid imams were infallible, since they were believed to have unlimited powers of insight and divination. Among the Shiʻis in general the imams' innate acquisition of this knowledge was explained through the doctrine of *nur Muhammadi*. According to this belief an eternal luminous prophetic light was transmitted via genealogy from Adam to Muhammad and then to ʻAli and his progeny from Muhammad's daughter, Fatima. Alongside Muhammad's light, ʻAli also came to be seen by the Shiʻis as the recipient of *nur Allah* (the light of God), a light encapsulating all divine spiritual virtues and eternal knowledge, the permanence of which was to be continued via ʻAli and the imams in his line. In addition, among the Shiʻis and the Ismaʻilis in particular the modality of how this light would pass on from one imam to the next was resolved by the principle of *nass*. Being infallible and all-knowing, the incumbent imam had the power, exclusive knowledge and sole prerogative to appoint his successor.

At the heart of this true knowledge was the imam's unique ownership of the inner meaning thought to be behind the literal text of the Qur'an. The belief in the existence of an esoteric version of the Qur'an was rooted in prophetic traditions ascribed to Muhammad according to which, alongside the outer Qur'anic revelation, Muhammad had also received the knowledge of its hidden, esoteric meaning. These and other narratives led to a belief in some quarters in the existence of a book containing this secret wisdom. In one tradition, for example, Muhammad is reported as saying, 'Verily, I was given the Book and with it something like it,' the latter expression interpreted to mean esoteric knowledge.[2]

References to the existence of a secret written book that was circulated among the Prophet's household members generated speculations on the content of this text, the practical means by which it was preserved and how it was passed on. Fatima stands out as a locus of esoteric knowledge to the point of being credited with having had her own *mushaf* (lit. 'codex', but typically intended to mean a written copy of the Qur'an). According to Shi'i transmitters of prophetic traditions, that is, those who, mainly through travel, learned about and exchanged *hadith*s, this was a book consisting of a corpus of texts in which the angel Gabriel consoled Fatima in the aftermath of Muhammad's death by disclosing to her future events. For this reason, this book, whose physical existence remained elusive, came to be ascribed divinatory power. Another narrative reported that the Prophet gave a book written by himself to one of his wives, Umm Salama, who then passed it to 'Ali, credited to have said that the book contained new knowledge beyond what featured in the Qur'an and the traditions.[3]

The promise to disclose this esoteric knowledge among the Isma'ili believers made it incumbent on them to strive to attain it as much as possible in order to gain guidance on spiritual and temporal conduct towards the ultimate fulfilment of their faith. The imam in turn released this wisdom to his followers in stages, and in part on the basis of their inner spiritual and intellectual strengths. However, the imam's willingness to share at least part of this knowledge with his community was hampered by a practical obstacle: although omnipresent in a metaphysical sense, in practice the physical imam was located in one place, meaning that he could not be reached by all, at all times, irrespective of whether he was hidden or manifest. The limitation imposed on believers by lack of proximity to the imam was however overcome thanks to the belief that, while the imam was the ultimate holder of the esoteric knowledge, his closest associates – the highest-ranking propagandists, the *da'is* – once authorized by the imam and under his instruction, could disseminate the imam's exclusive wisdom through the power of decoding they were delegated with.

Allegorical or esoteric interpretation, *ta'wil*, refers to the exegetical practice of going back to the primal meaning behind the manifest Qur'anic revelation. By extension this method applied to the power of capturing the true meaning behind ambiguous verses of the holy book and, beyond the scriptural context, to extracting the ultimate true significance behind every aspect of mundane life. Through the *da'i*, the knowledge released via the application of *ta'wil* could be shared among those deserving believers on the basis of their stage of personal advancement. As a prime spiritual envoy, the *da'i* was invested with the authority of carrying out activities in the imam's name, aimed at establishing his universal rule. The *da'i* was therefore the gate through whom the Isma'ili follower could enter the path to the attainment of a superior wisdom and, with it, benefit from an enhanced state of existence. Over time, the figure of the *da'i* came to encompass a number of roles: teacher, community leader, propagandist and political as well as spiritual agent.

Begun as the operational network of an underground movement dedicated to the cause of Isma'ili imams in hiding out of safety concerns, the *da'wa* became an organized instrument of the state following the open inauguration of the Fatimid dynasty in 909. While the 'Abbasids dismantled their propaganda machine once in power, for the Fatimids the *da'wa* continued to function as the ideological militant arm that the regime needed to fulfil its ultimate aspiration, the unseating of the 'Abbasids and the attainment of universal rule.

The organization of this organ of the state comprised a number of professional ranks arranged in descending order. The chief *da'i* had responsibility for preparing lectures which were approved by the imam. Copies of the sermons were then distributed to all the *da'is* operating in all the Isma'ili communities. In the territories that came to be under direct or indirect Fatimid control, the *da'is* were given authority to recruit followers, administer oaths of allegiance and deliver lectures to them during learning sessions. While Cairo became the *da'wa* headquarters, Isma'ili propaganda was also operational in Syria and Palestine. In regions outside the Fatimids' control, the *da'wa* continued to be active underground. The areas where this secret mission was carried out were divided into twelve so-called islands, each with an appointed high-ranking *da'i* called *hujja*, proof. In the tenth century, al-Qadi al-Nu'man named these regions as Arabia, Byzantine-controlled territories, Slav regions, Nubia, the land of the Khazars (today part of

Russia, Ukraine, Crimea and Kazakhstan), India, Sindh, sub-Saharan Africa, Abyssinia, China, Berber territories and Daylam in Iran.[4] In the latter, important cells came to be established in Shiraz, Rayy and the Caspian Sea area.

The lowest rank among those who served in the *da'wa* organization was that of the *mukasir*, the breaker. His task was to engage possible adepts in debates and refutations in order to sow doubt in them about their beliefs. In territories outside the boundaries of the Fatimid empire, to ensure that the right persons were dispatched to fulfil this role, the *da'i* sent activists familiar with local languages and customs in order to persuade the population. *Da'i*s were expected to travel to inspect the islands in order to familiarize themselves with the nature of people's beliefs and the kind of discussions they would respond to. The *mukasir*s then moved in, identified those likely to pledge allegiance to the imam and, resorting to arguments, broad knowledge, dialectic and rhetoric, sought to break them. In this respect the Isma'ili propagandist also acted as a cultural broker, dispatching his message but also acquiring and even adopting the cultural traits of the people he operated among, if only for purposes of disguise.[5]

The taking of an oath of allegiance granted formal entrance into the Isma'ili community and participation in the activities of the *da'wa*. The elusiveness surrounding the content of the Isma'ili oath and the means by which it was administered have been the subject of much speculation and defamation among anti-Isma'ili polemists. Conspiracy theories, stories about secret societies and fantasies of masonic-like initiations have surrounded the Isma'ilis to this day. Taken at face value, the protocol of entering the Isma'ili fold was instead rather prosaic. After the *mukasir* had succeeded in his task, three days passed before the oath could be taken by the novice. At the ceremony both *da'i* and adept underwent purification rituals, with two prayer-like prostrations completing the procedure. The *da'i* then started to praise God and the imam and to seal the oath and *baya* (homage) to the imam of the time as prescribed in the text of the pact. At some point the formula of this credo became gender-specific. The *da'i* pledged the adept to believe in God, the angels, the imams as representatives of Muhammad and 'Ali down to the imam of the time; to adhere to the exoteric and the esoteric realms of existence; to obey and stand up for the imam; to not reveal the secrets of the religion to unauthorized persons or non-Isma'ilis; to be loyal to brothers in faith; to be the friend of friends and the enemy of enemies of the imam. The *da'i* then swore the new adept to the imam. Once initiated, the novice was to be nourished with knowledge, stage by stage, based on its degrees of complexity. Upon progressing, the believer became known as *mustajib*, the one who responds when summoned. Since *mustajib*s displayed different abilities from each other, the *da'i* educated them in different rooms of his house – sometimes at particular times – according to specific syllabi. Irrespective of abilities, the syllabus at this stage included knowledge of the unity of God, the prophets and the imams; the ranks of the *da'wa*; the structure of celestial spheres and their respective metaphysical correspondences to the *da'wa* hierarchy. The *da'i* had a duty to answer questions in relation to the appropriate level of knowledge delivered. In some cases, the *da'i* had to research his answer before giving it to the adept.

Once advanced at *mustajib* stage, the initiate could progress to take an active role in the *da'wa* as *ma'dhun*. This figure assisted the *hujja*s operating in clandestine conditions outside the sphere of the Fatimid empire. The *ma'dhun* was allowed, under supervision, to give tuition to *mustajib*s, having attended training sessions designed for this rank. From among the *ma'dhun*s the *da'i*s selected the candidates who showed more promise to progress to the level of *da'i*, a stage that, once reached, was sanctioned by final approval from the community and leaders. Until that moment, although the *ma'dhun* could operate with some degree of independence, he still had to be supervised until deemed suitable to take charge of an island as *hujja*. The *hujja*, working far from the fountainhead of wisdom, received the imam's instructions from the chief *da'i* in Cairo. In some cases, either from the provinces of the empire or the regions where cells operated, the most talented *da'i*s or *hujja*s were summoned or made their way to Cairo for special training or to contribute with their knowledge and writings to the intellectual life of the *da'wa* headquarters. When not in person, the exchange of communication between the seat of *da'wa* in Cairo, the imam and remote cells took place via couriers who travelled under the guise of merchants or pilgrims. However, since the circulation of correspondence could be slow and unsafe, local *da'i*s were granted some degree of independent decision making.

Before the open disclosure of the line of the imams in North Africa and in those territories outside the *dawla*, all *da'wa* activities had run undercover. To that end Isma'ilis were allowed to resort to religious dissimulation, *taqiyya*, that is, outwardly pretending to adhere to another Islamic school of thought.

Treatises written by Isma'ilis for Isma'ilis between the tenth and eleventh centuries, the study of which became open to non-Isma'ilis only from the early twentieth century onwards, give insight into the profile of the ideal *da'i* and his responsibilities towards his community. The *da'i* was expected to make his house the forum around which local Isma'ili communities gathered. For this reason, the *da'i* had to have a large household and be wealthy, enjoying the support of his family as well as that of servants and assistants. The *da'i*'s wife and children had to be examples of probity. The hiring of the doorman required extensive scrutiny since this person had to be discreet about the goings-on in the house and proper in conduct towards the guests. Since the house of the *da'i* had to be open to all believers including women and children, the doorman had to be respectful to women and not harass them. The *da'i* was expected to be a knowledgeable and well-integrated person within the wider community he lived among, able to establish close connections with the local elites. In his house, the believers joined the *da'i* in the recitation of the Qur'an and prayers. He educated them as well as admonished them. No jokes could be cracked during these sessions. The *da'i* had to ensure that the social life of his community was based on solidarity and mutual care. Those who stirred hatred for the brothers in faith could face being expelled from the community. Believers were expected to obey the imam, love him and give to him in kind. In return the *da'i* took care of the needs of the community and, if necessary, acted as intermediary between the believer and the imam, provided that requests were appropriate.[6] The *da'i*, though not a ruler or judge, was delegated judicial authority in his community and therefore the believer had to obey his verdict. If an offence was committed, the *da'i* had the authority to reprimand and punish. If the imam gave an order, his followers had to obey him and the *da'i* was responsible for ensuring that was done. During learning sessions, the *da'i* had to reassure the believers in times of trouble, promising joy and reward. In turn initiates had to play their role in stopping anyone suspected of wanting to deceive the imam. A *da'i* was instructed to keep a close eye on each member of the community to evaluate each person's reliability, but also to identify those suitable to advance in the reception of higher knowledge. Traits to look for included ambition, intelligence, respectability and outward adherence to the prescribed law. This talent scouting was vital to secure the future of Isma'ili leadership in remote communities. The *da'i* was in charge of the money needed to finance the cause of the imam. It was his duty to collect dues in the imam's name, sending part of the money to the Cairo headquarters and retaining some to redistribute at local level to finance the organization of the *da'wa*.[7] Against all the odds, the *da'wa* grew into a smooth operation that functioned for centuries. In Cairo and a few other locations, some *da'i*s excelled in recording allegorical insights as reflected in their production of theological, doctrinal and legal literary works. Benefitting from their closeness to the imam and access to the libraries the Fatimids became famous for, these *da'i*s-cum-scholars went on to contribute to the formation of what, to this day, constitutes the foundational canon of Isma'ili doctrinal and devotional literature.

Religious and legal instruction for the subjects of the regime took place in different settings depending on whether the recipient was an Isma'ili or not. The chief *da'i* was expected to be knowledgeable in all the doctrines relating to the family of the Prophet on which he would lecture. From at least the first quarter of the eleventh century the chief *da'i* was assisted by a number of secretaries who, twice a week, helped him in the redaction of a sermon that he then submitted to the imam for final approval and countersigning. Given the secrecy surrounding the sharing of esoteric knowledge, for Isma'ilis in the Cairo court the learning sessions were conducted in the palace on Thursdays. During them the chief *da'i* delivered the lectures to men while sitting on a special chair in the grand hall. He addressed the women from a separate room. At the end of the sessions the believers kissed his hand, an act to which he responded by touching their heads with a scroll bearing the signature of the imam-caliph. In return for the blessing the chief *da'i* proceeded to collect money to be given to the imam. Affluent Isma'ili faithful could ask for personalized blessings in return for a more generous fee. Names and amounts paid were recorded in account books. Ordinary believers listened to sermons in al-Azhar.[8] Those who were not Isma'ili needed to know about the Fatimids' take on the application of the outer aspect of the law governing the state. They were instructed via sessions held every week in the mosques across the capital and the Fatimid domains.

The figure that bridged the gap between the realm of the imamate for Isma'ili devotees and that of the caliphate for the subjects at large was the chief judge, *qadi*. During the North African days of the dynasty, the figure of the *qadi* blended with that of the *hakim*, a junior jurist role that grew in importance through management of the practical handling of people's petitions. Once in Egypt, and for most of the duration of the Fatimid regime, the figure of the *qadi* took centre stage and gained a sharper focus when the roles of chief *da'i* and chief *qadi* became embodied, in many instances, in the same person. With a few exceptions at the end of the Fatimid regime, the chief *qadi* was an Isma'ili who – bar some notable exclusions during al-Hakim's reign – had jurisdiction (in some areas only nominal) over all the territories under direct or indirect Fatimid rule. On the whole, this role came to be retained within the same families, with the Nu'mans being the ultimate example of monopoly over Isma'ili jurisprudence passed on through a dynastic line. The last of the Nu'mans, al-Qasim, was reputed to have been not as brilliant as his ancestors in the role of judge as well as head of the *da'wa*, but he retained his position for some twenty years nonetheless.

The formal investiture of the chief *qadi* was an elaborate affair that took place at the royal palace and at al-Azhar Mosque in the presence of the imam-caliph and the high dignitaries of the state. For example, in 976 'Ali, son of al-Qadi al-Nu'man was appointed *qadi* at a public ceremony in al-Azhar to advertise the judge's role in the state as part of the ruling establishment, with executive powers symbolized by the insignia bestowed upon him. In general, the ceremony involved the reading of the diploma of conferment, after which the appointed person stood up, bowed his head and kissed the ground each time the name of the imam was mentioned. At the palace, the new *qadi* received ceremonial gifts, which included a robe of honour, gowns, a sword, a turban and grey mules, a colour associated with this dignitary. In procession, preceded by witnesses, the nominated *qadi* was escorted to al-Azhar where one of his relatives read the diploma again and, after that, the same was repeated at the 'Amr Mosque.

After this ceremony the chief *qadi* had the authority to appoint deputy judges as well as certified functionaries whose role was to bear witness to court proceedings. Although the *qadi* had discretion in deciding how many court sessions to hold, in practice these took place between two and four times a week, in the city's two main mosques. The rest of the week was devoted to administration and a day of rest. Staff assisting the *qadi* included two chamberlains standing by his office, two porters at the main gate of the court and one chaperon to escort litigants to the presence of the *qadi*. Four secretaries transcribed the proceedings and one valet held the *qadi*'s silver inkwell. In front of the *qadi*, who had the right to punish any disruption of procedure or misconduct, litigants could be represented by agents. In turn the *qadi* availed himself of the prerogative of consulting jurists from other legal schools if needed. In time, though, he administered justice on the basis of Fatimid law.

The Fatimid chief *qadi*, exempt from jurisdiction over the army, had responsibility for the theoretical formulation of jurisprudence, the oversight of the administration of justice and the performance of religious rituals and preaching in mosques. Though in theory the handling of petitions became the chief *qadi*'s responsibility, de facto the vizier administered them. In Cairo the office of petitions was for some time located in an annex to the Ibn Tulun Mosque, but by the end of the eleventh century it had been moved to a corner of the royal palace. There the vizier chaired the sessions, assisted by the chief *qadi* with two certified witnesses. The vizier was flanked by a secretary of the imam-caliph and a senior financial inspector, faced by the imam's chamberlain and the head of the military. At other times the sessions might be chaired by a lower-ranking officer who held court by the Golden Gate at the palace. The start of proceedings was announced by a crier inviting the plaintiffs to submit their complaints. Oral complaints were transcribed, to be dispatched to relevant judges for deliberation. A secretary handled written petitions sent from outside the capital. The chancery took care of submitting the letters to the imam, who had his verdict recorded on the back of the missive or written in interlinear spaces. The chancery then returned the letter to the original sender. According to Nasir-i Khusraw, 'The chief justice receives a monthly stipend of 2,000 *dinar*s, and thus every judge down the scale so that the people need not fear venality from the bench.'[9]

In time, and in response to contingencies, the chief *qadi* took up a number of roles and functions that stretched beyond the judiciary. In the tenth century, for example, this high officer monitored the correct application of the inheritance laws; oversaw the mint, controlling the purity of gold and silver coinage; checked the production of weights and measures, and, sometimes, managed pious endowments. The Nu'man family even came to oversee the production of *tiraz* textiles and their delivery to the court. At times, the roles of the chief *qadi* and that of the chief of police (an independent officer in charge of the criminal justice system) overlapped, with consequent friction between the two institutions. Also blurred was the boundary between the head of the judiciary and that of the *hisba*, an office that dealt with market inspection but that under the Fatimids also served to keep order and control in other areas of public life.

The chief *qadi* was the head of a network of jurists appointed across the Fatimid domains to ensure that the Fatimid interpretation of Islamic law was applied across the empire. In Egypt, in the early years of the dynasty's instalment, a parallel system was kept in place with Sunni jurists taking care of the needs of the majority non-Isma'ili population. At one level, this arrangement was in keeping with Jawhar's promise made to the population after his arrival in 969. However, it was also a pragmatic move since the regime had not yet trained enough Isma'ili jurists to take posts on a large scale. Over time a number of Sunni *qadi*s continued to serve the needs of the Sunni population while working for the Isma'ili regime. They were required to apply Fatimid law in matters of state governance and whenever there was disparity of opinion with the other schools of law. In the tenth century, under Ibn Killis, the vizirate rivalled the judiciary. The vizier resorted to measures aimed at curtailing the power of the Nu'mans by, for example, establishing that each *qadi* was independent in his decision and that no one was allowed to appeal to other judges. This measure was intended to curb what had become a popular practice, resorted to by dissatisfied defendants who hopped from a *qadi* of one school to another seeking to have unfavourable judgements overturned. The power game between the vizirate and the office of the *qadi* underscored tensions at the heart of the Fatimid administration that lasted until the end of the dynasty, with viziers taking over the headship as *qadi* and chief *da'i* as well, or demoting the role of chief *qadi* to that of deputy vizier. In the twelfth century a radical change was introduced into Egypt's judicial system with the appointment of four judges, each representing a school of law: Shafi'i, Maliki, Isma'ili and Imami Shi'i. By that time, the primacy of Isma'ili law at the heart of the regime was over.

The figure of prestige ranked closest in importance to the *qadi* and the *da'i*, associated with Islamic public life, was that of the *muhtasib*, the market inspector. The *hisba*, an office with pre-Islamic antecedents, was at its core a religious institution since it was tasked with the practical implementation of the Qur'anic commandment to uphold the right and forbid the wrong.[10] Upon arriving in Egypt, Jawhar took care of restoring order in the markets and controlling prices to address the economic collapse left behind by the Ikhshidids. He appointed to the task Sulayman b. 'Azza as *muhtasib* of Fustat. The Fatimid *muhtasib*, chosen from among the ruling elites by the chief *qadi* with grand pomp and the bestowal of robes of honour, operated across the empire via delegates. As for his tasks, in addition to those performed by counterparts across the Islamic territories, the Fatimid *muhtasib* had to enforce additional morality and religious prescriptions as designated under Isma'ili law. In Cairo, every other day the head of this office held court at the two main mosques of the capital. The role of *hisba* and the police could somewhat overlap, but the two institutions catered for two separate spheres. It was the duty of the police to combat crime and administer punishments, including the death penalty on criminals and apostates, upon the imam's authorization. The *hisba* instead had exclusive responsibility for the inspection of markets to ensure the standards of products were respected and that no cheating took place in vendor–customer transactions. For example, the *muhtasib* played a particular role in safeguarding the interests of women involved in the textile cottage industry.[11] The Fatimid *muhtasib*'s responsibility extended to checking state-issued weights and measures to ensure they had not been tampered with; supervision of the public conduct imposed on non-Muslims such as wearing distinctive items of clothing; ensuring that beasts of burden were not overloaded; securing clear passage and cleanliness of the city's roads; ensuring no fouling compromised the sanctity of the mosques; regulation of water distribution; monitoring of the grain trade and the supply of bread in times of shortage.[12] In Fustat, where the main market for the sale of bread was located, a head of breadmaking was in charge of supervising the quality of what was sold. Frauds were frequent with, for example, vendors wetting loaves to make them heavier to cheat customers on weight. The vast majority of people relied on market vendors for their needs since buying flour to make dough and bake it at home was only done in upper-class households that had a private oven. It was also common to prepare the dough at home and then take it to the bakers in return for payment. The *muhtasib* checked that goods at fixed prices were indeed sold that way. When wrongdoing was detected, this figure had executive roles such as administering punishments to offenders: public beating and shameful parading were the norm. More often than not the *muhtasib* was caught in a catch-22. During al-Zahir's reign, in times of crisis, the market inspector banned the slaughtering of cattle.

Lacking bread, hungry people were consuming meat instead, which meant that fewer cattle were available to farmers to work in the fields. However, the butchers complained since it became expensive for them to keep animals which were no longer used for work but that still needed feeding while being deprived of their expected income.

The *hisba* often worked in tandem with the police, *shurta*. Until at least the mid-eleventh century in the capital there were three separate police forces. The Upper and the Lower ones were in Fustat. Separate from both was the Cairo police. These were merged in the time of crisis that engulfed Cairo and Egypt during al-Mustansir's reign. In terms of prestige, in the hierarchy of state offices, the police occupied the lowest rank, as shown in public parades and protocols where the chief of police came last, although still ahead of the non-Muslim servants of the state. Ordinary policemen, often no more than errand boys, were recruited among the lower classes. The chief, who had to be Muslim, was selected from among the eunuchs of the court and high-standing slaves in the imam's entourage. He was ranked among the people of the sword, that is, a government official with executive authority. A secret police existed with examples of informants – often women – reporting back to the high dignitaries being frequent. However, the inner workings of this special force has remained obscure to this day. Under the Fatimids the police became a paramilitary arm of the state, managed by a dedicated *diwan* that was guided by religious law in the handling of criminal matters. The ideal policeman was expected to be even-handed with the rich and the poor; he had to uphold the rights of the victim and be committed to punishing crime irrespective of the status of the criminal. This, however, was only after having established firm proof of wrongdoing. In practice a whiff of suspicion that someone had committed a crime was enough to seal this person's grim fate. The police were also in charge of enforcing moral standards. For example, the police intervened to curb prostitution, which though not illegal since prostitutes were taxed was nevertheless discouraged. In this realm of criminality, an example of an offence that was met with punishment was the interplay between Muslims and non-Muslims: a husband-and-wife pimping enterprise was accused of having non-Muslim clients; a Christian man was executed for having been found with a Muslim lady of the night. The moral squad's sphere of action extended to the surveillance of weddings to ensure that separate wedding halls were used by male and female guests.

In theory, besides combating crime, the main role that people expected the police to play was the maintenance of public order. Thanks to Ibn Killis's reform that gave the police greater powers, the imam-caliph capitalized on the people's appreciation of combating crime and receiving help in time of need. Police intervention had proved, at least in some instances, to be effective in curbing riots that had escalated into looting. People could exercise citizen's arrest but would have to take the apprehended person to police headquarters to be dealt with. Beyond these instances, in practice the maintenance of public order was something that on many occasions the police seem to have failed to do. As an institution appointed by the regime, the *shurta* served the interest of the ruling class on which its fortunes depended. Therefore, while the estates and commercial ventures from which the royal family and the elite drew their wealth were protected, the police were useless in intervening when ordinary people found themselves exposed to mass looting, rioting and crime. Ethnic-based biases and inadequate strength also meant that ordinary people were left to fend for themselves, abandoned to the mercy of the army's intervention, something that often made things worse.

Falling on the wrong side of the police landed you in jail. In Fatimid Cairo there were a number of prisons notorious for the appalling conditions in which inmates were kept. Common criminals ended up in a prison called *habs al-ma'una* while political prisoners and disgraced dignitaries (at least around the mid-eleventh century) were marched off, often for a one-way trip, to a prison that in Cairo had been a repurposed caliphal warehouse.[13] Other figures entrusted with civic duties were vigilantes, that is, those in charge of the surveillance of local boroughs. These would intervene in cases of low-level trouble but also hastened people in the areas under their remit to attend the caliphal public parades.

The Secular Institutions

If the *da'wa* and the judiciary functioned as the executive arms of the imam-caliph in matters of Isma'ili faith and conduct, once in Egypt, the vizirate became the office to which the imam delegated the executive function of coordinating the administration of the state. Based on the dominant method of intervention in the administration of the state, the vizier might be a vizier of the pen, that is, operating via the civil service, or a vizier of the sword, managing via military enforcement. The imam-caliph had authority over the vizier and controlled his actions but, as we will see, in time the Fatimid viziers overstepped their mark, usurping their masters to assume outright power. In response to this threat imams like al-Hakim suppressed the hegemonic aspirations of the vizier's office, while those like al-Mustansir succumbed to it. In the Fatimid context the office of vizier is linked to the figure of Ibn Killis, the first, most famous vizier of the pen ever to serve the regime. In general, the vizier was a mediator between the ruler and his subjects, as well as the head of the central administrative apparatus that controlled and managed the functioning of the empire through departments or *diwan*s. At times this office was catered for by acting viziers or the holders of a go-between office called *wisata*. The Fatimid administration mirrored in many ways the *diwan* system already adopted by the rival ʻAbbasids, but departed from them by adding bureaux to cater for Fatimid-specific needs. The number and dedicated sectors in which these *diwan*s specialized changed over time, with a significant shift occurring during the caliphate of al-Zahir's successor al-Mustansir. At some point these departments amounted to more than twenty, of which at least six dealt with financial affairs.[14] A typical bureau employed about seventeen people, each with rank and title to match the function they were employed for. At the top was a supervisor, followed by an executor whose role was to organize the work within the department. An agent, sometimes with an assistant, kept track of progress at work and reminded staff of deadlines. The office had a scribe who made copies of incoming and outgoing mail to archive all correspondence, while another scribe collected dues. A bookkeeper monitored expenditures and a witness verified that correct records were kept. Each officer had a deputy who could step in if necessary. Where relevant, a cadastral surveyor reported his findings to the relevant *diwan*, which in turn helped an officer to keep a record of names of landholders and the amount of their land so that taxation could be worked out. In some departments a controller monitored the use of certain products and their production, while a keeper was responsible for storing goods like foodstuffs, recording the quantity. A squeezer was the officer charged with checking that *dhimmi*s, that is Christians and Jews, complied with dress codes, payment of taxes and regulations imposed on them by the regime. Above all of these dignitaries was the head of the departments who was third in hierarchy after the imam-caliph and the vizier. He had ultimate authority to distribute funds within each bureau as well as to receive and answer requests for budget increases for the *diwan*s.

The *diwan*s were in charge of (among other services) ceremonies, granting of benefits and robes of honour, registration of gifts received and delivered and the audit of state expenditure registers. The *diwan al-rawatib* dealt with paying salaries to troops and civilians. The provision of arms and uniforms fell to other departments. The *diwan khass* was dedicated to the upkeep of the palace and the caliphal household, although the boundary of what was the property of the imam, state property and private property outside what was owned by the regime was blurred. The *bayt al-mal*, the treasury, formed a separate department.

The chancery, the *diwan al-insha'*, issued edicts and state correspondence. The expansion of the empire and offices to run it meant an increase in personnel. Scribes with a distinctive know-how, such as knowledge of specific formulae when writing formal correspondence, decrees and documents and of appropriate calligraphic styles, were sought after. Sometimes recruited among Copts and Sunnis, the scribes or *kuttab* formed a special class of trained personnel who came from families that had served in that position for generations. Their skills ranged from calligraphy to bookkeeping. Most important was their command of the language and written protocol to translate into formal edicts and decrees the state directives that were to be circulated across the empire. For this reason, the chancery was one of the most important departments in the state administration. The office dealt with the release of a wide spectrum of policy documents, from issuing licences to admonitions. The head of the chancery, who had to be an eloquent writer, dealt with incoming correspondence for the caliph, discussed the content with him, answered on behalf of the caliph and sealed it with his seal. Under the Fatimids this sensitive position could nevertheless be occupied by a non-Muslim. Also belonging to this office was a private secretary to the imam-caliph who might be present at events involving the vizier. During these confidential sessions a scribe took minutes that the secretary signed, to be countersigned by the vizier or the caliph. Once all signatures were collected the document was released. The mail bureau ensured that all correspondence issued by the chancery reached its point of destination. Mail was sometimes dispatched by pigeon post but more often through boxes transported by caravans, the *barid* system. The mail department also served as an intelligence bureau.

Not long after their arrival in Egypt the Fatimids reorganized the administration of the provinces by dividing them into four main units: Upper Egypt, East, West and Alexandria. Beyond Egypt, Syria and North Africa also became administrative units. At some point Syria had a dedicated *diwan* appointed to it. A special office was established for the Hijaz in order to deal with all the affairs relating to the Fatimids' patronage of the pilgrimage to Mecca. These units were managed through regional offices under the authority of *wali*s who answered to the vizier and/or the imam-caliph. In the provinces, bureaux were also established to address local matters like farming, canal clearance and irrigation, the coordination of tax collection and the payment of salaries, among other things. In Sicily, after their conquest, the Normans relied for a generation or so on the administration that had been implemented by the Kalbids in the parts of the island they controlled. After that phase, until the mid-twelfth century the Normans adapted and changed it to fit their needs, replacing Arabic-speaking staff with Greek Christian administrators. Particular care was taken to review neglected or inaccurate cadastral records. However, the Normans modelled their system on that of the Fatimids, a blend of approaches that reinvigorated a once-depleted administrative machine.[15]

Military-related departments included those of the army, the land grant, the office of supplies and that of clothing. They dealt with the provision of outfits for the army and the administrative personnel. In term of responsibility, the boundary of competence between departments was often blurred and overlapped. A typical interdependence was that which linked the departments of army, salaries and transport (horses and mules). Alongside state ones, the establishment of private *diwan*s was notable, such as those managing the affairs of royal women which became centres of power. Many men who became powerful figures in the regime had forged their careers while serving in these private departments. All the *diwan*s were subject to oversight to curb potential corruption and embezzlement of funds.

The department dealing with the army handled the needs of the various elements that composed the Fatimid military.[16] This office took care of equipment, ammunition, supplies and ship building. It was the department with the highest budget. Its head, who had to be a Muslim, was also responsible for military logistics, from transportation to knowing who was where at any time. Of all the departments, the army had most investment in the office issuing salaries, the usual way soldiers were paid. Higher-ranking officers received in addition land grants, a method which secured cultivation of the land, revenues for the state and the upkeep of soldiery under their command. The practice of issuing these grants survived the end of the Fatimids and remained in use during the Mamluk sultanate, until the sixteenth century. The cavalry was better paid than the infantry, as horses enjoyed a special place in Fatimid ceremonial protocol as well as in warfare. Nasir-i Khusaw's description of the expenses the imam-caliph incurred to finance the soldiers appointed to escort the pilgrimage caravan from Cairo to Mecca gives us a glimpse of the eye-watering costs the regime faced for its upkeep:

> The daily disbursement to the soldiers for fodder is one thousand dinars, over and above the twenty dinars each man receives per diem for the twenty-five days until they reach Mecca, where they stay for ten days. Thus, with the twenty-five days it takes them to return, they are gone for two months, and sixty thousand dinars are spent for provisions, not counting miscellaneous disbursements for rents, bonuses, stipends and camels that die.[17]

Much care went into the management of the caliphal stables, which did not house black horses given the association of the colour with the 'Abbasids. At least five senior officers were employed in the stables of the imam-caliph, aided by specialized personnel which included those who trained horses for dressage, staff in charge of security and grooms. Each stable was well equipped with wells and food storage, the provision and distribution of which was monitored by the imam-caliph himself. Beyond the palace, as the army expanded so did the provision of riding and pack animals to ensure the mobility of the troops. When in 996 al-'Aziz was preparing for yet another anti-Byzantine campaign in Syria he is reported to have deployed tens of thousands of horses and camels. The Kutama were given 4,000 horses and funds to buy a thousand more. Each animal was equipped with saddles, harnesses and riding fittings that from al-Mu'izz's time were kept in a dedicated storage space in the palace. Every year the cavalry held a dressage parade in front of the imam-caliph and the high dignitaries of the state. Also dating from the caliphate of al-Mu'izz, army parades, *'ard*, were organized once a year, a practice continued by his successor. In the 'Abbasid context, these military tattoos were orchestrated by the master general, an officer who was also responsible for disbursing the troops' pay. It is plausible that a similar arrangement might have been in place under al-'Aziz.

The laws of patronage, underpinned by the bond of reciprocal advantage that shaped the relationship between master and servant, were at the heart of the social contract between the Fatimid regime and its army. The survival of the caliphate was dependent on the support and loyalty of the army and, in turn, the army depended on the prosperity and stability of the ruler to reap material benefits from him. In many ways the history of the Fatimids is a tale of a fragile balancing act between two interdependent powers, and of the dire consequences when the balance between the two was subverted, or indeed broke down altogether.[18]

The army unit that, par excellence, was linked to the origin of the Fatimids' fortunes was the one composed of Kutama Berbers. As the earliest group to pledge en masse their support for the cause of the hidden Isma'ili imam, the Kutamas were instrumental in enabling the manifestation of the imam in the figure of al-Mahdi. Although dominated by Berbers, in Ifriqiya the Fatimid military saw a gradual growth of Arab elements. Forming the Fatimid military elite, the Kutamas continued to enjoy preferred status in the eyes of the dynasty following its relocation to Egypt. In Cairo they were at the forefront of the regime's military expeditions for territorial gain, as well as marching against enemies and aggressors like the Qarmatians. However, the regime's difficulties in securing its hold in Syria and Palestine dented its expansionist aspirations, which resulted in a drastic change in state military policy. The need for more varied fighting skills and a greater number of soldiers led to greater ethnic diversification in the composition of the army divisions. Whether through absorbing defeated armies, defections, purchase or attracted by better patronage, over time large numbers of eastern elements came to fight on the Fatimids' side. From the reign of al-'Aziz onwards the Kutamas found themselves having to fight off ethnic rivals to defend their status. In these confrontations it was they who lost out in the end. By the twelfth century the Kutamas had dwindled as a distinct military group and were absorbed into the civilian population across the empire. Along with the Kutamas, other troops of North African origins included the Barqiyya and the Batiliyya who, having arrived in Egypt with Jawhar's army, featured as horsemen in military tattoos. The *qasriyya* or *qaysariyya* is best known for its involvement in Sitt al-Mulk's attempted coup against al-Hakim.

Around 1020 this militia and other corps rioted in the capital, looting and burning the market. More references to the *qaysariyya* coincide with the economic crisis of 1024–5, during al-Zahir's reign. On that occasion their commander intervened to prevent looting by an armed gang consisting mainly of Black slaves known as *jawwala*.[19] Later however, *qaysariyya* and *jawwala* joined forces to rob a North African caravan. The *qaysariyya* fought and robbed members of the Turkish contingent in the Fatimid army, an action that prompted the Turks' retaliation. Petitions against the *qaysariyya* were presented to al-Zahir by the Kutamas.[20] The early Fatimid army also included Greeks and other soldiers of European origin, known under the denomination of *Rum*. These were acquired via cities like Venice, or when captured during incursions along the Italian coast, or in the course of fights with the Byzantines. There were also North Africans like the Zawila who fought against Abu Yazid. They followed Jawhar into Egypt and their quarter was by one of Cairo's gates which became known after them, Bab al-Zuwayla. Then there were the Saqaliba. Both in North Africa and in Egypt elements of this group, many of them eunuchs, rose to prominence as high-ranking officers who worked close to the imams. There were Saqaliba commanders in both the naval and land forces. They formed a military group in the army of Jawhar (himself a Saqaliba from Sicily), and in both Palermo and Cairo they had a quarter to themselves.

The Turks arrived in Cairo following al-'Aziz's victory over Alptakin and his allies in Syria and Palestine, when several thousand Turks were absorbed into the Fatimid army. At the expense of the Kutama, the Turks were given a privileged position, and special bonds of patronage tied them to the regime. Headed by a commander, these Turks were freedmen who established their own quarter in Fustat. Other major players included the Daylamis originating from the Caspian Sea area, and the Kurds. The Daylamis, of Persian origins, also came to serve the Fatimids after the victory over Alptakin. They were recognizable in parades by their javelins, and Nasir-i Khusraw says that it was this contingent that formed the imam-caliph's private guard, at least at the time of his visit to Cairo. Several military chiefs who defected to the Fatimids from the Hamdanids also arrived in Cairo with their troops. Members of this group were nominated as governors in Palestine, with troops stationed in Ramla, Syria as well as in Cairo. The violent fighting for supremacy between *maghariba*, *mashariqa* and the other

34 Drawing of two Fatimid soldiers, 11th–12th century, ink on paper.

major military group, the Blacks, became a regular feature of city life throughout the eleventh century (illus. 34).

Having inherited them from the defeated Aghlabids, the Fatimids used Black slave troops from the inception of their reign in Ifriqiya, along with the Kutamas. Of sub-Saharan origins, Black troops remained part of the Fatimid army once the dynasty moved to Egypt, where their numbers expanded during the reign of al-Hakim. Though they were bought on a large scale as slaves, this imam-caliph also freed many of them. Their extensive incorporation into the Fatimid army had a destabilizing effect on the civilian population as well as on other military groups. Regular outbreaks of military infighting saw the population caught in the middle, both in the capital and in the provinces. Besides being engaged in action, the Black military also featured in parades and protocol with those who belonged to one unit, *al-sa'diyya*, being appointed to ride the royal horses and being known as 'the holders of the bejewelled swords'. They might have been the same as *al-rikabiyya*, Black slaves who formed part of al-Hakim's escort and received his patronage. In 1014 three of al-Hakim's *al-rikabiyya* took presents from Byzantine envoys. Taking the acceptance of the gifts as a sign of possible betrayal, al-Hakim had the three killed. In 1024, *al-sa'diyya* were involved in quelling turmoil caused by price rises in times of food crisis. The market supervisor of Fustat trusted them with the policing of the grain trade.[21]

The number of Black soldiers was still considerable by the end of the eleventh century, thanks to Rasad, consort of al-Zahir and mother of al-Mustansir, who brought a large number of Black soldiers into the Fatimid army. With this intake the balance of power within the military was once again disturbed, with almost fatal consequences for the dynasty. Black officers and soldiers formed many units. One of them was the *'utufiyya*, named after its leader, 'Utuf. As a *ghulam*, 'Utuf was no mere slave but rather a person who enjoyed privileged status in his relationship with his master. In general, the soldier *ghulam* owed his training, equipment and privileged place in society to the care and interest of his patron, who acted as a foster parent to the *ghulam* from adolescence.[22] Training included inculcation of obedience to the master. The *ghulam*'s gratitude for these benefits was strengthened by a general ethic of respect and filial duty. In the Fatimid context, these sentiments between the master and military personnel in general were enshrined in legal theory and advice to the ruler in the work of al-Qadi al-Nu'man. Al-'Aziz and Ibn Killis became major patrons of military slaves, a tradition that was continued by al-Zahir. In chronicles for the year 1005, the *'utufiyya* is listed among those divisions that were issued decrees of protection by al-Hakim. As was typical for important *ghulam* commanders of this period, 'Utuf had a large number of *ghilman* at his service. As 'Utuf is described as Black, we can assume that the *ghilman* forming his corps were also Black slaves, since there is no evidence of multi-ethnic contingents in the Fatimid army. The *'utufiyya* was probably an infantry division, since in general the Fatimids appointed Black soldiers to that role. In 1010, 'Utuf was killed by Turkish military on the order of al-Hakim. His legacy, however, lived on in a quarter of Cairo named after his unit that became known as one of the best districts in Cairo, with impressive houses, *hammam*s, *suq*s and mosques.[23]

By the end of the eleventh century, the Armenians had become the dominant ethnic group in the Fatimid infantry, following the arrival in Cairo of the Armenian commander Badr al-Jamali from 'Akka, the city that the Crusaders called Acre. He had been summoned by al-Mustansir to restore order as his reign was falling apart. Their predominance continued until the end of the dynasty.[24]

A special army division was appointed to act as security guards of the caliphal palace. Every evening, for an hour at the call of prayer, the sound of trumpets, drums and cymbals announced the start of the rounds which lasted the whole night. The practice had been in place since the early years of the Fatimids' arrival in Egypt and the protocol was only modified by al-Hakim when he prohibited the playing of musical instruments.

The Fatimids had at their disposal significant naval power, which, consisting of military and commercial fleets, gave them control of parts of the Mediterranean while competing for supremacy over other areas with rivals such as the Umayyads of al-Andalus and the Byzantines. The importance the Fatimids gave to their maritime presence is witnessed by the large space given in the *Book of Curiosities* to maritime affairs and maps. The apogee of their naval force, whether deployed for military purposes or trade, dates to the North African years of Fatimid history. The move to Egypt brought about a period of lower Fatimid influence due to fewer resources and the resurgence of the Byzantines' maritime power. However, the Fatimid military navy saw a revitalization of its role when the Cairo regime employed it against the Crusaders' advance. On the whole, during this phase, more impetus was given to its commercial use. In addition to a sea-going fleet, the Fatimids developed a riverine one for internal trade and transportation along the Nile. On the Red Sea coast, the Fatimids had fleet destined for commerce only.

In the course of Fatimid history, the fleet underwent developments in its organization and naval architecture, and in the size, type and number of vessels that comprised it. In the early decades of the Fatimid presence in Ifriqiya, there is no evidence of systematic management of the maritime forces, be they military or civilian. Specialist staff to take care of specific tasks appear to have been absent. Commanders took various roles and shifted from military to commercial positions and back, according to where they were needed. The dynasty became active in the Mediterranean sea in both naval, military and commercial contexts with the establishment of al-Mahdiyya. Trade-wise, ships were engaged in commerce on behalf of the imam. The imams' fleets sailed from various ports: Alexandria, but also Tripoli on the eastern Mediterranean coast and Tinnis. The eunuch Jawdhar testified in his memoirs to frequent naval transportation of goods to and from Sicily.[25] Royal women were also known to have owned ships for trade operated via their agents.[26] As for fleets used for military purposes, the warships that formed them came in different sizes: large ones called *usul*, medium war galleys called *shini* and small vessels called *markab harbi*.

Around 950, during the reign of al-Mansur, the Fatimid fleet, whether military or commercial, began to be managed in a more systematic way. As this development coincided with the transfer of the capital from al-Mahdiyya to al-Mansuriyya, the establishment inland of an office devoted to the navy must be understood as part of a process of centralization in the management of the state. Under al-Mansur the command of the fleet came to be assigned to one person (or members of the same family) who led every expedition, instead of a new commander being appointed for each mission. From this time, the Banu Kalb coordinated naval operations on the imam-caliph's order. With the admiralty set up, personnel came to be organized in a hierarchical order: at the top was the *sahib al-bahr*, the marine master, who was responsible for the administration of maritime affairs. Below this rank was the person responsible for the storage of naval provisions. Those in command tended to be chosen from among the Saqaliba and Arabs who were descendants of old families established in North Africa. When deployed for military purposes, rather than for combat at sea, vessels at this time were used as means of transport for land troops, military equipment and supplies. There are however instances of military ships involved in sea combats. For example, the Fatimids fought the Umayyads along the coast near Almeria by using incendiary devices, only for the Umayyads to retaliate in the same way on the Tunisian coast not long after.[27] Sea skirmishes between Byzantine and Fatimid fleets also occurred. In Egypt, the administration of the navy appears to have become more systematic from the twelfth century onwards. By this time there was a bureau of naval affairs responsible for ship building, keeping records of personnel and payment of salaries to the sailors. It also dealt with labourers employed by the *diwan* and granted authorizations to smaller government vessels for civil use to exit the arsenal. Its head was assisted by deputies who in turn had sergeants under them. Their role included general recruitment and calling sailors to report for duty, as well as logistics such as the boarding of personnel and military equipment. The office responsible for purchasing materials to build ships for war was separate from the one in charge of acquiring materials for the commercial fleet. Overall, investment in the development, upkeep and organization of the workforce of the military fleet was prioritized over that for the commercial navy. Towards the end of Fatimid rule the head of the naval bureau also became responsible for the oversight of port facilities in coastal cities in Fatimid territories to ensure that they were fit for purpose. In time the administration of the fleet and the naval command fell under the control of an independent high officer who was chosen from among the elite of the regime. This was a prestigious and powerful position, but one that did not require specialist or maritime knowledge. That expertise belonged to the admirals of the fleet who were the true commanders of operations. Ships' crews consisted of mercenaries and slaves as well as conscripts, recruited or bought along the coastal areas and chosen for their knowledge of the sea. A mixed bunch, the Fatimids struggled to secure their long-term loyalty, unlike the Kutamas, whom they trusted and employed on vessels but who were not natural seamen. These crews, which became professionalized after the move to Egypt, included Christians and Jews.[28]

From the highest ranks of state management to the lowest of the low among the marginalized, slaves were at the heart of the practical functioning of the Fatimid state machine as well as everyday life. Those individuals who lived as slaves in Islamic territories were originally non-Muslims who in many instances subsequently converted to Islam. As already observed, the Saqaliba are emblematic of slaves who, whether eunuchs or not, formed a class that came to occupy a position of prominence and power in society. However, apart from this group, only a few slaves gained acceptance at the highest level in the corridors of power. The vast majority served the court as well as affluent social elites holding menial positions.

The imam-caliph al-'Aziz's entourage might have included up to 10,000 slave women and eunuchs. In general, slaves were bought and sold, exchanged as part of gifts, or acquired as captives. Like their male counterparts, slave women were among the goods the Fatimid royals swapped in diplomatic transactions with their vassals. However, during the reign of al-Hakim the trading of slaves was prohibited for some time. Upon resumption of this trade, from Cairo slaves were even exported to rival Baghdad, where mixed-race female slaves were sought after. Under al-Mustansir in 1077 thousands of women who were members of a rebellious Berber tribe were sold in Cairo's markets. Some girls and boys were born into slavery or bought along with their mothers, while others were acquired as part of an inheritance or dowry. Sometimes slaves were freed under specific circumstances. For example, manumission was often granted by male masters to slave women who gave birth to their free master's child. In this instance the child was considered freeborn. Some women were freed by a master on his deathbed. However, even when released from bondage during the lifetime of the owner, in many instances these women maintained in general a solid attachment to the former master after emancipation. This was particularly so in cases when a personal and intimate relationship had developed between the two or when, though having become free, these women were still financially dependent on the former master. The direct voice of elite women is rarely heard in Muslim medieval sources – even less so that of ordinary ones and female slaves. Narratives of manumission centre around the intention and wishes of the master (and more rarely the mistress), thus making it hard to detect how those women who saw their status changing from slavery to emancipation reacted and adapted to their new social position. Irrespective of male or female, manumission of slaves happened en masse in times of economic crisis and famine when the master or mistress could no longer afford to fulfil his or her obligation to provide for the enslaved servants.

Manuals were written that dealt with legal obligations and guidelines on how to buy and treat a slave. The eleventh-century Christian Iraqi physician Ibn Butlan (d. 1066), who composed a treatise on the purchase of slaves, perhaps while in Cairo, recommended women slaves for cooking food. In his view they were better than men because of their consistency in the job and their understanding of cooking secrets: they were good at balancing flavours and at making sauces.[29] Irrespective of the method of acquisition, slaves were considered human beings with rights protected by law. Owners had to treat them well and provide them with food, drink and clothes. Their work had to be within limits and they could only be disciplined for good reason. Slaves were allowed to keep their faith, and the master should respect their religious practices. On one occasion some slaves among the embroiderers were reported to have apostatized – the gravest sin in Islam – after becoming Muslim. The imam-caliph al-Mu'izz ordered restraint in punishment if they repented.

Slaves had rights to ownership, could keep what was given for their services and could own slaves in turn. However, when children were born to a couple where both parents were slaves, the status of the child was that of slave too. Notwithstanding their rights, and even if they converted to Islam, slaves remained and were treated as second-class citizens. Slave women were categorized in legal theory based on racial stereotypes: Berber women were good for housework, sex and childbearing; Black women were docile, robust and good wet nurses; Byzantine women were honest and could be entrusted with valuables; Persian women were reputed to be excellent childminders; and Arab women were noted for their singing ability, while Indian and Armenian women had a reputation for being hard to manage and were therefore seen as unsuited for slavery. The price was high and only rich people could afford to buy a slave, although lower prices applied to slaves with disabilities or the elderly. In the twelfth century a young woman slave could cost up to twenty *dinar*s, a price out of reach of most. After purchase the slaves were brought to their masters' residences where they would – especially if female – work as servants, cooks, nurses, singers and dancers. A female slave often had more room for manoeuvre than the free lady of the house she worked for; unveiled, she could go out and about running errands.

With a few exceptions, many Jewish and Christian officials worked at all levels in the Fatimid state apparatus. A number of bureaux dealt with the affairs of the *dhimmi*s when they intersected with the interests of the state. Following the standard legal attitude of Muslims towards non-Muslims, in the Fatimid domains no churches or synagogues could be newly built or restored without state approval. These permits were granted to the extent that al-Mu'izz and al-'Aziz gained a reputation as patrons of churches.[30] Al-Hakim allowed many churches to be built, which contrasts with his portrayal as a destroyer of non-Muslim places of worship. In Egypt, these communities – Christian Copts, Melkites and Byzantines, and Jewish Rabbanites, Karahites and Samaritans – were managed by their own institutions, headed by patriarchs and rabbis. Among the Jews it was the Karahite community that, throughout the history of the dynasty, managed to position itself with some of its members among the highest officers in the service of the state. In the second half of the eleventh century the Fatimid regime instituted an official dedicated to Jewish affairs, a community leader known as the head of the Jews. Appointed by the imam-caliph by formal letter, the holder of this position was a Jew experienced in finance, or a physician.[31] Beyond the terms imposed by Islamic law on non-Muslims, the state did not interfere in the day-to-day life of the ordinary people belonging to these communities. Christians and Jews avoided the intervention of Muslim courts or the government in dealing with their internal affairs. The Fatimid regime did meddle in the internal affairs of the Coptic Church, for example, in the second half of the eleventh century. In fact, the regime was instrumental in having the headquarters of the Coptic patriarchate transferred from Alexandria to the Church of Saint Michael near Cairo. However, only on rare occasions did the regime force its hand on key matters that were solely under church jurisdiction. Government involvement, when it happened, was at the Christians' instigation, to mediate in internal disputes. The most common type of request the Fatimid authorities received was for involvement in the appointment to a bishopric. The Fatimid regime imposed its choice of patriarch on only two occasions. The first was when al-ʿAziz nominated his two Melkite brothers-in-law as patriarchs, one in Fustat, then Alexandria, and the other in Jerusalem. This small Christian group accepted the patriarchs, as they saw their appointments as a sign of official favour towards the community on the part of al-ʿAziz. The second instance of imposition was when, towards the end of his reign, al-Hakim – by then in an expansive mood towards the Christians – was asked by Nicephorus, a Greek slave who worked in the palace as a carpenter, for permission to become the patriarch of Jerusalem. Al-Hakim approved and the carpenter took up his new post in the Holy City in 1021.[32] Bar the occasional aberration or the shared public festive occasions, ordinary Muslims and non-Muslims lived most of the time in parallel universes with interactions between the two communities confined in general to trade transactions.

As far as Ismaʿili expectations were concerned, in Egypt, and wherever the authority of the Fatimids was recognized, the imam-caliph had indeed proved to be the fountainhead of a harmonic system actualized on earth according to the will of God. The self-image of a confident dynasty that knew its place in the world became visible not only through the institutions of the regime but through the soft power of the arts and cultural artefacts that, by their very existence, these Fatimid institutions had been instrumental in helping to produce.

8

The Making of a Golden Age: The Cultural Life and Its Industry

With so much resting on owning knowledge of the ultimate eternal truths as the pre-eminent sign of the imam's right to spiritual and temporal leadership, the Fatimid age became defined by the paramount importance given to learning. Whether it was directed towards sharing the Isma'ilis' claimed monopoly of esoteric wisdom, sponsored by the state to uncover new scientific grounds, or as a pursuit cultivated by intellectual elites irrespective of affiliations, literary production occupied a prominent place on the cultural scene of the Fatimid domains. Under the Fatimids, book production and the circulation of knowledge took place within three main intellectual spheres: one formed by Isma'ili authors; another comprising non-Isma'ili Muslim writers whether under the patronage of the Isma'ili regime or independent of it; and one which included non-Muslim scholars active in Fatimid-controlled lands. Given the esoteric and secretive character of Isma'ili literature, intended for circulation among initiates only, the last two groups were barred from tapping into Isma'ili literary output. Conversely, nothing prevented the Isma'ili literati from having access to Islamic and non-Islamic texts of any sort if they so wished.

Literary Production and Intellectual Interactions

A number of Isma'ili sources point to the existence of proto- and early Isma'ili doctrinal works having been in circulation among sworn affiliates during the phase of the imams' concealment prior to the manifestation of their line in Ifriqiya. Early propagandists like Mansur al-Yaman in Yemen, as indeed the hidden Isma'ili imams themselves, were credited with having composed works of esoteric content.

According to some, the encyclopaedic work consisting of epistles dealing with all aspects of knowledge, written in Basra by a mysterious collective with Isma'ili inclinations known as Ikhwan al-Safa', originates from this early period and context. Following the establishment of the dynasty in North Africa, more Isma'ili scholars produced literary works, with figures like the son of Mansur al-Yaman, Ja'far, the *da'i* Ibn al-Haytham and al-Qadi al-Nu'man standing out as representative of this phase. Works ranged from doctrinal writings on the allegorical interpretation of verses of the Qur'an to personal memoirs by those serving the imams and explanations of the need for an Isma'ili imam in this world. Compendia collecting the imams' deliberations were compiled, as well as historical accounts retracing the steps that resulted in the rise of the Fatimids. Some of these works became Fatimid foundational narratives, reconstructing as they did the official history of the dynasty's origins from an inside perspective. Some became the basis for Isma'ili law manuals. From an early date, the imams had asserted their authority as overseers of these works by approving them before they could be released into circulation among the Isma'ili faithful. Once in North Africa, the imams also disclosed themselves as authors, with works attributed to them ranging from prayer books to theological explanations on the nature of the imamate.

Once in Egypt, with the *da'wa* having become a fully fledged organ of the state apparatus, Isma'ili literature was produced to serve as the official voice of the regime in matters of law, doctrine and ritual. This had taken official form through being shared during lectures and preaching sessions, as well as through the circulation of books restricted to the Isma'ili community. Special emphasis was given to instructive books on jurisprudence and its esoteric decoding. Works on philosophy, cosmology and metaphysics focused on drawing parallels between cosmological hierarchies and those of the *da'wa* in order to validate the latter by way of demonstrating it to be the terrestrial projection of a divinely designed transcendent scheme of things. Imams' sermons and responsa were gathered in books that functioned as sources of authority. Besides al-Qadi al-Nu'man, with his monumental work on Isma'ili jurisprudence, the tenth and eleventh centuries saw the rise of thinkers who became household names at the Fatimid court. Both al-Sijistani and al-Kirmani, in their respective ways, blended Neoplatonic philosophy into Isma'ili doctrines, thus giving shape to a distinctive strand of Isma'ili thought. Through his writings al-Sijistani had been instrumental in bringing part of the eastern *da'wa* of Iran into the fold of Fatimid Isma'ilism (illus. 17). Al-Kirmani had arrived in Egypt from Iraq (where he acted as *hujja* in the name of the Cairo imams), having been summoned to inject the *da'wa* with renewed intellectual vigour. As well as writing what has been considered to be the most significant corpus of Isma'ili philosophical literature, he was also the author of works in defence of al-Hakim's imamate, and against the extremist tendencies that grew around this imam. From Iran, al-Nishaburi arrived in Cairo, to systematize in his writings, aspects of the *da'wa* organization as no one had done before. In the eleventh century Iranians like Nasir-i Khusraw and al-Mu'ayyad fi'l-Din al-Shirazi became the most prominent Isma'ili authors of their age. Unlike Nasir, al-Shirazi settled for good in Cairo, where he became a key figure of the Fatimid regime and the last great Cairo-based Isma'ili thinker before the fall of the dynasty. From the twelfth century onwards, representatives of the revived *da'wa* in Yemen, in addition to preserving the bulk of the Fatimid literary canon, continued to produce Fatimid-style Isma'ili literature in terms of themes, doctrinal direction and content. In the fifteenth century the Yemeni Isma'ili religious leader and scholar Idris 'Imad al-Din (d. 1468) authored, among other works, the first major coherent pre-modern history of the dynasty written by an Isma'ili. The often-precarious state of the Fatimids' hold on Syria and Palestine meant that Cairo-endorsing literary production to serve the local *da'wa* was significant in content, to the point of forming a distinctive corpus, but it was limited in quantity and in its impact on Fatimid Isma'ili thought in general.

While the classification of Isma'ili literature is understood to apply to works produced by and for the *da'wa* that were doctrinal and legal in character, the Fatimid intellectual environment also produced authors who were Isma'ilis, or at least Fatimid sympathizers, who contributed to a belles-lettres body of literature. Isma'ili poets and panegyrists, while serving an Isma'ili court, became nonetheless accessible to wider audiences. The Andalusian poet Ibn Hani' was a panegyrist of the Fatimid imams in North Africa, but his verses were also read in Baghdad. In Cairo, Tamim, son of al-Mu'izz, composed poetry for the enjoyment of the Isma'ili court, but his verses rang sufficiently agenda-free to be appreciated by wider audiences. In the eleventh century, from his place of exile in Central Asia, Nasir-i Khusraw became acknowledged as a great poet and a literary figure who contributed to the canon of Persian literature, notwithstanding his Isma'ili affiliation. During the same period in Cairo, al-Mu'ayyad fi'l-Din al-Shirazi's writings included religious texts and collected sermons. His poetry collection became the official voice of the regime in verse. His autobiography was a prose mirror of the age he lived in. Beyond poetry, Isma'ilis authored works to nurture the erudition, curiosity, imagination and thirst for learning of Fatimid princes destined for succession, choosing to remain anonymous themselves. Might the eleventh-century *Book of Curiosities* have been one such work? On a more practical level, Isma'ili scholars, besides indoctrinating the *mu'min*s, had to reach out to the *muslim*s with legal compendia and manuals designed to instruct non-Isma'ili subjects (the majority of the population) on the laws and procedures governing them under the rule of the Isma'ili regime.

Many scholars, a few bona fide Isma'ilis but several not so, found themselves serving the Fatimid regime, whether attracted by patronage or forced by circumstances. In Ifriqiya the Fatimids brought together locally authored books belonging to the imams which were circulated through the *da'wa* network and collected via *da'i*s who had come to settle in al-Mansuriyya. This material formed the foundation on which the collections of the famed Fatimid libraries were built and expanded. In North Africa the Fatimids also inherited the literary corpus of the departed Aghlabids. In Egypt, collaboration between several Sunni scholars and the Isma'ili regime became in many instances intentional, agreed and formalized. The vizier Ibn Killis was a prominent promoter of literature, besides being an author of legal works himself. State-sponsored investment in the study of sciences – intended here in the broadest possible sense – was considerable. Al-Hakim's *dar al-'ilm* was the ultimate example of a purpose-built academy intended for cross-disciplinary exchange of knowledge. Al-Musabbihi, an enthusiastic contemporary court chronicler, described the setting up and purpose of this institution:

> On this Saturday . . . the so-called House of Knowledge in Cairo was inaugurated. The jurists took up residence there, and the books from the palace libraries were moved into it. People could visit it, and whoever wanted to copy something . . . could do so; the same was true of anyone who wanted to read any of the material kept in it. After the building was furnished and decorated . . . lectures were held there by the Quran readers, astronomers, grammarians and philologists as well as physicians. Into the house they brought

> all the books that . . . al-Hakim ordered to bring there . . . manuscripts in all domains of science and culture . . . He allowed access to all this to all people . . . he granted substantial salaries to all those who were appointed by him to do service there, jurists and others. He also donated what people needed: ink, writing reeds, paper and inkstands.[1]

Among the Egyptian Sunni scholars ʻAbd al-Ghani b. Saʻid, indicated as having headed the *dar al-ʻilm*, is one of few authorities to be associated with that institution by name, irrespective of denomination. Born in 944 to a family of prominent transmitters of *hadith*s, ʻAbd al-Ghani studied with several important scholars. Prior to taking his post at the *dar*, where he taught traditions of the Prophet of Islam, the imam-caliph al-ʻAziz had already instructed him to compile a collection of praises in honour of ʻAli b. Abi Talib. This was part of an effort by the regime to glorify Islam, to appease Muslims who had shown popular discontent at the appointment of Jews and Christians as high dignitaries at court. In 1008, out of fear of al-Hakim ʻAbd al-Ghani escaped to Palestine, only to return to Egypt in 1012 to resume teaching the following year. Back in office, he joined an escort for the emissary of a Byzantine ambassador. He died in 1018 and was honoured with a solemn funeral. However, ʻAbd al-Ghani's reputation was tainted among some of his Sunni contemporaries, as his close associations with the Fatimids put his Sunnism in doubt.[2]

Under the Fatimid regime's patronage Sunni authors produced major works on topics ranging from astronomy and medicine to music theory and grammar. Chroniclers close to the court recorded events in books that became source material for later historiographers. Envoys on diplomatic missions wrote travel reports for strategic government use. One example was the account that al-Aswani wrote following his diplomatic mission in 969 to George II, the Christian king of the Nubians, on behalf of the Fatimid general Jawhar.[3]

Some works were desired in order to fill knowledge gaps in the imam's personal library collections, or for pure pleasure. Al-ʻAziz's librarian wrote on Christian monasteries. His keeper of falcons wrote a book on falconry at his master's request.[4] The Cairo intellectual scene produced polymaths who put their erudition at the imams' service. Besides Ibn Ridwan's contribution to the corpus of scientific literature, the Shafiʻi Muhammad al-Qudaʻi (d. 1062), who served the Fatimid regime as *qadi* for the Sunni population, wrote many works including a compendium on the teachings and sayings of ‘Ali. Another major figure was al-Mubashshir b. Fatik, a wealthy scholar who must have occupied a high position at the Fatimid court. Author of a biography of the imam-caliph al-Mustansir (now lost), al-Mubashshir met scientists like Ibn al-Haytham and Ibn Ridwan, and was a prolific author in his own right. In 1048 he wrote what is now his only known extant work, *Choice of Wise Sayings and Fine Statements*. This was a selection of quotations from the sages of Late Antiquity – the mysterious Egyptian-Greek Hermes Trismegistus being one – accompanied by short biographical annotations. Popular throughout Muslim intellectual circles, this work was translated into Latin as well as other languages, and circulated in medieval Europe.[5] Al-Mubashshir has been suggested, among others, as a possible author of, or contributor to, the *Book of Curiosities*. In the twelfth century the Yemeni poet, jurist and chronicler ‘Umara (d. 1174), whose affiliation with the Isma‘ilis was somewhat questionable, adjusted his voice to the tastes and inclinations of his patrons in volatile times. During his service to the Cairo regime the scholar and diplomat Usama b. Munqidh (d. 1188) composed non-committal verses in a fluctuating political climate. During this century, everyone from secretaries to viziers had a go at writing poetry to serve different masters, thus producing verses of mediocre quality.

The accepted view is that the Fatimids' religious tolerance, and their patronage of scholarship through the establishment of institutions of learning, were the two factors that contributed most to the vibrancy of intellectual life in Egypt during their reign. The relative economic prosperity and socio-political stability that the Fatimids secured for the region provided a suitable context for this pluralistic intellectualism to thrive. If Sunnism had to wait until the fall of the Fatimids and the advent of the Ayyubids in 1171 to be restored as the state religion in Egypt, from a cultural and intellectual point of view it had never gone away. At least some five hundred named Sunni scholars were active in Egypt under Fatimid rule. Some were itinerants who came to Egypt during their peregrinations across the Islamic territories; others were native to Egypt but are also known to have travelled eastward to lands loyal to the ‘Abbasids. Sunni scholars often came to Egypt as part of journeys undertaken in search of knowledge, *rihla*, understood to mean a quest for narrations of prophetic traditions. Frequently these travels coincided with the pilgrimage to Mecca.

Some spent only a few years in Egypt, while others made it their permanent home and died there. Between the tenth and eleventh centuries, from al-Andalus, Sicily, Baghdad, Damascus, Nishapur, Ramla, Kufa, Aleppo, Raqqa, Isfahan, Herat, Shiraz, Basra, Rayy, Balkh and more locations, a multitude of scholars representing the four Sunni legal schools (some of them Sufis) converged on Fatimid Egypt at some point in their lives. The vast majority of them are recorded as having gravitated to Fustat and the surrounding region. Tinnis became the second most important centre of Sunni learning, followed by Damietta and Alexandria, which dominated the Sunni intellectual scene towards the end of the dynasty. Some important scholars are also associated with provincial centres like Qulzum, Akhmım, Aswan and Edfu. The traffic of savants, many of them Malikis travelling back and forth between al-Andalus and the lands under Fatimid control, had been significant since the reign of al-Mu'izz. It continued to grow until it became a cause of major concern during the reign of al-Hakim, who faced the most challenging revolt against his rule at the hands of Abu Rakwa.

In Ifriqiya the Fatimid regime had adopted a somewhat repressive and adversarial stance towards Sunni scholarship, which nevertheless continued to be active. In Egypt, beyond occasional friction, a notable feature of Fatimid rule was the lack of religious-ideological barriers between traditionists in pursuit of knowledge. Sunni subjects did suffer sporadic forms of repression at the hands of the Fatimid regime during the reign of al-Hakim, but the motivation appears to have been driven by politics rather than dictated by theological divergence. One instance was in Egypt in 973, when for political reasons the imam-caliph al-Mu'izz sentenced to death a Syrian traditionist. A case of censorship relates to a scholar who had moved to Egypt from Ifriqiya during the reign of al-'Aziz. Having become close to the court, he agreed to write a historical work on the Umayyads and the 'Abbasids, which he did in flattering tones towards both dynasties. When in 987 the vizier Ibn Killis found out, he sought to alienate this man from al-'Aziz. He confiscated the work and had its author put to death in 995. In 991 or 992 a man was beaten up because he was found in possession of a copy of *al-Muwatta*, the jurist Malik's compendium that formed the basis of the legal school he founded. There is however no overt indication that the Fatimid regime was involved in this act of repression. In fact, the episode could be situated in the context of inter-confessional rivalries between Malikis and Shafi'is. During al-Hakim's reign, in

1008, transmitters of *hadith*s were put to death. A key to understanding al-Hakim's ambivalent attitudes towards Sunni theologians – from him appointing several to lecture in the *dar al-'ilm* in 1004 to having them killed four years later – can be found in his concern about growing pro-Sunni sentiments, a result of having almost failed to halt Abu Rakwa's revolt. Courting Sunni scholars in 1004 served to appease the populace when the revolt was gathering momentum; eliminating them a few years later was part of the purge that followed its quashing. The infrequency and contingent nature of these repressive acts lends support to the portrayal of the Fatimid regime as mostly benign towards their non-Isma'ili Muslim subjects and the cultural artefacts they produced. However, this religious tolerance might have been determined by pragmatism rather than ecumenism, since the Fatimids, as foreign rulers representing a minority creed with Islam, could not afford to alienate or silence the voices of their Sunni majority subjects.

A category of scholars who found Fatimid Egypt an attractive professional destination was that of the Qur'an reciters. While the act of receiving remuneration for reciting the Holy Qur'an had been met with contempt in early Sunni circles, the Fatimid dynasty stood out not only for looking favourably on this profession but for encouraging it through handsome payments for reciters hired to perform at royal funerals. The promotion of professionalism among these reciters resulted in the added benefit of producing skilled performers who attracted students from various parts of the Islamic world. Many of the Andalusians who went to Egypt in this period were apprentices of this discipline. As for theological and *hadith* studies, the ongoing exchange of knowledge relied on the mobility of the transmitters. Travelling in quest of knowledge and for pilgrimage provided the ultimate context for intellectual exchange. In the Fatimid period, Mecca, Medina and the Hijaz feature as the centres where contacts among scholars were established, and then rekindled in Egypt or in other regions. Both types of travel were long and expensive and could only be undertaken if the traveller was confident of securing financial support while on the way. Apart from those few who served the courts and received patronage, by and large scholars functioned in a private capacity, receiving no emoluments, and had to support themselves in a variety of ways. In the first 470 years of Islam a substantial proportion of them derived their livelihood from commerce and trade. A commercial axis that stretched by land from Baghdad to Damascus and Tyre (Ar. Sur), and by sea from

Tyre to Tinnis or Damietta and, via the Delta, to Fustat, was one of the routes along which intellectual exchanges took place.[6] In Egypt, learning pursuits could be combined with practical needs of a material and commercial kind. It is no coincidence that most of the seekers, memorizers and transmitters of *hadith* who gravitated to Egypt earned their living as merchants and traders. A factor that added to Fatimid Egypt becoming an attractive destination for itinerant savant merchants was the Fatimids' securing of the land route for the pilgrimage via Egypt and Syria. This resulted from their victory over the Qarmatians, who had disrupted the pilgrimage routes for decades with their pillaging of caravans and demands for ransoms. Nasir-i Khusraw, himself a visitor to Egypt while travelling to Mecca, described the Fatimids' organization of the caravan to Islam's holiest city:

> It is customary for the representative of the sultan to appear in the mosque in the middle of the month of Rajab and proclaim the following, 'O company of Muslims! The pilgrimage season is at hand, and the sultan, as usual, has undertaken the outfitting of soldiers, horses, camels, and provisions'. During Ramadan this proclamation is repeated, and from the first of Dhu'l-Qa'da people set out for the appointed meeting place. At the middle of Dhu'l-Qa'da the caravan moves out.[7]

He observed that in the year prior to his arrival the caravan had not been organized due to drought and a scarcity of supplies which made it unwise for pilgrims to make the journey. Twice a year, however, the imam-caliph still sent the covering for the Ka'ba, as was customary. Another factor affecting the transmission of Sunni learning in Egypt was the relative health of the Egyptian economy under al-'Aziz's reign. The emergence of Tinnis as a centre of Sunni intellectual exchange is noteworthy at a time when the Fatimids had raised the city's status to that of an international industrial hub, famous for its textile production.

In Egypt under the Fatimids – as elsewhere prior to the establishment of the *madrasa*s – prophetic traditions were shared in private homes, mosques and in the markets. A representative of the travelling scholar in quest of traditions who was present in Egypt throughout most of al-Hakim's reign is the Sufi Abu Sa'd Ahmad al-Malini (d. 1021), who became a pupil of 'Abd al-Ghani. A Shafi'i of Afghan origin, he travelled to Iraq, Iran and Syria, went to Mecca, and came to Fustat, where he stayed until his death. He also travelled to Upper Egypt, where he interacted with other Sufis. Rated by his contemporaries as a great scholar of *hadith*s and the author of several works, al-Malini is a rare example for this period in Egypt of someone being described as a Sufi. In the tenth and eleventh centuries, the eastern Islamic territories had become the pre-eminent centres of Islamic mysticism. It was in those lands and in that period that classical Sufism became consolidated, thanks to the appearance of a body of literature that was to define the doctrinal and practical contours of the Islamic mystical tradition. While the history of Sufism in the ʻAbbasid territories is well documented from the end of the twelfth century onwards, as far as Egypt is concerned the presence of Sufis is less known. Contrary to common belief Sufism was present in Egypt throughout the Fatimid period, both as an expression of personal piety and as an organized form of devotion.[8]

The Fatimid regime facilitated a cultural climate that promoted triangulated exchanges between Twelver Shiʻis, Sunnis and Ismaʻilis. The religious-political activities and ritual practices of Twelver Shiʻis in Fatimid Egypt are well attested and so is their legacy in the post-Fatimid history of the region. In Egypt there was home-grown Imami Shiʻism even before the Fatimids' arrival. Those belonging to this faction were often conflated or confused with ʻAlids, that is, those who traced their lineage to ʻAli b. Abi Talib. These people supported ʻAli's cause and honoured him, but not all joined the Shiʻa, the distinctive religious-political faction that formed in his name. However, many Twelver Shiʻi scholars whose presence is attested in Egypt under the Fatimids came from elsewhere. An example of this type of Shiʻi itinerant savant was Muhammad al-Karajiki (d. 1057), a prolific author whose interests spanned jurisprudence and *hadith* transmission to astronomy, medicine, grammar and lexicography. From Tripoli, the port city on the eastern Mediterranean coast, he travelled in quest of learning, visiting Egypt on a number of occasions. Al-Karajiki first came to Cairo during al-Hakim's reign when the *dar al-ʻilm* had been operating for some ten years. His reported experiences as a user of that institution in his most famous work, *Kanz al-fawaʼid*, constitute a rare eyewitness account of the activities which took place there. For example, he stated that in the *dar al-ʻilm* he saw an autograph copy of a compendium on astrology, *al-Mughni fi ahkam al-nujum*, by the mid-tenth-century Christian author Ibn Hibinta. This work became popular in Europe thanks to having been quoted by other Muslim authors. However, today only a few complete manuscripts of this text are known to be extant. Parts of this compendium show similarities with sections of the *Book of Curiosities*. In exploring the relationship between the two works, al-Karajiki's witness statement confirming the *Mughni*'s presence in a Fatimid state-sponsored library adds an important piece to the puzzle that is the formation of the *Book*.

In Egypt al-Karajiki attended lectures on topics ranging from the use of analogy as a law-making tool with a Maliki jurist, to enquiring with an Isma'ili scholar about the principle of imamate transmission and the sequence of the imams. While there al-Karajiki collected *hadith*s through meeting Iranian Twelver Shi'is who also travelled to Cairo. He was in the Fatimid capital during the reign of al-Zahir, forming connections with Fatimid elites which he would cultivate once resettled in Syria. While in Cairo he wrote many treatises, including summaries of al-Qadi al-Nu'man's main works. After leaving Egypt al-Karajiki settled in Ramla and then Tripoli, where he continued to maintain his links with high-ranking officials attached to the Fatimid regime in Cairo. Back in Syria and Palestine he composed works on commission, or dedicated to various local rulers whose lives were intertwined with Fatimid politics in Egypt. One family of jurists he served in particular was that of the Bani 'Ammar, credited with founding a *dar al-'ilm* in Tripoli modelled on the Cairo one. There is some indication that al-Karajiki was a librarian in that institution. He may have served as *qadi* in Fatimid-controlled Syria and Palestine before dying in Tyre in 1057. Over time, Twelver Shi'is built a significant presence in Upper Egypt. A fourteenth-century local historian stated that in Fatimid Aswan, Afsun and Armant the Shi'a presence was strong and that in Edfu many people were either Isma'ilis or Twelvers. Despite long-term home-grown Shi'ism in Fatimid Upper Egypt, there is no evidence of a significant intellectual legacy in that region.

The typical mechanisms by which books were purchased, owned and collected consisted of copying them, presenting them as pious donations, trading them but also passing them on through inheritance as family heirlooms.[9] Books were an expensive commodity to the point that, at least according to a custom documented among Jews living in Fatimid Egypt, written sale contracts were drafted when books were traded, a practice that otherwise was applied only to the purchase of houses and slaves.[10] The *warraq* served as a paper vendor, seller of writing tools, copyist and scholar in his own right. This person could occupy varied positions on the social scale from marginal to distinguished scholar. The *kutubi*, in contrast, was the wholesaler or broker of volumes already in circulation.

In eastern Muslim lands by the eleventh century the *madrasa* had become the obvious hub for book production, trade and circulation. In Cairo, *madrasa*s appeared under the Ayyubids, while in Alexandria this institution was established during the last phase of Fatimid rule. The opening of Sunni theological schools in the Mediterranean port city coincided with the arrival of prominent foreign Maliki and Shafiʿi transmitters who enjoyed patronage there. One of them, the Shafiʿi scholar Abu Tahir al-Silafi, amassed an extensive personal library and engaged with the most important booksellers of his time.

From at least the middle of the eleventh century to the end of the Fatimid period and beyond, in the capital the *suq* of the books was located in an alley in Fustat, near the ʿAmr Mosque. It was in this alley that Ibrahim al-Habbal (d. 1089), a famous bookdealer of eleventh-century Egypt, could be found. A Sunni, connected to the family of al-Qadi al-Nuʿman, al-Habbal's mentors included ʿAbd al-Ghani b. Saʿid. Al-Habbal's fame and influence must have generated anxiety within the Fatimid establishment, as at some point the regime forbade him from transmitting *hadith*s, threatened him and controlled his movements. The reason for these restrictions is not known. Al-Habbal's stock of volumes was kept in over five hundred special wooden cases which he sold for 5 *dinar*s each. When five hundred *dinar*s worth of books got spoilt by rain, al-Habbal was advised to build storage to contain his stock but he quipped that a repository the size of the ʿAmr Mosque would be needed to house his collection. He was a trendsetter in storytelling; it was reported that in 1095 al-Darrab's *Book of Marvels* was recounted in his style.

Al-Habbal built his enviable book stock thanks to the extensive network of scholars to which he belonged. Above all, however, al-Habbal's bookselling enterprise must have benefited from the massive number of books that flooded the Cairo market following the plundering of the Fatimid caliphal libraries during a severe economic crisis that hit Egypt during al-Mustansir's reign. On that occasion, unpaid Fatimid troops ransacked the palaces and the royal libraries, dispersing the contents for money. In the aftermath, the book market became so saturated that dealers sent volumes to sell in Alexandria, North Africa and as far as Baghdad. Royal books found their way into private hands.

According to an anecdote, in one of those dire days, Fustat's chief of police gifted two loaves of bread to his children's tutor. The man then sold one loaf to his mentor and the other in the market of the lamps for 14 silver *dirham*s. With the money, he then approached the guards at the entrance to the palace library who sold him books at one *dirham* each. Back at his home, the teacher hid the books in a hole that he had dug in the ceiling. In times of cash-flow crises books also entered the market through being released from the royal libraries to serve as collateral in lieu of the salary that the regime owed to government officials.

In the late Fatimid period, another figure at the heart of the distribution of knowledge was Ahmad al-Fasi (d. 1165). A Maliki Qur'an reciter and *qadi*, al-Fasi, helped by his wife and daughter – like him, renowned calligraphers – established a cottage industry in book-copying on commission or for sale. Specializing in works on jurisprudence, *hadith*s and literature, the family's quality trademark was their refusal to sell a finished book if it contained even one orthographic error.

Perhaps the most effective way for an ordinary person to buy books at reasonable prices was through auctions. At the end of Fatimid rule a figure who dominated the auction market was the Fatimid–Ayyubid high official al-Qadi al-Fadil (d. 1200), one of the most discerning book collectors of the time. He was credited with having spent almost a year's worth of his revenues to purchase for 30,000 *dinar*s a large Qur'anic manuscript believed to have been one of the codices put in circulation by the third caliph 'Uthman. Al-Qadi al-Fadil was known to buy books on every subject from everywhere. In his days the most prominent Cairo bookseller was Ibn Sura (d. 1210). This trader used to conduct his business from the vestibule of his mansion on Sundays and Wednesdays, selling books to men of rank and learning. Ibn Sura had built a reputation as a vendor who could be trusted to meet the demands of the most discerning customer. One day al-Qadi al-Fadil asked him for a copy of a popular anthology of the time, *al-Hamasa*, for his child to read. Ibn Sura proceeded to show his customer 35 manuscripts of the work from his stock. Al-Qadi al-Fadil went through each copy, recognizing the hand of the copyist of each manuscript, but concluded that none was of a standard adequate for his child, so he ordered Ibn Sura to procure him a copy for a *dinar*. Ibn Sura's status as the pre-eminent twelfth-century Cairo bookseller was secured when, in Alexandria, he bought one of the most important private book collections of his time upon the death of its owner, Abu Tahir al-Silafi.[11]

An additional chance to siphon books from the Fatimid royal collection en masse came in 1171 with the end of the dynasty and its rule.[12] Once again, al-Qadi al-Fadil managed to position himself as the right person at the right time.

Jews played a prominent role in the book trade of the Fatimid period.[13] Evidence gathered from the Cairo Geniza documents shows that it was typical of physicians to dedicate themselves to this commerce. Wholesalers included trading in books among a diverse array of products they dealt with, such as flax, silk, olive oil, spices and metals. Within the context of a small Jewish community, the activities surrounding book production and exchange were concentrated in the hands of a close-knit intellectual elite among the merchant and civil servant classes.[14] As for literary production and intellectual agency, Judeo-Arabic became the dominant literary language for prose, while Hebrew remained the preferred language for poetry. An example of the shared use of language and literary styles in the works of the same author can be found in the Alexandrian Karahite poet Moses Dar'i, active in the late Fatimid period. The Cairo Geniza documents reveal a substantial literary canon of secular and liturgical poetry being produced and circulated during the Fatimid period. In the twelfth century the wealthy Jewish community of Fatimid Fustat paid a hefty ransom to retrieve the Aleppo Codex, the oldest known complete manuscript of the Torah, that the Crusaders had stolen in Jerusalem. The subsequent vicissitudes of this codex have been surrounded by mystery to this day, with part of the manuscript having disappeared and the remaining section kept in the Shrine of the Book in Jerusalem (illus. 35).[15] Towards the end of Fatimid rule it was among the Jewish community of Fustat that the Cordoban Jewish philosopher Maimonides (d. 1204), one of the most influential thinkers of all time, settled and thrived.

There is reason to believe that Christian scholars too had their own networks through which books changed hands via family legacy, copying and trading. However, by this period Coptic literature output had suffered a general decline. One of the most significant developments in the Coptic literary production of the Fatimid period was a linguistic shift from the use of Coptic to Arabic as a writing medium of choice. First through translations from one language to another, and then through direct use of Arabic, Copto-Arabic monastic, hagiographical, homiletic and liturgical literature came to incorporate idioms of other Arabic literary production it encountered. It was in response

35 Folio from the Aleppo Codex (Deut. 28:17–45), Shrine of the Book, Jerusalem.

to the adoption of Arabic as the language of the Egyptian Christians that Gabriel II, Coptic Patriarch of Alexandria, had the Bible and other sacred literature translated into Arabic in 1131.[16] The gathering speed of this linguistic change during the Fatimid period has been interpreted as an effect of the power relation that high-ranking Copts had established with the regime. At elite level, working for the state administration implied having a full command of written Arabic, the use of which went beyond the production of state documents. The language shift was also the result of a gradual demographic decline in the Coptic population, which through conversion, inter-marriage and other factors became assimilated with the Muslims of Egypt. The most important Coptic work in Arabic for this period was translated in English with the title *History of the Patriarchs of the Coptic Church of Alexandria*. Ascribed to Severus b. al-Muqaffa (d. 987), it was in fact produced over an extended period of time by several authors, the Alexandrian Mawhub b. Mansur b. Mufarrij being the most prominent, covering the eleventh and twelfth centuries.[17] This semi-official history of the Coptic Church is also a valuable first-hand source of information on Fatimid history in general. The linguistic Arabization of the Christians of Egypt also affected the Armenian community, which grew in size and social impact in the twelfth century. Among the Melkites, a distinguished literary figure was Sulayman al-Ghazzi (d. after 1027), active in Palestine in the first half of the eleventh century, who authored poetry and theological works.[18]

Visual, Applied and Decorative Arts

In keeping with a trend that was typical of the medieval art world anywhere, artists and craftsmen active in Islamic territories followed the money. The lavishness that the Fatimids had brought to their court and the lifestyle of social elites meant that artists set aside political, ideological and religious divides in pursuit of Fatimid patronage. Craftsmen flocked to Egypt from Iraq, Iran and Central Asia to offer to new masters their skills ranging from know-how in lustreware manufacture to rock crystal carving, a craft apparently not known in Egypt before the reign of the imam-caliph al-ʿAziz. The Fatimid regime sought every opportunity and means to upstage the ʿAbbasids, Umayyads and Byzantines in court splendour and market affluence. Combined with the contribution of local talent, the outcome was the production of thousands of objects ranging from ceramics, metal, glass, stone and textiles to ivory, wood, paper and rock crystal.[19] To this day extant artefacts produced under the Fatimids bring to life accounts of the lavish lifestyle enjoyed at the time by both royals and urban elites. This is how Nasir-i Khusraw described what he saw in the lamp market by the 'Amr Mosque:

> Every sort of rare goods from all over the world can be had there. I saw tortoise-shell implements such as small boxes, combs, knife handles, and so on. I also saw extremely fine crystal, which the master craftsmen etch most beautifully. I saw elephant tusks . . . a type of skin . . . that resembled leopard, from which they make sandals . . . In Old Cairo they make all types of porcelain, so fine and translucent . . . they make cups, bowls, plates, and . . . paint them to resemble bulanqamun [a type of lustrous fabric similar to taffeta] so that different colours show depending on how the article is held. They also produce a glass so pure and flawless that it resembles chrysolite, as it is sold by weight.[20]

The fortunes of the Isma'ili propaganda system that led to the establishment of the Fatimid caliphate are linked to the production and distribution of textiles. The Isma'ili imams of the ninth century hid their identity behind the guise of cloth wholesalers. The *da'is* conducted their undercover operations in support of the imam's cause by working as itinerant traders in textiles. The revenues from the sale of fabrics provided most of the financial support that was necessary for the propaganda network to succeed in Ifriqiya. Textiles were the major industry in the medieval Mediterranean, a production that the Fatimids came to dominate in terms of both quality and the quantity of items circulating at home and through international trade. Indeed, the Fatimids' economic affluence was built on the production and distribution of fabrics, as they became famous for their export of flax and linen cloth. Nasir-i Khusraw observed, 'I saw a caravanserai there called Dar al-Wazir, where nothing but flax was sold, and on the lower floor there were tailors while above were specialists in cloth repair.'[21] Above all the Fatimids established themselves in the textile trade for the quality of their inscribed *tiraz*. *Tiraz* is a word of Persian origin used to indicate a textile featuring embroidered – or in the case of the Fatimids, woven – inscribed bands. Typical inscriptions featured on a *tiraz* consisted of benedictory and laudatory formulae, the name of the ruler and his ancestry, the name of the ruler's vizier, the nature of the production workshop (private or public), and the place and date of production. The word *tiraz* was also used to indicate the type of workshop where such textiles were produced (illus. 26).

In Egypt these ateliers were already established in the ninth century to serve the needs of the 'Abbasid court, but it was under Fatimid rule that the industry reached its zenith. From the main Egyptian factories in Tinnis, Alexandria, Cairo and the Fayyum region, the most expensive *tiraz* would feature laudatory inscriptions enriched with gold, silver and silk threads.[22] Besides writing in bold Arabic font, designs on fabrics ranged from representations of mythical and exotic animals and birds to humans in varied settings and also images of the Islamic paradise, including its ever-virgin inhabitants, the *huri*s. Beyond the Islamic context and characteristics applied to the textiles, in Egypt it was Coptic craftsmen who transferred, in their productions for their new masters, the designs and motifs they had relied on for centuries before (illus. 41). Beyond clothing, *tiraz* also came to be used as an architectural term to denote friezes on buildings.

Irrespective of religious denomination, the textile industry was the most common area of employment for women. Factories of various sizes existed in most cities of the Islamic middle period, and these ateliers employed slaves, forced labourers and paid male and female workers at various stages of the production process. Notwithstanding regional variants, most of the working population and the trading community were engaged in this branch of the economy. Working the spindle was the most widespread labour occupation that women are known to have engaged in across the Islamic lands in this period. Women of all ranks and backgrounds spun, either for personal need, as a pastime, to earn, out of marital duty, or to serve a religious-political cause. Within the Fatimid court, for example, Rashida, the spinster daughter of the imam-caliph al-Mu'izz, occupied herself with spinning. Typical of those who spun for money were spinsters, widows, divorcees, orphans and the poor, that is, women who lacked the financial support that men were expected to provide. Among Jews in Fatimid Egypt, custom and statutory law recognized spinning as one of the duties of a wife, as shown in some Jewish marriage documents from the Cairo Geniza.[23]

The most common yarns that women used for their work were flax and wool. Flax became the main crop cultivated in Egypt, privileged even above grain since flax fed the profitable linen industry. It was grown in winter, joined by summer crops such as cotton and sugarcane, using water from the river Nile that in low season was drawn by mechanical means. Silk was imported from Tunisia, Sicily and the Iberian Peninsula in form of cocoons which were then processed in Egypt. In turn, raw flax was exported to Sicily, Ifriqiya and further afield.

These yarns were supplied by vendors in the bazar. The gendered character of spinning meant that female customers had to interact with male traders, a proximity that – in a society bent on enforcing gender separation – led to the devising of a code of conduct and regulations. In medieval Islamic manuals for market inspectors instructions are given on how the transactions between male vendors of yarns and female buyers should be conducted. The potential risk of sexual misconduct occurring between men and women during such trade encounters was not lost on medieval observers, who saw spinners and weavers as akin to prostitutes.[24] As for silk, a common practice across all silk-growing areas was for women to nest silk worms in their bosom in order to support their incubation with the warmth of their bodies. Women unravelled, reeled, spun, wove and dyed silk threads, that is, they were occupied in activities that demanded high levels of skills.

Spindles were the obvious essential items that women needed in order to spin. These were purchased in markets, and as such the trading of spindles had to be regulated too. Market inspectors manuals set out not only a code of conduct but specific standards to ensure that spindles met the appropriate quality specifications, thereby preventing women from being duped by being sold tools of inferior quality. In Fatimid Cairo the making of spindles in itself evolved into a thriving industry.

After spinning, embroidery was the second most popular activity that links women to textile production in the medieval Mediterranean. Embroidered items were not only for personal use but were traded, with women reported to have occasionally sold their needlework products in markets through female brokers. However, large-scale professional embroidery, and its supervision in workshops, was a male preserve. Since embroidery patterns commissioned by clients were copyrighted, whoever was tasked with carrying out the work of transferring a particular pattern onto cloth by needlework had to swear not to replicate the same design elsewhere without the permission of the client.[25] The imposition of such an oath meant the embroiderer had to be in a position of seniority, which women did not occupy in that sector.

Also, large-scale weaving and dyeing for industrial production was a male preserve when the use of gold and silver threads was involved. In Fatimid Egypt, the use of gold for textile production was supervised by a government-appointed high dignitary, since the handling of gold thread was related to the activities of the mint, a male-dominated realm.

It is unclear how much of the large-scale textile work was done by women in workshops and how much work was done individually or in small groups at home. The Fatimids established an administrative department, the *dar al-tiraz*, that oversaw the work of two categories of factories: those that specialized in the production of textiles to serve the imam-caliph and his court and those that, while belonging to the ruler, produced textiles for the general public. Women working in ateliers that served the court were given a distinctive title that pointed to them belonging to a specific professional class. Following his arrival in Cairo, in 973 the imam-caliph al-Mu'izz ordered the establishment of a special government tailoring department known as *dar al-kiswa* which served as an official bureau overseeing the production, storage and distribution of costumes for the court members and the palace staff. The imam-caliph was responsible for supplying each courtier in his service and his family with complete sets of clothes every season of the year. Over time, the great demand generated by the court's needs caused the exponential growth in staffing, size, number and productivity of state textile factories in Egypt, which were supervised by officials who controlled the quality of the products. The importance that the Fatimid regime gave to fabrics as a potent signifier of majesty is reflected in the extreme care given to the choice of uniforms and furnishings in parades and diplomatic receptions at the palace. For the ceremony of the opening of the canal Nasir-i Khusraw observed that:

> a large pavilion of Byzantine brocade spun with gold and set in gems [was] assembled . . . for the Sultan . . . ten thousand horses with gold saddles and bridles and jewel-studded reins . . . all . . . with saddle-cloths of Byzantine brocade and buqalamun . . . in the borders of the cloth are woven inscriptions bearing the name of the sultan of Egypt.[26]

On other occasions elephants were decked with saddlecloths in red embroidered fabrics, bearing palanquins furnished with matching cushions, pillows, carpeted seats, curtains and spreads of silk brocade. The imam-caliph's ultimate sign of his endorsement of an individual of high rank was his personal bestowal of the *khil'a*, the robe of honour. The Fatimids, with their excellence in textile production, more than other dynasties elevated this garment as a potent device for the public display of royal favour.[27]

The wardrobe of the imam was attended to by a person who held the title of *zayn al-khuzzan* (ornament of the treasurers). This supervisor had oversight over some thirty female workers and of the handling of the most precious robes reserved for the court. Towards the end of the Fatimid dynasty the *zayn al-khuzzan* was known to have been a female slave of Byzantine origin, thus indicating that neither gender nor social status nor religious affiliation stood in the way of a woman occupying such a sensitive position at the heart of the court. What did the imam-caliphs wear? The apparel worn by rulers and high officers in public ceremonies and parades is known since it is often described in chronicles and historical accounts. For example, Nasir-i Khusraw described the attire of al-Mustansir at the opening of the canal ceremony:

> the sultan, a well-built, clean shaven youth with cropped hair . . . is mounted on a camel . . . and wears a white shirt, as is the custom in Arab countries, with a wide cummerbund . . . called . . . dabiqi in Egypt . . . On his head he has a turban of the same colour . . . At the sultan's side rides the parasol-bearer with a bejewelled, gold turban and a suit of clothing worth ten thousand dinars. The parasol he holds is extremely ornate and studded with jewels and pearls.[28]

The written recollections of courtiers working within the private sphere of the imams give us an insight into their master's informal and domestic attire, the one worn away from the public eye. In his memoir Jawdhar, the arch-secretary and confidant in Ifriqiya of the first four Fatimid caliphs, described the informal clothes they wore. Al-Mu'izz donned angora wool leggings and a lined coat in cotton from Marw (a city in Iran which was famous for the superior softness of that fabric), with a tunic underneath. Al-Mahdi owned a lined coat in plain colour in silk cloth and tunics. Al-Qa'im instead sported tunics, trousers, a turban and a white trouser band in sought-after Armenian cloth. Al-Mansur also had a robe in fabric from Marw like that of

36 Fatimid ivory carved 'frame', 12th century.

37 Fatimid bronze deer-shaped jug for hand washing, late 10th–early 11th century.

38 Fatimid ivory 'doll', 10th–11th century.

39 Fatimid ewer, late 10th–early 11th century, rock crystal, enamelled gold. This work is one of seven surviving rock crystal ewers made for the rulers of Cairo during the Fatimid period. It was set with gold mounts (top, handle and base) by the goldsmith Jean-Valentin Morel in 1854 in Sèvres, France.

40 Detail of the 'The Veil of St Anne', an early 12th-century Fatimid textile.

41 Lovers in the Garden, Coptic, Egyptian, Fatimid Period, 11th century, wool and linen.

42 Badr al-Jamali's wooden pulpit now in the Ibrahimi Mosque in Hebron.

43 Wooden cenotaph believed to have been used to transport al-Husayn's head to Cairo, 12th century.

44 Fatimid wooden *mihrab* of the Mashhad of Sayyida Ruqayya. Dating from 1154–60, it was commissioned by 'Alam al-Amiriyya.

45 Queen Arwa and the Sulayhids in the game expansion *Crusader Kings® II: Sword of Islam* (2012).

46 Queen Arwa's shrine in Dhu Jibla, Yemen, 12th century.

al-Mu'izz. All these garments Jawdhar had received from the latter as gifts, intended as a sign of his blessing.

The ownership of clothing and textiles enabled the women of the court to exhibit agency and power. The vast quantities of the finest textiles and dresses recorded as having belonged to the royal Fatimid princesses indicate that such items were not only intended for personal use but in fact traded as commodities. Royal women are reported to have relied on commercial brokers acting on their behalf. In general textiles were desirable assets for women (and men) because they maintained their value, were durable and were easily movable products that could be exchanged for cash if necessary. Among ordinary women, the textiles and fine garments of their bridal trousseau, beyond the bride's personal use, were considered an investment which was often passed from parents to children and could be converted into money. Documents from the Cairo Geniza show that a bride's dowry consisted in general of objects, with textiles being by far the most common type. In times of need, selling a piece from her wardrobe could provide a woman with months of sustenance. The practice of exchanging textiles for cash was quite widespread and women were known to dispense with home furnishings to pay debts. Even well-to-do ladies sold, through eunuchs, items from their wardrobe in Fustat's second-hand clothes bazar.[29]

Represented or extant, Islamic or Coptic, Fatimid textiles are a rich source of information on the use of colours in decorative arts concerning dyes, techniques and desirability. Some colours, for example, were preferred over others: blue, because of the high cost of indigo, was suited to luxury goods; red was also much in demand; yellow was unpopular due to negative connotations associated with it (the Prophet Muhammad disliked it); black, the colour favoured by the 'Abbasids, was avoided by the Fatimids who instead adopted white for their trademark flags. Though favoured by the Prophet and associated with the 'Alids, green cloth was a challenge to sell because this pigment did not print well and faded fast, limitations that made it unattractive for long-term investment in textiles of this colour.

More details on the applied use of colour schemes during the Fatimid period emerge from the description of the interior decoration of some important Fatimid mosques like the one built by Durzan, the consort of al-Mu'izz and mother of al-'Aziz, in al-Qarafa. The most outstanding extant example of the use of colours in paintings that may have echoed an artistic vocabulary also in use in Fatimid palaces can be found on the ceiling of the Cappella Palatina in Palermo, built between circa 1132 and 1140 (illus. 27).[30] In terms of books, the tenth-century gold calligraphed Blue Qur'an set the tone in terms of the Fatimids' penchant for grandeur in advertising themselves as the ultimate Muslim leaders. Once in the library of the Great Mosque of Qayrawan, it became dispersed, with loose folios ending up in art collections around the world.[31] Beyond this unique Islamic masterpiece, as objects at the intersection of codicology and art history, miniatures in Fatimid manuscripts would have provided us with the best visual reference to the use of colours in the figurative arts of the time. Vast numbers of illustrated books enriched the Fatimid libraries but only a handful of examples of illustrations on paper produced in the Fatimid period have survived. The extant items also present problems of attribution and function. The most impressive is a full-figure drawing of a nude woman. The purpose and contextual production of this artefact is unknown (illus. 25). Other well-known surviving pieces include a paper leaf with a woodcut image of two warriors; block printed amulets in Cairo's Museum of Islamic Art; the images of a lion and a hare on a paper folio at the Metropolitan Museum in New York, and a fragment of a coloured drawing in the Keir Collection, at present in the Dallas Museum of Art.[32]

The most encountered examples of Fatimid decorative figural motifs occur in the recognizable glazed earthenware bowls, plates, jugs and ceramic pieces that in the Islamic middle period flooded the markets of Egypt, those of Cairo-controlled regions and far-flung destinations. A large number of these objects was found during archaeological excavations in Fustat between 1965 and 1981. Precious and exquisite as this lustreware production was, its wide circulation in medieval Egypt indicates that this type of manufacture was intended for the wealthy bourgeoisie and the general public rather than just royal use. To date, the largest ceramic dish from the Fatimid past known to be extant is in Cairo's Museum of Islamic Art. It was made for Ghabn, a commander who served al-Hakim between 1011 and 1013. For themselves the Fatimid royals preferred Chinese porcelains, stoneware jars and footed marble basins. But although in Ifriqiya the use of Chinese ceramics was a taste the rulers acquired by making use of what the Aghlabid *amir*s had left behind, in Egypt Chinese porcelain was part of a state-endorsed importation of luxury goods. Trendy urban bourgeoisie caught up with the court by adopting imitation Chinese pottery.[33]

Beyond quality homeware made for the elites, the greatest amount of pottery was left unglazed and destined for the daily use of ordinary people. Also, urban production was more refined than the provincial. Among surviving fragments and sherds of mass-made pottery are pierced clay water filters that, plugged in the neck of a jug, stopped rubbish floating in the water passing through into the container. Quality lustre Fatimid ceramics were decorated – often using gold paint – with animals, birds, hunting scenes, musicians, dancers, entertainers, wine-drinking dignitaries, wrestling fighters, cockfights, rope dancing and duels (illus. 21). Under Fatimid rule, al-Qadi al-Nu'man enshrined in law the permissibility of artistic figural representation, something that might have favoured its proliferation. However, apart from some distinctive Fatimid features, these images were part of a visual vocabulary shared across the courts, aimed at projecting a sense of the positive, hedonistic mood prevailing at the time. The extent to which these scenes can be considered a faithful representation of reality has been the subject of debate.[34] Nevertheless, the images on the many plates and bowls visible to us constitute a catalogue of styles and tastes in vogue under the Fatimids. While there was an overlap of themes and motifs across religious affiliations, Copts and Jews also

47 Fatimid lustreware ceramic shard decorated with an image of Christ, 10th–11th century.

devised distinctive motifs for ceramics destined for their respective communities (illus. 47).

Metalware with conclusive attribution to Egypt or Syria during the Fatimid period is rare. Nevertheless, recent findings of Fatimid metal artefacts in the Mediterranean sea, such as large hoards from Spain, Caesarea and Tiberias, testify to their international desirability.[35] The dominant type of production in this period consisted of bronze objects for domestic and ritual use such as lampstands, ewers, buckets, pans, amulet boxes, braziers and animal-shaped incense burners, as well as fountainheads, monumental pieces and weaponry. A bronze lion-shaped fountain piece can be admired in Cairo's Museum of Islamic Art. Water dispensers in the shape of a deer were popular everyday artefacts (illus. 37). A Fatimid miniature bronze gazelle dating to the late tenth or early eleventh century sold by Christie's in 2011 became one of the most expensive Islamic art objects sold at auction in recent years.

The use of luxury objects, adornments and jewellery in gold and silver was common at court and among the elites. Eleventh-century fine Fatimid filigree jewellery pieces with their distinctive granulation motif are among the most prized possessions of public and private collections. Precious metals were also used to make coins. The 24-carat *Mu'izzi dinar* was the finest in circulation at the time, across a vast territory well beyond the Fatimids' borders. The *dinar* was used as reserve, or for large purchases such as lands or properties. The *dirham* was for regular use. The introduction of the Fatimid currency as the official trading monetary denomination in the domains under Cairo's control caused the collapse in value of the previous currencies; those who had savings in pre-Fatimid money suffered massive losses. After the arrival of al-Mu'izz only his *dinar*s were accepted for trading. Market volatility occurred when, to address an economic crisis, a new *dinar–dirham* exchange rate was imposed during al-Hakim's reign. This caused such an instability in the value of currency that, in time, it brought about economic stagnation. The regime intervened by injecting new *dirham*s into circulation and by ordering the withdrawal of old ones. Prices went up and fraud and speculation on the sale of goods ensued. The regime policed and punished accordingly.[36] An added difficulty that affected monetary policies was that while the Fatimids had plenty of gold thanks to their access to and control of gold mines in Upper Egypt, silver was scarce. This made *dirham*s more expensive to produce, due to high demand, though lower in value when compared with the *dinar*. The relative scarcity of silver coins in circulation was addressed with single *dirhams* being cut up and chipped away to generate small change.

Specific use of language and inscribed formulae gave Fatimid buildings, objects and coins a distinctive Isma'ili imprint and identity. The use of a particular Arabic font known as floriated Kufic served to brand surfaces with epigraphic panels that were recognizable to all, irrespective of literacy levels or religious inclination. When, in the twelfth century, for propaganda purposes, the need arose for writings on the walls to become clearer to wider audiences, an easier to read font appeared on public buildings.[37] The use of symbolism served to advertise the dynasty's credentials as sole rightful universal leader. Significant in this respect is the insistence, irrespective of medium or artefact, on the use of astronomical references as a decorative motif. One example is the occurrence of the six-pointed star – evocative of the seal of Solomon – which made its appearance on both objects and architecture throughout the duration of the dynasty. Its use signalled the paradigmatic link the dynasty had established between itself and light, as well as the cyclical sequence of six imams whereby the seventh was the culmination of a cycle. Representations of the crescent moon, a standard symbol associated with Islam, acquired Fatimid-specific meanings. The Fatimids had made the moon a term of reference that distinguished Isma'ili ritual practice from that of all other Muslims. By Fatimid law, in fact, the rise of the new moon that signalled the start and end of the fasting of Ramadan was determined by astronomical calculation and not, as with all other Muslims, by eye observation. However, the frequent representation of a crescent moon in groups of three may point to the Fatimids' adoption of the symbol for its eschatological significance. In Islamic belief one of the signs announcing the eschaton is a triple eclipse of the moon. In keeping with their messianic self-image, the three moons that the Fatimids showcased as a decorative motif were not simple crescents but rather the visible slice of the eclipsed moons predicting a messianic era, the advent of which the dynasty claimed to have fulfilled.

In terms of workmanship, the definite contours of what constitute unique Fatimid artistic expressions are difficult to draw. The cosmopolitan nature of the imported human capital that came to produce artefacts for the Cairo regime meant that craftsmen not only brought with them technical skills but transferred to a Fatimid context

48 Fatimid-style Sicilian ivory casket (detail), 11th–12th century.

imagery and tastes matured to meet the aesthetic and ideological expectations of different audiences.

Nevertheless, the Fatimids, by creating through patronage a climate that stimulated the blending of foreign styles and techniques with local pre-Fatimid artistic vocabulary, gave impetus to the production of a spectacular number of distinctive artefacts, the superb quality of which became sought after across the Mediterranean and in markets further afield. Some of these artistic expressions transferred to Sicily where they were embraced and even promoted by the Normans once in power.

Small objects like Sicilian ivory caskets as well as grand projects such as the paintings on the ceilings of Cefalù's cathedral and Palermo's Cappella Palatina are a remarkable example of this transfer (illus. 48). In the Palatina, looking up at the ceiling we enter moments of eleventh-century Arab everyday life: veiled women going for errands travelling in a palanquin perched on a camel; elsewhere two chess players enjoy the game in the privacy of their home; some women dance, others play musical instruments. From the ceiling looking down on the visitors a bearded Norman king, Roger II, wearing a three-pointed 'crown', is seated legs akimbo, holding a cup and entertained by a musician. The image resembles one previously made in marble, found in the ruins of al-Mansuriyya, representing a Fatimid imam-caliph flanked by a flute player. In turn the Fatimids in Ifriqiya had adopted styles left behind by their predecessors. What might have been the image of a Byzantine king was carried forward to become that of an Isma'ili imam-caliph, only to return to represent Christian royalty in Palermo. Such a fusion of styles may be so remarkable that it can be hard in some cases to determine the exact purposes and cultural affiliation of an object: a carved ivory oliphant, is it Fatimid? Norman? Southern Italian? And what was it for? Another example of such a transfer of craftmanship and taste is a huge lion's head made of carved rock crystal in the Fatimid style, once used as a fountainhead in one of the Norman palaces in Sicily.[38]

To this day the art world agrees in celebrating the artistic output of the Fatimids as representative of the Islamic golden age. It is the exquisite quality and lavishness of this production that frames this written portrait of the Fatimid age (illus. 36).

9

Being a Woman in the Age of the Fatimids

In wishing to add female faces with definite contours to our portrait of the Fatimid age, the unveiling of women's lives in Cairo requires the patient and careful lifting of several layers. In general, to tap into the Islamic past represents a major challenge due to the general lack of extant documentary and archival evidence to complement material and literary sources. This means that, in most cases, when it comes to women, we can only infer what their life experiences might have been. The Fatimids, however, offer us opportunity for an insight into women's lives that is not available to the same extent when looking at the lives of women under other Islamic dynasties. Being the only long-lasting independent Shiʿi Ismaʿili dynasty to reign over an extensive territory during an Islamic middle period that was dominated by Sunni rulers, the Fatimids attracted the attention of the historians and chroniclers of the time. They commented on the affairs of male-dominated political and social elites, but in the process they also included information on aspects of women's lives and deeds in their narratives.

In keeping with the vast majority of medieval sources, none of the primary material at our disposal that contains details on women's affairs was written by women and, as a whole, male writers did not deal with women as their primary concern. To a large extent what is known about women in medieval Islam is more revealing about men's perceptions of them than about the women themselves. Sources are revealing about how male writers – and the male protagonists they wrote about, or for – viewed women, and what they thought relevant to report based on their worldview, backgrounds and aims. As a result, in evaluating the quality of information we derive from these informants, we need to bear in mind the social, political and cultural contexts that impacted on the writers' perspectives.

Wading our way through a maze of mixed-quality writings from different genres, armed with a few documents and carrying the occasional object, we can nevertheless position our easel in the palaces and streets of Fatimid Cairo to capture some aspects of the women who lived in the city and other relevant territories.

Inside the Court

Throughout the North African phase of Fatimid history, we find women – whether royal or commoners – making only shadowy cameo appearances in the events that shaped the Fatimid age of that period. With the arrival of the caliphal family in Cairo, thanks to the expansion and greater formalization of court life women gained a prominence that translated into deeds which in turn granted them greater visibility. In Fatimid Egypt women emerged in narratives as figures with defined contours, something that testifies to a shift in the way their place in society came to be perceived, whether at court or in the street.

The first royal woman to emerge as a noteworthy figure was Durzan, consort of al-Muʿizz and mother of his successor al-ʿAziz. She also became famous as Taghrid (Twittering), on account of her melodious voice. According to some sources she was a slave of Arab descent, to others a cousin of the imam, and from being described as a diminutive figure who sang at her son's private parties, she rose to become one of the most visible female figures of the Fatimid period, thanks to her reputation as a prolific architectural patroness.[1] To date, Durzan is one of only two women of the Fatimid royal family for whom we have not just literary but also direct material sources testifying to their existence. An extant inscribed limestone slab refers to Durzan (indicated as the mother of al-ʿAziz) as the commissioner of a building. The other material evidence relating to a Fatimid royal woman is the mausoleum dedicated to Sayyida Ruqayya, one of ʿAli's daughters, the construction of which in the Qarafa area started in 1133. A plaque in its interior identifies ʿAlam al-Amiriyya, consort of the twelfth-century Fatimid caliph al-Amir, as the commissioner of the wooden tomb in its interior believed to preserve the dedicatee's remains. ʿAlam is also named as the patron behind the wooden niche pointing to the direction of Mecca, *mihrab*, that was made for that shrine (illus. 44).

Other than the buildings ascribed to Durzan and the remarks on her singing talent, little is known of her life. She may have been the first Fatimid royal woman recorded to have been addressed in public with the title of Sayyida. The honour signalled an order of seniority of a woman over men, at least in given circumstances; it was this Sayyida who summoned the high dignitaries of the regime, including Ibn Killis, to the bed of her dying consort. Durzan herself died in 995. Upon hearing of his mother's death, al-'Aziz, who was out of Cairo at a military encampment, returned to the capital to perform the funeral prayer for her.

Durzan's association with architectural patronage relates to structures erected outside the city walls over a period of more than twenty years. In Fustat the *manazil al-'izz*, pleasure pavilions built in 973–5, are attributed to her, although some sources ascribe the patronage of this structure to the imam-caliph al-Mu'izz, claiming that he had it built for one of his sisters. Rated as one of the finest buildings in the area, but no longer extant, it was described as a belvedere by the Nile. On one side it faced Rawda island and on the other it looked at a wall of the Qasr al-Sham, the citadel that in time became known as Coptic Cairo. This latter complex, not far from the 'Amr Mosque, included the monumental Mu'allaqa Church and the Ben Ezra Synagogue of Geniza documents fame.

Durzan's link to the mosque and *qasr* (castle, fortress) built in 976–7 in al-Qarafa is uncontested; the construction was managed through an official that today we would call a project manager. Neither is now extant. The mosque was built as part of a regeneration policy of the area, on the site of a pre-existing one known as Masjid al-Qubba. The mosque and the castle served a number of purposes: to provide new facilities for residents; to accommodate the needs of an area growing in population; and to mark with a Fatimid imprint the landscape outside the royal city. Claiming this area helped to reinforce the strategic link between establishment Cairo and commercial Fustat. The muscular quality of Durzan's constructions was in keeping with other regenerative projects of her time. By 975, the Fustat bridge had been repaired, allowing people to cross again after years of disruption. In the same year, in light of the reopening of this important point of transit along the pilgrimage route, it was announced that the caravan heading for Mecca would proceed by land after having been suspended for some time.

A *muhtasib* appointed to carry out the work, in this context, in addition to being a market inspector, acted as a municipal officer whose responsibilities stretched from repairing houses and erecting shops to public safety, street cleaning, maintenance of the city walls and ensuring the quarter's water supplies. As for the Fatimidization of the landscape beyond Cairo, this took the shape of advertising the dynasty by marking the territory with buildings associated with the regime, such as Durzan's mosque, reported to have been built in the style of al-Azhar. According to an eleventh-century description,

> The Mosque of the Qarafa was decorated with paintings in blue, vermillion, verdigris and other colours and, in certain places, painted a uniform colour. The ceilings were entirely painted in polychrome and the intrados and the extrados of the arcades resting on the columns were covered with paintings of all colours. This decoration is the work of the painters of Basra and of the Bani Mu'allim, of whom Kutami and Nazuk were the masters.[2]

Opposite one of the mosque's doors there was a *trompe l'oeil* of a stepped fountain. Of all this beauty only a green mihrab escaped a fire that at some point ravaged the building. A mausoleum that was built next to it is also attributed to Durzan. The extant limestone foundation slab referring to her might have belonged to this structure. Durzan's architectural patronage played a significant role in transforming al-Qarafa into an upmarket, sought-after area to the point that, in Fatimid times, the nobility was known to gather at her mosque. The area around her *qasr* became a favourite meeting point for the palace entourage during festivals.

Durzan is also believed to have commissioned a well, a *hammam*, at least two gardens, a cistern, a basin for ritual ablutions and a hydraulic pump that would be renovated by her daughter Sitt al-Malik. A basin or fountain built in 995 in the centre of Ibn Tulun Mosque courtyard is attributed to her. As most of the writers who reported on Durzan's building activity were not contemporary to the events they described, it is possible that constructions that became known by Durzan's name might not have been commissioned by her after all. For the dynasty to advertise itself by this unusually extensive use of a woman's name signalled something about how the ruling family wanted to project itself to its subjects. Building activity associated with Durzan coincided with her becoming queen mother of the reigning ruler al-ʻAziz, an event that occurred at a significant time in Fatimid dynastic history. With her consort al-Muʻizz having died only two years after moving to Cairo, as the mother of his successor Durzan found herself to be the most prominent woman in the court, though not one with power. In fact, it was her contemporary, ʻA'isha, a concubine of ʻAbd Allah, the first intended heir apparent of al-Muʻizz, whom sources point to as one of the most powerful women of this court.

Al-Muʻizz's death occurred during a time of transition for the Fatimids, from being a North African provincial dynasty to becoming, once in Cairo, one with imperial clout. This transformation manifested itself in the upgrading of the court ceremonial, in the rapid urban expansion of Cairo and in greater complexity in the management of the regime. At this juncture Durzan was the first Fatimid queen mother in a new royal court, the organization and functioning of which was overseen by the vizier Ibn Killis.[3] Did he guide Durzan's hand in the building activities attributed to her? The architectural works ascribed to Durzan constitute the first known major public buildings erected by the Fatimids outside the walls of the royal city. Durzan's buildings can therefore be regarded as the earliest known attempt on the part of the Fatimids to leave their urban mark on a broader landscape. The imam's name graced the glorious buildings of Cairo. Outside it, Durzan, as queen mother, was propelled to become a symbolic locus of power. At this junction, Durzan was the only senior royal other than the imam-caliph whose name could be used to advertise the dynasty to non-Ismaʻili subjects. To ascribe buildings to royal brothers, thus risking signalling their power, was asking for genealogical trouble; to promote the imam's children through architecture was ineffective since, without open appointment and until the actual moment of ascent to the throne, the outcome of the succession choice was open. The queen mother was therefore the only royal figure whose loyalty could not be questioned, since her own status was sanctioned by the blood link with the reigning imam-caliph. For the high dignitaries at the Fatimid court, to project and promote Durzan as a figure of prestige through architectural patronage meant marking with a royal stamp a strategic landscape, while advertising the dynasty in a safe way.

As for Durzan being described as an Arab singing girl, we are perhaps dealing with one of the gender stereotypes that were typical of literature of the Islamic middle period. Was Durzan an Arab and therefore assumed to be a good singer? Was she a good singer and therefore assumed to be an Arab? She might have been both. We have plenty of visual references, on ceramics and ivories, to female entertainers at the Fatimid court. However, the sheer abundance of objects from the Fatimid period featuring the female entertainer as decorative motif reinforces the view of Durzan's portrayal conforming to stereotypes of her time.

One of Durzan's granddaughters was Sitt al-Mulk. Known also by other honorific titles and maybe named Sultana, this princess rose to a fame that transcended the boundaries of Fatimid history, a rare occurrence for a woman of medieval Islam. The life of Sitt al-Mulk was in many ways defined by her relationships with the men of her time, be they family members, courtiers or servants. Her ambivalent relationship with her half-brother al-Hakim escalated to cast an air of suspicion around her as the mind behind his disappearance. The allegation stuck, and while it was her making in turning her into a chronicler's diva, it also somehow overshadowed other aspects of her life and character. Suspicions aside, Sitt al-Mulk deserves her place in history as a rare example of a woman who wielded considerable influence in an Islamic court. Throughout her life she acted as political adviser, ruler, diplomat and broker, not to mention architectural patron of public baths, gardens and more. Sitt al-Mulk was born in 970 in the former Fatimid capital al-Mansuriyya. In keeping with a Fatimid regime policy that seems to have been imposed on the royal princesses, she never married. Before Sitt al-Mulk, Fatimid royal spinsters of note were al-Mu'izz's daughters Rashida and 'Abda, both known to have been wealthy. At their death the sisters' estate consisted of tens of thousands of textiles, 2 million *dinar*s, rock crystal ewers, jewels, precious stones, armoury, silver pieces and hundreds of large jars full of perfumes. Like them, royal and court women owned vast quantities of camphor, rose water, musk and violet oil along with spices. The wholesale quantity of these items indicates that they were not intended for personal use but as stock for trading. According to some, Rashida owned a priceless relic: the black silk tent in which the 'Abbasid caliph Harun al-Rashid had died while in the Persian city of Tus in 809. Like these and other princesses, Sitt al-Mulk grew fabulously rich thanks to land grants and state-sanctioned allowances allocated to her as a senior female royal. The princess had thousands of slaves at her service, among them Taqarrub (d. 1024), who became her most trusted confidant and spy. This servant died a wealthy woman, was buried in al-Qarafa and her possessions were entrusted to another servant of Sitt al-Mulk, al-Maliha, a Black slave identified as the possible muse for some saucy poetry in her days.

Sitt al-Mulk lived in Cairo in the Western Palace assigned to her by her father, described as including four halls and water pools (illus. 49). Served by a military company, *al-qasriyya*, her ascendancy extended to other military units like the *'utufiyya*, a connection that came to be celebrated in verse. During her father's reign, her influence at court became evident when the Christian vizier 'Isa b. Nasturus sought her intercession to regain favour with the imam-caliph. Her influence stretched as far as Syria where she owned extensive estates. A Christian civil official there who took care of her affairs alerted the princess to the locals' resentment against the governor of Aleppo, who had been appointed by al-Hakim. As this governor was also showing pro-Byzantine leanings, Sitt al-Mulk conspired to replace him by exploiting the breakdown in the relationship between this man and his former protégé. Some saw in Sitt al-Mulk's plot against the governor the revenge of a spurned woman.

Her power did not go unnoticed among the Jarrahids in Palestine. Hassan, the head of this tribe (which was in the habit of shifting alliance for and against the Fatimids) rose up against al-Hakim. Threatened by the imam-caliph with severe retaliation, Hassan backed off and sought forgiveness via his mother's intercession with Sitt al-Mulk. This the princess did, but when Hassan later entered into an alliance with a renegade Fatimid commander who aspired to control Palestine, Sitt al-Mulk had this officer killed and Hassan narrowly escaped her wrath.

The year 1021 saw Sitt al-Mulk at the centre of al-Hakim's disappearance. Whatever her role – if any – in the days following it was to Sitt al-Mulk, rather than the high dignitaries of the regime, that the army

49 Wooden frieze with depictions of animals from the palace once inhabited by Sitt al-Mulk. The panel dates from the time of the imam-caliph al-Mustansir, who renovated the palace in the mid-11th century.

and people appealed for an investigation into the imam-caliph's fate. In response, Sitt al-Mulk mobilized, manipulated and controlled the military into securing the succession of her nephew, al-Zahir, avenging the death of al-Hakim, and gathering consensus for al-Zahir's reign and her role as regent. In fact, in the month during which al-Hakim was reported lost but not declared dead and al-Zahir could not yet be formally recognized as his successor, she was the uncontested ruler.[4] That capacity gave her the mandate to eliminate the alleged conspirators behind al-Hakim's disappearance. She is reported to have extracted, at knife point, a confession out of six Black guards who had accompanied al-Hakim in his last outing. She neutralized the Kutama high dignitary of the court Ibn Dawwas, the man named by some as being behind the conspiracy against the lost imam. Sitt al-Mulk summoned the officer in charge of a loyal military unit and ordered him to kill Ibn Dawwas and have his head presented to her. She then completed the purge by instructing the same officer to eliminate all the men who formed Ibn Dawwas's entourage and dump their corpses at the gate of the palace. In due course the executors of her orders were eliminated too.

Sitt al-Mulk then turned her attention to al-Hakim's appointed heir, his cousin 'Abd al-Rahim b. Ilyas. Upon al-Hakim's disappearance, Sitt al-Mulk enticed him to Egypt – or had him brought to Cairo – and then had him killed. To secure the loyalty of the army to her as regent on behalf of the new imam-caliph, Sitt al-Mulk proceeded to distribute privileges, money and gifts to the troops. In return, the army pledged loyalty to her through an oath of allegiance.

Sitt al-Mulk was credited with having charisma. Part of this was due to her wealth. The imam-caliph al-'Aziz followed in his father's footsteps in allowing his daughter to accumulate riches that, in time, continued to grow through investments, revenues from land grants, real estate and commodities, as well as the odd diversion of treasury money to her *diwan*. Sitt al-Mulk also had genealogical capital. With the demise of al-Hakim her power became more palpable, since she gained physical control over the succession by sheltering in her palace al-Hakim's son and his mother. We can assume she must have recognized him as the sole legitimate heir to the throne by virtue of birthright. As the guardian of a youth with strong imam-caliph potential, Sitt al-Mulk became an attractive figure for the military to back. Once al-Zahir was enthroned, she reinforced their loyalty once again by a great dispensation of money, gifts and favours. In return, al-Zahir's accession to the throne was announced on the authority of 'our lady', and it was she who bestowed upon the new caliph the crown-like turban that had belonged to al-Mu'izz. Despite all this power, Sitt al-Mulk's name never appeared on state insignia such as coinage, which was struck in al-Zahir's name.[5]

Throughout her adult life her influence extended to several men. Besides 'Isa b. Nasturus who sought her intercession, Sitt al-Mulk was close to the *qadi* Malik al-Fariqi, whom al-Hakim eventually eliminated. Al-Jarjara'i, who later became one of the great Fatimid viziers, began his career working for her. As regent Sitt al-Mulk authorized every project undertaken. Her authority was recognized outside the palace among ordinary people, so much so that, as Geniza documents show, it was to her that petitions were submitted to seek her intervention to redress wrongdoings.[6] She entered into correspondence and exchanged gifts with her Zirid female regent counterpart in North Africa. In 1022 she entered into diplomatic relations with the Byzantine emperor, sending the Melkite patriarch of Jerusalem as her envoy to negotiate the restitution of confiscated churches in exchange for a resumption of trade relations.[7] Sitt al-Mulk's leadership, whether overt or from behind the scenes, was cut short by her death from dysentery in 1023. Poets sang her life. Others mourned her death, chanting, 'Living under the sovereignty of Sitt al-Mulk/ We Have shared the comfort of its shadow . . . Don't be surprised by the night-like gloom of today/ [from] what were yesterday's gifts from her'.[8] Some have interpreted the picture of a woman wearing a crown-like headgear featured on a pottery plate in the Museum of Islamic Art in Cairo to be a portrait of this princess.

While Sitt al-Mulk's path to authority was paved by kinship and privilege of birth, Rasad's rise to power was that of a parvenu, since her fate changed when al-Zahir bought her as a slave from the Jewish merchant Abu Sa'd al-Tustari. From being a mere concubine, Rasad's status changed on becoming *umm al-walad*, mother of al-Zahir's son. When al-Zahir died in 1036 and this son became his successor as al-Mustansir, Rasad became queen mother. From that moment, for the next forty years or so, Rasad was the most powerful woman of the regime. The effect of her interference in the core institutions of the state would have long-lasting consequences for the fortunes of Fatimid rule. Rasad influenced army politics; made and broke men's careers in the administration of the state; was involved in the top appointments of the justice system and the *da'wa* organization; and used her personal *diwan* as means of patronage to secure loyalty. Upon al-Mustansir becoming imam-caliph at the age of seven, al-Jarjara'i acted as the effective ruler of the Fatimid state. It was following this dignitary's death in 1045 that Rasad rose to prominence as de facto regent for her young son. In the years that followed many viziers were hired and fired until it was the turn of Sadaqa al-Fallahi, a Jewish notable who had converted to Islam and had been al-Jarjara'i's aide. However, the regent Rasad favoured her former master, al-Tustari, whom she had made head of her *diwan*, a sector of the palace known as the gate to power. In time the rivalry between al-Tustari and al-Fallahi escalated, with – as we will see – dire consequences for both. Rasad put the management of her affairs into Jewish hands when she employed Ibn 'Usfura, a philanthropist known to have donated clothes to the poor of al-Qarafa in 1058.

A young and ambitious officer who rose to power by serving Rasad was Abu Muhammad al-Yazuri. When this dignitary moved onwards and upwards career-wise, so coveted was a position in Rasad's *diwan* that he tried to have his son appointed to his former post. She turned him down on the advice of another courtier, Abu'l-Barakat, who had already appointed his own son to al-Yazuri's place in her service. In time al-Yazuri, as a plenipotentiary of the state, reclaimed the office and gave it to one of her protégés, a head of the military administration. Rasad influenced *da'wa* appointments too: al-Mu'ayyad fi'l-Din al-Shirazi had hoped for her intercession to become head of the propaganda bureau but she preferred an old member of the Nu'man dynasty.

During the years of political and administrative chaos that marked part of al-Mustansir's reign, Rasad played a central role in the ethnic in-fighting that erupted among rival military factions. In 1062 she sponsored with money and equipment the army's Black contingent which she had expanded in order to rebalance the Turks' and North Africans' dominance within the army which had created an ethnic imbalance. Rasad's measure backfired as the confrontation between these rival military contingents set in motion a chaos in which many historians saw the beginning of the slow decline of the dynasty. Some alleged that in 1069 Rasad escaped with her daughters to Baghdad to seek refuge from the economic collapse that had hit Egypt. In 1071 in Cairo she was confined within the court and had all her assets confiscated, an act that ended her direct influence on affairs of state. Relegated to a diplomatic role, in 1078 Rasad, seated by the side of al-Mustansir and his sister at the palace, greeted Cyril on the occasion of his consecration as the new

Coptic patriarch. During this period, she exchanged official letters with the ruler of the dynasty that acted as the Fatimids' vassal in Yemen, the Sulayhid queen Arwa. Rasad was the last Fatimid queen mother to act as regent; later, even when caliphs ascended the throne at a young age, the viziers succeeded in sidelining their mothers. Throughout her time in the limelight the importance of courting Rasad's favour is reflected in the quality of gifts she is reported to have received: a silver-decorated boat made for her by al-Tustari; lavish presents from Byzantine emperor Michael VI (d. 1057); a rare precious stone credited with healing powers donated to her by the mother of her courtier Abu'l-Barakat. She was made the custodian of family heirlooms including thousands of saddles with silver ornaments. Although she was addressed by the title *malika*, queen, there is no evidence that she was manumitted from slavery during her husband's life, something that did not prevent her from surrounding herself with 5,000 slaves in her personal service. As in the case of Sitt al-Mulk, events that centred on Rasad were reported in medieval Muslim Sunni sources on the Fatimids but were on the whole absent from Isma'ili narratives.[9]

After the royal aunt and the slave queen mother, in Arwa we have an example of a woman who, having started her royal ascent as the wife of a king, once widowed, became a monarch in her own right. One of the Isma'ili Sulayhids of Yemen, Arwa was first queen consort, then acting queen on behalf of her sick husband, al-Mukarram. She then became regent for her son, al-Mukarram Jr. At the death of the latter and with no other male offspring alive – having become a widow again after a second marriage – Arwa became absolute monarch, ruling until her death in 1138. Born around 1048, her full name was Arwa bint Ahmad b. Muhammad al-Sulayhi, but she became best known as al-Sayyida al-Hurra, the Noble Lady. Following her mother's death Arwa had been raised by her uncle 'Ali, founder of the Sulayhid dynasty, and his wife Asma'. Asma' had exercised considerable influence on her husband and played a significant role in the life of the dynasty. She had secured the appointment of her brother as governor of the Tihama region and she delivered to her husband dues pretending they came from her brother. 'Ali was known to consult his wife, favouring her opinion until his death in 1067, when he fell victim to tribal rivalries. After 'Ali was killed, Asma', with other female relatives, was imprisoned in a cell from where she was made to look at the impaled head of her husband. A story goes that to rally her son and 'Ali's successor, al-Mukarram, to rescue her and the other women, Asma' sent him a letter, which she hid in a loaf of bread and smuggled out via a beggar. In it she urged al-Mukarram to act before she gave birth to the child of her captor. It was a ruse that worked. Once freed and back in Sanaa, as queen mother Asma' became so influential that from Cairo al-Mustansir granted her the title of mother of the chosen princes. The celebrated thirteenth-century biographer Ibn Khallikan reported on Asma''s craftiness in his treatment on the Sulayhids. During this period Asma' gained strategic information on the state and managed financial matters by controlling the payment and distribution of tributes from the provinces. Her virtues aside, seeking her patronage might have inspired a poet who sang that the splendour of the mythical Queen of Sheba would pale in Asma''s comparison. However, according to Yemeni popular lore Asma''s greatest accomplishment was that of having groomed in her palace Arwa, the girl who married al-Mukarram in 1065–6. For the occasion 'Ali al-Sulayhi gave the future daughter-in-law as dowry the revenues from the tributes paid by the city of Aden, amounting to about a hundred thousand *dinar*s a year. This payment dried up after al-Mukarram's death.

According to Yemeni Isma'ili sources, as queen consort Arwa received correspondence in 1069 from al-Mustansir's wife al-Sayyida al-Malika, campaigning in favour of her son al-Musta'li as the future heir of the then incumbent imam-caliph. However, Arwa lived in the shade of her mother-in-law until 1074–5, when the latter died. When al-Mukarram was hit by paralysis Arwa took the reins of government as acting monarch. To shelter from rebellions that broke out across Yemen during this period, and to provide her ill husband with a more salubrious environment, Arwa moved the Sulayhid capital from Sanaa to the remote hill village of Dhu Jibla. When al-Mukarram died in 1084 Arwa, from her new capital, became regent for her son, al-Mukarram Jr. Her formal appointment to that role came from Cairo in the form of letters of condolence, preserved in the Yemeni Isma'ili literary tradition. In these letters al-Mustansir and his sister, a figure who would play a part in the succession crisis that followed her brother's death, confirmed Arwa's son as ruler, enjoining the princes and believers of Yemen to obey the queen and her son. Meanwhile Arwa had been receiving Isma'ili religious instruction from the Yemeni *qadi* and *da'i* Lamak, following his return from Cairo where he studied under the leadership of al-Shirazi. Lamak and other Yemeni *da'is* brought back from Cairo not just their learning but copies of the books of the *da'wa*. It was thanks to this scriptorial enterprise that a distinctive Yemeni Isma'ili literary tradition developed which preserved and perpetuated the canon of Fatimid Isma'ili literature for future generations.

Unlike her Cairo-based counterparts, Arwa was not only a queen, but one to whom al-Mustansir had granted the second most important religious rank in the *da'wa* hierarchy. According to Yemeni Isma'ili sources, in one of the letters al-Mustansir exchanged with Arwa the imam-caliph proclaimed her to be his *hujja*, proof. No other woman before or since has been accorded the honour of occupying the highest rank in the Isma'ili *da'wa* hierarchy after the imam.[10] This and many other letters exchanged with the Fatimid royals became foundational to Yemeni Isma'ilism's literary and doctrinal canon. In practice, the position turned out to be more political and organizational than spiritual. Shortly before her son's death, in a letter dated 1088, al-Mustansir had assigned to the queen the oversight of *da'wa* in India, as she had informed him of the death of the *da'i* operating in that region. The imam-caliph therefore instructed Arwa to take care of affairs in those territories and in Oman, to support the spread of Isma'ili propaganda. Arwa obliged. In line with the mores and expectations of the time, to make her position tenable, al-Mustansir instructed Arwa to marry the Fatimid *da'i* Saba. His sons were already married into Arwa's family, one to her daughter Fatima (d. 1139) and the other to her sister. It seems that Arwa, who could not disobey al-Mustansir's order, only agreed to marry Saba as a formality, refusing to consummate the marriage.

As sole ruler in practice, Arwa was faced with many problems due to increased tribal rebellions. In 1097 her nominal husband, who had acted as her commander-in-chief, died. It would take another ten years for Cairo to send someone else that Arwa would appoint as commander and place in charge of civil affairs. However, when this person arrived in Yemen the relationship between the two soon soured, to the point that she had him imprisoned and sent back to Cairo in disgrace. In the meantime, in 1094 al-Mustansir had died. In the succession dispute that ensued that brought about a split between those who supported the imamate of his eldest son, Nizar, and those who backed the succession of his brother al-Musta'li, Arwa endorsed the latter. After al-Musta'li's death his son and heir al-Amir engaged with Yemen by exchanging regular letters with Arwa. According to Yemeni sources, in one of these letters, dated 1130, al-Amir informed Arwa of the birth of a son who, according to Yemeni Isma'ili scholars, was called al-Tayyib. Upon al-Amir's death, some maintained that this child was his designated successor but that he had gone into hiding for safety, a claim that was challenged by a rival group. However, in Yemen Arwa, as well as some Musta'lian supporters in Egypt and Syria, advocated al-Tayyib's imamate. Out of yet another succession dispute, a new religious-political faction emerged: the Tayyibi Isma'ilis. Though credited by her Isma'ili subjects as having spiritual charisma, Arwa nevertheless delegated spiritual leadership to a religious figure who was given the title of *da'i mutlaq*, absolute *da'i*. In doing so, Arwa established a line of spiritual authority that from her day onwards would become embodied in an uninterrupted sequence of religious and spiritual leaders that has lasted to this day, with some internal divisions, within the Da'udi, Sulaymani and 'Alawi branches of the Bohra communities.

Unlike Sitt al-Mulk and Rasad, Arwa makes frequent appearances in Tayyibi Isma'ili sources. Her hagiographers lauded her knowledge of the Qur'an and her erudition. As for her style of rule, she is portrayed as preferring diplomacy over military confrontation and centralized power rather than devolution. Her political virtues are described to have included domestic pragmatism, and acumen in her relationship with Cairo. She was implacable when it came to avenging other women in her family. Some accounts show us Arwa exhibiting the head of Asma''s captor to his imprisoned wife, mirroring this man's conduct to her mother-in-law. Having found out that her son-in-law had rejected her daughter Fatima for another woman, Arwa sent an army against the philanderer in response. In the siege, Arwa's daughter camouflaged herself as a man among the soldiers sent to rescue her and was able to return to her mother. After days of siege the son-in-law was at last expelled from his domains.

Arwa's death in 1138 brought to an end the rule of the Sulayhid dynasty in Yemen. Elegies singing her praises abound. She was buried in the Friday Mosque of Dhu Jibla – a destination of devotion to this day – which had been built around 1087 in Fatimid style by her order (illus. 46). As well as the mosque in Dhu Jibla she commissioned the construction of her palace. Before the move to her new capital, she is credited as having sponsored at least two mosques in Sanaa, one known as *masjid al-hurra*, which is variously ascribed to her or to her mother-in-law. The mosques, no longer extant, might have been located by one of the city gates on what is today the Hadda road. In Sanaa Arwa has also been credited with repairs to the Great Mosque and the decoration of its eastern ceiling. Two inscriptions that are still visible on the mosque's walls name her, but they appear to have been transferred from elsewhere, thus making unclear her role as patron of this building.[11] Arwa's name is also associated with the foundation of the Grand Mosque of 'Ibb. She was named in the Friday sermon but coins issued during her reign continued to indicate al-Mukarram as the ruler.

According to Tayyibi authors her loyalty to the Tayyibi cause extended beyond her death, since it is claimed that in her will Arwa made al-Tayyib the symbolic heir of her estate. The bequest listed 44 items including golden tiaras, swords, necklaces, bracelets and anklets, brooches, rings, gold ingots and seals, as well as precious stones once owned by her father-in-law 'Ali al-Sulayhi, reputed to have been a collector. Arwa, one of the longest reigning queens in history along with Queen Elizabeth II of the United Kingdom, is in today's Yemen still a much-loved and revered figure who is often featured in literature and popular lore with the sobriquet little Queen of Sheba.[12]

As in every Islamic court, the concubine came to play a central role in the life of the Fatimids. A concubine was a slave woman, non-Muslim or converted to Islam, with whom the master engaged in sexual intercourse according to a pre-Islamic custom that was permitted – subject to conditions – under Islam. The rise and subsequent expansion of the Islamic empire meant that a growing number of concubines came into all royal, aristocratic and well-to-do households, acquired as booty or war captives, as gifts and through purchase. Ownership of a large number of concubines became a symbol of dynastic power and prestige. It was this figure who, more than most, conjured up images of romantic and erotic liaisons with the master. Beyond sentimentality, and as we have seen, on many occasions, concubines exercised significant power in court politics. This was especially true if she gave birth to the master's progeny, especially sons thus becoming an *umm al-walad*. As mother of the master's children, the concubine could not be sold, and she would acquire free status at his death. Her children were considered freeborn and legitimate, and if the master was a ruler, to give birth to a boy could place an *umm al-walad* and her offspring in the succession race. The 'Abbasids were the first dynasty to raise the status of the concubine as a means of royal reproduction. On many occasions it was the children of concubines who came to succeed their fathers as caliphs and *amir*s, at the expense of sons born within marriage. The

Ottomans stand out as the rulers who, more than others, championed this type of dynastic succession. Concubinage among the Fatimids followed similar patterns in many ways. The boundary between who was a wife and who was a concubine is often blurred in sources, as only on rare occasions do we have descriptions of contracted marriages. Also, varying terminology to indicate a concubine points to differing status depending on their closeness to the master or their place in the hierarchical ranks within the harem. As with other dynasties, several Fatimid imam-caliphs were sons of *umm al-walad*. Imam-caliphs married or had non-Muslim women as life partners; non-Muslim wet nurses breast-fed their children.

The Islamic court institution associated with women's lives was the harem, intended as a physical space in the palace inhabited by the complete network of a man's female kin and in-laws as well as relatives acquired through marriage, his concubines, and their female free and slave servants. This area was only accessible to few male family members. All administrative and practical management of the harem that required the intervention of a non-related male fell to eunuchs, one of whose roles was to bridge the liminal space that separated the secluded harem from the rest of the palace. For many eunuchs, serving a prominent lady of the harem opened the way to careers that reached the top of the state administration or the military.[13] Comprising women of different backgrounds and origins, with concubines often exchanged from court to court as gifts, or incorporated into a ruler's harem after the defeat of an enemy, this feminine universe – which at any given time might amount to thousands of women within the royal court (but also within the household of a rich master among the elites) – was multi-religious and multicultural. Many women were Christian and remained so; some were Jewish; most were Muslim through conversion or by birth having been born to converted slave parents. Arabic became the lingua franca. Given the inaccessibility of the harem to outsiders, descriptions of its interiors are approximate. The Fatimid jurist al-Qadi al-Nu'man advised that the harem should be decorated and furnished with carpets, no doubt to create a warm and welcoming atmosphere for the master. On occasion, women who came to be added as captives to the harem of Fatimid imam-caliphs made requests to satisfy their practical needs, thus giving a hint of what type of objects might have been in use on a day-to-day basis. These might range from precious clothing and furnishing to jewellery and musical instruments. Artefacts of the Fatimid period abound with images of pursuits conducted in the privacy of the harem.

Outside the Palace

Outside the royal city, stepping into the streets of Fustat and surrounding areas we would have a major problem in observing ordinary women engaged in daily chores as lived in the privacy of their homes. Reliable accounts of everyday female domesticity are seldom found in medieval Islamic sources. Some glimpses emerge from documentary evidence provided by the Cairo Geniza material, but this is too fragmentary to allow us to draw patterns of behaviour that would apply to most women, irrespective of differences in faith and social standing. When looking for women we are better served by heading to typical female gathering places: markets and cemeteries. However, were we to take this stroll at some point during the reign of al-Hakim we would be disappointed, due to his orders limiting women's freedom of movement. From around 1004 onwards al-Hakim issued a series of decrees including several that, intermittently, forbade women to go out at night, to gather at cemeteries, to hang around in the streets or to go to markets. Given these prohibitions we must assume that, prior to them, women must have engaged in these activities. By 1008 the situation had escalated further, and in 1013 a total lockdown on women was imposed. As a measure to enforce this policy, it is claimed that al-Hakim went as far as forbidding the manufacture of female shoes. Bells and street criers would announce curfew times. These restrictions were partly lifted a year or so later.

Contrary to common belief, al-Hakim was neither the first nor the last ruler to impose mobility restrictions on women. While he was vilified for it, state control of women's movements was fairly common in Muslim territories at his time and beyond. After the fall of the Fatimids, in Mamluk Egypt women were occasionally prevented from going to markets and could only use the public baths at night. For example, according to al-Maqrizi, in the context of the plagues that hit Egypt in the mid-fifteenth century, these measures were imposed on women to limit the spread of the pandemic. Many medieval manuals on policing and morality recommended seclusion for women, warning against the perils of letting them loose in cemeteries and markets. Al-Hakim's restrictions appear to have impacted on the urban population. They were imposed within the context of other decrees affecting various aspects of everyday life for his subjects, irrespective of gender; sometimes they were also applied to men, or did not affect all women. Women of high social status hardly went out anyway, due to their rank. Their affairs were conducted by their husbands, their agents, their male and female servants as well as labourers. It was those who occupied low social ranks, as well as male and female slaves, who comprised the larger part of the population on the city streets. Categories of women exempt from al-Hakim's restrictions included widows, the washers of corpses, spinsters, paupers, women needing to submit petitions to the court and women on pilgrimage or travel. However, on occasion some of these too are reported to have been punished for being found out and about.

Some commentators have detected an innate misogyny in al-Hakim's character, perhaps on account of his fraught relationship with his half-sister. Others have interpreted his controversial gendered measures in light of his personal inclination towards asceticism, and his attempt to enforce morality. Al-Hakim's ban on festivals, fun activities and singing by the shore of the Nile points to a curbing of mixed-gender activities. Al-Hakim's control of women's movements was focused on three areas: visiting cemeteries, taking part in entertainments and frequenting baths and markets. These activities were often part of the day-to-day pursuits of a typical, ordinary woman of the time. Many commentators on urban life at the outset of al-Hakim's reign gasped at the number of women who crowded the streets of Cairo. Crowds in general, and crowds of women in particular, were perceived to have an impact on public order, public health and the circulation of money, all areas that demanded careful monitoring in the context of volatile economic, social and political factors, such as those prevailing in al-Hakim's reign. With frequent famines, epidemics and food shortages to contend with, did al-Hakim – in keeping with the prevailing mindset of his day – see the free movement of women as a public hazard? Restrictions may have been motivated by a perceived need to regulate market forces; fearing food shortages women had a habit of hoarding, thus worsening the situation. In times of monetary devaluation and chronic silver shortages, women spending too many of their *dirham*s caused further currency instability and inflation. Epidemics were often seen as a physical evil resulting from relaxed morals, something that – according to widespread medieval belief – the free movement of women helped to spread.

Rather than being a misogynist, was al-Hakim in fact a clumsy financial and moral interventionist who targeted a particular section of society as one of several measures at his disposal to secure some socio-economic stability for his domains? Draconian and reprehensible on many levels as the measures were, al-Hakim's lockdowns seem to have worked in preventing starvation and disease: from 1009 to 1024 Egypt was almost free of famines and epidemics. Restrictions were reintroduced by Sitt al-Mulk when, at a time marked by a severe bread crisis, riots broke out due to price rises and fraud in the weight of baked goods. As a result, shops were closed and fraudsters arrested. In 1024 a full-scale famine erupted and both men and women went on a rampage, pillaging houses and attacking the police with stones.

Information about women working outside the palace is infrequent. Chroniclers and historians whose work depended on patronage made only rare references to the lives of ordinary people in their writings, especially women. Yet it can be inferred from the scanty records that women were active in many areas with varying degrees of responsibility. The most typical areas associated with female work were those in which gender separation and modesty required women to serve other women as doctors, midwives and wet nurses. Being highly skilled professions, these female workers would have undergone an apprenticeship or induction upon taking up their roles, details of which are unknown. Some practices were passed on from mother to daughter. Some women are known to have acted as teachers to others. In the medical profession we can assume they may have belonged to families of physicians. Records show a relatively high number of female ophthalmologists. When women found themselves forced by circumstances to consult male doctors, they indicated to them the areas of their bodies where they felt discomfort by pointing to small carved figures of bone or ivory (illus. 38).[14]

To be a midwife went beyond helping a woman in labour; it also carried legal implications. The midwife was the sole witness to a birth, or to the death of a mother or a stillborn child, with potential consequences in matters of succession and inheritance.[15] Wet nurses established a semi-permanent familial relationship with the family that employed them. Milk brotherhood was held in many respects to be full brotherhood, and in some cases in the Fatimid court, a milk brother might receive preferential treatment over a blood one. A brother was a rival in the succession race; a milk brother was not. In Zirid North

Africa wet nurses were entitled by contract to bedding, a full set of clothes, linen, good food and living conditions. Other gender-exclusive professions included working as a washer and hair remover in the *hammam*. Social rituals also required the creation of professions that could only be carried out by women for women: marriage brokers and counsellors, bridal hairdressers, body washers for the burial of deceased women and professional mourners. This last category of female professionals was frowned on by the Fatimid regime, but the practice persisted to the point that some performers had become rich and famous by the end of the Fatimid period. One of them was Khisrawan (or Khusruwan), who performed the lamentations at the funeral of one of the last Fatimid viziers.[16] A female slave known for her wailing abilities could be resold for double her original price.

Women were a major part of the workforce in textile production, engaged at various levels from wholesalers and brokers to embroiderers and spinners. They also participated in cottage industries, making food or other products to be sold in the street. Women who prepared their merchandise at home relied on other women of lower social standing to act as intermediaries between their commissioners and the vendors selling home-made products in markets. The presence of women in market areas meant that transactions involving them had to be kept under control by a special police force. By the end of the Fatimid period, there was at least one inspector operating in Cairo and women were employed by the state to be supervisors in markets. Some of these women acted as spies for the regime too. At the end of the eleventh century a woman was put in charge of closing, every year, the wine shops in the capital at the end of the Islamic month of Jumada II, warning against the purchase of wine. This month was revered, by the Fatimids in particular, because it was in Jumada II that the daughter of the Prophet Muhammad, Fatima, was born. Women could also be found working as prison guards overseeing female inmates. In Ifriqiya under the Zirids this figure was the *amina*, an unmarried woman or, if married, one who would be trusted to act as a prison guard on account of being the wife of a man of high social standing. There are references to female tax collectors whose task was to retrieve revenues from working women. Some women ran their businesses by themselves in the streets, rather than through agents. One, for example, was the trader encountered by Nasir-i Khusraw in Cairo who rented out jugs for the collection of water. However, the most famous female entrepreneur of Fatimid Fustat was the Jewish woman Karima (d. 1104), known as al-Wuhsha. Married young, she was divorced by her husband while pregnant by another man. Expelled from her synagogue for her transgression, she supported herself by acting as a commercial broker. She died a wealthy woman, leaving her possessions to her son and charities. To her child's biological father, she left in her will a promissory note for payment of a debt amounting to 80 *dinars*.[17] Records show women as international maritime traders, owning commercial boats and involved in the buying and selling of grain through male commercial agents.

And then there was the oldest profession in the world. Islam disapproved of prostitution, and those involved, sex workers and pimps, were considered lawbreakers. Yet, wearing their distinctive cloaks and red shoes, prostitutes solicited in market areas, caravanserais and ports. A popular spot in Fatimid Cairo was the wheat merchants' market, frequented by male wholesalers with cash to spend. Prostitutes carried out their trade from home, but also in brothels. In 1024 in Cairo the police beat up a transgender pimp who was found running a brothel with five women in his house. As both during and after the Fatimid period prostitutes' earnings were taxed, we can assume that repressive measures were applied in cases of real or presumed public displays of obscenity. In tenth- and eleventh-century Cairo the most frequently reported punishment for prostitutes and pimps was flogging. Cross-religious encounters were targeted. In the case of Muslim women consorting with Christian and Jewish clients, the man could be condemned to death while the woman would be flogged and paraded.[18] Female entertainers such as musicians and singers were often conflated with the figure of the prostitute. Besides those serving within the royal court, there were many who formed part of the entourage of high-ranking men as well as those who provided entertainment in tavern-like venues. The vast majority of them were slaves, with singers cast as being of Arab origin and musicians defined as lute players, pipers and percussionists. The adulteress also fell within the realm of sexual misconduct and impropriety. In Islamic law female adultery, when witnessed by four trustworthy people, can result in the death of the woman by public stoning. Though discussed in legal manuals, so far no evidence has emerged from the sources that such a punishment took place in practice under the Fatimids.

One day a great commotion was heard by the house of the savant al-Mubashshir b. Fatik. He had just died, and a woman was yelling from within the inner courtyard, the noise accompanied by the sound of splashing water. The woman in question was his widow, whose cries were not of grief, but to vent her resentment against her husband who, when he was alive, had dedicated more time to his books than to her. In retaliation, now he was dead, she was throwing all his volumes into the courtyard's fountain. This anecdote gives us an excuse to look inside the houses of families of scholars who lived in the main cities of Egypt during Fatimid rule. Although Isma'ilism was the official religious denomination endorsed by the regime, the vast majority of the population of Egypt remained Sunni, and Sunni scholarship continued to be cultivated alongside Isma'ili erudition.

Throughout most of their reign, the Fatimids promoted lectures and preaching sessions dedicated to court and ordinary women, whether Isma'ili or not. In most cases, these sessions are reported to have taken place in formal settings, in accordance with regime-endorsed procedures and based on gender-specific pedagogical methods. Non-Isma'ili sermons that gave guidance on aspects of the law for all to comply with were delivered in mosques by state-appointed high officers for the benefit of men and women alike. Beyond state-sponsored instruction, Sunni learning continued as a domestic, mosque-based, private affair. In this male-dominated environment, learned Sunni women played an important role as bonding agents, fostering cohesion between networks of Sunni scholars in Egypt and elsewhere, and also as genealogical links in the transmission and preservation of intellectual capital in family lineages. At home, wives and daughters often shared the knowledge of their savant husbands, fathers and brothers, and in many instances contributed to its perpetuation.[19]

In the early phase of Fatimid rule in Egypt, Umm Habib Safwa (d. *c.* 989) was the matron at the heart of a family of scholars from Fustat characterized by an important network of female members as transmitters of *hadith*s. Knowledgeable about the family of the Prophet, Umm Habib became a renowned contributor to the dissemination of 'Alid traditions. However, the woman of this period who appears to have earned the greatest prestige for her learning was Umm al-Khayr al-Hijaziyya. Active as a preacher at the 'Amr Mosque, she had a convent dedicated to her in al-Qarafa. Similarly renowned for her piety was her contemporary Fatima al-Basri, whose mausoleum became a well-known site of popular piety. Al-Mubashshir's daughter Khafrita (d. 1133) became famous as one of the most distinguished female scholars in eleventh- and early twelfth-century Cairo. Possibly born in Damascus, once in Egypt she earned the respect of the most prominent male Sunni scholars of her age.

Growing female participation in *hadith* scholarship can be linked to the arrival in Alexandria around 1097 of the Andalusian Maliki scholar al-Tartushi. His wife, a devout and wealthy woman, founded the first *madrasa* in Egypt in her two-storey house. This woman – a widow whose son, disapproving of her marriage to the scholar, tried to kill them both – also ensured that al-Tartushi established links with the Alexandrian intellectual elite. Another learned woman in his circle was Zaynab, the daughter of al-Tartushi's most prominent student, who became a renowned transmitter of prophetic traditions and a student of jurisprudence.

Sunni scholarship in Fatimid Alexandria expanded with the arrival in the city, in 1117, of Abu Tahir al-Silafi. Once in Egypt, al-Silafi too married an affluent Egyptian woman, Sitt al-Ahl, whom he described as pious, and belonging to a family of distinguished scholars on her mother's side. Al-Silafi's mother-in-law, Turfa, was an authoritative *hadith* transmitter, and her sister Khadija was praised for her ascetic life. In Fatimid Egypt, for women who like Khadija chose to devote themselves to a life of worship there existed a convent-like institution called *ribat*. This provided shelter to widows and elderly women who either chose seclusion or resorted to live in this institution due to lack of family support. Al-Silafi and Sitt al-Ahl had a daughter, also Khadija (d. 1226), who, in keeping with her family lineage of distinguished female traditionists, achieved fame as *shaykha*, that is, a highly revered person in a position of prestige, in this case on account of her religious knowledge. In Alexandria a woman named Shuhda bint Abi Nasr granted diploma-like certificates to other women, a rare occurrence in this period.

In the late Fatimid period, the most prominent female *hadith* transmitter was Fatima bint Sa'd al-Khayr (d. 1203). Born in either Xinghian or Iran, she lived in Baghdad and Khurasan, and moved to Egypt from Damascus following her husband, also a trader-cum-scholar. Belonging to a mercantile family that originated in al-Andalus and settled in China, Fatima's itinerant life epitomizes the cosmopolitanism that was typical of the merchant families who filled the Fatimid cities. Having received learning certificates from prominent male and female scholars, once in Damascus and Cairo Fatima affirmed herself as an authoritative transmitter, and many distinguished male scholars boasted of having been her student.

In a social world dominated by rules of gender seclusion and decorum, female scholars are shown to have acted in close proximity with men. The sources do not tell us – outside the context of familial relations – what mechanisms were in place to ensure that gender boundaries were maintained or negotiated between male mentors and female students, or vice versa. Since childhood, seniority and commitment to celibacy or asceticism rendered women unthreatening to the social order, in some cases these factors might have facilitated cross-gender interaction.

Women's engagement with learning was not limited to being transmitters of prophetic traditions. We find women active in the material production of knowledge as calligraphers, copyists of books and secretaries. In Zirid Ifriqiya women donated precious Qur'an manuscripts to the mosque of Qayrawan, and one acted as intermediary on behalf of a court woman in the registration of her bequest. Some of these codices are in part still extant.[20] Other women found more creative ways to make money out of learning. When, in Cairo, Ibn Ridwan sought to become an *ante litteram* Pygmalion by trying to educate a young slave girl in his service, he found that she had robbed him of all his money and vanished. Across social classes literacy levels among women were not uniform. Geniza documents include letters exchanged between Jewish women and their husbands and fathers, but there is no evidence to prove that they wrote the correspondence themselves. Literacy and learning were on the whole discouraged for Jewish women in Fatimid Egypt but in practice they were not always neglected. The documents also reveal that some Jewish fathers were proud of their daughters' command of the Torah, and there is evidence in Cairo's Jewish community of bequests where money was ring-fenced for educating daughters.[21] Among Christian communities such as the Copts, female participation in higher forms of learning is understood to have been of a religious nature taking place in the context of monastic life. Women who chose convent life served their churches in various roles, and some advanced in their careers to the rank of deaconess. Coptic female saints like St Marina were inspirational, and a focus of devotion among Christians in Fatimid times and afterwards.[22]

The intimate link the Fatimids had with Fatima, the mother of the imams, shaped the dynasty's attitudes towards women. Beyond the exaltation of Fatima as a role model, events in her life served as precedents that impacted on the formation of Isma'ili law – especially Shi'i law – that granted special privileges to women when compared with Sunni jurisprudence. For example, Fatima's right to inherit land from her father, endorsed by the Shi'is and opposed by Sunnis, became an Isma'ili law that allowed women to inherit real estate. This precedent extended to the practice of favouring women's accumulation or acquisition of wealth. Within the court, the Fatimid regime implemented a policy of providing royal and elite women with money allowances and allocation of properties. Outside the court, women could be participants in, as well as beneficiaries of, investment opportunities for financial returns. The belief in Fatima's role as a repository of esoteric knowledge inspired positive attitudes towards women as recipients of learning. In addition to those relating to Fatima, the narratives underscoring many of the events that marked the history of the Fatimids were filled with stories of reverence towards 'Alid women. With these premises, we can appreciate why, for the Fatimids, the idea of female leadership, spiritual or otherwise, could not have been an alien concept. Setting aside the time in al-Hakim's reign when women were targeted by restrictive decrees, under the Fatimids women gained visibility and agency the extent of which finds no parallels in other medieval Islamic dynasties.

In the second part of the eleventh century and the century that followed, the vicissitudes of a changing world catapulted the regime into uncharted territories. To confront the challenges that arose, royal mothers, sisters, wives and aunts mobilized themselves in dramatic fashion. Child-caliphs and the grown men of the regime challenged them at their peril.

10

High Drama: The Long Reign of al-Mustansir

Having been designated heir apparent at eight months old, al-Zahir and Rasad's son was aged seven when he succeeded his father as imam-caliph with the royal name al-Mustansir. He ruled first with his mother as his regent for nine years and then by himself for a total of 58 years, thus becoming the longest-serving imam-caliph of the Fatimid dynasty (and ruler overall) in Islamic history thus far. His reign was marked by high drama: great achievements but also near annihilation; economic revival as well as Isma'ili *da'wa* expansion but also a shrinking sphere of political influence; new political friends but also the collapse of old alliances.

Problems started almost at the outset. At the time of al-Mustansir's accession to the throne the Fatimid regime was still managed by his father's capable vizier, al-Jarjara'i. The latter's death triggered a period of government instability which was nevertheless somewhat eased by the appointment of Sadaqa al-Fallahi to replace him. Nasir-i Khusraw described Sadaqa as a person excelling in asceticism, piousness, trustworthiness, truthfulness, erudition and intellect. He must also have been a man of exquisite taste if we go by a superb silver-gilt and niello casket made for his treasury that is now in the Real Colegiata de San Isidoro in León, Spain.[1] However, it appears that these qualities were not appreciated by Rasad who, on the strength of being regent for her son, intervened in court politics by flanking al-Fallahi with her former master, Abu Sa'd al-Tustari. Al-Tustari's brother was put in charge of finance. Based on Geniza documents, Abu Sa'd became known as the 'superintendent of all the affairs of the state'.[2] The Tustaris soon proved unpopular: they were accused of favouring Jews, and blamed by the North African and Turkish army factions for discrepancies in their respective pay. The general discontent with al-Tustari was expressed (though he was not named) in satirical poetry of the day, with verses like 'The Jews of this time have attained their uttermost hopes . . . O people of Egypt, I advise you, turn Jew, for the heavens have turned Jew!'[3]

In this volatile climate Rasad further exacerbated rivalries in the military by privileging the Blacks' army contingent. In 1047 Abu Sa'd al-Tustari was murdered, the result of a conspiracy for which Sadaqa al-Fallahi was blamed. Nasir-i Khusraw, who was in Egypt at the time of these events, described Abu Sa'd and his fate:

> There was once a Jewish jeweller who was close to the sultan. He was very rich, having been entrusted with buying the sultan's jewels. One day some soldiers attacked this Jew and killed him . . . The murdered Jew was named Abu Sa'id, and he had a son and a brother . . . They also say that he had on the roof of his house three hundred silver pots with fruit trees planted in them so as to form a garden. The brother then wrote a note to the sultan to the effect that he was prepared to offer the treasury two hundred thousand dinars for protection. The sultan . . . said . . . 'No one will harm you'.[4]

In 1049 Abu Sa'd's brother, Hersed, who had been a scribe of the Fatimid commander in Palestine, was assassinated after being accused of treason and espionage. In the meantime, Rasad had al-Fallahi eliminated in reprisal for his alleged involvement in al-Tustari's death.

The vacuum of power was filled by al-Jarjara'i's brother who took over as vizier, but he too soon turned out to be an unpopular disciplinarian, and he was exiled to Syria. Despite this administrative instability, the public image the Fatimid regime projected remained unaffected when seen through the lens of supporters like Nasir-i Khusraw who, claiming to have been received at court, provided a description of the interior of the royal palace:

> The sultan's palace is in the middle of Cairo, encompassed by an open space so that no building abuts it . . . As the ground is open all around it, every night there are a thousand watchmen . . . who blow trumpets and beat drums at the time of the evening prayer and then patrol until daybreak. Viewed from outside the city, the sultan's palace looks like a mountain because of all the different

> buildings and the great height. From inside the city, however, one can see nothing at all because the walls are so high.[5]

The royal complex housed in twelve separate blocks a population of mixed ethnic background, with many women. The harem had ten gates, each known by a specific name such as Golden, River, Wind and Emerald. The ruler used subterranean passages to move from building to building unobserved, riding donkeys or mules managed by a female servant. As for internal decoration, one of the twelve square structures was plastered in gold on three sides of its interior, with decorations featuring hunting and sporting scenes as well as fine epigraphic panels. It was furnished with made-to-measure carpets and cushions of Byzantine brocade. Along the sides there was a latticework gold balustrade, accessible via a silver staircase.[6] What Nasir might have seen on display was part of a lavish gift including brocades and textiles that the Byzantine emperor Constantine IX (d. 1055) had sent to al-Mustansir in 1046.[7]

In due course Nasir's loyalty was rewarded by him being appointed *da'i* to carry out Isma'ili propaganda on al-Mustansir's behalf in Iran and Central Asia after his journey back from Mecca in May 1051. The reach of his mission stretched as far as Yumgan in northeast Afghanistan, a region where he took refuge to escape Sunni persecution and where he lived in exile until his death in circa 1088. Today Isma'ilis living in the mountain regions of Central Asia root their tradition in Nasir-i Khusraw's propaganda in the area. A figure at the centre of strong popular devotion, the Pir or Hadrat-i Sayyid, as Nasir is referred to, is believed to be buried in a mausoleum situated in the Yumgan valley.[8]

Contrary to Nasir's assessment, administrative stability did not return to the Fatimid reign until 1050. In that year Rasad favoured the appointment as vizier of the former administrator of her private affairs, al-Yazuri. Originally from Palestine, he was the son of a farmer who rose in status by becoming one of the many Sunni *qadi*s who served the Fatimids there as local administrators. According to an anecdote, when al-Yazuri went on pilgrimage a piece of masonry from the Prophet's mosque in Medina fell on his shoulder. This was taken as a portent of a luminous career to follow. Indeed, having fled Ramla following a quarrel with the city governor over his audacious proposal to have their respective children joined in matrimony, al-Yazuri arrived in Cairo where his ascent to power was launched. The Tustari brothers, with whom al-Yazuri had already established a connection in Palestine, might have been instrumental in attracting him to Cairo in the first place. In Egypt he not only served the court but soon accumulated wealth of his own. By 1048 he owned boats that Jewish merchants used for the transportation of flax on the Nile.

Al-Yazuri's career is emblematic of the reciprocal advantages but also the mutual dependency triggered by the patronage system underpinning power dynamics at the Fatimid court. Having started his career in Cairo by serving Rasad, he remained dependent on her support even when he became vizier.[9] Al-Yazuri continued to consult Rasad on state affairs, with her sitting behind a screen. Installed in 1050 in what had once been Ibn Killis's house, al-Yazuri became the most powerful man of the regime, occupying the positions of vizier, chief *qadi* and chief *da'i* – a Sunni as the head of Isma'ili institutions, and the first dignitary in Fatimid service to hold these three offices at the same time. His appointment as head of the judiciary and propaganda offices ended once and for all the al-Nu'mans' monopoly of those roles. At the same time, being a Sunni, he had to rely on a high-calibre Isma'ili scholar to assist him in delivering sermons at *majalis* that would conform to the official doctrine endorsed by the regime. This scholar was al-Mu'ayyad fi'l-Din al-Shirazi. Besides working in al-Yazuri's chancery and writing his sermons, al-Shirazi had access to the imam and participated in affairs of state on sensitive diplomatic missions. Al-Yazuri, however, kept him at arm's length, and al-Shirazi's ambition to head the *da'wa* would only be fulfilled after this vizier's death.

At the height of his power, for a brief period al-Yazuri was granted the unusual honour of having coins minted in his name alongside that of al-Mustansir. At home the vizier retained the state organization and personnel left behind by al-Jarjara'i, a stabilizing move that nevertheless did not spare him from bouts of severe economic crisis brought about by the toxic combination of low Nile floods, administrative naivety, bungled diplomacy and mercantile profiteering. In 1052 an economic crisis erupted that caused riots, leading to part of Fustat being destroyed. Like his predecessors, al-Yazuri was caught in the abstruse bread policies that could make or break even the most valiant of viziers. The state granaries had become empty. By and large, the imam and the state (the two being in essence one and the same) obtained grain in two ways: through the imam's private estates and crown lands, and by buying it on the free market. The Fatimid practice was to acquire grain from the market for around 100,000 *dinar*s a year with a view to storing it as backup for lean years, but also to resell it for profit. Al-Yazuri sought to take a balanced approach by trying to help the poor by ensuring that bread would be affordable, safeguard the regime's financial interests and ensure fair competition among traders. This balancing act worked at first but in the end it backfired in spectacular fashion. On one occasion for example, al-Yazuri responded to a crisis that caused the bread to become expensive with measures that forced bakers to apply low prices. This policy however triggered a downwards price war with catastrophic consequences. People went en masse to buy cheap bread, with the result that the grain reserves were soon depleted. At the same time state granaries, as the main distributors, suffered heavy financial losses, being forced to undersell provisions first bought at a higher price. Also, bakers became disincentivized in selling bread due to revenues having become too low. In turn this meant that unsold grain stored in the state granaries rotted. A new, more profitable tactic was adopted in 1054–5 when, due to a low Nile flood, grain merchants started speculating on the price of grain. On that occasion al-Yazuri bought their grain himself. He then stored it in state granaries and released it to the market in a way that brought prices down, much to the relief of people who by then had gone hungry again. A whiff of insider trading? Perhaps, but Cairo and Fustat received enough grain to feed the needy while ensuring that bread was available for sale to the general public. After this lesson, to spread the risk the vizier introduced a diversification policy for state investment: to offset potential losses from state grain sales he promoted, along with wheat, the resale for profit of non-perishable goods which were less prone to price fluctuations. The consequences of this financial tactic would be felt in years to come.[10]

However, it was foreign and diplomatic policies that defined al-Yazuri's vizirate and the first part of al-Mustansir's reign. From 1048 onwards, in Ifriqiya the Zirids under the leadership of al-Mu'izz b. Badis magnified their switch of allegiance from the Fatimids to the 'Abbasids. White flags came down and black ones went up, the Friday sermon hailed the caliph in Baghdad and coinage also changed. Maliki Sunnism became the official creed in Zirid territories and Shi'is suffered persecution. The Fatimids tried but failed to regain their former vassals' support and in the end the Ifriqiya province was lost. In retaliation for this betrayal, the Banu Hilal and the Banu Sulaym, Arab tribes based in Upper Egypt, were instigated by the Fatimid regime to invade the lands of their former North African vassals. By 1052 the Banu Hilal, with other lesser tribes in tow, had brought devastation to the Ifriqiya countryside, having defeated the Zirids that year in the Battle of Haydaran. In 1057 the invading tribes looted Qayrawan, forcing the Fatimids' former vassals to retreat to al-Mahdiyya.[11] Thirty years later, in 1087, worse befell what had been the first purpose-built Fatimid capital when the Pisans and the Genoese raided the city and its surrounding area.[12] Knowing they could not hold on to al-Mahdiyya in the long term, the Italians gave it back to the Zirid ruler in return for a tribute which was shared between the city-republics. The Pisans spent part of the indemnity they received on the cathedral of Pisa and the new church of St Sixtus. It has been suggested that the Pisa Griffin, the largest medieval Islamic metal sculpture known – housed today in the city's cathedral – was among the goods taken during this campaign.[13] It is noteworthy that the Norman king Roger I did not join these campaigns, out of fear of losing control of Sicily's export of foodstuffs to North Africa. His successor, Roger II, continued this policy by allowing the export of grain to Ifriqiya.[14] This state of affairs continued until 1148 when al-Mahdiyya fell to Norman attacks; Roger II held it for twelve years.

Once abandoned, the splendid al-Mansuriyya palace was levelled to the ground by the people of Qayrawan, who used its ruins as quarry. Today al-Mansuriyya's archaeological site bears witness to its tragic end. The Hilalian invasion of Ifriqiya brought chaos on a wider scale: pilgrimage routes via North Africa and Egypt became unsafe once again; economic devastation in Ifriqiya worsened and an already precarious situation in Egypt deteriorated further with the disruption of inter-regional trade and exchange of supplies. Beyond bringing devastation, the Hilalian presence in North Africa impacted on the region's demographics and way of life as, once settled, the Banu Hilal warriors aided the rise of subsequent Sunni dynasties that ruled in North Africa. The extent to which the imam-caliph himself was behind the mobilization of these tribes is unclear, but it was al-Yazuri who was blamed for a strategy that backfired. In Sicily the Fatimids' Kalbid vassals (in fact independent), though struggling, remained in power until 1053. Following a number of incursions in 1057 the Norman Roger de Hauteville, in aid of his brother, conquered Calabria, the region at the boot of Italy from where, in 1061, the brothers launched a Norman campaign to Sicily. Palermo was lost to the Normans in 1072, and the last Muslim foothold in Sicily fell to them in 1091.

If nothing more could be done to keep Ifriqiya and Sicily, al-Yazuri took preventive measures in Nubia. When he suspected defection by the Christian tributaries of that region, the vizier had the Coptic patriarch in the capital imprisoned. The latter was alleged to have incited the Nubian king to withhold the tribute the Fatimids had imposed. For good measure, al-Yazuri sent a military expedition to Nubia and doubled the tribute. Churches were closed, bishops were imprisoned alongside the patriarch and heavy levies were imposed on Christians all round.

The Fatimids' hold on their eastern provinces continued to remain tenuous. In 1055 the Seljuq Tughril Beg had entered Baghdad, bringing the Shi'i Buyids' rule to an end. That same year Turkoman groups linked to the Seljuqs had appeared in Syria and Palestine. Their arrival set in motion a process of destabilization in the region that, by the end of al-Mustansir's reign, would result in the Fatimids' final loss of those provinces to the Seljuqs, with the exception of a few coastal towns. In the meantime, the appearance in the eastern Mediterranean of a common enemy strengthened the relationship between the Fatimids and the Byzantines. Back in 1038, with Aleppo still in Fatimid hands, yet another truce had been confirmed which included the go-ahead to rebuild the Church of the Holy Sepulchre as had been agreed during al-Zahir's reign. The Byzantine emperors remained on good terms with the Fatimid imam-caliphs for some time. In 1053 Emperor Michael VI sent al-Mustansir gifts that arrived loaded on a warship and a cargo boat. The presents included a large number of slaves, a menagerie of white birds to honour the Fatimids' colour of choice, bears trained to play musical instruments, dogs and some 7,000 chests of 'fine things'.[15] In return, al-Mustansit ensured that the Byzantine emissary, having to travel through territories under Fatimid control, was escorted by the Fatimid army in order to safeguard him. In fact, this Byzantine envoy had with him a large number of gold objects as a gift to the Church of the Resurrection in Jerusalem that Michael VI had instructed him to deliver on his behalf. Honouring a previous agreement of mutual support, the following year Byzantium sent al-Mustansir a supply of grain when famine hit Egypt.

Given the historic rivalry between the Fatimids and al-Andalus, it is at first glance surprising to find that in 1055 Iqbal al-Dawla (d. 1076), the ruler of Dénia – one of the many principalities into which Islamic Spain had disintegrated – sent to al-Mustansir a cargo

50 A hoard of Fatimid metalwork from Tiberias, 11th century.

of food supply in aid. The two monarchs exchanged correspondence until at least 1059. This assistance from al-Andalus was consistent with long-established trading relations that relied on Dénia as a convenient port for all involved, irrespective of politics. The offer of help was also in keeping with a favourable attitude towards the Fatimids previously adopted by al-Mujahid and his son ʻAli, rulers of Dénia and the Balearic Islands; dating back to 1009, this would last until 1076. Behind this cooperation was the formation of a united commercial front against mutual rivals: Pisa, Amalfi, Genoa and Barcelona. As a token of appreciation for the food supply received, the imam-caliph was reported to have sent to Iqbal al-Dawla a boat full of gifts.[16] In recent years in Spain there has been growing speculation that among the presents al-Mustansir sent to Iqbal was a cup reputed to be the Holy Grail. According to popular belief, at some stage the Muslim ruler of Dénia, having received the relic, sent the cup to the Christian king Ferdinand I of León as part of a peace agreement. Today an onyx cup encased in a jewel-encrusted chalice, housed in León's Basilica of San Isidoro, is believed to be the gift that al-Mustansir sent to Dénia, and is therefore venerated by many pilgrims as the cup that Jesus drank from at the Last Supper.[17] On more solid ground, also regarded as part of al-Mustansir's reward for the help received is a large number of eleventh-century fine Fatimid bronze artefacts, discovered under a street in Dénia in 1920. A similar hoard dating to the same period was found in the eastern Mediterranean region (illus. 50).

Meantime, also in 1055 but in Constantinople, with Theodora Porphyrogenita having become Byzantine empress the bonhomie between Cairo and Constantinople came to a sudden end. If al-Yazuri had previously shown acumen in preventing famine by releasing to market grain from the state granaries, this policy had by now backfired, and the regime and people were running on empty. However, when the Fatimid regime pleaded with Byzantium for help, this time Theodora refused to send a cargo of wheat to al-Mustansir.[18] The Fatimids responded to this affront by threatening war, to no avail. The incident brought to a head what proved to be the Byzantines' cooling down of relations with the Fatimids and their warming up to the Seljuqs. This Seljuq–Byzantine entente was signalled in 1055 by a change in the sermon of Friday prayer in Constantinople's mosque, naming the 'Abbasid caliph instead of the Fatimid imam.[19] In retaliation, al-Mustansir took all the property of the Church of the Holy Sepulchre in Jerusalem. To some, it was in the context of this confiscation that the Fatimids came into possession of the cup that later acquired mythical status in León.

The Conquest of Baghdad

More by fortuitous circumstance than deliberate design, it was towards the end of his vizirate that al-Yazuri was instrumental in turning into reality a dream that had become no more than a theme for propaganda rhetoric: to have the Fatimid imam-caliph's authority recognized in Baghdad. The Seljuq Tughril's instalment as sultan of Baghdad and the demise of the Buyids had been met with resistance at various levels. This ranged from dissent among the Seljuqs themselves to protests at the looting of the city by Seljuq troops and resentment on the part of peripheral military figures who had done well under the Buyids. One such was al-Basasiri (d. 1060), a Turkoman slave-soldier who had risen through the ranks in Iraq and, at some point, even managed to bring several towns under his semi-independent control. With the new Seljuq–'Abbasid alliance, al-Basasiri – who had shown some Shi'i leanings under his former masters – feared complete obliteration. Rather than succumbing, the commander took the only countermeasure available to him: he offered to conquer Baghdad in al-Mustansir's name in return for military help. Taking advantage of a climate of civil hostility against the Seljuqs, the Fatimids responded to this call in 1056 by sending al-Mu'ayyad fi'l-Din al-Shirazi – rich in diplomatic skills but also gold and military equipment – to Syria and Iraq to plan a successful strategy with al-Basasiri. In the aftermath of this mission Fatimid troops and al-Basasiri's military supporters advanced on several Iraqi cities, where the sermon that accompanied the Friday prayer came to be delivered in al-Mustansir's name. Galvanized, the Fatimid regime sent more money and weapons, which arrived at a propitious time.

In 1057 Tughril was faced with a revolt by his half-brother in Iran. Seeking to seize the sultanate for himself, this half-brother was said to have colluded with al-Basasiri and the Fatimids. Forced to go on military campaign to quash the rebellion mounted by his sibling, Tughril left Baghdad unprotected, thus giving al-Basasiri the chance to enter the city. This he did, with overall popular support, in December 1058. As promised, the pulpits of Baghdad's mosques rang with the sermons in al-Mustansir's name. The Fatimids had fulfilled their destiny: Baghdad had been conquered at last. In Cairo al-Mustansir had the Western Palace restored to host the deposed 'Abbasid caliph al-Qa'im during what was expected to be his lifelong exile. However, al-Basasiri had made other arrangements for the caliph, interning him in the town of Haditha on the Euphrates.[20] He sent only the caliphal insignia to Cairo as a mark of subjugation. After Baghdad, al-Basasiri was on course to expand his domains even further in the name of the Fatimids when Cairo signalled a sudden U-turn. Al-Yazuri did not live to see the fruits of the conquest of Baghdad that he had been instrumental in engineering, and his successor was no longer prepared to send money and support to al-Basasiri. Meanwhile Tughril was ready to return to Baghdad. Having offered alliance to al-Basasiri, on his refusal and departure the Seljuq reconquered Baghdad and restored Caliph al-Qa'im to the throne. By December 1059 the Fatimids' nominal recognition in Baghdad was over.[21] By January of the following year al-Basasiri was dead and Iraqi Shi'is were being persecuted.

Life of Luxury at the Fatimid Court

As a recipient of patronage himself, al-Yazuri knew the benefits of attracting loyalty by bestowing favours on others, be they political figures or artists. A keen bibliophile with an interest in illuminated books, he was a generous patron of the arts. On one occasion, al-Yazuri engaged in competition the most famous painters of the day, the Iraqi Ibn 'Aziz and the Egyptian al-Qasir, challenging them to produce the most realistic *trompe l'oeil*. One painted a dancer in red against a yellow background who looked as if she was entering the room through the wall. The other artist instead painted a dancer in white against a black background, who looked as if she was fading into it. Their mastery was considered equal and both won robes of honour and gold.[22] A Sicilian poet, 'Abd al-'Aziz al-Ballanubi (that is, from the farmstead of Villanova), who had left Sicily for Cairo, dedicated three laudatory poems to al-Yazuri in 1055.[23] A gourmand, al-Yazuri loved a good feast. In his seating arrangements for the banquets of the imam-caliph, each seat was furnished with three floor cushions carpeted in white silk brocade, under a pavilion, costing 5,000 *dinars*. Rock crystal dishes for condiments and carved rock crystal jugs for drinks, described as having been part of al-Mustansir's treasures, may have been used to serve and impress the guests. Al-Yazuri's penchant for lavishness – something al-Mustansir frowned on, according to anecdotes – was in fact consistent with the luxurious standards of the period. Al-Yazuri was reported to have had a tent made that portrayed all the known animals of the world.[24] He was also a lover of music. Of only a few surviving Fatimid-period manuscripts there is one featuring a text on the practice of music, a compendium of learning and lore. It was written by Ibn al-Tahhan (eleventh century), already active under al-Zahir and known to have taught the female musicians in the service of this vizier.[25] Al-Yazuri's patronage fast-tracked others' political careers to unexpected heights. Among those he favoured was his scribe, 'Abd Allah al-Babili. A scholar and mathematician, this protégé betrayed his benefactor and became vizier for brief intervals over several years.[26]

Despite all his efforts, the reality was that under al-Yazuri's vizirate the Fatimids' political and territorial holds outside Egypt had suffered: Ifriqiya was lost, the Seljuqs had advanced in Syria and the trumpeted taking of Baghdad turned out to be an expensive whimper. Their hold on Sicily was, in practice, gone too. The once-allied Byzantines were now siding with the Seljuqs. At home a short but brutal famine had left its mark. This state of affairs jarred with messianic expectations that grew around al-Mustansir. Some saw him as the inaugurator of a new cycle, that of his seven predecessors having come to completion.

Since the imam's powers could not be questioned as he was believed to be infallible, a scapegoat for these failures had to be found. Once the apple of the regime's eye, al-Yazuri was accused of a series of wrongs. He was blamed for having squandered funds to finance the Fatimids' taking of Baghdad. In the best revisionist style, what had been seen as a smart move approved by the imam-caliph became the action of an unscrupulous vizier who caused a crisis that affected whatever control the Fatimid regime had left over Syria and Palestine and allowed the Seljuq advance. Accused of having secreted embezzled treasures in Jerusalem and Hebron (Ar. al-Khalil) while preparing to escape to Baghdad, al-Yazuri was denounced as a traitor when correspondence judged to be suspicious was intercepted. On these charges al-Yazuri was executed in Tinnis in 1058. Post-mortem, the fiasco of the Hilalian invasion in Ifriqiya was blamed on him too. After his death, in an effort to reaffirm the imam-caliph's direct authority over the management of the state, al-Mustansir sought to undermine the position of vizier.[27]

New Directions for the *Da'wa*

Following the death of al-Yazuri, the political administration of the regime fell into even deeper crisis, with viziers hired and fired in quick succession and the queen mother Rasad still calling the shots thanks to the strength her private *diwan* had acquired. Rasad's employees had grown in favour at the expense of others, a situation that caused court rifts and jealousy. Seeking to separate state and religious administrations to reclaim control of a core organ of the state, al-Mustansir took to directing the affairs of the *da'wa*. He can be credited with having reinvigorated and expanded its activities. In 1058 he appointed as chief *da'i* al-Shirazi, who established his headquarters in the *dar al-'ilm*, the learning institution founded by al-Hakim which had been left inoperative for some time. In the *dar* al-Shirazi received *da'is* for training and instruction. At his death in 1078 the chief *da'i* was buried in the *dar*. The advance of the Isma'ili cause in the east provoked a Sunni reaction spearheaded by the formidable Seljuq vizier Nizam al-Mulk (d. 1092), who became the effective ruler of the 'Abbasid domains under Seljuq control. He established a network of Sunni learning centres called *nizamiyya*s that employed high-calibre scholars of the day to produce, among other intellectual contributions, doctrinal refutations of the Isma'ilis. The most famous of these scholars was the Sunni mystic and theologian Muhammad al-Ghazali (d. 1111), who wrote a number of works that count among the most powerful rebukes to Isma'ilism.

With mounting anti-Isma'ili hostility in the eastern 'Abbasid territories and the Mediterranean, as well as the religious-political but also commercial implications that resulted, al-Mustansir looked to new horizons in seeking support (and trading partners) for the Fatimid cause. Yemen, once the cradle of the Isma'ili *da'wa*, had been all but forgotten. But when a local Yemeni ruler came forward around 1047 who set out to relaunch the *da'wa* there and conquer territory in the imam-caliph's name, al-Mustansir endorsed his mission. This man was 'Ali al-Sulayhi (d. 1067), the son of a Shafi'i judge in the Haraz region who had converted to Isma'ilism. With the support of the Cairo regime, he set out to create a tribal following for the conquest of Yemen. Soon fortresses were established and Sanaa capitulated. More cities were to fall under the pressure of al-Sulayhi's advance: Aden, Zabid and the Tihama region were added to what became, by 1063, a whole new dominion of the otherwise depleted Fatimid empire. From Cairo, as a sign of alliance, al-Mustansir took to sending to 'Ali al-Sulayhi the first animal he killed on the occasion of the festival of sacrifice. 'Ali al-Sulayhi, however, expected more than just sacrificial meat. On several occasions he asked to be received in person by the imam-caliph at his court in Cairo. On each occasion al-Mustansir turned down 'Ali's requests.

One of the main reasons for such a refusal must have been that al-Mustansir did not want al-Sulayhi to witness the conditions into which his reign had fallen. At the end of 1058 the streets of Cairo had been filled with singing and drumming by Nasab, a woman stationed outside the palace who was appointed to advertise the Fatimid victory in Baghdad. Described as somewhat masculine, so pleased was al-Mustansir with her service that in the same year he gave her land grants. Festivities continued for weeks. But while the name of the imam was celebrated in Iraq and Yemen all was far from well at home. The Mamluk historian al-Maqrizi described these celebrations in Cairo as the last happy moment in the history of the Fatimids. In fact, despite all his efforts and well-meaning policies, al-Mustansir had been unable to bring order to all the branches of the state administration after al-Yazuri's death. He had tried to project his hold on public order by raising the profile of the police, choosing its chief from among the eunuchs of his household. These chiefs, however, often delegated to their slaves the actual job of safeguarding security. If this line of action created public reassurance on one level, on another al-Mustansir failed in his obligation to deliver justice through the handling of petitions, the ultimate glue between the ruler and his subjects. Deluged with the submission of about eight hundred petitions a day, the imam-caliph gave up on the task. In other departments the tensions between civil servants and the military continued, in most cases due to pay issues. With salary discrepancies or periodic lack of wages, soldiers grew restless and disaffected towards the ruling class.

The Cairo regime had hit a cash-flow problem due to a combination of adversity and mismanagement. For example, with only nominal control over provinces like Syria, local governors there no longer felt duty bound to send tributes to Cairo, diverting them instead to their own pockets or to other political beneficiaries, rivals of the Fatimids. No taxes reaching the capital meant no cash available to pay the army. With the Seljuqs' advance and the Byzantines' shift of alliance, the dwindling Fatimid grip on Syria and Palestine meant further loss of revenues for Cairo, due to the disruption of the delicate balance of trade exchanges in the Mediterranean region and beyond. Competition over limited financial resources exacerbated pre-existing internal rivalries among the various army factions. The Turks, the Blacks and the North Africans all opposed one another, with each group having internal divisions of its own. What started as a petty scuffle between rival soldiers came to be identified as the first major symptom of a malaise that would escalate into the full-blown collapse of all the state institutions. The scale of devastation experienced at all levels was such that this crisis was recorded by historians under a specific title: *al-shidda al-'uzma*, the terrible calamity, or *al-shidda al-Mustansiriyya*.[28] In 1062, a year in which he arbitrated the succession of Mecca's next *sharif*, 'Ali al-Sulayhi dispatched from Yemen to Cairo a substantial gift for the imam-caliph which included a large number of pearls. In Aswan and again in Asyut the caravan carrying the gift was seized by some 30,000 soldiers of the Turkish and Black contingents, who quarrelled over which should oversee its shipment to Cairo. Within a short time, the confrontation got out of hand, degenerating into a fight between rival groups that spilled across Egypt until it reached the capital.

'The Terrible Calamity': The *Shidda* of al-Mustansir

The squabble around the gift remained an isolated incident while resentment between the Turks and the North Africans on one side and the Blacks on the other continued to simmer, with the Blacks' corps still favoured and even expanded by Rasad. But by 1066 full-blown conflict had erupted between these factions, leading to a civil war that launched a crisis lasting until 1072–3. By this time Lawata nomads had settled in the Delta region and their neglect of the irrigation system further aggravated a bad situation.[29] Long-term unreliable Nile floods, food shortages, disease and plague, though experienced across the population to different extents, added to the grief that marked this period. In desperation, starving people resorted to atrocities, including, according to some historians, cannibalism. Churches were destroyed and monks killed across Egypt. The cities were devastated and the countryside depleted. The population of Egypt halved, and beasts of burden were decimated by famine or butchered for food. With no labour force or farm animals, the land remained uncultivated, a factor that drove even further out of control the shortage of consumable crops. While attempts were made to maintain a public face, the royal household was not spared the devastation. Unpaid and angry soldiers ransacked the royal palaces, looting its treasures, including the throne that alone weighed 515 kilograms (81 stone/ half a ton) in gold and was studded with 1,560 precious stones. According to an inventory based on an eyewitness account, the looted items included a gold peacock studded with gemstones, with eyes of ruby and feathers of glass enamel inlaid in gold; a gold rooster with a gem-studded crest; a life-size gazelle made of gold, pearls and precious stones; a large golden palm tree; and an entirely gilt and niello miniature garden similar to one that, years before, Sitt al-Mulk had gifted to al-Hakim. Eighteen thousand pieces of rock crystal and cut glass were removed from the palace, together with a large number of bejewelled gold and silver knives, valuable chess and backgammon pieces, various types of decorated hand mirrors, and 6,000 vermeil perfume bottles, not to mention carved ivories and ebony. Many items had the name of the 'Abbasid caliph Harun al-Rashid inscribed on them. Gone were translucent egg cups in which to put soft boiled eggs for the celebration of Easter, a festivity in which Muslims participated on account of Jesus being revered as a prophet sent by God in Islam. Within the Fatimid court, the celebration was also relevant to the many Christians who served it. A box with seven emeralds worth 300,000 *dinar*s found its way to the jewellers' market for five hundred. For a necklace worth 80,000, only 2,000 was paid for the piece to be taken apart and the stones resold. Gone were items of furniture, carpets – like the one on which Buran undressed for her husband, the 'Abbasid caliph al-Ma'mun (d. 833) – curtains and wall coverings, many embroidered in gold. The looters pushed the smaller items down their trousers, inside their turbans and into their bags. Bejewelled barges with all their ceremonial fittings, used by the court for leisure trips on the Nile, were taken too.[30] The royal mausoleum was not spared: the precious world map that hung by al-Mu'izz's tomb and all the treasures in other shrines also disappeared.

The books in the royal libraries were stolen or dispersed. By the time of the 'terrible calamity' the palace library consisted of forty rooms, each decked with bookshelves, labelled on each door and arranged in compartments by subject. Looted books included 18,000 volumes of ancient science and 2,400 boxes of Qur'an manuscripts. In 1068 the incumbent vizier had arranged for 25 camels laden with books to take the load to his residence, having accepted books in lieu of salary. A month later the same books were stolen from the vizier's house. A story goes that some of the books stolen in Cairo later came into the possession of North African tribesmen who turned their leather bindings into sandals. The books were then piled high and burnt, with the smoke filling the air for days. Only a few of all the manuscripts associated with the Fatimids' royal libraries and produced under their patronage have reached us: one intact Qur'anic manuscript dated 1037, one folio of the same text attributed to the dynasty and, among the non-religious texts, the manuscript of part of a compendium on music by Ibn al-Tahhan.[31]

According to anecdote, in those days the imam-caliph survived on a bowl of soup prepared every day for him by a charitable woman. The women of the royal family were reported to have sought refuge in Baghdad, with many not making it there due to starvation.[32] The occurrence in 1068 of one of the strongest earthquakes ever recorded in Palestine, Syria and the eastern Mediterranean region added further disruption, hampering the availability and circulation of goods and people that, under other circumstances, might have alleviated the effects of the crisis. Pilgrimage routes were diverted and the caravan from Cairo was suspended altogether. Eventually the military dispute ended with the Turks prevailing in the capital, the North Africans controlling the

Mediterranean coast and the Blacks driven away, some to Alexandria and most to Upper Egypt. Having taken control of Cairo, different factions among the Turks fought among themselves for supremacy. One group was headed by Nasir al-Dawla b. Hamdan (d. 1073). He was a former Fatimid-appointed superintendent of Tripoli and then governor of Damascus. In Cairo Nasir al-Dawla became de facto ruler in 1071 while the imam-caliph was relegated to a minor dwelling and reduced to living on a pension. While in power Nasir al-Dawla made the most of enjoying his new position by taking possession, along with his troops, of whatever was left of of the palace's most treasured items, among them an 8-litre rock crystal jar decorated with images carved in high relief.[33] Nasir al-Dawla also pushed for a restoration of Cairo's Friday prayer sermon in the name of the 'Abbasids, thus bringing the Fatimid caliphate to an end. It was a step too far. The Turks, not ready to gamble on the privileges the Fatimids had given them, killed Nasir al-Dawla in 1073. Meanwhile, reacting to the Seljuqs' successes and expecting the Fatimids' imminent downfall, in 1069 the *sharif* of Mecca shifted his allegiance to the 'Abbasids in return for a generous pension.[34] The alliance with the Fatimids was soon resumed, but recognition of Cairo's authority in Hijaz was lost again. Meanwhile, in 1070 the Seljuqs had taken control of North Syria from the Fatimids and handed it to the 'Abbasids. In 1071 they defeated the Byzantine army in battle at Manzikert, in Anatolia. The battle, which has acquired mythical status among many past and present historians, had significant long-term symbolic and geopolitical repercussions for these two contenders. For the Fatimids the battle turned out to be a life-saving stroke of good luck. The Seljuqs, emboldened by their success in Syria, had intended to attack Egypt that year. However, they were forced into a sudden change of plan to confront the Christians, having learned of a Byzantine advance towards Aleppo against them. Was it not for Manzikert this book might have ended here.

Badr al-Jamali: Enter the 'Vizirate of the Sword'

By 1072 the Fatimid cause appeared to be lost. But the regime had one last card to play: to appoint a strong man to head the administrative apparatus and restore order in the domains. There was only one person who had shown the level of skills and loyalty required for the task, the Armenian commander Badr al-Jamali, who – stationed at that time in 'Akka – had governed Damascus for the Fatimids since 1063. In his youth Badr had served as a slave of the Fatimid-appointed ruler of Tripoli, Jamal al-Dawla b. 'Ammar, hence his name al-Jamali. In Egypt the year 1073 had marked a turning point at last, with a good harvest after years of misery. It was then that al-Mustansir summoned Badr al-Jamali from Syria to Cairo. The commander arrived in January 1074 with about a hundred ships filled with thousands of men from his private contingent of Armenian troops and military slaves. He proceeded to quash each rebellious group one by one, eliminated the old military elites by confiscating their properties, purged ineffective administrators and potential military rivals, phased out Rasad's influence and introduced tax incentives that protected the interests of the merchant classes. The Amalfitans, who by this stage had surpassed the Sicilian Kalbids in their volume of trade with Egypt, were back in favour, having been granted permission to build in Cairo a complex that included religious and non-religious structures such as lodgings and storage warehouses. Around 1077 Badr reduced the number of provinces to four main ones, subdivided into districts to improve their management. His administrative division of Egypt coincides by and large with the one in place today. Order was restored across the rest of the country. The Fatimid regime was back in business.

Best known by the title *amir al-juyush*, Commander of the Armies, Badr's instalment as a military figure at the head of the civil, judicial and religious administrations brought about a fundamental change in the nature of the vizirate, which went from being led by 'men of the pen' to being in the hands of 'men of the sword'. For the first time in the history of the Fatimid regime Badr al-Jamali – who we would call today a military dictator – rose through the ranks, not thanks to the patronage system, but with the support of his own power base, embodied in his private army. In 1078, at an unprecedented ceremony of its kind, before the notables of the *da'wa* and the *dawla*, al-Mustansir appointed Badr as the sole executive administrator of the state via a decree in his handwriting that was kept in a golden case. A copy of this official decree was sent to the vassal Sulayhid ruler in Yemen and parts of it were circulated in Syria. The imam-caliph al-Mustansir bestowed on Badr the all-important white robe, the formal Fatimid symbol of honour and investiture as well as a sign of the imam's blessing. On that occasion Badr received the sword of the state, though this was no longer Dhu'l-fiqar, 'Ali's mythical sword that the Fatimid royals had claimed to own. In his plenipotentiary role Badr embarked on a programme of major fiscal, agricultural and administrative reforms with a view to securing income for the state's coffers and also solving the pressing problem of paying the army on which the regime's survival depended.[35]

Though Badr had converted to Islam, most of his Armenian soldiers were Christians who, from Anatolia, had entered the Fatimid army in Syria. Many had fought in Byzantine cavalry and infantry divisions, but under Badr these Christian soldiers served a Muslim ruler. Their arrival in Egypt added a new thread to the tapestry of Christian minorities already in the region. During Badr's rule, Muslim and Christian Armenians continued to settle in Egypt in large numbers, impacting on the ethnic diversity of the country. To serve the needs of this growing Armenian Christian community Badr became a great sponsor of the Armenian church in Egypt, a preferential treatment that caused some tensions with the Copts. When in 1086 the Coptic bishops turned to Badr to complain about their patriarch, Cyril II, he ordered them all to convene in his presence and asked the assembly to draw up canon laws to manage the civil and religious rights of the Coptic community.[36] This was duly done, the dispute was settled and the corpus served as a blueprint for the establishment of personal status laws for Coptic Christians that remained relevant until modern times.

Badr was instrumental in restoring peace and relative prosperity to Egypt. Meanwhile the imam-caliph, reduced to a symbolic role, retreated to the palace and was no longer visible at parades, processions or excursions. His household and entourage became reduced and disempowered. In addition to his military-cum-administrative leadership Badr was entrusted with the oversight (alongside the judiciary) of the *da'wa*, a position that had been left vacant after the death of al-Shirazi in 1078. That Badr's role in this position was no mere formality is indicated by al-Mustansir's instructions to his Yemeni vassals to address to the commander all questions of faith. Badr became the public face of the regime and the effective leader of the state for all to see, with his extensive list of titles engraved on public foundational inscriptions and his name associated with architectural projects carried out at his behest. Via architectural inscriptions he made sure that the caliph's endorsement was there for all to see, dropping al-Jamali in favour of al-Mustansiri.[37]

Badr's presence in Egypt is tangible to this day as the patron of city walls, mosques, shrines and inscriptions dotted across the capital and Egypt. In Cairo, between 1087 and 1092 he replaced what was

51 Fatimid restoration inscription of Badr al-Jamali on Ibn Tulun Mosque, Cairo.

left of the old wall built by Jawhar (and modified since) with a stone structure and imposing gates, Bab al-Nasr, Bab al-Futuh and Bab al-Zuwayla being the most outstanding. He also extended the walls' perimeter and added more entrances. These constructions were raised by workforces that included Syrian, Byzantine and Armenian master builders who added their styles and skills to Fatimid imperial architecture. Badr's city ramparts are regarded as a masterpiece of Islamic military building design. Al-Hakim Mosque became incorporated within the city walls; beyond Bab al-Zuwayla royal Cairo was no longer separated from commercial Fustat, with the two parts now forming an interconnected city in terms of commercial exchange, administration and the staging of Fatimid public ceremonies. Where once the people of Fustat needed a permit to enter Cairo, now they could not only go back and forth but settle there. The Darb al-Ahmar quarter, today restored under the patronage of the Aga Khan Development Network and one of Cairo's most visited tourist landmarks, is an example of an area that formed part of Badr's urban regeneration. To this day the quarter is the centre of one of Cairo's most popular celebrations with its festival in honour of the birthday of Fatima, daughter of the Prophet, taking place there.[38] Badr's urban interventions gave today's Old Cairo its characteristic layout. His restoration programme included rebuilding the part of Fustat that had been destroyed during al-Yazuri's vizirate, as well as changes to the mosque of Ibn Tulun and, in 1089, to the mausoleum of Sayyida Nafisa (illus. 51). Founded in 825, the shrine had already undergone several restorations, but it was transformed by Badr. The Nilometer on Rawda island underwent works, and in 1092 a new mosque was built nearby. The *amir al-juyush* gave himself a new residence, north of the Western Palace, to replace the one where Ibn Killis and subsequent viziers had lived. The memory of Badr still dominates Cairo from a shrine known today as the Juyushi Mosque which he built in 1085 on the top of the Muqattam hills, perhaps in memory of a dead rebel son. The minaret of this mosque features what has been described as the earliest known example in Egypt of the use of *muqarnas*, a stalactite-like architectural feature associated with eastern Islamic building constructions. As the resting place for himself and the rest of his family Badr built in 1087 a shrine in the area outside Bab al-Nasr that was already in use as a cemetery. The mausoleum would one day house the remains of his son and successor, al-Afdal, and his grandson Kutayfat.

Badr al-Jamali is also named as the sponsor of a splendid carved wood pulpit dated 484 in the Islamic calendar, corresponding to the year 1091–2, commissioned initially for a new mosque in ʻAsqalan. This city was a strategic outpost for the Fatimids, situated at the head of a line of ports connecting the eastern Mediterranean coast to Cairo via the western Delta. The mosque was commissioned to house a relic, the head of Muhammad's martyred grandson al-Husayn, which Badr claimed he had miraculously discovered in that city.[39] The mosque was completed by Badr's son and successor al-Afdal in 1097. Having been perfumed and kept in a case in the intervening years, al-Afdal in person positioned the relic in its dedicated mausoleum. Today Badr's wooden pulpit is in the Ibrahimi Mosque in Hebron (illus. 42). As for the relic itself, it was taken in a casket to Cairo after ʻAsqalan fell to the Franks in 1153 (illus. 43). Once in Egypt, the relic was buried in the grounds of the Turbat al-Safran funerary complex within the Fatimid royal palace. This site then became the heart of al-Husayn Mosque, built in 1154, where the head is believed to be to this day. Al-Husayn Mosque dominates the square to the right of the entrance into Khan Khalili market and is a focus of Muslim popular devotion. In recent times the Da'udi Bohras of Gujarat have reclaimed the Ismaʻili connection to this relic by staging pilgrimages to ʻAsqalan. Thanks to a collaboration between the fifty-second *daʻi mutlaq* of the community and an Israeli tourist entrepreneur, a marble open prayer platform has been erected for the use of the Bohra community to mark the site believed to be that of Badr's original shrine.[40] Another miracle associated with Badr relates to the shrine in Cairo of al-Shafi'i, the founder of one of the four Sunni legal schools. According to a story the Seljuq vizier Nizam al-Mulk had sent a letter, accompanied by presents, to Badr al-Jamali asking for the body of the great jurist to be exhumed in order to be reburied in Baghdad. Against the wishes of the people Badr proceeded to honour the request, but when the burial site was opened such a stench arose from it that the workers almost fainted. The occurrence was interpreted as a miraculous sign that al-Shafi'i was displeased with the move and the transfer was abandoned. The portent was reported back to Nizam al-Mulk, who proclaimed the episode an official miracle to be retold in all the mosques of the Seljuq domains.[41]

In 1074 Badr had scored a major diplomatic success, regaining Mecca's allegiance to the Fatimids (lost to the 'Abbasids since 1069) by resuming the supply of grain. However, it was not all plain sailing for the commander, and much as he tried to defend the Fatimids' interests some ventures were just no longer worth pursuing. The already tenuous Fatimid hold on Syria and Palestine was further weakened by allegiance being paid to the 'Abbasids with alarming frequency. In 1076, despite Badr's best efforts, Damascus and most of Syria fell once and for all to the Seljuqs. He repelled a Turkish-led attempted invasion of Egypt from Syria. Minor rebellions kept cropping up, including one led by one of his own sons in Alexandria in 1084. By Badr's time, control of Sicily through the Kalbids had become another lost cause. In the 1050s the Kalbids' grip on the island had weakened, leaving the way open to the Christian Normans' advance. At first spurred by the Byzantines' efforts to retake Sicily, the Normans later conquered the island for themselves between 1061 and 1091, with 1071 being a turning point. An independent Norman Christian kingdom was inaugurated in 1130. Following their arrival in Sicily, the Normans, lacking previous experience of ruling style, modelled themselves on the Fatimids in many aspects of court life. Notwithstanding rivalries, on the whole the Normans and the Fatimids maintained a cordial relationship marked by diplomatic exchanges, reciprocal gifts and trade well into the twelfth century. In Upper Egypt, Badr had to intervene to crush the ambitions of a tribe, the Banu Kanz, which from being loyal to the Fatimids began to show signs of dissent. In dealing with the Christian Nubians, he resorted to the help of Egyptian Christians, who in turn gained considerable prestige during his vizirate. Among them, of course, were the

Armenians, both those who were already resident in Egypt before Badr's arrival, and those who followed him when he moved there. In 1078–9 the king of Nubia went to Aswan to expand his church, was arrested and brought to Cairo. Greeted by Badr al-Jamali, this king later died before being able to return to his kingdom. In Iran, Iraq and Central Asia the Seljuqs were by now well established under the watch of Nizam al-Mulk, who, while serving the ruler Malik Shah (d. 1092), sought to convert various dominions into a centralized state.

Nizam al-Mulk launched an anti-heterodoxy campaign, not only through fighting and the physical and political persecution of the Isma'ilis but by devising an educational infrastructure for the promotion of Sunnism. Established in Baghdad, the *nizamiyya* was the first of a series of colleges designed to teach Sunnism as the orthodoxy of Islam and to form personnel to serve the government according to Sunni principles and laws. The Isma'ili *da'wa*, although in a clandestine way, continued nevertheless to be quite active and loyal to the Fatimid imam-caliph. This was to change when a convert to Isma'ilism, Hasan-i Sabbah, arrived in Cairo from Iran in 1078, aiming to meet al-Mustansir and the then chief *da'i* al-Shirazi. However, the latter had died by the time of his arrival. After a brief, turbulent stay in Egypt, Hasan-i Sabbah returned to Iran, where his activities were to revolutionize the Isma'ili *da'wa* while causing havoc in the Seljuq domains.

The Sulayhids of Yemen and New Trade Routes

Before Badr's arrival al-Mustansir had continued to be active as a religious leader by engaging in person in the *da'wa*. Between 1066 and 1069, despite the *shidda*, *da'is* from Yemen had come to Cairo, where they were trained by al-Shirazi and by the imam-caliph via his sermons. For those who could not receive instruction at the fountainhead of Isma'ili knowledge in Cairo, al-Mustansir fulfilled his guiding role by entering into didactic correspondence with leaders of distant propaganda networks. The epistolary exchange had far-reaching legitimizing consequences as far as the Fatimid *da'wa* in Yemen was concerned. When 'Ali al-Sulayhi died, he was succeeded as local *da'wa* leader and ruler of Sulayhid-conquered territories by his son al-Mukarram. But al-Mukarram fell ill, propelling first his mother, Asma', and then, in 1074, his wife Arwa to be leaders in his stead. In her new capital, Dhu Jibla, with the aid of *da'is* returned from Cairo, Arwa inaugurated a new phase in the history of the Isma'ili propaganda. Having been raised (via correspondence) to the rank of a proof of the imam-caliph, al-Sayyida Arwa was instrumental in the development of a distinct Yemeni school of Isma'ilism that, rooted in Fatimid Isma'ili scholarship, preserved its legacy, literature and traditions for future generations. Through epistolary exchange and the commuting of *da'i*s, under her rule Sulayhid Yemen became the launch pad for *da'wa* expansion and, with it, trade opportunities with India and its ocean regions. In 1067–8 the first Isma'ili *da'i*, 'Abd Allah, was sent from Yemen to Cambay in Gujarat. In 1083 two new *da'i*s were sent to Oman and India. The mission to Oman failed, but in Gujarat it gained momentum.[42] An Isma'ili-linked merchant community came to be established along the Indian Ocean coastline, with Aden becoming an important trade entrepôt of the Fatimid empire.

Elsewhere al-Mustansir's image as the ultimate leader of the Muslim community continued to be projected in the most significant shrines of Islamic sacred history. In Cairo's Ibn Tulun Mosque his name appeared in a stone inscription at the top of a prayer niche. To Jerusalem he sent as a gift silver lamps for the Dome of the Rock, decorated with 'al-Mustansir' written in gold letters on the underside of these objects for maximum visibility. Once again, a paradigmatic link between the imamate as embodiment of divine light and the Dome in Jerusalem was reinforced. Under his auspices, the Fatimid governors of Palestine carried out constructions in the Haram Sharif area, indicated by inscriptions found at the site. The Ibrahim shrine in Hebron was expanded, redecorated and enriched with gifts sent by al-Mustansir. Meanwhile in Bahrain, a coalition of local chiefs who received 'Abbasid and Seljuq support defeated the Qarmatians. This time the victory of the Fatimids' Sunni arch-rivals turned out to be a blessing in disguise: the remaining Qarmatians joined the Fatimid *da'wa* once and for all.

In 1094 al-Mustansir died after a long, eventful reign, leaving behind an empire that was reduced in territorial size but redirected in Isma'ili *da'wa* outreach and transformed in its political and commercial focus of interest. Having suffered from a combination of natural calamities, administrative misjudgements, the growth in power of political rivals, loss of allies and a large dose of bad luck, the regime had survived against all the odds and even returned to prosperity. Only a few months before the imam-caliph's demise, the old vizier Badr al-Jamali had also died, having secured his son al-Afdal's position as plenipotentiary vizier. As saviour of the empire, Badr made sure that his legacy would be safeguarded for generations to come. He not only changed the nature of the vizirate by shifting the management of the state from civil to military administration, but made the office hereditary for the first time in the Fatimid context. Also, from Badr onwards Armenian viziers and high officials would play a prominent role in the life of the Fatimid regime to its end.[43] As the twelfth century dawned there were already signs of the upheavals that would mark the history of the Fatimids and their involvement in many of the defining events of the era.

11

The Darkest Hours of the Fatimids

To say the events that marked the history of the Fatimids in the twelfth century are not for the faint-hearted is somewhat of an understatement. Murderous succession disputes followed by vicious partisanships; court assassinations avenged by bloodthirsty royal aunts; international conflicts marked by betrayals and false loyalties; failed military alliances and new religious horizons; royal children either killed or used as puppets on the throne. With more turmoil to come the Fatimids faced a geopolitical storm of epic proportions.

Succession Disputes: The Nizari–Musta'li Split

In the course of his life al-Mustansir had a number of children. Of these, two sons became figures of great importance in the destiny of the dynasty, with a wider impact on world history. One of them was known as Nizar. According to several Isma'ili sources it was this son that al-Mustansir had designated as his heir apparent. However, at the imam-caliph's death, Nizar's ascent to the throne was checked by the new vizier al-Afdal, the 'Akka-born son of Badr al-Jamali. This vizier backed as ruler Abu'l-Qasim Ahmad, a brother of Nizar who became known as al-Musta'li. He was al-Afdal's brother-in-law. Badr had married the prince to his daughter, thus binding by blood his vizirate dynasty to the caliphal one. Given the title of Sitt al-Mulk as her more famous namesake, for the royal wedding Badr gave his daughter a splendid trousseau and jewels that at some point al-Afdal took for himself. Later pro-Musta'li literature claimed al-Musta'li's appointment as heir by his father had taken place on the occasion of this wedding.

Al-Afdal installed al-Musta'li on the throne, an act that generated a split between those who supported Nizar's imamate and those who defended al-Musta'li's caliphate. Muslim historians report that al-Musta'li's brothers protested when faced with this fait accompli. Loudest of all was Nizar, who responded to the affront of having been defrauded of his rights by claiming to be in possession of a document signed by his father that confirmed the legitimacy of his claim to the throne.[1] Though determined to fight against the usurpers, Nizar was forced to leave Cairo. Lacking the backing of local notables and the army (which had sided with al-Afdal due to its Armenian elements), in 1095 Nizar left for Alexandria with a small group of followers including a brother and his right-hand man Ibn Ma'al. According to later sources written by supporters, he was also accompanied by two sons. Other children and brothers escaped to North Africa. In Alexandria Nizar mounted a revolt, and once he had secured the support of the city governor, its *qadi* and sections of the citizenry, he proclaimed himself imam-caliph with the title al-Mustafa li-Din Allah, The Chosen One for the Faith of God. The discovery in 1994 of a gold coin struck in Alexandria in Nizar's name shows that in the city, albeit for a brief period, Nizar's claim to the imamate must have been recognized (illus. 52 and 53). This initial success was to no avail. As al-Afdal and his army quashed the uprising, Nizar and his allies were captured, taken back to Cairo and imprisoned. In Alexandria the pro-Nizar chief *qadi* was persecuted.

52, 53 *Dinar* struck in the name of Nizar, son – and to his supporters, successor of – the imam-caliph al-Mustansir, al-Iskandariyya (Alexandria), dated 488 corresponding to the year 1095.

In Cairo, Barakat, a figure who had become prominent in the *da'wa*, led a dissenting group in favour of Nizar. In response al-Afdal closed down the *dar al-'ilm* where these agitators gathered and arrested this *da'i*. However, palace insiders helped Barakat to escape disguised as a woman, a strategy that allowed him to hold gatherings in secret. His female disguise was only discovered at his death.[2]

The confused circumstances of al-Musta'li's rise to power led to a strong defence of his right to rule on procedural grounds. In historical accounts produced for the Musta'lian side it was claimed that their champion had been appointed by al-Mustansir on his deathbed, and that the dying caliph's sister had been entrusted with this nomination. In response the counterargument sustained that there was no evidence of Nizar's initial appointment having been revoked. Also, it was impossible for an imam to change his mind about an heir's designation once it had been made public, as this action would invalidate belief in his infallibility.

The dispute snowballed to the extent that two rival branches of Isma'ilism emerged from it. The eastern Isma'ilis sided with Nizar's cause. In Iran the activist Hasan-i Sabbah (d. 1124) led a campaign in support of Nizar's imamate which resulted in the establishment of an altogether new *da'wa* network, with its headquarters in the fortress of Alamut in northern Iran, which became independent of Cairo. The ruins of the 'eagles' castle' stronghold, which became the setting for legends about Hasan-i Sabbah and his followers, are still extant and represent one of the main tourist attractions in the Qazvin province of Iran. Prior to the split, Hasan-i Sabbah had arrived in Egypt in 1078 seeking an audience with al-Mustansir. There are contradictory reports as to whether the meeting took place or not, with a likelihood that Hasan's wish went unfulfilled.[3] Badr al-Jamali saw a troublemaker in the ambitious and charismatic Hasan. There are conflicting accounts regarding the methods the vizier used to get rid of him. According to some, he had Hasan incarcerated in Damietta, from where he then escaped. Epistolary evidence indicates that the 'Abbasids, weary of Hasan's activities, had instigated Badr al-Jamali's opposition to the Iranian Isma'ili activist by sending emissaries and money to the Armenian commander in return for his capture.[4]

The succession crisis that emerged at the heart of the Fatimid dynasty coincided with a period when the Cairo regime, in crisis at home, had grown distant from the Iranian Isma'ilis whose survival was threatened by the Seljuq rulers of the region. Supporting Nizar's imamate offered Hasan-i Sabbah the opportunity to lead his co-religionists on a separate and distinctive doctrinal path in the name of their champion. Emboldened, the Nizaris – as the supporters of this faction were called – went on to acquire sympathizers among ruling elites, territories and more fortresses, thus succeeding in establishing a de facto state within the Seljuq domains. In time the imams in the line of Nizar, whom these Isma'ilis believed had gone into hiding for safety, re-emerged in Alamut. The Nizari brand of Isma'ilism went on to expand into parts of Iraq and was embraced by most of the Isma'ilis of Syria and Central Asia. To counteract persecution in those regions, Nizari militants resorted to unconventional warfare techniques that might entail suicide attacks on their enemies. These were the legendary Assassins. Accounts of their exploits, conflated with other dark tales, have been feeding the imaginations of Western audiences ever since. The Venetian merchant and traveller Marco Polo (d. 1324) indulged in his travelogue in stories about the Old Man of the Mountain whom he identified with Hasan-i Sabbah. In fact, the moniker referred to Rashid al-Din Sinan (d. *c.* 1192), the leader of the Syrian Nizari Isma'ilis, a community ensconced in impregnable mountain fortresses. Of these the most famous is Masyaf, in the Hama governorate, which functioned as the headquarters of this faction. The ruins of this castle are still extant and since 2000 have been undergoing restoration under the auspicies of the Aga Khan Trust for Culture's Historic Cities Support Programme. In the course of their history the Nizari Isma'ilis survived persecutions by various Sunni regimes, and the Mongols' onslaught in the mid-thirteenth century, by living as secretive communities in parts of Iran, Central Asia and the Indian subcontinent. Today the Nizari Isma'ilis constitute a flourishing, peaceful, pluralistic and cosmopolitan community of about 15 to 20 million. They operate worldwide under the spiritual leadership and community guidance of a dynasty of Aga Khans whom they believe to be imams in the Prophet Muhammad's direct line of descent via 'Ali and Fatima. If on the one hand the imamate was disputed between these two factions, on the other it was the rulers of the Fatimid line in Cairo that, being nominally in charge of the empire, continued to be recognized – even if only formally – as caliphs by their subjects and in diplomatic relations.

With the defection of the eastern Isma'ilis to the Nizari cause, the Fatimid rule continued in Cairo with al-Musta'li as nominal sovereign and his vizier al-Afdal as the effective leader of the state. Like his father, al-Afdal's priority was to secure order and prosperity in Egypt. He introduced significant land tax reforms which remained in place until the end of the dynasty. Al-Afdal also followed in his predecessor's footsteps in toning down public rituals and ceremonial that had the caliph at their centre. Like his father, he promoted himself via architectural patronage; in 1094 al-Afdal was behind the construction of a prayer niche in the Ibn Tulun Mosque. To this day it is one of the finest examples of stucco work and one of only two such niches in Cairo to feature the name of the donor in its inscriptions.[5] In the name of public safety nothing was left to chance, given the constant threat of Nizari attacks. In terms of state security, al-Afdal emerges as the figure who perhaps more than other Fatimid rulers made use of female spies. Resorting to women to gather intelligence goes back to at least al-Hakim's time, when elderly women were instructed to spy on others by visiting their houses and reporting back. Sitt al-Mulk's informant was her servant Taqarrub. After 1094, al-Afdal gained a reputation for sending his mother to markets, mosques and cemeteries to solicit people's opinions about the vizier and test their loyalty. Her method was to pass herself as the complaining mother of one of al-Afdal's soldiers to invite comments from her interlocutors. She then reported those who made negative remarks, with consequent painful outcomes for her naive informants. On one occasion, however, one of her interlocutors outsmarted her. Unaware of her identity – or pretending to be – the man reprimanded her for badmouthing the sultan of God on earth. When his mother reported what had happened, al-Afdal rewarded the man by embellishing an oratory named after him.

Outside Egypt, al-Afdal secured loyalty in Syria, which in the early years of his vizirate was in part under Fatimid control. He also took back Jerusalem from Turkish rulers with Seljuq affinities who had established themselves in Palestine. In Yemen an even stronger bond was established with the Sulayhid Queen Arwa, who promoted the Fatimid *da'wa* in her territories by heading a team of Cairo-trained Isma'ili propagandists. To add to his caliphal credentials, al-Musta'li's mother Sayyida Malika – a witness to the controversy that had surrounded her son's succession – engaged in correspondence with Arwa to reaffirm her son's accession to the throne by designation.

The Crusaders

Busy fending off possible Nizari attacks and asserting himself via his protégé caliph, al-Afdal did not see coming the most significant challenge the Fatimid regime was to face in the twelfth century. In fact, seemingly out of nowhere, mobs of thousands of armed Christians, from the poor to the nobility, descended from Europe on Syria and Palestine. Their intent was to liberate what to them was the Holy Land from those they saw as infidels, that is, Muslims and Jews. In time the European militants and adventurers who took part in these military enterprises became known in the West as Crusaders, from the Latin for 'those marked by the cross'. Muslims instead gave them the collective name *Faranji*, Franks, since they believed that they came from France. Having responded in 1096 to Pope Urban II's call, by 1098 the Crusaders had captured Antioch. It was here that the Fatimids first came face to face with them. From Cairo an embassy was sent to them seeking an alliance in pursuit of a common goal: joint control of Syria and Palestine at the expense of the Seljuqs. The delegation returned to the Fatimid court with presents accompanied by Frankish representatives, leading al-Afdal to believe that this unholy alliance might have worked. In that year, as a result of the disruption caused by the Crusaders' arrival, al-Afdal even managed to take Jerusalem. However, after checking a Seljuq attack in Syria, the Crusaders, led by Godfrey of Bouillon (d. 1100), did not stop there but fought their way on to Jerusalem, which they took from the Fatimids in 1099 along with, subsequently, Ramla and Hebron. The victory marked the establishment of what became the Latin Kingdom of Jerusalem, the first of the four Crusader states of Tripoli, Antioch and Edessa. These events were game changers in the geopolitics of the region, echoes of which have reverberated and tainted Christian–Muslim–Jewish relations since. The Crusaders embarked on an infidel-cleansing campaign with methods that ranged from mass killings and land occupation to the destruction or misappropriation of cultural artefacts.

Al-Afdal's reaction to the Franks' conquests at the Fatimids' expense was too little and too late. Soon 'Asqalan was under siege too, following a surprise charge by the Frankish knights. The defeated al-Afdal retreated to Cairo, while the Crusaders lifted the siege on 'Asqalan only because quarrels broke out among themselves over who should rule the city. On Christmas Day of 1100, Godfrey's brother Baldwin of Edessa (d. 1118) was crowned as the first king of Jerusalem. By 1101 the Crusaders had planted themselves in Palestine, having taken Haifa, Arsuf and Caesarea, while al-Afdal tried – and failed – to reach a deal with them. During the following 25 years, the establishment of a Crusader kingdom blocked all the Fatimids' hopes of bringing Syria and Palestine back under their control. At the same time, the Fatimids reformulated the ideological purpose of the dynasty as the one that would lead Islam in the war against the Christian infidels. In the name of this mission al-Afdal launched new campaigns to remove these foreign intruders from the Fatimid lands, but after a series of alternating fortunes, by 1109 Tripoli too was lost to the Franks, with 'Asqalan hanging in the balance.[6]

The Caliph al-Amir Reclaims the Stage

An additional setback to al-Afdal's attempts to reclaim Syria and Palestine was the death in 1101 of al-Musta'li, an event that forced the vizier to focus on dynastic politics at home. He proclaimed as the new caliph al-Musta'li's five-year-old son, with the royal name al-Amir. It is unclear if this boy was born from the union between al-Musta'li and al-Afdal's sister. In due course the vizier married this child to his own daughter, in line with Badr al-Jamali's plan to merge the caliphal and vizirate dynasties. Commenting in retrospect on this marriage, Ibn Khaldun remarked that it was forced and therefore invalid by Islamic law, the marriage contract having been redacted by al-Afdal.

To introduce the new caliph to the crowds al-Afdal held the child in front of him in procession while riding on a horse. An announcement was then read out to the assembled dignitaries, following which al-Afdal continued for some twenty years to be the effective ruler of the Fatimid state. During this period anti-Crusader expeditions were carried out, with some Fatimid military alternating fortunes in Ramla in 1102. However, from that year onwards Tartus, 'Akka, Tripoli, Sidon, and Tyre in 1124, were lost to the Franks, with only 'Asqalan left in Fatimid hands. In 1113 Baldwin I married Adelaide del Vasto (d. 1118), mother of Roger II of Sicily. The gold in the Sicilian-made textiles and carpets that constituted her dowry was so valuable that with it Baldwin was able to pay his debts and the salaries of his soldiers.[7] Thanks also to this cash injection, Baldwin invaded Egypt, reaching the Delta towns of al-Farama and Tinnis and heading towards Cairo. But a year or so into the campaign, in 1118, the king died, an event that forced the Crusaders to return to Jerusalem with the disembowelled body of their dead monarch cured with salt. Al-Afdal responded to these challenges with frequent raids against the Franks out of 'Asqalan, backed by naval expeditions to defend or retake the coastal cities along the eastern Mediterranean. During fifty years in Fatimid hands, 'Asqalan had been turned into a major fortress that functioned as a regional command centre from which to launch attacks against the Crusaders and patrol the route between Palestine and Egypt. The mid-twelfth-century Crusader historian William of Tyre described it as protected by a double wall semi-circling the city, with towers and gates opening on the direction of the coast, towards Jerusalem and the port.

In the aftermath of these defeats, al-Afdal undertook a reform in the composition and training of the army, from servile manpower consisting mainly of slaves to units comprised of professional free men. He did not live to see the potential results of his experiment. After a number of assassination attempts (for one of which he accused his own sons), in 1121 al-Afdal was murdered during a parade to celebrate the end of Ramadan. In the immediate aftermath of al-Afdal's death, his second in command Ma'mun al-Bata'ihi took control of the situation by returning the body of the murdered vizier to the palace and delaying the formal announcement of his death until the caliph had been informed. The next day al-Amir announced the appointment of al-Bata'ihi as the new vizier and led ceremonies to reaffirm his role as the effective head of state. Al-Afdal's adult sons were imprisoned, but other relatives of the deceased vizier were invited to the *'id* celebrations, participating in the traditional distribution of dates and food blessed by the caliph. Al-Afdal received a funeral appropriate to his rank and was laid to rest near his father in his mausoleum. In a number of sources, the caliph al-Amir and al-Afdal's lieutenant al-Bata'ihi are indicated as having been behind the assassination, on the grounds that the caliph wanted to rule by himself. Others point to Nizari agents as the perpetrators of a revenge killing. In some sources, these were part of a group called the Bad'iyya which al-Afdal had crushed. Al-Afdal's name appeared among those killed by Nizari militants in a list found at Alamut after the fortress fell to the Mongols in 1256. In any event, after his death al-Amir confiscated al-Afdal's considerable wealth. According to some, the vizier had amassed more property than any previous ruler, to the extent that it took forty days – likely to be a nominal figure used as literary device to indicate a long time – to move all the goods from his house, Dar al-Mulk, south of Fustat by the bank of the Nile, to the caliph's residence.

Al-Afdal was reputed to have been a cultivated man and a patron of the arts. News of his generosity reached Dénia in the Iberian Peninsula, from where the poet Abu'l-Salt al-Dani (d. 1134) travelled to the Cairo court in search of sponsorship.[8] Al-Afdal also had a taste for the novel and the unusual. In the hall where he used to relax, he had installed eight mannequin automata in the shape of women slaves facing each other, all fitted with expensive garments and bejewelled. Four of them were white, made of camphor, and four of them were dark, made of amber. When al-Afdal stepped into the room a mechanism at the door would cause their heads to bow down, while upon his sitting down, a device would make their heads rise. Known for his love of poetry, verses attributed to him reveal his personality as that of a passionate yet violent man consumed by jealousy. According to an anecdote, he had a favourite woman slave beheaded when he caught her looking out on to the street from the roof of the house. Al-Afdal gruesomely repeated the episode in verses chanting how her beautiful head was now nested on his lap.[9]

As a ruler determined to reassert full control over the state, Caliph al-Amir first sought to downplay the vizier's role, and then make sure everybody knew it. The most effective way to communicate this change of political direction to his subjects was to make himself visible as much as possible. In making his rule manifest, al-Amir was not only seeking to put his highest-serving officer back in his place but to challenge, with his attestable presence, the Nizari counterpropaganda rooted in the claim that the imam was in hiding. To achieve his goal in Cairo the Fatimid caliph resumed tried and tested tactics to make his presence felt: the staging of religious and secular ceremonies, public and private celebrations, palace protocol, diplomacy and patronage.

After decades of his father and grandfather living in virtual seclusion, al-Amir reclaimed his place as the personality at the centre of all festivals. His new vizier, al-Bata'ihi, basked in the shade of his master's splendour, a position that in turn advertised his role to the population. Al-Bata'ihi had advanced in his career on the back of his predecessor, al-Afdal, becoming one of his highest-ranking officers. While in that capacity al-Bata'ihi had proved himself to be an able administrator by masterminding land tax reforms and introducing agricultural policies (all of which al-Afdal took credit for) which in many ways helped to restore the Egyptian economy. Al-Bata'ihi was therefore used to operating in the background and, having witnessed how al-Afdal had been liquidated, he continued in his role as a smooth background operator even upon becoming vizier. When al-Amir returned as the front man of the regime, it was al-Bata'ihi who planned the events that served to exalt the caliph. It was this vizier who organized the celebrations of the ritual year, doing it in a choreographed way. These splendid affairs took place on the occasion of festivals such as New Year – the most lavish of them all – the Feast of Sacrifice, the Breaking of the Fast, the perfuming of the Nilometer and the commemoration of the day when, according to Shi'i belief, Muhammad had appointed 'Ali as his successor. Thanks to al-Bata'ihi, the celebrations for the birthdays of Muhammad and his closest family members, *mawlid*s, were resumed. The Fatimids had introduced these birthday festivals into Egypt some time after the first quarter of the eleventh century, but al-Afdal had abolished the practice for a period.[10]

With the addition of a new celebration – the birthday of the imam of the time – al-Amir became the fulcrum around whom the festive programme revolved. These occasions saw the Fatimids' sweet tooth in full display, with sugary confections produced and distributed in abundance. Taken together, these festivals served to reinforce the claim that the Musta'lian bloodline, not the Nizari, was the one that stretched uninterrupted from Muhammad to the current caliph. On these occasions the crowds could see the caliph, even though he was sitting behind the grille of a street-facing window of the royal palace. For the festival of lights, a Shi'i celebration falling in the middle of the Islamic month of Rajab, al-Bata'ihi invited al-Amir to reveal his figure in full from a palace window that was open for the occasion. Every possible soft power was deployed at these events to make the caliph look good. Alms were given to the poor, notables received robes of honour and inside the royal court banquets were given, courtesy of the caliph, in keeping with a code that, since time immemorial, fused kingship, religion and feasting. At the celebration that heralded completion of the Qur'anic recitation coinciding with the last night of Ramadan, the caliph bestowed his blessings on his entourage gathered for the occasion. The most distinguished women of the palace were present. Servants carried before the caliph and other participants dates, ice and containers filled with water so that the caliph's blessing would pervade them. New gold and silver coins were donated in abundance as part of the annual ceremonies.

In designing the programme for these pageantries al-Bata'ihi planned them in such a way as to link the palace city with Fustat, to ensure maximum participation beyond social and religious divides. In addition to formal events, the caliph's visibility was also enhanced through the public staging of private outings. Al-Amir's leisure trips to the Lu'lu'a pavilion on the Nile with his consorts, brothers, daughters and aunts were performative. The vizier undertook similar public outings with his own entourage, though on a smaller scale.

Palace protocol was modified to reflect this renewed focus on the manifest presence of the imam. Within the royal palace the throne was no longer hidden behind a screen in the great hall. At audiences, a curtain, when lifted, revealed the caliph in all his glory to those present. At the end of the session the curtain was drawn again. The vizier, as the person appointed to orchestrate this protocol, could flaunt his own power as the gateway for those who wanted access to his master. Under the direction of al-Bata'ihi, the troops' loyalty was reinforced with the oldest pleaser of all: salary increase. Fatimid palace women, whether consorts and family members of the caliph or related to high officials, gained greater visibility, with some occupying important positions in the palace bureaucracy. During this period women's presence is attested working in the treasury and as female attendants. For royal consorts and women of high rank a formalized dress code was devised to signal the position each held at court on the basis of the hierarchical status of their male relatives. In the budget for the year 1122 al-Bata'ihi mentions in order of importance the court women to whom the palace treasury had allocated expensive clothing. The value and complexity of the garments, of which every item was specified, shows they were proportional to the woman's standing. With reference to al-Amir's consorts for example, al-Bata'ihi listed first the concubine 'Aliya, who was allocated a long flowing gold-threaded garment made of fifteen pieces. Al-Amir's other known consort 'Alam al-Amiriyya was given a similar outfit. Women who occupied lower positions each received gold garments of only fourteen pieces, which were lower in value. Further down the scale, other women in al-Amir's entourage received gold garments of unspecified style and value. Women in the families of high dignitaries serving al-Amir were allocated a silk outfit each. The budget even specified how many shoes each got. In the twelfth century, with the revival of court life spearheaded by al-Amir, the palace administration and bureaucracy expanded to the point that a codification of rank by attire became necessary in order to project to audiences the correct hierarchy for ceremonial and protocol purposes. In his coordination of a complex and stratified court life, the vizier was aided by an ever-growing number of eunuchs who in turn reinforced their status as a powerful lobby within the royal court.[11]

The restored sense of prosperity that the regime conveyed to the populace was not enough, however, to crush the Nizaris' claims once and for all. Instead, the movement continued to grow, and signs showed their activities were infiltrating Egypt in secret. In response to these threats al-Bata'ihi devised new strategies aimed at defeating any potential challenge to al-Amir. In 1122 at the caliph's behest, the vizier staged a formal gathering at the palace during which Nizar's sister, from behind a curtain, testified against her brother's claims before an audience composed of the highest dignitaries and notables of the state, their children and relatives. She declared that she had witnessed al-Mustansir, on his deathbed, summoning al-Musta'li and blessing him. Then she heard him whisper his designation to al-Mustansir's sister, who in turn confided it to al-Afdal after the death of the old caliph. The reliability of this event and what was reported is tainted by the bias of those who had a vested interested in such a statement. The testimony, together with other evidence, was then written down in a document known as *al-Hidaya al-Amiriyya* that was read out across Egypt. Given its importance, the redaction of this document was entrusted to one of the most experienced and distinguished scribes in the Fatimid chancery, Ibn al-Sayrafi (d. 1147). Besides being the author of chancery manuals, he also wrote a book on the history of the Fatimid vizirate up to his time. The *Hidaya* was also sent to Syria, where local Nizaris refuted it in writing. The propaganda reached Yemen accompanied by gifts to Queen Arwa. Al-Amir's rights were acknowledged in North Africa by the Zirids who, after a long period of alienation, sought a rapprochement with the Fatimids in return for help in checking the Norman threat. In 1124 al-Bata'ihi conducted a census of Egypt's population, relying among others on the services of women going house to house. Beyond its demographic purpose, the process was in effect an intelligence-gathering exercise intended to unmask covert Nizari sympathizers and potential anti-regime conspiracies. Under his watchful eye entrants into Egypt were scrutinized, suspects were arrested and, if necessary, executed.

As nothing was left to chance, symbolism also became part of a wider programme of public advertising by the regime, through urban regeneration under the auspices of royal and court patronage. During this period, we witness the restoration of palaces and shrines, including those linked to Muhammad's ancestry, in popular locations such as cemeteries. A new caravanserai was built to attract merchants into the city and, to inspire trust in the regime, a new regulatory system was set in place to ensure the metal purity of coinage, in order to put a stop to the production of forgeries entered into circulation by the Franks. The *dar al-ʿilm*, closed by al-Afdal, was reopened. Regeneration projects extended to new housing in quarters between Cairo and Fustat that had become derelict. Al-Bata'ihi also ordered the renovation of pavilions opposite the Lu'lu'a one, and the clearance of houses built by Sudanese troops in the eleventh century but later abandoned. The owners of derelict houses were forced to renovate them, under threat of state confiscation. Investment in the restoration of seven mosques in the Qarafa area, including Durzan's, was especially significant and charged with symbolism. Repairs extended to the shrines of women in the Prophet's family. As part of the plan to enhance the capital's landscape and ritual significance, al-Bata'ihi built a major new mosque, the Aqmar, still standing today on al-Muʿizz street in Cairo. Demonstrating the best example of keel arch use – a distinctive feature of Fatimid architecture – al-Aqmar's facade was designed with embedded propaganda that summarized in decorative and scriptural form all that was at the core of Fatimid Ismaʿilism (illus. 54). The message that the Cairo imam was the heart of a spiritual and religious power stemming from his direct descent from the Prophet's family was on full display. The writing on the wall was as much for his subjects in Cairo to read as it was oblique propaganda against the Nizaris' counterclaims.

The year 1125, with the inauguration of the Aqmar Mosque, should have marked al-Bata'ihi's crowning as the most efficient vizier of his caliph. Instead, it was in the aftermath of this event that al-Bata'ihi's downfall began. He went an act of patronage too far: al-Bata'ihi had a new observatory built and named after himself, which displeased the caliph who read in the gesture a sign of the vizier's self-aggrandizement. The observatory was destroyed and never mentioned again. Al-Bata'ihi and thirty others, including his brother, were

54 Facade of al-Aqmar Mosque in Cairo, 12th century.

arrested and, in 1128, crucified. Al-Amir's jealousy and fear of betrayal have been interpreted as the causes behind al-Bata'ihi's fall from grace. However, it has also been observed that while al-Bata'ihi managed to reshape a positive image of the dynasty at home, he failed on the foreign policy front. Under his vizirate the Franks took Tyre, an important eastern Mediterranean coastal outpost that the Fatimids had managed with great effort to bring back under their control in 1122. Al-Amir would never forgive his vizier for this loss.

After al-Bata'ihi's death al-Amir found himself ruling without a vizier. The caliph tried to recruit staff to supervise the state departments but failed. With headhunting having acquired a somewhat sinister meaning, it is no wonder that one prospective candidate turned down an otherwise coveted royal appointment by self-confessing incompetence. In time al-Amir managed to form a team of tax collectors, comprised of a Muslim and a Jew with a Coptic bureaucrat, known as the monk, as supervisor. This figure, however, terrorized people and pursued a policy of mass property confiscation that made him unpopular to the point that the caliph was threatened with rebellion. In 1129 al-Amir resorted to his preferred problem-solving method: dismissal and imprisonment.

The Coptic offical was then subjected to a humiliating death by shoe beating. Once nailed to a wooden board, his beheaded corpse was made to float down the Nile out to sea. Al-Amir took the exceptional step of apologizing to his subjects by freeing slaves, giving to the poor and adding two extra months of fasting to that of Ramadan. The caliph's contrition was to no avail. In fact, al-Amir's display of cruelty had made things worse and the caliph's public image was now in tatters. One day in 1130 al-Amir went to Rawda island to celebrate the Nile having reached a promising height for the forthcoming flood. Having completed the customary blessing rituals al-Amir left his pavilion, heading for the river's bank. Once he was on the narrow bridge that linked the island with the mainland, his escort failed to protect him. It was at this junction that nine Nizari agents stabbed him to death.

With regard to his private life, al-Amir was described as a man of learning, having earned a reputation as a Qur'an memorizer. He is known to have had many consorts and concubines, with some becoming prominent female court figures in their own right. In keeping with an established practice among Fatimid royal women, some of them emerged as architectural patronesses. Soon after al-Bata'ihi's death, one was credited with having sponsored the building of the Bitter Orange Mosque near al-Qarafa. The most celebrated royal consort of this period was 'Alam al-Amiriyya, whose patronage became visible after al-Amir's death. Another woman of note in the caliph's life was 'Aliya, from Upper Egypt, gossiped about in the sources as a capricious woman with a penchant for luxury goods, and as the author of saucy verses intended for her true love, who was not al-Amir but her male cousin. Vignettes about al-Amir's private life include one in which the royal consort used to lock her bedroom at night, opening it to al-Amir only after he gave her gifts. Either the caliph was a frequent visitor or his gifts were generous because, according to the story, over time the woman accumulated 100,000 *dinars*. During his reign the extravagant palace lifestyle extended to food consumption, with the meat of some 5,000 sheep said to have been consumed each month.

The Caliphate of al-Hafiz

By his consorts al-Amir had a number of children. From 'Alam he had at least a daughter. Another girl was born to him from another woman who was pregnant when he died. Given the implications for succession, it was the circumstances surrounding the existence of male offspring that drew particular attention to al-Amir's private life. Sources point to the birth of a son having been celebrated in Cairo for two weeks. It was said that for the occasion the capital was festooned and that a copious amount of food was distributed to the jubilant population while the royal palace was filled with fruits and sweets. The troops received new uniforms to mark the event. The *'aqiqa* ceremony, the ritual animal sacrifice to celebrate a newborn, accompanied the weighing in gold or silver of the baby's newly cut hair. The celebration took place in front of the caliph, officiated by the chief *qadi*. The gold and silver were donated for charity. According to epistolary evidence preserved in the literary canon of the Isma'ilis of Yemen, al-Amir announced the arrival of this boy to Queen Arwa. Among these Isma'ilis the child became known as al-Tayyib. Apart from references to his birth, in Egypt nothing more was heard of this baby or his whereabouts, a predicament that left the door open for dynastic disputes. On the death of al-Amir in Cairo, his cousin al-Hafiz came forward to take charge of the caliphate. At first, he claimed to be acting as regent on behalf of an unborn child that one of al-Amir's concubines was pregnant with. In fact, he might have been behind the mysterious disappearance of al-Amir's male offspring. Al-Hafiz's position was challenged by Kutayfat, one of al-Afdal's sons, who staged a coup with the backing of the army. He arrested al-Hafiz, placed himself on the throne and, being a Twelver Shi'i, went as far as abolishing the Fatimid dynasty altogether.[12] The move proved unpopular and Fatimid loyalists soon responded with a countercoup which succeeded in getting rid of the usurper. With the physical absence of a royal son and no vizier to account to, in 1132 al-Hafiz proclaimed himself imam-caliph with the backing of self-interested high officers at court. The victory that led to the restoration of the dynasty would be celebrated every year until the end of the Fatimid caliphate. It was perhaps the vacuum of power created by the confused transfer of the caliphate that led another claimant, identified by some as a son of Nizar, to come forward. He launched an attack on the capital which was soon quashed.

Al-Hafiz based his claim to the throne on having been nominated as heir apparent by al-Amir before his death. Although this succession between cousins (previously attempted by al-Hakim) was a first in Fatimid dynastic history, in defending it al-Hafiz had recourse to the ultimate precedent: Muhammad's appointment of his cousin 'Ali as his successor. In Yemen, however, al-Amir's announcement to Arwa of al-Tayyib's birth was taken to imply that the baby had been appointed as heir apparent. While some local rulers recognized al-Hafiz's caliphate, most of the Yemeni *da'wa* rejected his claim and backed the imamate of the infant whom they believed to be living in occultation. Out of this dispute yet two more branches of Isma'ilism emerged: the Hafizis in Egypt, Nubia, Syria and Palestine, and the Tayyibis in Yemen. In time this latter group gathered around the spiritual guidance of a religious authority called *da'i mutlaq*, absolute *da'i*, whom they saw as the exclusive representative of al-Tayyib's hidden imamate. Across the centuries, through trade, the Tayybi propaganda reached India where these Isma'ilis grew into a small yet prosperous community amounting today to about 1.5 million people. In the Indian subcontinent and wherever they were present those who belonged to this offshoot of Isma'ilism became known as the Bohras. In 1589 the Bohras divided into Da'udis, Sulaymanis and, later, Alawis, with each group endorsing a separate line of spiritual leadership. Of these, today the Da'udis represent the largest community, which has its strongest base in India.

Born in 'Asqalan from a brother of the imam-caliph al-Mustansir, al-Hafiz remained a fairly obscure figure until the day he came forward as a pretender to the caliphate, partly on the grounds of being the oldest male in the dynasty around at the time. Against all the odds, al-Hafiz lasted on the throne for some twenty years and, for once, he died of natural causes. During his reign he had to defeat repeated challenges to his right to rule from the Nizari and Tayyibi factions. In his management of the state al-Hafiz contended with a series of ambitious men who aspired to become his viziers in order to sideline him. One of these was his own son al-Hasan who, having prevailed over rival brothers, forced his father to nominate him as vizier in 1134. Once in office al-Hasan launched a campaign of terror which within a year led to revolts calling for his death. These army-led rebellions grew to the point of threats to burn the royal palace if the request to eliminate al-Hasan was not met. Al-Hafiz tried to buy time by summoning the governor of a province in the western Nile Delta, Bahram al-Armani, to back his son. But the crisis increased and, on al-Hafiz's instruction, al-Hasan was poisoned before the governor arrived. Not satisfied, the rebel troops asked to inspect al-Hasan's dead body and stabbed it several times for good measure.

In 1135 Bahram, a Christian Armenian, arrived in Cairo to take up the vizirate after al-Hasan's death. The only Christian among several

Armenian viziers and the only Christian to head the Isma'ili *da'wa*, he placed his own people in key positions in the state administration, with the result that both high-ranking Muslim officials and Muslim subjects resented him.[13] During the period of Bahram's vizirate, there were almost 100,000 Armenians as well as more than thirty Armenian churches and monasteries in Egypt's major cities. This period was also marked by growth in the building of private chapels. Between 1137 and 1140 the Muslim population embarked on anti-Armenian atrocities, with people massacred and houses pillaged and burnt. The acts of violence extended to Bahram's family: a brother's tomb was desecrated and his other brother, Vasak, the governor of Qus in Upper Egypt, was murdered. The corpse was then mutilated, tied to a dog's carcass and thrown on a rubbish dump. Al-Hafiz tried to safeguard his vizier by not admitting him to Muslim religious ceremonies, replacing him with the chief *qadi* and removing from him the leadership of the Isma'ili *da'wa*. At a personal level al-Hafiz did not seem to harbour anti-Christian sentiments, counting among his friends an Armenian patriarch who, on numerous occasions, visited the palace to hold lectures for the caliph.

By this time the Egyptian merchants had lost access to vital markets on the eastern Mediterranean coast, and the Fatimid fleet was reduced due to a lack of supply bases. However, on the foreign policy front Bahram enjoyed a welcome respite and even some success. The Crusaders had to divert their attention from the Fatimids to address the rise to power in Syria of a new contender: the Sunni Zengid Turkic ruler of Aleppo. In 1131 (during al-Afdal's son's short-lived coup) the Fatimids sent peace-offering presents for the coronation of Fulk, Count of Anjou (d. 1143) as the new king of Jerusalem, including an ivory tau, or T-shaped cross. This was later used in Angers as a sceptre during the inaugurations of the counts of Anjou.[14] After a brief period of non-belligerence conflict resumed but with the advent of Bahram, perhaps on account of the shared Christian faith, relations with the Crusaders eased somewhat. The Crusaders, among whom Bahram was known as Vahram '*le seigneur des Armeniens*', responded to his negotiation by releasing three hundred men taken captive during the Battle of Ramla in 1102. Likewise, under his watch the Fatimid regime enjoyed positive diplomatic relations with the Normans. In 1130 Count Roger II became king of Sicily. Gifts were exchanged and the Fatimids even sent Roger a jewelled parasol modelled on that of the Fatimid caliph. In turn, the Normans had embraced a Fatimid style in most areas of court life. In

Sicily, Arab and Muslim craftsmen of the former Fatimid regime now served Norman masters, with Roger making the most of their skills. Arabic inscriptions and Islamic dating adorned his royal ceremonial mantle, made in Palermo in 1133/4. Bearing a political message with its image of a mirrored pair of lions devouring two camels, this luxury item made of red silk, embroidered in gold with pearls and jewels, was later used as a coronation cloak by the Holy Roman emperors (illus. 55).[15] In Norman Sicily *tiraz* textiles embroidered with Arabic inscriptions were used for the court outfits; administrative documents were written in Arabic in the style of the Fatimid chancery. Roger II became a patron of Arab scholarship, which culminated with the completion in 1154 of one of the most famous geographical treatises of all time, the *Book of Roger* originally written in Arabic by Muhammad al-Idrisi (d. 1165). Islamic art and architecture, echoing Fatimid details, were adopted in the building and decoration of Norman palaces.

Capitalizing on mounting anti-Christian sentiment directed at the vizier, Bahram's rivals at court plotted for his removal. One such opponent was the Sunni Ridwan b. Walakhshi, who unseated him in 1137, having marched against him with highly visible pro-Muslim banners: his soldiers had pages of the Qur'an pinned on top of their spears. The deposed vizier took refuge in Upper Egypt where, after attempting some resistance, he retreated to the White Monastery near Aswan. Ridwan took over the vizirate with a significant difference compared to his predecessors – as well as retaking control of the judiciary and the

55 King Roger II of Sicily's coronation mantle, Royal Court Workshop, Palermo, 1133–4, samite, silk, gold, pearls, enamel, filigree, precious stones.

da'wa, rather than *wazir* he called himself *malik*, that is, king, a title that implied independent ownership of power rather than ministerial service to the caliph. Ridwan found a way to signal his self-appointed status to his subjects on the occasion of the *'id*, where he appeared in public wearing a robe in a style reserved for kings.

Once securely in office Ridwan took to persecuting Christians by hitting them with punitive taxes. The mostly Christian Armenian troops who formed Bahram's powerbase were disbanded. In Alexandria, Ridwan became a staunch patron of Sunni learning with the establishment of the first formally appointed *madrasa* in Egypt. On the foreign policy front he reached out to the Zengid lords who now ruled in parts of Syria, to form a common front against the Crusaders and establish an alliance that would lead to the deposition of the Shi'i Fatimid regime he pretended to serve. Al-Hafiz, however, smelt a rat when he realized that his vizier, the *malik* Ridwan, was in fact liquidating his closest aides one by one. The caliph therefore recalled Bahram from his monastic retreat and, in defiance of Ridwan, installed him in the royal palace. This action forced Ridwan to come into the open about his real intentions, and having surrounded the palace with his forces he called for al-Hafiz to abdicate in favour of a son whom Ridwan had taken under his control. Since the realpolitik of the circumstances did not allow for sentimentality al-Hafiz had this son killed too. Not only did the caliph not budge; he was also able to rally military and popular support in his defence, to such an extent that Ridwan fled to 'Asqalan. From there he attempted another anti-Fatimid campaign but, having failed, he surrendered to al-Hafiz's troops. Once brought back to Cairo the caliph imprisoned him in a room next to Bahram's lodgings.

After Ridwan, from 1139 onwards al-Hafiz ruled without viziers until the end of his reign. He tried to reappoint Bahram but the Armenian refused, offering his consultancy instead. The relationship between the two remained strong and, at Bahram's death in 1140, the caliph declared three days of mourning and led the funeral procession in tears. Bahram was buried at the monastery of al-Khandaq in Cairo. From this time until the end of al-Hafiz's reign, the affairs of state were managed by a number of secretaries of mixed ethnic and religious backgrounds who had no links to the military and were therefore dependent on the caliph's favour. In the civil servant hierarchy, the head of the chancery occupied a position that gave him vizier-like privileges, such as wearing the tail of his turban in a style reserved to high-ranking palace eunuchs, or attending to the caliph during the Friday prayer. Having been betrayed by so many men in his service, al-Hafiz employed women in positions that involved working in his physical proximity. One was the supervisor of the caliphal inkwell, an important insignia of sovereignty. Assisted by a eunuch at her service, Sitt al-Ghazal had a reputation for knowing everything about pens, inkwells and cotton tufts but being ignorant of everything else.[16] Another woman was known to be on standby to wait upon al-Hafiz's needs. Both became wealthy patrons of mosques.

With the Franks preoccupied with the Zengids, al-Hafiz could concentrate on maintaining cordial relations with his Norman counterpart in Sicily. For the sake of securing good trade relations for mutual benefit, the Fatimids showed restraint when Roger II showed signs of expansion towards Ifriqyia, following his taking of the island of Jarba (present-day Djerba in Tunisia) in 1135. By 1148 the Normans had control of the coastline from Tripoli to al-Mahdiyya, thus ending the Ziridis' rule. In 1138, in Yemen, Queen Arwa died, a demise that brought the Sulayhid dynasty to an end. Al-Hafiz sought a rapprochement with the Yemeni *da'wa* but the Tayyibis remained steadfast in their support for their hidden imam, carrying forward the pre-al-Hafiz Fatimid spiritual and literary traditions which they were to preserve for future generations. In Syria, the Fatimids had woken up to the threat posed by the Zengids, now in control of most of their former territories. In 1147 a Fatimid delegation went to Syria to try to form an alliance with the Crusaders against the Zengid ruler, Nur al-Din (d. 1174), to no avail. In due course the Fatimids and the Crusaders would pay the consequences of their failed joint mission against this common enemy.

However caliphal life was not all doom and gloom for al-Hafiz. Among the women in his entourage were the slaves Bayyan, a singer and lute player, and Rayhan. As his favourites, both had mosques named after them. He had a daughter, Sayyida Sharifa or Sitt al-Qusur, whose court manoeuvrings will become apparent later in this chapter. Of the mothers of al-Hafiz's children we know of *umm al-walad* Sitt al-Wafa' or al-Mana', who gave birth to the boy who became al-Hafiz's successor with the name of al-Zafir. Though not a candidate for a 'father of the year' award given his treatment of his other sons, the intimate portrayal of al-Hafiz is that of a man soft at heart. According to an anecdote, having fallen asleep while listening to Bayyan playing the lute, al-Hafiz dreamt of going to the treasury for a box in which there was a gem. On waking up he went to the treasury, and sure enough found the box with the jewel he saw in the dream. Al-Hafiz gave the jewel to the woman, and after that he repeated the same gesture on that same day every year.

Dreams and portents appear as frequent topos associated with al-Hafiz's actions in other contexts. Stories of his night visions feature in accounts of his motivations in promoting the restoration of mosques and shrines, mostly carried out under the auspices of royal female patrons. The woman who emerged as the most prolific architectural sponsor during al-Hafiz's reign was 'Alam, the consort of the deceased al-Amir. She is named as the person behind works carried out under the supervision of prominent eunuchs who were in her service. These included works for the Andalus Mosque and its complex in al-Qarafa, the oratory of Mughafir and the Ruqayya shrine. According to a story, in 1133 al-Hafiz had been prompted to build a mausoleum dedicated to the latter, having dreamt of a woman who, wrapped in a cloak, identified herself as 'Ali's daughter, Ruqayya. Al-Hafiz ordered an excavation in an area coinciding with the one he saw in the dream and, lo and behold, a tomb was found which he recognized as that of the granddaughter of the Prophet Muhammad. 'Alam al-Amiriyya was credited with doing the rest. The wooden *mihrab* made in her name for the shrine is still extant. Inscriptions in this building feature 'Alam's name. Under its dome, an arabesque-decorated wooden tomb bears the inscription that it was built in 1138–9 by order of 'Alam al-Amiriyya via her eunuch, the servant of al-Hafiz.[17]

In 'Alam, a widow with no investment in dynastic politics, al-Hafiz found a safe partner through whom to showcase in public the dynasty he represented. Epigraphic evidence on constructions dating to this period indicate that, beyond meeting ritual needs, these works were carried out as part of a well-orchestrated pro-al-Hafiz visual advertisement. This was aimed at reiterating the legitimacy of his accession to the throne in the eyes of questioning or disaffected Shi'is. As for restoration carried out in al-Hafiz's name, in 1137 the shrine of Sayyida Nafisa was repaired, and the following year the caliph ordered a major refurbishment of al-Azhar Mosque in Cairo. The keel-shaped arches and carved stuccos decorating the courtyard, as well as the dome at the central entrance of the prayer hall, go back to his time. Al-Hafiz is also linked to the construction of the Shrine of Light. A story relates that during his caliphate the people of Fustat saw a column of fire rising in the al-Qarafa area. The caliph, having been informed, investigated the event. He ordered people to dig on the spot where the flame had appeared, and believed they uncovered the funerary remains of an 'Alid woman who was identified as a descendant of al-Hasan, the grandson of the Prophet. Al-Hafiz instructed a shrine to be built on the site.[18]

A notable detail of al-Hafiz's reign is the care he took to ensure the protection of the Christian monks of Mount Sinai. Between 1130 and 1136, first as regent and then as outright caliph, al-Hafiz issued a number of decrees instructing Fatimid officials to protect the community, not to claim taxes from the monks or deprive them of their grain entitlement. Due in part to the intercessions of Armenians in government, the caliph's eagerness to please can perhaps also be interpreted in light of the presence of the Crusaders further east. By going the extra mile to protect these monks he might have hoped to ensure that, although Christian, they would still prefer to remain his subjects.[19]

The last years of al-Hafiz's reign were marked by a constant struggle to stay afloat and alive. Ridwan, having escaped from his house arrest, tried again to seize power but, having failed, he was killed with his brother near the Aqmar Mosque. In Alexandria a presumed son of Nizar gathered support among the Lawata tribesmen in the city and launched a rebellion against al-Hafiz. He was defeated and his head was paraded in Cairo. Over the years rival military factions clashed in the streets, causing havoc and pillaging that added grief to the lives of people in the capital. At one point the dead resulting from these fights were so many that Cairo's streets became congested. As if all these upheavals were not enough, the Nile's performance between 1139 and 1148 was either too low or too high, causing crops to fail with consequent regular bouts of famine and disease. In 1149, around the age of 75, after such a convulsed reign, death by disease must have come as a relief to al-Hafiz.

Puppet Caliphs

One of al-Hafiz's sons lived in spite of murderous disputes among his brothers and his father's drastic measures to retain the caliphate at the expense of at least two of his children. At al-Hafiz's death this sixteen-year-old youth rose to the throne with the name of al-Zafir. Overwhelmed by court pressures, al-Zafir appointed a vizier, Ibn Masal (d. 1150), while he indulged in court entertainments. He amused himself, for example, by listening to a white parrot that could recite Qur'anic verses. Ibn Masal was an old man of Berber origin who had been a high-ranking civil servant during al-Hafiz's reign. This vizier juggled factionalism within the army which he controlled with the promise of donations and protection. Nevertheless, he became the target of al-'Adil b. Sallar (d. 1153), the governor of Alexandria, who launched a campaign against him. After only a few months in office Ibn Masal, despite strenuous resistance, succumbed to Ibn Sallar, who paraded his head across the capital. Al-Zafir was left with no choice but to appoint Ibn Sallar as the new vizier. In reality the caliph mistrusted him and conspired to have his new vizier killed. Ibn Sallar, however, found out about the plan and launched a purge of all those appointed to be the perpetrators of the conspiracy against him. If on the one hand this vizier attracted the enmity of the men of the palace, on the other he seems to have enjoyed the backing of the Fatimid royal women. Perhaps it was in view of reaching out to his female supporters that in 1152 Ibn Sallar's wife Ballara was showcased as a patron through her sponsorship of a mosque known as *masjid* Umm 'Abbas.[20] To date, this is the last known building linked to female patronage in Fatimid Egypt.

While Ibn Sallar was in Cairo, in Jerusalem King Baldwin III (d. 1163) sought to reinforce the Franks' presence in Gaza as a launch-pad from which to take 'Asqalan, a strategic outpost suited to Frankish incursions into Egypt. Between 1136 and 1150 the area saw a dramatic rise in the building of Crusaders' castles, a development that signalled the Franks' expansionist plans for the region. To counter their advance Ibn Sallar courted an alliance with the Zengid ruler Nur al-Din, via the mediation of a distinguished Arab poet, nobleman, knight and diplomat, Usama b. Munqidh (d. 1188).[21]

Usama, whose historical writings became one of the most frequently quoted Arabic sources on the Franks, belonged to a family originating from northern Syria. A Shi'a sympathizer – maybe more out of convenience than conviction – Usama had been an itinerant courtier in Syria, switching sides as necessary. Having gone one intrigue too far, he was expelled from Damascus in 1144. In quest of patronage, he moved to Fatimid Cairo, where he found favour with al-Hafiz who allocated to him a stipend, comfortable living quarters and other amenities. Now, under Ibn Sallar's instruction, Usama's mission was to agree the launch of a Zengid–Fatimid combined attack: Nur al-Din would fight the Franks in Tiberias on the Sea of Galilee while the Fatimid fleet would assault Frankish positions on the Mediterranean coast. The plan, however, came to nothing; the Fatimids' gold, meant to entice Nur al-Din, never reached the intended recipient, while the Franks pre-empted the Zengid attack, forcing Nur al-Din to retreat. The Fatimid fleet did raid the harbours of all the main Frankish ports but Nur al-Din's lack of intervention contributed to rendering the effort in vain. For all the anti-Christian rhetoric of the Muslim powers of the day, the Fatimids had in fact been left to their own devices in facing the brunt of the Franks' invasion. Having failed in his mission, Usama b. Munqidh returned to Egypt.

When in January 1153 Baldwin III launched the siege of ʻAsqalan, in response Ibn Sallar instructed his stepson, ʻAbbas, and the latter's son Nasr, to gather an army to relieve the city. Instead, as ʻAsqalan fell to the Franks that year ʻAbbas and Nasr, in collusion with al-Zafir, plotted to murder the vizier so that ʻAbbas could replace him. Once back in Cairo Nasr, rumoured to have had a more than affectionate relationship with al-Zafir, murdered Ibn Sallar in his sleep, thus opening ʻAbbas's door to the vizirate. Some saw Usama b. Munqidh as the *éminence grise* behind this conspiracy. As for ʻAsqalan, the fortress at last surrendered to the Franks on terms that allowed its entire population to emigrate to Egypt. As they left, they took with them, among other things, what was believed to be the relic head of al-Husayn, discovered by Badr al-Jamali in 1091.[22] Meanwhile in 1154 in Cairo, ʻAbbas, having grown suspicious of al-Zafir's true feelings towards him, instructed his son to catch the caliph in a love trap. Nasr invited the caliph to his living quarters, murdered him and dumped his body into a well. Once again Usama b. Munqidh's shadow lurked behind this regicide.

Not long after the murder, ʻAbbas – after pretending to search for the missing caliph – carried on his shoulder al-Zafir's five-year-old child, al-Fa'iz, to sit him on the throne. In the meantime, the vizier eliminated the boy's uncles, having accused them of al-Zafir's murder. ʻAbbas's reign of terror in the palace escalated to the point of triggering a frantic call for external help. Fearful for the child-caliph's life, the royal aunts took al-Fa'iz under their protection, becoming the strongest bastions of resistance against the power of the bloodthirsty vizier. In desperation, they urged Tala'iʻ b. Ruzzik (d. 1161), a Twelver Shiʻi Armenian military commander and governor in Upper Egypt, to come to Cairo to rescue the situation. In 1154 the women of the palace cut their hair and sent the locks to him as a signal of their extreme despair.[23]

As Tala'i' b. Ruzzik advanced, 'Abbas and his son Nasr escaped to the Zengids, having first looted the royal palace. Usama b. Munqidh, in tow, gambled his way towards new alliances. It was in the course of his travels as negotiator among various forces between Egypt and Syria that – much to his regret – Usama lost his entire library, which fell into the Crusaders' hands.

From Cairo, al-Zafir's sister Sitt al-Qusur, seeking revenge for the murder of her brother, pleaded for the Franks in 'Asqalan to intervene against 'Abbas, who was caught and executed. Nasr, sent back to Cairo in exchange for a ransom, met the fury of the harem's women, who beat him with their clogs, mutilated him, forced him to eat his own flesh, hanged him while still alive and then crucified him. The fierce spirit of these women was celebrated by the Yemeni court poet 'Umara who, in seeking patronage, courted rival rulers of his day as convenient. Having marched in triumph through Cairo with the locks of the royal women waving in the air from the top of the army's spears, Tala'i' b. Ruzzik became vizier and de facto ruler throughout al-Fa'iz's reign. Like Ridwan, he adopted the title of *malik*, but unlike his most immediate predecessors he did not want to overthrow the dynasty. Instead, he revived the ceremonial of al-Hafiz's days. In keeping with his Shi'i beliefs he built a new mosque to serve as mausoleum to house the relic head of al-Husayn, and supported the *ashraf* notables of Egypt as well as Hijaz and Iraq. Around 1155 Tala'i' b. Ruzzik faced a number of challenges, ranging from difficulties caused by grain shortages and price rises to the Frankish fleet launching from Sicily a successful attack on Tinnis and other Egyptian coastal cities. A year before, the Fatimids had broken an agreement with Roger II by entering into commercial relations with Pisa.[24]

Tala'i', nevertheless, sought to pursue the Fatimids' wish to be seen as saviours of Islam against the infidels by launching an expensive campaign across the Mediterranean against the Franks. The Fatimid navy was sent to Tyre in 1155 and to Beirut in 1158, while the army marched towards Jerusalem in 1157 and 1158. Along with the expenses for these expeditions Tala'i' also spent money on weapons and subsidies destined to Nur al-Din, seeking again to seal an alliance with the Zengid ruler of Aleppo and Damascus against the Frankish threat from 'Asqalan and Gaza. To please Nur al-Din, Tala'i' even composed poems dedicated to him which he sent via Usama b. Munqidh who, now in Damascus, could act as a go-between. Yet despite this charm offensive, no deal could be reached. These failures took the shine off Tala'i' b. Ruzzik in the eyes of the harem women, who grew dissatisfied with him, accusing him of mismanagement and abuse of power. Tala'i', who saw what was coming, in response arrested high dignitaries and royal family members for having entertained correspondence with al-Zafir's sister, one of the women who had summoned him in the first place. In 1157 the vizier crushed a plot against him led by this aunt of al-Fa'iz. As a result, the vizier had her executed along with her eunuchs and private guards.

If he failed in Syria, Tala'i' b. Ruzzik's diplomatic efforts produced a better outcome when he worked on strengthening the Fatimids' influence in the Red Sea region. In 1155 the vizier welcomed in the Golden Hall the ambassador of the *sharif* of the Holy Places, the already mentioned Yemeni poet but also jurist 'Umara. 'Umara then headed back to Mecca, loaded with money and grain, with instructions to secure the loyalty of several Yemeni locals to the Hafizi *da'wa*. 'Umara, a Sunni, returned to Cairo in 1157, settling in the palace as chronicler of the events of his day and as court poet. Whether in prose or in verse, he became an important informant on Fatimid–Frankish campaigns. Among his eulogies, for example, he dedicated a laudatory poem to Tala'i' b. Ruzzik (or his son) to congratulate him on halting a Frankish attack on Egypt.[25] Al-Fa'iz, who never recovered from the trauma of witnessing the murder of his family members, died of an epileptic fit in 1160 at the age of eleven, having spent most of his life in seclusion.

The End of the Fatimids and the Beginning of a Myth

With the caliph having died at a pre-pubescent age there was no heir from his line who could be installed as caliph. Tala'i' b. Ruzzik therefore put on the throne al-'Adid, a nine-year-old cousin of al-Fa'iz, celebrating his succession with his own poetry, chanting 'Two Imams in the hand of God; a mystery in which one is taken, the other raised up by Him'.[26] At some stage, the vizier married al-'Adid to his daughter, to secure his power with yet another attempt at merging the caliphal and vizirate dynasties. The story goes that Tala'i' had al-'Adid imprisoned until he agreed to marry the girl. The wedding took place in the vizier's palace and was officiated by one of Tala'i''s sons, also called Ruzzik. However not everybody in the family rejoiced at the union since another son of Tala'i', 'Adil, had this sister killed when he suspected her of plotting to murder her own father. As well as the threats that originated within his close circle, Tala'i' as vizier continued to attend to the business of protecting the reign from internal dissent and external perils. A new challenge he had to face was the appearance on the scene of a certain Muhammad b. al-Husayn who, having claimed to be the grandson of Nizar, pretended to be enthroned as the rightful imam. This claimant's venture was short-lived, as he was soon eliminated.

By this stage the relationship between Tala'i' and what was left of the royal family had broken down. The vizier, rather than seeking a rapprochement, moved all the wealth of the palace to his residence and took full control of a source of prime palace revenue, grain supply and distribution. With this manoeuvre Tala'i' ring-fenced for his personal advantage access to finance destined to pay the troops, thus securing their personal loyalty to him. But Tala'i' only delayed the inevitable. In 1161 the princess Sitt al-Qusur – for the sum of 15,000 *dinar*s – had palace personnel assassinate him in an ambush, which took place in a palace corridor while he was on his way to his customary greeting to the caliph. The temporary vacuum of power that followed Tala'i''s death was soon filled by the appointment of his son, Ruzzik, to the vizirate. This Ruzzik had Sitt al-Qusur strangled with her own headscarf while all the other conspirators were hunted down one by one. The caliph al-'Adid was placed in the care of yet another princess, who somehow convinced the new vizier of her innocence regarding her involvement in the plot against Tala'i'.

Ruzzik junior sought to promote his image in a positive light by being lenient towards high-ranking officers his father had arrested, and by sending gold to Mecca. During his vizirate he made one important appointment by placing al-Qadi al-Fadil, who had served first in the chancery, at the head of the army department. A Sunni born in 'Asqalan, al-Qadi al-Fadil would continue to occupy a position of high prestige under the Sunni regime that followed the demise of the Fatimid dynasty. He chronicled the transition from one dynasty to the next, besides gaining a reputation as one of the greatest bibliophiles and book collectors of his time.

In 1163 Ruzzik junior was killed by Shawar, a governor in Upper Egypt, whom his father had warned him against.[27] Shawar rose to the vizirate, but only for a few months, as he was expelled from Cairo by a Fatimid officer, Dirgham, whose prestige rested on him having defeated the Franks in Gaza. The fight between Shawar and this officer escalated to the point of impacting on relations between Egypt, the Crusaders and Nur al-Din, something that in due course triggered the circumstances that would determine the downfall of the dynasty. On the run from Cairo, Shawar took refuge at the Zengid court in Syria where he asked Nur al-Din to help him to regain the Fatimid vizirate. Nur al-Din's promise of help to the deposed vizier prompted the Frankish king Amalric I (d. 1174) in Jerusalem to invade Egypt in 1163, the Franks having entered it before. Tala'i' b. Ruzzik had negotiated the payment of an annual tribute to the Franks in return for a truce, a tribute that continued to be honoured by his son. Perhaps Shawar halted the payment? Whether as an excuse to force resumption of the tribute, or indeed as a full conquest, Amalric invaded Egypt. The Fatimids had to resort to breaking the dams along the Nile in advance of the appointed time to cause a flood as a stratagem to stop his advance.[28] In 1162, out of concern at the Franks' attempts to conquer Egypt and acting on behalf of the caliph al-'Adid, the Fatimid royal women and children had once again cut their hair, this time dispatching the distress call in a horse nosebag to Nur al-Din.[29] After some hesitation, in 1164 Nur al-Din answered Shawar's appeal and the women's call for help by escorting Shawar back to Egypt flanked by a military force. This was led by Asad al-Din Shirkuh (d. 1169), a commander of Kurdish origins who, along with his brother Ayyub, had served the Zengids. On that expedition Asad al-Din Shirkuh took with him a nephew, the son of his brother Ayyub, called Salah al-Din (d. 1193). A legend was born: the Saladin of European chronicles and Crusades fame entered world history and myth.

The mission succeeded; Dirgham was defeated and Shawar reinstated as vizier. Hedging his bets to fend off threats of either a Frankish or a Zengid takeover of Egypt, Shawar lasted for some time in office, during which he switched sides by trying to enter into alliance with Amalric I. This policy succeeded for a while, in that it pitted the Frankish and Zengid armies against each other, while other factions fought in the Fatimid caliphate's name. It was in the context of these arrangements that in 1167 Amalric I dispatched Hugh of Caesarea (d. 1168 or after) to collect tributes from al-'Adid, an occasion that left the Franks' delegation amazed at the splendour and ceremonial of the Fatimid court. Hugh of Caesarea described al-'Adid as a handsome sixteen-year-old youth with impeccable manners. The Frank was astonished by the way he was welcomed, with an elaborate and meticulous protocol which the Christian envoy subverted by making al-'Adid shake his hand. Hugh commented that al-ʿAdid had a large number of wives, more likely to have been mostly concubines. Shawar's conciliatory attitude towards the Franks was conditioned by the fact that they had carried out their first major attack against Alexandria. Up to this time the Crusaders had left Alexandria alone because the city was too valuable a trading post for their own interests to warrant disrupting its international traffic of goods by military expeditions. Merchants from Italian cities on which the Franks depended for much of their naval power and supplies relied on access to Alexandria to import, among other goods, alum and natron, both vital minerals for Italian textile production. Pisans and Amalfitans had hostels and depots in the city. The Franks did not want to disadvantage their allies, so when they did attack Alexandria it was not by plan but in response to a set of circumstances.[30]

This arrangement between the Fatimids and the Franks worried the Zengids a great deal. Now weary of Shawar's diplomatic games, in 1168 Nur al-Din backed a second expedition led by Shirkuh accompanied again by Salah al-Din. The official excuse for the expedition was that it had been prompted by Shawar and al-ʿAdid, due to their mounting concerns about the Franks' presence in Egypt. In reality Nur al-Din had his own designs. Once in Cairo Shirkuh, having pushed back the Franks, sought to eliminate Shawar. In 1169 Salah al-Din arrested the vizier and had him killed, possibly with al-ʿAdid's consent. At this point the caliph had no choice but to nominate Shirkuh as vizier, with the title *al-malik al-mansur*, the victorious king. During his rule this vizier – with the aim of strengthening the loyalty of Christians on Fatimid Egypt's eastern frontier – continued the policy of issuing decrees that guaranteed the protection of the monks of Mount Sinai and their bishop, thus reaffirming arrangements dating back to the reign of al-Hafiz.

When in a short time Shirkuh died, Salah al-Din took over the vizirate following his investiture by the Fatimid caliph. In keeping with his Zengid master's objectives, Salah al-Din, now in power, prepared the ground to bring the Fatimid regime to an end and rule in its territories in the name of the ʿAbbasids. Salah al-Din built a loyal military force around him while disbanding the Fatimid army factions by burning down their quarters and rooting them out in Upper Egypt. He replaced Egyptian state civil servants with Syrian ones. He imposed anti-Ismaʿili policies by abolishing Shiʿi aspects of the ritual and closing down Ismaʿili institutions of learning such as the holding of the sessions of wisdom. Sunni *qadi*s and jurists were now in charge of the law in Egypt, at the expense of Isma'ili and Shi'i jurisprudence and the judiciary. He fought off yet another Frankish–Byzantine attempt to invade Egypt. Having taken over the caliphal palace (by this time inhabited by some 12,000 staff and their families), Salah al-Din put a formal end to the Fatimid dynasty on Friday, 10 September 1171. On that day the sermon in Cairo's mosques was read in the name of the 'Abbasid caliph al-Mustadi' (d. 1180).

The populace was too exhausted by decades of political turmoil to care either way. Nevertheless, Salah al-Din took no risks, staging a display of strength with a grand parade of his troops through the capital. He also delivered an explanation of why and how the Fatimid dynasty had to come to an end. Following the death of al-'Adid shortly after his takeover, at his funeral Salah al-Din announced that he had informed Da'ud, the young son of the deceased caliph, that since his father had not declared him as his successor according to the rules established by the dynasty itself, he could not inherit the caliphate and that therefore the line had to come to an end.

Salah al-Din was now on course to make himself independent of Nur al-Din, and in 1174 he founded a new dynasty named Ayyubid after his patronymic. In time, from the ranks of the slave soldiers who served this dynasty another emerged in the mid-thirteenth century, the Mamluks. Their sultanate lasted until 1517. After the death of the last Fatimid caliph, the rest of the royal family was kept in captivity in areas of the palace and in isolated quarters. The royal treasures were divided among the new ruling class. The Fatimid libraries, which had almost been restored to their former glory after the looting of the *shidda* years, were dispersed once and for all. Isma'ilis were persecuted. Many went into hiding in Upper Egypt, where they created pockets of resistance against Salah al-Din. Soon claimants to the Fatimid throne came forward, advancing their rights on the basis of lineage. Al-'Adid's son Da'ud was recognized by some as heir apparent, but he died in a Cairo prison in 1207–8. In 1174 former Fatimid notables including members of the Ruzzik and Shawar families, as well as a few of Salah al-Din's officers, sought help from Amalric I and the Normans of Sicily to mount an attack to overthrow Salah al-Din. In the process Alexandria was besieged, but the uprising was crushed, with many conspirators killed or exiled to Upper Egypt, a region that became a hotbed of anti-Ayyubid protest. There, between 1175 and 1177 more pro-Fatimid revolts were suppressed by Salah al-Din's brother and future successor, 'Adil (d. 1218). Meanwhile in Syria, the Nizaris had become a force to be reckoned with under the leadership of Rashid al-Din Sinan. Fighting against the Zengids and the Ayyubids to secure their own survival during the siege of their fortress of Masyaf in 1176, the Syrian Nizari fighters made attempts to assassinate Salah al-Din. According to an anecdote one night some strange lights and movement of people was noted in the Ayyubid camp. As Salah al-Din jolted out of his sleep he saw with the corner of his eye a figure sneaking out of his tent. Then, there, near where his head had rested, was a note pinned with a poisoned dagger warning him that he would be killed if he did not lift the siege. Troubled that Sinan himself might have been the figure he had spotted in the tent, Salah al-Din not only abandoned the siege plan but considered entering into an alliance with the Syrian Nizaris to prevent them joining forces with the Crusaders.

During the hundred years or so that followed Salah al-Din's instalment as sultan, the existence of remaining members of the Hafizi line in the Fatimid royal family is recorded. At Da'ud's death the Hafizis asked to mourn the prince in public. The Ayyubis agreed so that they could identify them, arrest them all and take their properties. Prince Da'ud in turn had a son, Sulayman, conceived in prison, who died in Cairo in 1248. More descendants of al-'Adid are reported to have been alive as late as 1298 when more claimants came forward. Fatimid Isma'ilism was reported as being observed in some villages in Upper Egypt and also in Syria's mountain villages until the early fourteenth century.

In 909, having unseated the Sunni Aghlabids, the Fatimid dynasty had inaugurated their reign by taking over the possessions left behind by the deposed ruler on the run. Among many artefacts in the royal palace in Raqqada the new Fatimid occupants found a whoopee cushion that caused much hilarity and scorn at the foolishness of the Aghlabid rulers. When in 1171 Salah al-Din and his troops entered the Fatimid royal palace they seized its treasures, among them a jacinth described as being the size of a mountain and a huge emerald carved in the shape of a handle. In al-'Adid's private quarters Salah al-Din's soldiers found a drum. Upon hitting it, one of the men was startled by the fart-sounding noise the drum produced. Another man then had a go at the toy and the same thing happened. And then another, and so on. Before long the men had turned into a jovial bunch, all amusing themselves with the drum until one of them dropped it and, much to the regret of all, broke it.[31] Like their Sunni predecessors in North Africa 262 years before, the once-roaring Shi'i Isma'ili Fatimids exited the religious-political stage on a whimpering sound.

Salah al-Din had the last laugh.

12

The Legacy of a Golden Age

Forgotten, ignored, even snubbed for centuries, the Fatimids have been making a steady comeback in recent times. Not as a political entity with neo-imperialist ambition but as representatives of an age that has inspired interest in various contexts, from academia to popular culture. Traces of the legacy the Fatimids left behind can be spotted in surpising contexts and in unexpected ways. The vicissitudes that marked the history of the dynasty and the age it represented intersect with the rest of the known world of their day. As such, the history of the Fatimids can be counted as an integral part of that medieval world at large. Today their status as the patrons and producers of outstanding cultural artefacts is affirmed globally, thanks to the surviving array of exquisite objects belonging to the Fatimid period that grace public and private collections. The variety of artistic, literary and performative expressions in which the Fatimids are showcased testifies to the power of their era as an ongoing source of creative inspiration. Within the Muslim sphere of action features that made the Fatimids stand out, such as tolerance, inclusivity, learning, artistic patronage and cosmopolitanism, continue to be – in different ways and to different extents – integral to the ethos of today's Shiʿi Muslim communities that trace their origins and heritage back to the dynasty and its reign.

Erasing, Obfuscating and Camouflaging the Fatimids

In 1171, Salah al-Din al-Ayyubi, having served as vizier for the Fatimid caliph al-ʿAdid, brought Fatimid rule to an end, thus inaugurating the Ayyubid phase of Egyptian history. He proclaimed allegiance to the ʿAbbasids and restored Sunnism as the state religion. Al-ʿAdid, aged twenty, died soon after the takeover and his extensive family, including his son and heir Da'ud, was kept under house arrest. Then the new ruler set out to erase the Fatimids' image as well as the Isma'ili presence in his acquired domains. The restoration of Sunnism as the state religion took many forms, such as the institutional repurposing of buildings. Salah al-Din turned the *masjid* of al-Hakim into the main Sunni mosque of the city, while houses that had belonged to members of the old regime were turned into *madrasa*s. Also systematic was the purging process that took place through cultural cleansing, physical persecution and economic reforms that moved away from the model which had been at the heart of the Fatimids' wealth.

Cultural cleansing took the form of dispersing the Fatimid royal libraries. To oversee the task Salah al-Din appointed the high official al-Qadi al-Fadil. A bibliophile and book collector, al-Qadi al-Fadil was known to have amassed over time a personal library of some 120,000 books. Anecdotes on his handling of the sale of books from the disbanded Fatimid royal libraries show him secreting the best and most valuable books for himself, even to the extent of manipulating to his advantage the auctions, which took place twice a week, through which the books were sold. Before the sale he would damage the exterior of a volume so that bidders would be deterred, leaving him to buy the item at a low price. The practical handling of the dispersal of the Fatimid palace library had been delegated to the eunuch Qaraqush al-Asadi, deemed to know nothing about books. Al-Fadil was not the only official close to Salah al-Din to siphon books. In 1177 his deputy, the scribe 'Imad al-Din al-Isfahani (d. 1201) – who in due course grew close to Salah al-Din and wrote works detailing aspects of his biography – took possession of royal volumes by dispatching them to Syria in eight camel-loads. Manuscripts once in the royal Fatimid libraries are recorded to have resurfaced in Damascus in the collection of al-Qadi al-Fadil's son. From Cairo other books ended up in Iran. The Iraqi-born thirteenth-century Shi'i scholar Radi al-Din b. Tawus (d. 1266) is believed to have owned copies of works by al-Qadi al-Nu'man, and some Ikhwan al-Safa' epistles.[1]

The other purge was the persecution of Isma'ilis and pro-Fatimid supporters. Most of them took refuge in Upper Egypt, which became a hub of pro-Fatimid subversive action against the new Sunni regime in Cairo. Over time genuine descendants in the line of the last Fatimid caliph as well as false claimants came forward to uproot those they saw as usurpers. Not long after an attempt at overthrowing the Ayyubids, culminating with the siege of Alexandria in 1174, in Upper Egypt the pro-Fatimid general Kanz al-Dawla launched another revolt that was soon quashed. Two years later a man claiming to be al-ʿAdid's son, Da'ud, appeared in Qift, where he attracted a substantial number of supporters. The Ayyubids killed about 3,000 people to quash the uprising. In 1181, also in the south, two men from Esna once again called for the return of the Fatimid caliphate. As late as 1297–8 a man who had presented himself in the same region as a descendant of the last Fatimid caliph failed in his campaign to re-establish Fatimid rule. More claimants to the Fatimid crown appeared elsewhere: in North Africa a presumed child of al-Mustansir's son Nizar gained some following. The Nizari Ismaʿilis of Iran linked the continuation of the imamate in Nizar's line of descent to one such son whom they claimed had lived in hiding.

In Egypt deliberate attempts to silence the country's Fatimid past – its Shiʿi Ismaʿili character in particular – continued over the centuries. By the nineteenth century Egypt had affirmed itself, among the Arab nations, as the pre-eminent cultural, intellectual and academic champion of Sunnism. By this time al-Azhar, founded as a Fatimid mosque and developed into a centre of Ismaʿili preaching as well as legal training, had become the most prestigious Sunni theological university in the world, a position it still occupies today. On the strength of these Sunni credentials, in Cairo a number of strategies to erase the Fatimids from collective memory were therefore adopted, which we see reflected in the ways in which the foreign-protected Ottoman regime of Egypt chose to represent the country to its subjects and the world. In Cairo the respective agendas of the European colonial and Ottoman imperial spheres converged in 1881 with the formation of the Comité de conservation des monuments de l'art arabe (Committee for the Preservation of the Monuments of Arab Art) established to list all the Arab monuments in Egypt that this body considered worthy of preservation. The establishment of the Comité led to the foundation of the National Museum of Arab Art. In the introduction to the 1885 first catalogue of the museum's collection, a brief chronological outline of Islamic Egypt is provided in which the Fatimids are featured as one of the ruling dynasties of the past. Though referred to as caliphs, the nature of their caliphate is not explained and no mention is made of the Ismaʿili brand of Islam the Fatimids embodied. The establishment of the museum contributed to a rebranding of the Egyptian capital into the committee's version of an authentic Medieval Cairo, one that gave the Ottomans the chance (among other agendas) to obfuscate the Shi'i origins and history of the city. The outcome of this process was a crystallization of Medieval Cairo as Mamluk in essence, something that on the whole Egyptians came to accept as representing the national past. On the international scene a tangible example of the canonization of Cairo's urban past as a Mamluk construct can be found in shows such as the universal exhibitions staged in Europe and the USA between the early 1860s and 1900s. One such extravaganza was the 1889 Exposition Universelle of Paris, where a pavilion called '*Rue du Caire*' was installed consisting of the reconstruction of an imaginary street lined by 25 replicas of historic Islamic buildings located in Old Cairo. None was Fatimid except a copy of one of al-Azhar mosque's gates that was included to reflect a time when this institution had already been transformed into a beacon of Sunni learning. Alphonse Delort de Gléon (d. 1899), promoter and curator of the display, did not mention the Fatimids at all in his catalogue for the exhibition.[2]

In 1952 Jamal 'Abd al-Nasir (d. 1970), or Nasser as he became known around the world, led the Free Officers' revolution that overthrew the Egyptian monarchy and ended the colonial presence, thus opening the way for him to become prime minister of the Republic of Egypt in 1954 and its president in 1956. In 1969 Nasser staged a lavish set of celebrations to mark 1,000 years since the foundation of Cairo. One event was the hosting in Cairo of a symposium titled *Colloque international sur l'histoire du Caire*. In their inaugural addresses neither Nasser nor the minister of culture who was behind the initiative mentioned the Fatimids.[3] In the conference proceedings the space given to the dynasty is somewhat peripheral and incidental, in sharp contrast to the Fatimids' foundational role in Cairo's history. In one contribution the Fatimids are reduced to being classed as a forgettable bold attempt that came to nothing.[4] A separate celebration volume was published in several languages as a souvenir of the occasion for international audiences. It features an introduction in which the Fatimids' contribution to Cairo's history and artistic splendour is acknowledged as a prelude to the Mamluks' achievements, and as a way to sharpen contempt for the Ottomans and colonial powers. The author goes as far as crediting the Fatimids for bringing the caliphate to Egypt, thus turning the country from that time onwards into the leading heart of Arab-Islamic culture and political life. What is not mentioned, however, is the Shi'i Isma'ili character of that caliphate.[5]

Re-Inscribing the Fatimids into the Present for the Future

In the late 1970s and early 1980s the Egyptian government granted the India-based leadership of the Shi'a Isma'ili Da'udi Bohras permission to undertake a massive Bohra-financed restoration programme of some of the little that was left of the Fatimid landmarks in the capital. With their distinctive, if controversial, approach to conservation the Bohras spearheaded this initiative as a way to reassert their claim over the Fatimid past through taking symbolic ownership of Cairo's Fatimid architecture.[6] The Da'udis' move was in part dictated by competition with the Nizari Isma'ilis in reclaiming the historical past of the same landscape. Moreover, the nature of the project, made visible on an international stage, served to advertise the Da'udis' assertion of their leadership rights against those claimed by rival Bohra branches, that is the Sulaymanis of Yemen and Saudi Arabia and the 'Alawis of Baroda in Gujarat. Irrespective of these divisions, which emerged in the sixteenth and seventeenth centuries over leadership disputes, through the replication of real or imagined Fatimid-era architectural motifs, the Bohras today add extra authoritativeness to the aesthetics of their new mosques with their adoption of what has been called a neo-Fatimid style. This phenomenon has evolved into a unifying visible vocabulary shared across their scattered cosmopolitan community.[7] Beyond architecture, the weaving of a Fatimid identity into the lives of the Bohras has found application in a sustained, continuous adherence to ritual, law and personal conduct based on textual authorities going back to the Fatimids. The 'Alawis proclaim their *Faatemi* way of life in protecting manuscript copies of Fatimid literature as well as in books published for their community. Mundane aspects of everyday life are not exempt from the Bohras' celebration of their Fatimid belonging: the term *Faatemi* can be found advertised on shopfronts in the quarters of cities, mostly in India, where they live.[8] To this day the Bohras use an Islamic calendar to determine the months of the year that is based on arithmetical rule rather than astronomical observation. They call it Misri, that is, Egyptian, claiming that this method was first developed by the first imam, 'Ali, and perpetuated as a state calendar by the Fatimids. This tabular scheme was the basis for the development of Microsoft's so-called Kuwaiti algorithm which has been used for its online Islamic calendar converter.[9] Apple has also developed a Misri calendar app.

Among today's Nizari Isma'ilis too, the direct nexus with their Isma'ili past and the Fatimid age in particular is made visible through higly symbolic architectural landmarks and projects. When arriving in the Egyptian city of Aswan the visitor can't help noticing a shrine on the top of a hill on the western bank of the Nile. The domed structure is the mausoleum of His Highness Sir Sultan Muhammad Shah Aga Khan III (d. 1957), the 48th Isma'ili imam and the grandfather of the late Aga Khan IV. In expressing his wishes about his choice of burial site HH Muhammad Shah designated Aswan as his final resting place so that he could – as he stated in his memoirs – return to the land of his fathers. Following the death in a car crash of Prince Aly Khan (d. 1960), grandfather of today's fiftieth Nizari imam, this proclamation of the family bond with its early history was signified by his burial in a purpose-built shrine in Salamiyya, the Syrian city where the movement for the Isma'ili imams' cause took shape and their line became manifest. The Aga Khan II, who died in Pune in 1885, was entombed in the family mausoleum in the Iraqi city of Najaf, the holiest site and pre-eminent resting place of choice for Shi'i devotees, since it is there that 'Ali b. Abi Talib was buried. Also, highly symbolic as a testament to the modern history of the Nizaris is Hasanabad, known in India as Mumbai's Taj Mahal, the shrine that hosts the remains of the first Aga Khan (d. 1881). At the time of his death, Mumbai was the headquarters of the Nizari Isma'ili community. In fact, following the re-emergence of the line of Nizari imams in Alamut in the twelfth century, after centuries of Nizari permanence in Iran, the 46th imam – the first to carry the title of Aga Khan – transferred the imamate to India. There the Nizaris have been known as Khoja Isma'ilis ever since.

HH Sir Sultan Muhammad Shah's authoritative claim to Egypt as the ancestral home of the Aga Khans is today echoed in the work of agencies that operate under the umbrella of the Aga Khan Foundation. Part of the foundation is the Aga Khan Development Network (AKDN) which is renowned for its work in the conservation of Islamic historic landmarks around the world. In Cairo the AKDN stepped in with its agency, the Aga Khan Trust for Culture, to carry out projects designed to bring about a holistic regeneration of areas affected by social and economic deprivation. Over a twenty-year period the agency's Historic Cities programme took charge of turning a 30-hectare (74 ac) rubbish dump into the spectacular al-Azhar park, inaugurated in 2005. Adjacent to the park are the Darb al-Ahmar and Bab al-Wazir areas, which have come under the agency's conservation oversight for several years.[10]

Symbolism and doctrines associated with the Fatimids are today embedded in the culture and architecture visible in the mountainous regions shared between Tajikistan, Pakistan and Afghanistan. Here the landscape is dotted with shrines, *qadamgah*, signposting spots where locals believe Nasir-i Khusraw, the figure who brought Isma'ilism to the area, stood or stopped. To this day houses in Pamir called *chid* are built based on a traditional design that reflects in structure and decorative motifs the fusion between Fatimid Isma'ili Neoplatonic cosmology and ancestral pre-Islamic beliefs. In these houses the highest seat is reserved for the most important community and spiritual leader of the village when he visits. Otherwise, the seat is left empty and is called 'the chair of Nasir-i Khusraw'.

Among the Druzes, most of them living in scattered communities across the Middle East, their Fatimid ancestry is celebrated with the ultimate symbol of their identity and creed: a multicoloured five-pointed star. They trace back their adoption of this symbol to the imam-caliph al-Hakim in whose cult their faith has its roots.[11] The star stands as a visual rendition of Druze cosmological doctrines. They believe that the ultimate esoteric meaning of this multicoloured star is disclosed to only a select few within the community.

Beyond the situation of contemporary Isma'ili or Fatimid-linked communities, in early 2007 the Cairo dynasty hit the news in the context of discourses reflecting the political polarization surrounding Sunni–Shi'i rivalries that have dominated the geopolitics of the Middle East. At that time an unexpected apologist for the Fatimid dynasty and its age came forward in the person of the late Libyan leader Mu'ammar al-Qadhdhafi (d. 2011). Although himself a Sunni, al-Qadhdhafi emerged as a champion of the Fatimids in a series of speeches in which he glorified them as examples of tolerance and cultural advancement.[12] To al-Qadhdhafi the only triumph the descendants of the Prophet achieved was the realization of the Fatimid empire in North Africa, proclaiming that Fatimid Shi'ism was part of the North African identity and culture. Al-Qadhdhafi saw Egypt as the heart of the Fatimid caliphate that spearheaded a cultural dominance which the country had enjoyed since. Al-Qadhdhafi's agenda behind his pro-Fatimid rhetoric was to launch an oblique derogatory comment against other Arab governments of his day, the Saudi one especially. By endorsing the Fatimids the Libyan leader sought to imply that the direct descendants of the Prophet had more right to rule than the Saudi royal family.

The Saudis walked straight into the provocation by condemning in local media al-Qadhdhafi's glorification of the Fatimids. In response, the Saudi Permanent Committee for Scholarly Research and Deliverance of Formal Legal Opinions slammed the Fatimids in a legal opinion, *fatwa*, of 8 April 2007, according to which '[Fatimid rulers] were infidel, godless, depraved atheists who renounced Islam and believed in Zoroastrianism'.[13] The *fatwa* alarmed the community of Sulaymani Isma'ilis based in Najran, on the Saudi–Yemeni border. To these Isma'ilis the formal opinion was a cause of grave concern since taking aim at a period of Islamic history relevant to their identity could be used by the Saudi regime as an expedient for repression against them. Instances of Saudi abuses against the Isma'ilis of Najran featured in a 2008 report by Human Rights Watch.[14] Even religious scholars in Egypt, though Sunnis, rebuked the *fatwa* which in their eyes debased an important chapter of their country's history.

The Fatimids Are All Around Us

Under the Ayyubids and the dynasty that followed, the Mamluks, industrial crops for textile production became more diversified, with cotton becoming more dominant. Fur, brocade and wool became preferred to linen and silk *tiraz* for the production of clothing intended to indicate class distinction. The growth of the textile export industry in Europe was a game changer in the international trade of fabrics which in time contributed to the diminished desirability of large-scale Fatimid-style production and stock surplus. After the Fatimids' demise, the legacy of their style in fabric design and techniques survived for a further century or so in Norman Sicily until the reign of Emperor Frederick II Hohenstaufen (d. 1250). Under his rule Sicilian silk production declined after 1220 due to, among other factors, the exodus (forced and deliberate) of skilled Muslim silk workers from the island.[15] Over the centuries most of the Fatimids' luxury fabrics vanished. To many the value of these clothes lay in their gold and silver threads, resulting in their destruction to extract precious metals. Already during the years of the *shidda* it was noted that 'Everything woven with or fashioned from gold and silver was burned and its gold melted down.'[16] Today the oldest known extant dated Fatimid textile is a *tiraz* from 354 AH, that is, 965 CE, proclaiming al-Mu'izz's place in 'Ali's line of descent.[17]

Despite their scarcity, some Fatimid robes (or clothes in their style) resurfaced in Europe, where they acquired new functions and cultural identities. Besides the mantle of the Norman king Roger II, another Arabic-inscribed Fatimid-style embroidered cape found its way to the Museo Diocesano of Fermo Cathedral in Italy. It is believed to have belonged to the Archbishop of Canterbury, St Thomas Becket (d. 1170), who in turn gave it to a friend. Fatimid *tiraz* made a surprising reappearance in thirteenth- to fifteenth-century Italian paintings in the shape of the figural representation of veils and cloaks which adorned the Virgin Mary. Inscribed bands of gold as ornament that in Muslim contexts were signifiers of power and glory were replicated by Italian artists as pseudo-Arabic inscriptions devised to ornament Mary's outfit. This time they symbolized her spiritual majesty, as well as evoking the eastern origins of the sacred family. Up to the end of the fourteenth century, Islamic textiles continued to reach northern Italy and northern Europe from the eastern Mediterranean regions, though in lesser quantities. Before that, another important factor for the presence of Islamic fabrics in Europe was the contribution of Crusaders who brought back textiles, among a variety of other artefacts, that they often presented (or passed) as holy relics. It is significant to note that the only pieces of Fatimid clothing known to have survived in their entirety are items that have been preserved in Europe which had arrived through that channel. Both in France, one is a shroud preserved in the Abbey of Cadouin in Perigord. It dates to the Fatimid caliph al-Musta'li's reign and was brought back to France by Crusaders. The other – the most sumptuous of the Fatimid textiles to have come down to us – is associated with Anne, the mother of Mary and is known as the Veil of St Anne. A linen overgarment woven with gold and silk, it is preserved in Apt Cathedral in France, where it was venerated as a relic until the nineteenth century. The Arabic text on it contains the Muslim faith formula, the name of the Fatimid caliph al-Musta'li and that of his vizier al-Afdal, as well as the place where the textile was woven: Damietta, Egypt. It was produced around 1096 or 1097. It too arrived in Europe following the first Crusade, maybe brought back by Raimbaud de Simiane, Lord of Apt, or Guillaume de Sabran, Lord of Ansouis (illus. 40).[18] With the exception of these and a few other superb pieces, the majority of extant Fatimid textile fragments are found today via archaeological digs in burial sites. Fine examples including Coptic artefacts from Egypt are exhibited in major museums around the world.[19]

As a result of the final convulsive phase of the dynasty's rule and its aftermath, royal and court artefacts associated with the Fatimids became dispersed, with many reaching Europe. For example, on occupying the palace of the last Fatimid caliph, Salah al-Din found the jewel used to adorn the royal turban worn during celebratory processions. This ornament then came into the possession of the Norman king William II of Sicily (d. 1189), who in turn gave it to the Almohad ruler Abu Ya'qub (d. 1184). Beyond the politics of gift-giving, Christian and Jewish merchants from Europe and Crusaders returning home were instrumental in this transfer of precious goods. Often sold as souvenirs and relics from the Holy Land (or repurposed as such), exquisite Fatimid ceramics, carved rock crystal jugs and perfume bottles, as well as textiles, ivories and jewellery, ended up in monasteries, churches, royal and patrician houses. Fatimid artefacts shaped the taste of the Italian Renaissance: Lorenzo de' Medici (d. 1492) is thought to have been a collector. In Italy, France, Germany and more these masterpieces – by then deprived of their Fatimid identity – became treasured possessions, objects of worship and a source of artistic inspiration. Fatimid ceramic vessels even came to be used as decorative features on the external walls of some Italian churches. The eleventh-century Fatimid *bacini* that can still be seen on the exterior of a number of churches in Pisa are famed.[20]

Over two hundred rock crystal objects are among the outstanding Fatimid artefacts that today grace museums, diocesan treasuries and private collections worldwide, or are found in the international art market. A number of these objects are known to have been commissioned by Fatimid caliphs or their close associates between the tenth and the first half of the eleventh centuries. Among these masterpieces are the superb Fatimid crystal ewers that are known in the art world as the Magnificent Seven. Two are in St Mark's Cathedral in Venice; one of these is inscribed with the name of the imam-caliph al-'Aziz. Another is in the Louvre in Paris, from the treasury of the Abbey of St Denis where it had been since the twelfth century. This is believed to be the flacon that Thibaut, Count of Champagne, acquired from Roger II of

Sicily and gave to Abbot Suger (d. 1151) of Chartres.[21] Others are in the Victoria and Albert Museum in London[22] and in the Keir Collection on display at the Dallas Museum of Art. The latter was at first mistaken for a worthless claret jug (illus. 39). The smallest of the group is the ewer in the Museo degli Argenti in the Palazzo Pitti, Florence.[23] In 1998 this jug broke into pieces when a gallery assistant dropped it on the floor. It has since been restored, regaining most of its original allure. The seventh is in the Museo Diocesano of Fermo cathedral.

Elsewhere small Arabic-inscribed crystal bottles and flasks became containers for saints' relics, framed in elaborate gold or silver holders. In Italy examples include one in St Mark's in Venice that functions as a reliquary for Jesus's miraculous blood. Other small crystal reliquaries can be found in the Bargello Museum in Florence, in the Basilica of Santa Chiara in Assisi (containing the saint's fingernail (illus. 56)), in the treasury of Capua's cathedral and a less refined one, probably

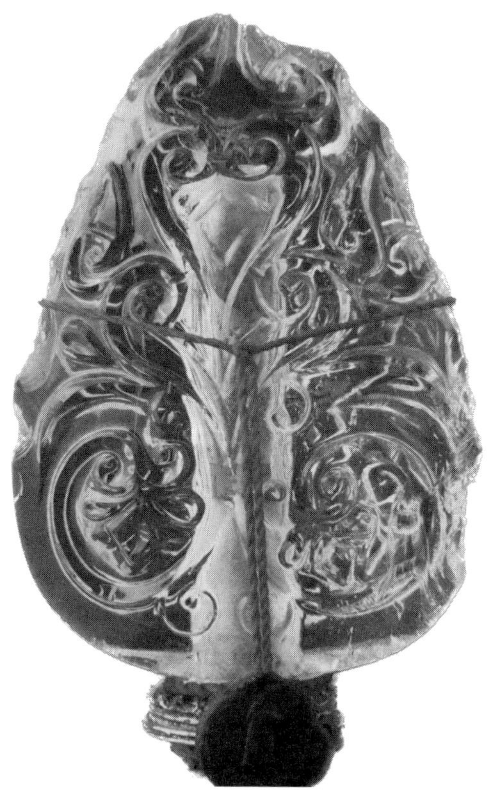

56 Reliquary containing the fingernail of St Clare made with carved Fatimid rock crystal, Egypt, 10th–11th century.

made in Fatimid Sicily, which holds the finger of St Gerlando, patron saint of Agrigento.[24] Further examples include a small bottle believed to have contained a hair of the Virgin Mary which is now part of the Islamic art collection in the British Museum in London.

The Fatimids in Fiction, Films and Popular Lore

The Fatimids have proven to be fertile ground from which to harvest material for fiction in a variety of media. From literature to popular lore, theatre and films to videos and digital games, animations and cartoons the dynasty and the age it embodied have made regular appearances in plots, as central features or as extras.[25] The Fatimids first entered modern Western written fiction by default, within the genre of poems, popular stories and novels that had the Crusades as their central theme. A Christian-centred literary canon devoted to stories of adventures in the Holy Land developed in Europe from the Middle Ages onwards. In modern times an early example of the Crusader–Fatimid theme in Western fiction can be found in one of the eight classic adventures by the American novelist Robert H. Howard (d. 1936). Collected under the title *Gates of Empire and Other Tales of the Crusades*, they were first published individually in the 1930s. The power struggles between Shawar, one of the last Fatimid viziers, the nominally Fatimid General Shirkuh (uncle of Salah al-Din) and the Crusader Amalric I set the tone for the last tale in the series, *Gates of Empire*.[26] Behind the intrigues that drive the plot is Giles Hobson, a noble Englishman who backs Shawar against Shirkuh.

The Fatimids are described in positive tones in Ellis Peters's mystery novel, *The Leper of Saint Giles*, set in 1139.[27] The Benedictine monk Brother Cadfael – the main hero of the book series to which this novel belongs – thinks them worthy of respect. He recognizes their nobility and honour on hearing that his companion, Guimar de Massard, having been captured in Egypt and succumbed to leprosy, was treated well and restored to health by Fatimid physicians. The novel was a great success and was adapted as a TV drama in 1994. Staying within the Crusader genre but from a narrative perspective that privileges the Muslim voice, the Fatimids enter the plot as the backdrop to the rise of Salah al-Din in the 1998 novel *The Book of Saladin: A Novel* by the British-Pakistani political activist and writer Tariq Ali. Kamran Pasha in his 2010 book *Shadow of the Swords: An Epic Novel of the Crusades* takes a similar perspective in downplaying the Crusades despite the title announcement.

In more recent times a classic of the genre has been the *Assassin's Creed* pulp novel series, published in the 2000s as part of the Ubisoft franchise that includes films, comics and animation based on the homonymous video and digital games. In the series, several of the plots conflate Crusader and Templar tales with legends about the Isma'ilis of Iran and Syria, against the backdrop of a late Fatimid pseudo-historical context. The Fatimids and the Isma'ilis of Iran are also fused in Scott Oden's 2010 *The Lion of Cairo*, a pulp novel set in the last days of the dynasty.

Besides the Crusader–Fatimid–Salah al-Din theme, the imam-caliph al-Hakim has been a popular source of inspiration for fiction. In 2007 the Austrian writer Johanna Awad-Geissler published *Die Schattenkalifin* (The Shadow She-Caliph). Based on the life of the Fatimid princess Sitt al-Mulk, it is – so far – the only historical novel written for a Western audience dedicated to a female figure of the middle period of Islamic history. In 2017 the American Bradley Steffens published a novel, *The Prisoner of al-Hakim*, centred on the vicissitudes of the eleventh-century polymath Ibn al-Haytham while in the service of the imam-caliph. In *Le maître du Nil*, published in 2019, Philippe Ward tells the story of the imam-caliph's rule while under the influence of the *jinn* 'Amr. Al-Hakim has inspired contemporary poetry, for example a work published by Eric Ormsby in the *New Yorker* in 1996. The Beat Generation poet Philip Lamantia (d. 2005), who visited the mosque named after this imam-caliph in Cairo, was also intrigued by this figure.

Early examples of Fatimid-related fiction in Arabic can be found in the corpus of the *Arabian Nights*. In modern times Jurji Zaydan (d. 1914) authored the most popular Fatimid-centred novels to appear first in Arabic. In 1912 he published *Fatat al-Qayrawan* (The Girl of Qayrawan), a story about the forced marriage of Lamya, daughter of the governor of Sijilmasa, to al-Husayn, the son of General Jawhar. The following year Zaydan published in Cairo a novel inspired by Salah al-Din in which the plot revolves around the final days of the Fatimids with a fictionalized princess, Sitt al-Mulk, presented as the sister of the last caliph. Here we follow the vicissitudes of the princess as she tries to disentangle herself from the web of intrigues masterminded by two rival men who compete to marry her for their respective political ends. Zaydan was a prolific and popular writer of the renaissance period of modern Arabic literature. Through fictionalized historical accounts like these, Zaydan intended to provide his readers with easy access to their own history. His novels, translated into many languages, first appeared serialized in the literary magazine he founded in 1892, *al-Hilal*. His works had a profound impact on shaping ideas of national consciousness and identity among modern Egyptians.

Zaydan's wave of cultural renewal found its match in the Egyptian theatre scene of the first half of the twentieth century. In the 1910s Ibrahim Ramzi (d. 1949), one of the fathers of modern Egyptian drama, wrote and staged *The Tale of al-Hakim bi-'Amr Allah* and *al-Badawiyya*, a drama revolving around a Bedouin girl from Upper Egypt who, in the play, resists the advances of Fatimid Caliph al-Amir. Around 1920 Ramzi wrote *Shawar ibn Mujir*, inspired by the above-mentioned vizier of the last Fatimid caliph. The Fatimids even featured in vaudeville shows poking fun at the dynasties that had ruled Egypt. However, the most famous playwright to contribute Fatimid-themed plays was 'Ali Ahmad Bakathir (d. 1969). His *The Secret of al-Hakim bi-'Amr Allah* was performed at Cairo's Opera House in 1947 to great acclaim. More recently Samir Sarhan (d. 2006) staged a drama titled *Sitt al-Mulk*, performed in Cairo at the National Theatre in 1987, with star actors Nour El-Sherif and Samiha Ayoub in the lead parts. Two years later his play was translated into English under the title *The Lady on the Throne: A Play*.

In 1989 we find the Fatimids again taking centre stage in Bensalem Himmich's historical award-winning novel *The Theocrat*, first published in Arabic and then translated into European languages. Using Arabic primary sources, mixing fact with historical imagination, the author uses this method to transform recorded instances in the life of al-Hakim and launch into a fantastic reconstruction of events. Overall, the plot revolves around the cliché of the imam-caliph as the villain whose rule is driven by madness.[28] Most of the book centres on the tension between al-Hakim and the rebel Abu Rakwa who sought to overthrow him. By the end of the novel the dark cloud over al-Hakim lifts when one of his supporters from Syria recognizes in him, rather than madness, the signs of divinity. Sitt al-Mulk once again makes her appearance in Himmich's book as the ultimate alter ego of her half-brother, lending her support to his son al-Zahir.

In 1991 the Egyptian author Khairy Shalaby published a novel later translated into English with the title *The Time-Travels of the Man*

Who Sold Pickles and Sweets. The story centres on the journey back in time of Ibn Shalabi. From the twentieth century we follow this vagabond through time in his encounters with various Egyptian historical figures. Among them are Fatimid imam-caliphs and high officers of the regime. A voice for the marginalized and the dispossessed, the author resorts to magic realism to comment on the state of society in his day, mirroring how ordinary people experienced the turbulent times that have defined the Egyptian past. Similar concerns are found in Reem Bassiouney's 2022 *Al Halawani: The Fatimid Trilogy*. Each part centres on defining figures who shaped Fatimid history and Egypt's past as a whole. These semi-fictionalized characters are the Fatimid general Jawhar al-Siqilli, the Armenian commander Badr al-Jamali and the Ayyubid Salah al-Din.

Novels and plays in Arabic featuring Fatimid-inspired plots located in regions outside Egypt include dramas by the Tunisian playwrights Ahmed Khéreddine (d. 1967) with *The Cub of the Fatimids*, and 'Izz al-Din al-Madani with two works, *The Revolt of the Man on the Donkey* inspired by the conflict between Abu Yazid and the imam-caliph al-Mansur, and *Fatimid Condolences*, staged respectively in 1970 and 1975. A contributor to Yemeni contemporary literature is Ramziyya 'Abbas al-Iryani (d. 2013) with her novella *Dar al-Saltana*. Published in 1998, it centres around the life of Queen Arwa al-Sulayhi, a figure that has been the source of inspiration for a variety of representations – from children's books to blog posts and more – in the contemporary Arab and Muslim worlds.

The age of the Fatimids forms a backdrop to Crusader genre films featuring plots embedded in the conquest of Jerusalem in 1099. Ignored by Hollywood, movies with this theme found a special place in Italian cinema, with productions ranging from Enrico Guazzoni's (d. 1949) 1918 silent *La Gerusalemme liberata* and the 1957 Carlo Ludovico Bragaglia's (d. 1998) film of the same title, to the TV miniseries *Crociati* of 2001, to name just a few. In these and others the stories are generally lifted from one of the best-known epic poems in Italian literature, *La Gerusalemme liberata*, first published in 1581 by Torquato Tasso (d. 1595). This poem recounts the events of the First Crusade in fictionalized fashion. Before being turned into film scripts, the stories in the poem were a popular subject for European paintings, music and operas from the sixteenth century onwards. Tommaso Grossi's (d. 1853) poem *I Lombardi alla prima crociata* formed the basis of the libretto for

Giuseppe Verdi's (d. 1901) opera of the same title. In the nineteenth century Tasso's epic inspired musicians like Donizetti, Liszt and Rossini, painters like Granet and Delacroix and poets such as Baudelaire.

The Arabs in general and the Fatimids in particular are an integral part of Sicily's cultural DNA. In today's Sicily the architectural, artistic and cultural legacy left by the Fatimids is often hidden under the label Arabo-Norman. On the island this heritage is celebrated in a broad range of popular culture artefacts. Oral plays centred on Christian heroes defeating Arab-Muslim foes are performed in public with their stories being integral to the Sicilian puppet theatre tradition that is today recognized as UNESCO Intangible Cultural Heritage. Projects such as film productions sponsored by the island's regional administration included in 2018 the web series *Indictus – La Terra è di Nessuno* (dir. Francesco Dinolfo), a fiction that pays homage to the Sicilian past by capturing one aspect of the struggle for supremacy between competing Arab and Norman forces. The drama unfolds within the context of the 1063 Battle of Cerami, an event that saw a small Norman army miraculously defeat a pro-Fatimid alliance of Sicilian Arab Kalbids and North African Zirids. In the series Count Roger I shines as the champion of the conquering Normans. However, against the grain of stereotypical negative representations, the Arabs are shown as seeking peace, an offer that the Normans reject. Moreover, events cause some Christians to appreciate their Muslim enemies' superiority in science and other fields of knowledge. The Fatimids, though not named, are present through references to Egypt as the distant homeland, home of esoteric knowledge. Prior to this cinematic rendition, the events of the Battle of Cerami caught the imagination of artists such as Prosper Lafaye (d. 1883), who depicted the battle in the orientalist style of his time. The painting is now in the galleries of the Palace of Versailles, France.

In different cinematic contexts (in both theme and place of production) the Fatimids formed the corollary of the 1947 Egyptian film *Abu Zayd al-Hilali*, which is based on an oral epic that is part of *al-Sira al-Hilaliyya*, set in the eleventh century during the reign of the imam-caliph al-Mustansir. The story of Abu Zayd and the Bani Hilal was turned into a play in 1978 by the Egyptian playwright Yusri Jindi. It was also serialized for Egyptian TV in the 1990s, and in Syria in 2005.

In films produced as contemporary video installation art pieces we find the Fatimids unnamed but nonetheless represented in the work of the Egyptian conceptual artist Wael Shawky (b. 1971). Shawky dedicated a film trilogy to the Crusades theme with his *Cabaret Crusades: The Horror Show File* (2010), *The Path to Cairo* (2012) and *Secrets of Karbala* (2015). All the short films feature, to different degrees and from different angles, a distinctive Fatimid presence in the way the artist chooses to tell his stories. The actors in the films are marionettes which enact narratives that move away from a Eurocentric representation of the Crusades to replace it with the stories of how Muslims experienced them. In the first instalment of the trilogy, one of the characters voicing these experiences is Usama b. Munqidh. 'The Path to Cairo' is a mythical interpretation of these events. Shawky's films are exhibited in museums and galleries around the world, accompanied by displays of the marionettes he used for the production. Arranged in thematic tableaux, the unanimated puppets add texture to the visual poignancy of the artist's power of storytelling. Shawky's installations evoke in some ways the agitprop play *Jerusalem Shall not Fall* by the Egyptian journalist and writer Sharf al-Shubashi (b. 1946). Staged in Cairo in 2002, this is a tragi-comedy that, as a way of commenting on contemporary international politics, deals with betrayals and intrigues set in the rivalry between the 'Abbasid and Fatimid regimes, with the rulers of both parties denounced as useless in the face of the Crusaders' advance.

Also in the contemporary art scene, the *Manifesta* 12 Biennial, held in Palermo in 2018, featured the project *I Racconti di Fatimide*. This is a collection of stories written by local children inspired by life in the Fatimide, the name by which an iconic city square of Palermo – Piazza Magione – was known in the past. Within the Fatimid-built Kalsa, this area is remembered as having once been a garden with plants from all over the world.[29]

At the intersection between written and cinematic fiction is the rich repertoire of illustrated publications that range from albums and commercial cards to games. In these productions Fatimid artefacts and sites – extant or known from descriptions in sources – have served as a source of reference for artists such as Adam Hook and Andrew McBride, among the world's most respected historical illustrators. In the early 2000s the Fatimids entered the world of strategy video games. From Creative Assembly's *Medieval II: Total War* (Sega) to Sid Meier's *Civilization* (Firaxis Games) game series and more the Fatimids can be played via modding, the process through which players can alter aspects of the game to meet their own specifications and strategies. For example, in Paradox Development Studio's *Crusader Kings® II Monarch's Journey* the Fatimids are also represented via the vassal Yemeni Queen Arwa turned into an avatar of choice (illus. 45). For most of these types of digital games the historical context is that of the conflicts, rivalries and alliances between Byzantines, Crusaders and Muslims in the eleventh to the thirteenth century. In the virtual realm, shifting across diverse histories and societies for solace as much as for ideological reasons, the Fatimids live on in a fantasy world where their glories are restored on a daily basis through the experiences of those gamers who choose to play with, through or against them. No longer relegated to a distant medieval past, in games the Fatimids acquire instead an ever-present dimension that perpetuates memory by generating new narratives which transcend traditional ones.

Post-9/11 those Muslims keen to correct the negative image often associated with Islam by non-Muslim observers look towards a vision of the Islamic past informed by intellectual interactions as well as fruitful cultural encounters that took place in a climate of tolerance. In the quest for models, there has been a growing interest in the Fatimids which in turn has generated flattering portrayals of the dynasty and its age in documentaries for terrestrial TV and online channels. Here the Fatimids are often evoked in connection with the protection of their subjects, tolerance and inclusivity, as well as values and attitudes appropriate for the twentieth and twenty-first centuries. Cartoons aimed at celebrating the achievements of Muslims for children belonging to the broader Muslim community glorify, for example, al-Muʿizz as a man whose great love for learning led him to invent the fountain pen.[30]

Today in Cairo the Fatimids' legacy also lives on in expressions of Coptic popular lore and devotion. Anachronistic stories tend to revolve around al-Muʿizz because of the role attributed to him in a legend involving the miraculous moving of the Muqattam hills to its present location. The hilly area of al-Muqattam in Cairo has been the site of devotion among the Copts of Egypt since time immemorial and Christian legends about miraculous events surrounding the mountain abound. According to the most famous of these tales, al-Muʿizz enjoyed convening gatherings of Muslims, Christians and Jewish savants to engage in intellectual debates. Having learned that according to Christian belief a mustard seed of faith would be sufficient to move mountains (Matthew 17:20) the imam-caliph asked the Coptic Bishop Afraham to prove it. If he failed, the imam-caliph would evict all the

Christians from the hills. The Copts asked for three days during which they prayed. When all seemed lost, they summoned the most devout Christian known at the time, a tanner called Simon. Thanks to his intervention the whole hills' range moved in three massive jolts and the Coptic community was saved. Al-Mu'izz and the bishop became enduring friends and in reward for the proven miracle al-Mu'izz granted permission for the rebuilding of a church. Today this legend, celebrated as a miracle with three days of fasting, is retold through various media. High-tech audio-visual effects are deployed during the festival day of St Simon at the Cave Churches on the Muqattam hills, where the Church of the Virgin and St Simon is extended with an open-air stage that seats 20,000 people. Besides live streaming the ritual ceremony, the audience is presented with a spectacular animation film showing al-Mu'izz on a horse, Bishop St Afraham in debate and St Simon's miraculous intervention in moving the hill. The screen simulation of the miraculous transformation of the landscape with the hills jumping three times is enhanced by booming sound effects resonating in the church.[31]

The story goes, within this community, that al-Mu'izz was so impressed by the miracle that he converted to Christianity. In the Church of St Mercurius there is a baptistry that is unlike those in other Coptic churches which is believed to have been used for the baptism of the imam-caliph.[32] From a historical perspective the legend poses problems of chronology, since al-Mu'izz and Bishop Afraham were not contemporaries. It is possible that in its written transmission, in the story al-'Aziz was replaced with al-Mu'izz.[33] Al-'Aziz was a contemporary of the bishop and also known to have allowed the Copts to rebuild the Church of St Mercurius after it had been turned into a sugar cane warehouse. Or could the ruler referred to in the story be al-Hakim instead? In dealing with al-Hakim's mysterious disappearance, it is narrated that the imam-caliph wanted to find a treasure and was deceived by being led to the Muqattam area where he was abandoned. As late as the seventeenth century foreign travellers narrated of being taken to visit the spot in the hills where Copts believed al-Hakim had gone in search of his treasure, described to be guarded by a crocodile. Besides the connection with the Muqattam area, in some Coptic stories al-Hakim converted to Christianity, a coincidence that has led to suggestions that over time the figure of this controversial imam-caliph was conflated with that of al-Mu'izz.

Dramatization can be found in performances attached to popular festivals introduced or promoted in Egypt by the Fatimids – such as birthdays of the Prophet and key members of his family – which are still celebrated in Cairo to this day. Until not too long ago, colourful sugar dolls were prepared on the occasion of the Prophet's birthday and sold in the streets, a treat believed to have originated in Fatimid times. Nowadays the popular perception of the Fatimid origins of these festivals has faded away, celebrated as they are in different ways, with different meanings and reclaimed under a different religious rubric.

Having started this book with sketches outlining the early traits of a movement that grew to the point of giving birth to an imperial dynasty, we have proceeded to depict the age that the Fatimids came to epitomize. As shown in this chapter, the cultural and artistic light the Fatimids nurtured, promoted and projected has outlived the dynasty's demise to find manifestation in many expressions in our time.

Epilogue

When confronted with this written portrayal would a reader see the sitter as the embodiment of success or failure? The appraisal of the Fatimids has been somewhat divided on this point and the verdict is still open. Seen from today's perspective the Fatimids distinguished themselves as a medieval Islamic dynasty that, on the whole, stood for tolerance and inclusivity. It conquered but did not subjugate; it did not succumb to the force of a rival military power; instead, it faded as the geopolitical climate around it changed. 'They moved away the highway,' as Norman Bates puts it in Hitchcock's film *Psycho*, when musing on how a transformed context caused the decline of his motel.

Today, whether introduced to us via museum artefacts or on screen, or as living history among some communities, the Fatimids and their age debunk a vision of Islam as monolithic and that of a world divided by rigid boundaries. In the same way the Fatimids became global players in the world they knew, today the dynasty and its age are part of a global history and heritage that defies geographical borders and cultural silos. Through formal and informal channels, the Fatimids have been finding their way from the past to today's audiences and this is no mean feat.

TIMELINE OF THE DYNASTY AND MILESTONES

‘Abd Allah al-Mahdi (r. 909–34)

921	Inauguration of the first capital al-Mahdiyya (Tunisia)
929	The Umayyad ‘Abd al-Rahman III proclaims himself caliph in Cordoba

al-Qa’im (r. 934–46)

944	The Khariji Abu Yazid stages a major anti-Fatimid attack

al-Mansur (r. 946–53)

946	Building of the second capital, al-Sabra al-Mansuriyya (Tunisia), begins

al-Mu‘izz (r. 953–75)

c. 960	al-Qadi al-Nu‘man completes his legal compendium, *Da‘a’im al-Islam*
969	Conquest of Egypt and foundation of third capital, Cairo
972	Foundation of al-Azhar Mosque in Cairo
973	al-Mu‘izz arrives in the new capital

al-‘Aziz (r. 975–96)

977	Ibn Killis becomes the first vizier of the Fatimid regime
978–88	First intermittent Fatimid conquests of Damascus

988	The Friday sermon is recited in the Fatimids' name in Byzantine Constantinople's mosque

al-Hakim (r. 996–1021)

1004–5	The Sunni Abu Rakwa launches an anti-Fatimid revolt
1009	al-Hakim orders the destruction of the Church of the Holy Sepulchre in Jerusalem
1011	The 'Abbasid Caliph al-Qadir issues in Baghdad an anti-Fatimid manifesto
1017	Supporters of al-Hakim proclaim his divinity: the rise of the Druzes

al-Zahir (r. 1021–36)

1021–3	The princess Sitt al-Mulk acts as regent for al-Zahir
1023	The Turkish Anushtakin al-Dizbiri secures control of Palestine for the Fatimids

al-Mustansir (r. 1036–94)

1036	Rasad, mother of al-Mustansir, rises to power
c. 1047	'Ali al-Sulayhi founds a Fatimid vassal dynasty in Yemen
1047	The Persian Isma'ili propagandist and thinker Nasir-i Khusraw arrives in Cairo
1058	The Fatimids proclaimed caliphs in Baghdad
1061	Beginning of the Norman conquest of southern Italy and Sicily
1066–72/3	The *shidda*, 'the terrible calamity', hits Egypt
1071	The Sunni Seljuqs defeat the Christian Byzantine army at Manzikert
1074	The Armenian commander Badr al-Jamali becomes vizier in Cairo

1076	Damascus is lost for good to the Seljuqs
1091	End of the Fatimid hold on Sicily
1094	The Nizari–Musta'li split occurs

al-Musta'li (r. 1094–1101)

c. 1097	Arwa, from regent, becomes Sulayhid Queen of Yemen
1099	The Crusaders conquer Jerusalem

al-Amir (r. 1101–30)

1130	The Hafizi–Tayyibi split occurs

al-Hafiz (regent 1130–32; caliph 1132–49)

1135	Bahram (d. 1140), a Christian Armenian, becomes vizier and the only Christian to head the Isma'ili *da'wa*

al-Zafir (r. 1149–54)

	The Sunni Zengid ruler Nur al-Din (d. 1174) rises to power in Syria
	The Fatimids lose 'Asqalan to the Crusaders

al-Fa'iz (r. 1154–60)

	The scholar, knight and diplomat Usama b. Munqidh (d. 1188) is active in this period on behalf of the Fatimid vizier Tala'i' b. Ruzzik

al-'Adid (1160–71)

1169	The Sunni Salah al-Din (Saladin) arrives in Cairo
1171	Salah al-Din brings the Fatimid dynasty to an end

REFERENCES

1 The Beginning of Shi‘a Isma‘ili Propaganda: From Covert Movement to the Unfolding of a Messianic Promise

1 Quoted in Stephen J. Shoemaker, *The Death of a Prophet: The End of Muhammad's Life and the Beginnings of Islam* (Philadelphia, PA, 2012), p. 91.

2 For an overview on Islamic eschatology, messianism and prophecy see Mathias Heiduk et al., eds, *Prognostication in the Medieval World: A Handbook*, 2 vols (Berlin and Boston, MA, 2021), vol. I, pp. 314–28, 356–70.

3 Bernard Lewis, *The Origins of Ismā‘īlism: A Study of the Historical Background of the Fāṭimid Caliphate* (Cambridge, 1940), pp. 25–6.

4 Ibid., pp. 30–31.

5 Michael Brett, *The Rise of the Fatimids: The World of the Mediterranean and the Middle East in the Tenth Century CE* (London, Boston, MA, and Cologne, 2001), p. 102.

6 Heinz Halm, *The Empire of the Mahdi: The Rise of the Fatimids*, trans. Michael Bonner (Leiden, 1996), pp. 12–13.

7 Ahmad al-Nishaburi, *Istitārul'-Imām* (full original title *Istitar al-imam wa-tafarruq al-du‘at*), trans. Wladimir Ivanow, *Ismaili Tradition Concerning the Rise of the Fatimids* (London, 1942), p. 162.

8 Lewis, *The Origins of Ismā‘īlism*, pp. 67–9.

9 Halm, *The Empire of the Mahdi*, pp. 6–9, 23.

10 Ibid., p. 14.

11 *A Code of Conduct: A Treatise on the Etiquette of the Fatimid Ismaili Mission. A critical edition of the Arabic text and English translation of Aḥmad b. Ibrāhīm al-Naysābūrī's al-Risāla al-mujaza al-kāfiya fī ādāb al-du‘āt*, ed. and trans. Verena Klemm and Paul E. Walker (London, 2012), pp. 35–76 (English text); and Wladimir Ivanow, 'The Organization of the Fatimid Propaganda', *Journal of the Bombay Branch of the Royal Asiatic Society*, new series, XV (1939), pp. 1–36 (pp. 34–5).

12 Halm, *The Empire of the Mahdi*, pp. 10–11.

13 Ibid., p. 15.

14 Among those supporting an early dating is the late Prof. Abbas Hamdani. One of his many works on the subject is 'Brethren of Purity, a Secret Society for the Establishment of the Fāṭimid Caliphate: New Evidence for the Early Dating of Their Encyclopædia', in *L'Égypte Fatimide, son art et son histoire*, ed. Marianne Barrucand (Paris, 1999), pp. 73–82.

15 This episode and others that follow are part of the account of ‘Abd Allah's residence in Salamiyya, his escape from the town and what happened next that forms the memoirs of his chamberlain. See [Ja‘far

b. 'Ali], *Sīrat Ja'far al-ḥājib* (full original title *Sirat Ja'far al-hajib: sirat al-hajib Ja'far b. 'Ali wa khuruj al-imam al-Mahdi min Salamiyya wa wusuluhu ila Sijilmasa wa khurujuhu minha ila Raqqada*), compiler Muhammad b. Muhammad al-Yamani. In Wladimir Ivanow, *Ismaili Tradition Concerning the Rise of the Fatimids* (London, 1942), pp. 184–223. The scene here described is at pp. 186–7.

16 The question of real, imagined, attributed and adopted names of the early Isma'ili imams is complex. For a valiant attempt to bring clarity to this onomastic conundrum see Abbas Hamdani and François de Blois, 'A Re-Examination of al-Mahdī's Letter to the Yemenites on the Genealogy of the Fatimid Caliphs', *Journal of the Royal Asiatic Society of Great Britain and Ireland*, 2 (1983), pp. 173–207.

17 Halm, *The Empire of the Mahdi*, pp. 58–62.

18 Farhad Daftary, *The Ismā'īlis: Their History and Doctrines*, 2nd edn (Cambridge, 2007), pp. 116–22; and Halm, *The Empire of the Mahdi*, pp. 62–6.

19 [Ja'far b. 'Ali], *Sirat Ja'far*, in Ivanow, *Ismaili Tradition*, pp. 192–3.

20 Daftary, *The Ismā'īlis*, p. 123.

21 On the history of the term 'fatimid/s' in Isma'ili and other contexts of its use see Maribel Fierro, 'On Fāṭimī and al-Fāṭimiyyūn', *Jerusalem Studies in Arabic and Islam*, xx (1996), pp. 130–61.

22 al-Nishaburi, *Istitāru'l-Imām*, pp. 172, 176–8.

2 The Inauguration of the Fatimid Dynasty in North Africa

1 Evidence of this belief can be found in devotional Isma'ili texts, for example, *Risala Sirat al-mustaqim*. Shafique Virani, 'The Right Path: A Post-Mongol Persian Ismaili Treatise', *Journal of Iranian Studies*, XLIII/2 (2010), pp. 197–221 (p. 211).

2 As a province, Ifriqiya became part of the Islamic empire in 703 following the Umayyad conquest of North Africa at the expense of the Byzantine empire. It comprised what today are Tunisia, eastern Algeria and, roughly, western Libya.

3 Heinz Halm, *The Empire of the Mahdi: The Rise of the Fatimids*, trans. Michael Bonner (Leiden, 1996), pp. 102–3.

4 Shafique N. Virani, *The Ismailis in the Middle Ages: A History of Survival, a Search for Salvation* (Oxford, 2007), p. 47.

5 al-Qadi al-Nu'man, *Iftitah al-Da'wa*, trans. Hamid Haji, *Founding the Fatimid State. The Rise of an Early Islamic Empire. An Annotated English Translation of al-Qāḍī al-Nu'mān's Iftitāḥ al-da'wa* (London and New York, 2006), pp. 44, 109. See also Delia Cortese, '"A Woman's Work is Never Done": Women and *Da'wa* in Early Ismailism', in *Egypt and Syria in the Fatimid, Ayyubid and Mamluk Eras*, ed. Urbain Vermeulen and Kristoff D'Hulster, vol. v (Leuven, Paris and Dudley, MA, 2007), pp. 68–70.

6 al-Qadi al-Nu'man, *Iftitah*, pp. 89–100.

7 Ibid., p. 113.

8 Quoted in Mark Littman, *The Heavens on Fire: The Great Leonid Meteor Storms* (Cambridge, 1998), p. 60.

9 See Ibn al-Haytham, *Kitab al-Munazarat*, in *The Advent of the Fatimids: A Contemporary Shi'i Witness Account of Politics in the Early Islamic World*, ed. and trans. Wilfred Madelung and Paul E. Walker (London, 2000).
10 Ibid., p. 108.
11 See Dwight Reynolds, 'Ziryab in the Aghlabid Court', in *The Aghlabids and Their Neighbors: Art and Material Culture in Ninth-Century North Africa*, ed. Corisande Fenwick, Glaire D. Anderson and Mariam Rosser-Owen (Leiden, 2017), pp. 144–60.
12 Ibn al-Haytham, *Kitab al-Munazarat*, p. 166.
13 See Aslisho Qurboniev, 'Traditions of Learning in Fatimid Ifriqiya (296–362/909–973): Networks, Practices and Institutions', PhD thesis, University of Cambridge, 2020, ch. 2.
14 [Ja'far b. 'Ali] *Sīrat Ja'far al-ḥājib* (full original title *Sirat Ja'far al-hajib: sirat al-hajib Ja'far b. 'Ali wa khuruj al-imam al-Mahdi min Salamiyya wa wusuluhu ila Sijilmasa wa khurujuhu minha ila Raqqada*), compiler Muhammad b. Muhammadal-Yamani. In Wladimir Ivanow, *Ismaili Tradition Concerning the Rise of the Fatimids* (London, 1942), pp. 184–223 (p. 207).
15 Delia Cortese and Simonetta Calderini, *Women and the Fatimids in the World of Islam* (Edinburgh, 2006), p. 48. My thanks to Dr S. Calderini, University of Roehampton, for reading and commenting on the first two chapters of this book. I am solely responsible for any mistakes or shortcomings.
16 Michael Brett, *The Rise of the Fatimids: The World of the Mediterranean and the Middle East in the Tenth Century CE* (London, Boston, MA, and Cologne, 2001), p. 103.
17 [Ja'far b. 'Ali], *Sirat Ja'far*, pp. 199, 201.
18 Ibn al-Haytham, *Kitab al-Munazarat*, pp. 153–4.
19 [Ja'far b. 'Ali], *Sirat Ja'far*, p. 211.
20 Paula Sanders, *Ritual, Politics and the City in Fatimid Cairo* (Albany, NY, 1994), p. 16.
21 [Ja'far b. 'Ali], *Sirat Ja'far*, pp. 217–19.
22 Halm, *The Empire of the Mahdi*, p. 146.
23 Cortese and Calderini, *Women and the Fatimids*, p. 79.
24 Brett, *The Rise of the Fatimids*, pp. 144–5.
25 The biography of this eunuch, *Sirat al-ustadh Jawdhar*, compiled by one of his contemporaries, represents one of the most important primary sources on the North African period of Fatimid history. See [Muhammad al-Jawdhari], *Sirat al-ustadh Jawdhar*, ed. and trans. Hamid Haji, *Inside the Immaculate Portal: A History from Early Fatimid Archives. A New Edition and English Translation of Manṣūr al-'Azīzī al-Jawdharī's Biography of al-Ustādh Jawdhar, the Sīrat al-Ustādh Jawdhar* (London and New York, 2012).
26 al-Qadi al-Nu'man, *Iftitah*, p. 227 and Halm, *The Empire of the Mahdi*, pp. 164–76; Brett, *The Rise of the Fatimids*, p. 110.
27 al-Qadi al-Nu'man, *Iftitah*, p. 124.
28 Muhammad b. Hawqal, *Kitab Surat al-ard* (Beirut, 1979), p. 73.
29 Heinz Halm, *The Fatimids and Their Traditions of Learning* (London, 1997), pp. 26–7.

30 Cortese and Calderini, *Women and the Fatimids*, p. 30.
31 Halm, *The Empire of the Mahdi*, p. 221.
32 See the chronicle of the Byzantine historian John Skylitzes (*fl.* eleventh century), trans. John Wortley, *A Synopsis of Byzantine History, 811–1057* (Cambridge, 2010), pp. 253–4.
33 Elsa Fernandes Cardoso, 'Politics and Diplomacy in the Mediterranean of the Tenth Century: Al-Andalus and Byzantium', in *The Medieval Mediterranean: Peoples, Economies and Cultures, 400–1500*, vol. CXVI: *Byzantium in Dialogue with the Mediterranean*, ed. Tamar Herzig et al. (Leiden, 2019), pp. 91–108 (p. 96).
34 'Abd Allah Muhammad b. al-Khatib, *Kitab A'mal al-a'lam*, ed. Émanuel Lévi-Provençal (Beirut, 1956), p. 32.
35 Farhad Daftary, *The Ismā'īlis: Their History and Doctrines*, 2nd edn (Cambridge, 2007), pp. 149–50.
36 Brett, *The Rise of the Fatimids*, pp. 156–7.
37 Muhammad b. 'Idhari al-Marrakushi, *Kitab al-Bayan al-mughrib fi akhbar al-Andalus wa'l-Maghrib*, ed. G. S. Colin and É. Lévi-Provençal, 2 vols (Leiden, 1948–51), vol. 1, p. 193.
38 al-Qadi al-Nu'man, *Iftitah*, p. 230.

3 New Imam-Caliph, New Capital, New Ventures

1 [Muhammad al-Jawdhari], *Sirat al-ustadh Jawdhar*, ed. and trans. Hamid Haji, *Inside the Immaculate Portal: A History from Early Fatimid Archives. A new edition and English translation of Manṣūr al-'Azīzī al-Jawdharī's Biography of al-Ustādh Jawdhar, the Sīrat al-Ustādh Jawdhar* (London and New York, 2012), pp. 57–8.
2 On al-Mansur's appreciation of Roman remains see Heinz Halm, *The Empire of the Mahdi: The Rise of the Fatimids*, trans. Michael Bonner (Leiden, 1996), pp. 325–8. Al-Mansur's impressions while touring Carthage are reported in al-Qadi al-Nu'man, *Kitab al-Majalis wa'l-musayarat*, ed. Habib al-Faqi, I. Shabbuh and M. al-Ya'lawi (Tunis, 1978), p. 201.
3 The tenth-century traveller Ibn Hawqal observed the commercial traffic from Fatimid-controlled lands towards the rest of the Mediterranean and beyond. See his *Kitab Surat al-ard* (Beirut, 1979), pp. 69–103.
4 [Muhammad al-Jawdhari], *Sirat al-ustadh Jawdhar*, p. 64.
5 This can be inferred from a passing reference in the list of contents outlined in an Arabic Isma'ili manuscript in the Ismaili Special Collections Unit, Aga Khan Centre, London. See Delia Cortese, *Arabic Ismaili Manuscripts: The Zāhid 'Alī Collection* (London, 2003), no. 108.
6 [Muhammad al-Jawdhari], *Sirat al-ustadh Jawdhar*, p. 103.
7 Paul E. Walker, 'Literary Culture in Fatimid Egypt', in *The World of the Fatimids*, ed. Assadullah Souren Melikian-Chirvani, exh. cat., Aga Khan Museum (Toronto, 2018), pp. 160–77 (p. 167).
8 H. H. 'Abd al-Wahhab Mujmal, *Ta'rikh al-adab al-tunisi min fajr al-'arabi li-ifriqiya ila al-'asr al-hadir* (Tunis, 1968), p. 97.
9 Respectively in Museo Arqueológico Nacional, Madrid (Spain), and Museo Diocesano Francesco Gonzaga, Mantua (Italy).

10 Delia Cortese and Simonetta Calderini, *Women and the Fatimids in the World of Islam* (Edinburgh, 2006), pp. 106–7.
11 [Muhammad al-Jawdhari], *Sirat al-ustadh Jawdhar*, p. 130.
12 al-Qadi al-Nu'man, *Kitab al-Majalis wa'l-musayarat*, p. 291.
13 Ibid., pp. 319–21.
14 Folios from this Qur'an are found in many museums as well as public and private art collections around the world. There is no overall consensus about the Fatimid origin of this codex. Alternative theories suggest, among others, al-Andalus or Iran as areas of provenance or influence in craftmanship.
15 Idris 'Imad al-Din, *'Uyun al-akhbar*, trans. Shainool Jiwa, *The Founder of Cairo. The Fatimid Imam-Caliph al-Mu'izz and His Era. An English Translation of the Text on al-Mu'izz from Idrīs 'Imād al-Dīn's 'Uyūn al-akhbār* (London and New York, 2013), pp. 85–6.
16 See Adam Mez, *The Renaissance of Islam: History, Culture and Society in the 10th Century Muslim World* (Patna, 1937), p. 3 based on the historian Ibn al-Jawzi (d. 1200).
17 al-Qadi al-Nu'man, *Kitab al-Majalis wa'l-musayarat*, p. 417.
18 Quoted in Yossef Rapoport and Emilie Savage-Smith, *Lost Maps of the Caliphs: Drawing the World in Eleventh-Century Cairo* (Chicago, IL, 2018), p. 198.
19 Farhad Daftary, *The Ismā'īlīs: Their History and Doctrines*, 2nd edn (Cambridge, 2007), pp. 202–3.

4 The Conquest of Egypt, Court Life and Imperial Expansion

1 Taqi al-Din al-Maqrizi, *Le traité des famines de Maqrīzī*, trans. Gaston Wiet (Leiden, 1962), pp. 12–14.
2 Shainool Jiwa, *The Fatimids*, vol. 1: *The Rise of a Muslim Empire* (London, 2018), p. 124.
3 Delia Cortese and Simonetta Calderini, *Women and the Fatimids in the World of Islam* (Edinburgh, 2006), p. 32.
4 For Fatimid–*ashraf* relations, see Shainool Jiwa, 'Kinship, Camaraderie and Contestation Fatimid Relations with the Ashraf in the Fourth AH/Tenth CE Century', *Al-Masaq: Journal of the Medieval Mediterranean*, XXVIII/3 (2016), pp. 242–64.
5 The full text is quoted in Taqi al-Din al-Maqrizi, *Itti'az al-hunafa' bi-akhbar al-a'imma al-fatimiyyin al-khulafa'*, ed. Jamal al-Din al-Shayyal and Muhammad Hilmi M. Ahmad, 3 vols (Cairo, 1967–73), vol. 1, pp. 103–7.
6 On both the Fatimids' *aman* and covenant (*'ahd*) see Shainool Jiwa, 'Inclusive Governance: A Fatimid Illustration', in *A Companion to the Muslim World*, ed. Amin Sajoo (London, 2009), pp. 157–76; Shainool Jiwa, 'Governance and Pluralism under the Fatimids (909–996 CE)', in *The Shi'i World: Pathways in Tradition and Modernity*, ed. Farhad Daftary, Amin Sajoo and Shainool Jiwa (London and New York, 2015), pp. 111–30, at 122–4 on the covenant.
7 Jonathan M. Bloom, *Arts of the City Victorious: Islamic Art and Architecture in Fatimid North Africa and Egypt* (New Haven, CT, and London, 2007), pp. 54–9.

8 Ibid., pp. 59–65.
9 [Qadi b. al-Zubayr] trans. Ghāda al-Hijjāwī al-Qaddūmī, *Book of Gifts and Rarities: Kitāb al-Hadāyā wa al-tuḥaf* (Cambridge, MA, 1996), p. 103.
10 Michael Brett, *The Fatimid Empire* (Edinburgh, 2017), pp. 82–3.
11 [Muhammad al-Jawdhari], *Sirat al-ustadh Jawdhar*, ed. and trans. Hamid Haji, *Inside the Immaculate Portal: A History from Early Fatimid Archives. A New Edition and English Translation of Manṣūr al-'Azīzī al-Jawdharī's Biography of al-Ustādh Jawdhar, the Sīrat al-Ustādh Jawdhar* (London and New York, 2012), pp. 116–17.
12 Ibid., pp. 106–7.
13 Maribel Fierro, 'Sacrifice, Circumcision and the Ruler in the Medieval Islamic West: The Ismaili-Fatimid Legacy', in *Intellectual Interactions in the Islamic World*, ed. Orkhan Mir-Kasimov (London, 2019), pp. 147–70 (p. 168).
14 [Muhammad al-Jawdhari], *Sirat al-ustadh Jawdhar*, pp. 156–8.
15 See Hugh Blake, Antony Hutt and David Whitehouse, 'Ajdābiyah and the Earliest Fāṭimid Architecture', *Libya Antiqua*, VIII (1971), pp. 105–20.
16 On this mosque see A. Abussaid, 'An Early Mosque at Medina Sultan', *Libya Antiqua*, vols III–IV (1966), pp. 155–60; and Geza Fehervari and Elizabeth Savage, author and ed., *Excavations at Surt (Medinat Al-Sultan) Between 1977 and 1981* (Broadstairs, 2002).
17 Taqi al-Din al-Maqrizi, *Itti'az*, vol. I, pp. 140–41, 230, among other references. See also Jonathan M. Bloom, 'Fatimid Gifts', in *Gifts of the Sultan: The Arts of Giving at the Islamic Courts*, ed. Linda Komaroff with contributions by Sheila Blair et al. (New Haven, CT, 2011), pp. 94–109 (p. 105).
18 Michael Brett, 'Al-Karāza al-Marqusīya: The Coptic Church in the Fatimid Empire', in Michael Brett, *The Fatimids and Egypt* (Abingdon, 2019), pp. 160–63.
19 For a concise discussion on the contents of this work see Sumaiya Hamdani, *Between Revolution and State: The Path to Fatimid Statehood* (London, 2006), pp. 63–84.
20 Olly Akkerman, *A Neo-Fatimid Treasury of Books: Arabic Manuscripts among the Alawi Bohras of South Asia* (Edinburgh, 2022), p. 67.
21 Cited from the historian Ibn Zafir (d. 1216 or 1226) in Heinz Halm, *The Empire of the Mahdi: The Rise of the Fatimids*, trans. Michael Bonner (Leiden, 1996), p. 159.
22 On this Melkite woman and the male members of her family who rose to prominence see Paul E. Walker, *The Fatimids* (Leiden, 2023), pp. 175–9, 286.
23 Cortese and Calderini, *Women and the Fatimids*, p. 223.
24 Respectively [Ja'far b. 'Ali], *Sīrat Ja'far al-ḥājib* (full original title *Sirat Ja'far al-hajib: sirat al-hajib Ja'far b. 'Ali wa khuruj al-imam al-Mahdi min Salamiyya wa wusuluhu ila Sijilmasa wa khurujuhu minha ila Raqqada*) compiled Muhammad b. Muhammadal-Yamani. In Wladimir Ivanow, *Ismaili Tradition Concerning the Rise of the Fatimids* (London, 1942), pp. 184–223 (p. 186) and Ibrahim al-Habbal, *Wafayat al-Misriyyin* (Riyad, 1408/1987), no. 48.

25 Michael Brett, *The Rise of the Fatimids: The World of the Mediterranean and the Middle East in the Tenth Century* CE (London, Boston, MA, and Cologne, 2001), p. 338.
26 Based on a Geniza document. See Mark R. Cohen and Sasson Somekh, 'In the Court of Yaqub ibn Killis: A Fragment from the Cairo Genizah', *Jewish Quarterly Review*, LXXX/3–4 (1990), pp. 283–314 (pp. 292–5).
27 Seta Dadoyan, *The Fatimid Armenians: Cultural and Political Interaction in the Near East* (Leiden, 1997), p. 84.
28 On high-profile Jews serving the Fatimid regime see Elinoar Bareket, *Fustat on the Nile: The Jewish Elite in Medieval Egypt* (Leiden, 1999), pp. 21–7.
29 Based on twelfth-to-thirteenth-century historian Ibn al-Athir as quoted in Adam Mez, *The Renaissance of Islam: History, Culture and Society in the 10th Century Muslim World* (Patna, 1937), p. 55.
30 For a full discussion on the codes and complexities governing patronage at the heart of politics in medieval Islamic courts see Roy Mottahedeh, *Loyalty and Leadership in Early Islamic Society* (Princeton, NJ, 1980).
31 Endre Tóth and Károly Szelényi, *The Holy Crown of Hungary* (n.p., 1996), pp. 57–60. My thanks to Prof. Istvàn Ormos for pointing out this sceptre to me.
32 The Àger chessmen represent one of the most prized medieval sets and one of the oldest extant in Europe.

5 The Imam-Caliph al-Hakim: Maverick or God Incarnate?

1 For a comprehensive assessment of al-Hakim and his reign see Paul E. Walker, *Caliph of Cairo: Al-Hakim bi-'Amr Allah, 996–1021* (Cairo and New York, 2012).
2 Delia Cortese, 'A Patron of Men: Sitt al-Mulk and the Military at the Fatimid Court', in *Guerre et paix dans le proche-orient médiéval (*XE-XVE *siècle)*, ed. Mathieu Eychenne, Stéphane Pradines and Abbès Zouache (Cairo, 2019), pp. 217–34 (pp. 218–19).
3 Michael Brett, *The Fatimid Empire* (Edinburgh, 2017), pp. 126–9.
4 James Heitzman and Wolfgang Schenkluhn, eds, *The World in the Year 1000* (Lanham, MD, New York and Oxford, 2004), pp. 52–3.
5 See Abu Ya'qub al-Sijistani, *Kitab al-Iftikhar*, ed. Mustafa Ghalib (Beirut, 1980), pp. 128–9.
6 Jonathan M. Bloom, *Arts of the City Victorious: Islamic Art and Architecture in Fatimid North Africa and Egypt* (New Haven, CT, and London, 2007), p. 79; Yaacov Lev, *State and Society in Fatimid Egypt* (Leiden, 1991), p. 150.
7 [Qadi b. al-Zubayr] *Book of Gifts and Rarities: Kitāb al-Hadāyā wa al-tuḥaf*, trans. Ghāda al-Hijjāwī al-Qaddūmī (Cambridge, MA, 1996), pp. 163–4.
8 Paula Sanders, *Ritual, Politics, and the City in Fatimid Cairo* (Albany, NY, 1994), pp. 58–60.
9 On the completion of the mosque and the building of these bastions see Jennifer A. Pruitt, *Building the Caliphate: Construction, Destruction and Sectarian Identity in Early Fatimid Architecture* (New Haven, CT, and London, 2020), pp. 73–86, 97–102.

10 Paula Sanders, *Creating Medieval Cairo* (Cairo and New York, 2008), p. 128.
11 Sanders, *Ritual, Politics*, p. 55.
12 Bloom, *Arts of the City Victorious*, p. 53.
13 Muhammad al-Musabbihi (eleventh century), quoted in Ibn Khallikan, *Biographical Dictionary*, trans. William Mac Guckin De Slane (Paris, 1843), vol. II, p. 365.
14 Heinz Halm, *The Fatimids and Their Traditions of Learning* (London, 2001), pp. 71–6.
15 On al-Hakim's attitude towards Christians and Jews see Paul E. Walker, 'al-Ḥākim and the Dhimmīs', in *Medieval Encounters. Special Issue. Non-Muslim Communities in Fatimid Egypt (Tenth–Twelfth Centuries CE)*, ed. Maryann M. Shenoda et al., XXI/4–5 (2015), pp. 357–63.
16 This practice, first carried out by the Sunnis in Egypt, was retrospectively commented on by the Shiʿi scholar Muhammad b. ʿAli al-Karajiki (d. 1057) who travelled from Tripoli to Egypt in the reigns of al-Hakim and al-Zahir. See his *al-Ta'ajjub min aghlat al-'amma fi masala al-imama* (Qum, 2000), p. 118.
17 Taqi al-Din al-Maqrizi, *Le traité des famines de Maqrīzī*, trans. Gaston Wiet (Leiden, 1962), pp. 17–18.
18 Shelomo D. Goitein, *A Mediterranean Society: The Jewish Communities of the World as Portrayed in the Documents of the Cairo Geniza*, vol. II: *The Community* (Berkeley, CA, 1999), pp. 86, 350.
19 Ralph Neuhaeuser, Carl Ehrig-Eggert and Paul Kunitzsch, 'An Arabic Report about Supernova SN 1006 by Ibn Sina (Avicenna)', *Astronomische Nachrichten*, LXXXVIII (2011), pp. 789–95.
20 Yaron Friedman, *The Shīʿīs in Palestine: From the Medieval Golden Age until the Present* (Leiden and Boston, MA, 2020), p. 11.
21 On Muslims celebrating Easter see Anna Chrysostomides, '"There is no harm in it": Muslim Participation in Levantine Christian Religious Festivals (750–1000)', *Al-Masaq: Journal of the Medieval Mediterranean*, XXXI/11 (2021), pp. 117–38.
22 Pruitt, *Building the Caliphate*, p. 1; for an interpretation of the circumstances that might have led to al-Hakim's destruction of the Holy Sepulchre and other churches, see pp. 106–13.
23 Quoted in Richard Landes, *Relics, Apocalypse and the Deceits of History: Ademar of Chabannes, 989–1034* (Boston, MA, 1995), pp. 43–4.
24 On the manifesto see Shainool Jiwa, 'The Baghdad Manifesto (402/1011): A Re-Examination of Fatimid-Abbasid Rivalry', in *The Fatimid Caliphate: Diversity of Traditions*, ed. Farhad Daftary and Shainool Jiwa (London and New York, 2018), pp. 22–78.
25 Sanders, *Creating Medieval Cairo*, p. 127.
26 Brett, *The Fatimid Empire*, p. 146.
27 Paul E. Walker, *Ḥamīd al-Dīn al-Kirmānī: Ismaili Thought in the Age of al-Ḥākim* (London, 1999), pp. 16–24.
28 Samuel M. Stern, *Fāṭimid Decrees: Original Documents from the Fāṭimid Chancery* (London, 1964), pp. 15–34.
29 Johannes Pahlitzsch, 'The Melkites in Fatimid Egypt and Syria (1021–1171)', in *Medieval Encounters*, pp. 485–515 (pp. 490–96).

30 Heinz Halm, *Die Kalifen von Kairo. Die Fatimiden in Ägypten, 973–1074* (Munich, 2003), pp. 315–24. On Mi'dad's activities see Michael Brett, 'The Execution of Ibn Badūs', in Michael Brett, *The Fatimids and Egypt* (Abingdon, 2019), pp. 77–9.
31 Heinz Halm, 'The Isma'ili Oath of Allegiance and the "Sessions of Wisdom"', in *Mediaeval Isma'ili History and Thought*, ed. Farhad Daftary (Cambridge, 2001), pp. 91–116 (pp. 107–8).
32 Nasir-i Khusraw, *Nāṣer-e Khosraw's Book of Travels* (*Safarnama*), ed. and trans. Wheeler M. Thackston Jr (Albany, NY, 1986), p. 74.
33 Paul Kahle, 'Die Schätze der Fatimiden', *Zeitschrift der Deutschen Morgenländischen Gesellschaft*, LXXXIX/14, nos 3/4 (1935), pp. 329–62 (p. 360).
34 See Avinoam Shalem, 'Jewels and Journeys: The Case of the Gemstone Called al-Yatima', *Muqarnas*, XIV (1997), pp. 42–56.
35 Lev, *State and Society*, p. 150.
36 Bloom, *Arts of the City Victorious*, pp. 81–3.
37 On al-Zahir's architectural intervention in Jerusalem see Pruitt, *Building the Caliphate*, pp. 136–43, 146–51.
38 Nasir-i Khusraw, *Book of Travels*, p. 27. See also Friedman, *The Shī'īs in Palestine*, p. 16.
39 On Fatimid–Zirid embassies from 992 to 1024 see Michael Brett, 'The Diplomacy of Empire: Fatimids and Zirids, 990–1062', in Brett, *The Fatimids and Egypt*, pp. 103–14 (pp. 112–13).
40 Carolina Doménech-Belda, 'The Fāṭimid Coins from Sicily in al-Andalus: The Jabonerías Hoard (Murcia, Spain)', in *5th Simone Assemani Symposium: Rome, 29/30 September 2017*, ed. Bruno Callegher and Arianna D'Ottone Rambach (Trieste, 2018), pp. 200–204.
41 Sulayman al-Ghazzi's verse, quoted in Pahlitzsch, 'The Melkites in Fatimid Egypt and Syria', in *Medieval Encounters*, pp. 485–515 (p. 511).

6 The Fatimids and the World as They Saw It in the Eleventh Century

1 Yossef Rapoport and Emilie Savage-Smith, ed. and trans., *An Eleventh-Century Egyptian Guide to the Universe: The Book of Curiosities* (Leiden and Boston, MA, 2014).
2 Nasir-i Khusraw, *Nāṣer-e Khosraw's Book of Travels* (*Safarnama*), ed. and trans. Wheeler M. Thackston Jr (Albany, NY, 1986), pp. 59–60.
3 André Raymond, *Cairo*, trans. Willard Wood (Cambridge, MA, and London, 2000), p. 55.
4 Michael W. Dols, ed. and trans., *Medieval Islamic Medicine: Ibn Riḍwān's Treatise 'On the Prevention of Bodily Ills in Egypt'* (Berkeley, CA, 1984), pp. 104–11.
5 For a detailed analysis of the topography of Cairo and Fustat during this period see Ayman Fuad Sayyid, *La capitale de l'Égypte jusqu'à l'époque Fatimide: al-Qāhira et al-Fusṭāṭ. Essay de reconstruction topographique* (Beirut, 1998).
6 Hassan Fathy, 'The Qa'a of the Cairene Arab House, Its Development and Some New Usages for Its Design Concepts', in *Colloque international sur l'histoire du Caire, 27 mars–5 avril 1969*, ed. André Raymond, Magdi Wahba and Michael Rogers (Cairo, 1972), pp. 135–52 (p. 136).

7 Ibn Ridwan, *On the Prevention of Bodily Ills in Egypt*, pp. 131–7.
8 Nasir-i Khusraw, *Book of Travels*, p. 74.
9 Ibid., p. 66.
10 A comprehensive survey of Fatimid gardens can be found in Stéphane Pradines and Sher R. Khan, 'Fatimid Gardens: Archaeological and Historical Perspectives', *Bulletin of the School of Oriental and African Studies*, LXXIX/3 (2016), pp. 1–30.
11 For a survey and description of extant Fatimid-era constructions in Cairo see Nicholas Warner, *The Monuments of Historic Cairo: A Map and Descriptive Catalogue* (Cairo and New York, 2005), entries nos 6, 7, 15, 33, 97, 109, 116, 352, 479, U10, U11.
12 For a broad contextualization of the Fatimids' role in the history of the Mediterranean Sea see David Abulafia, *The Great Sea: A Human History of the Mediterranean* (Oxford, 2011), pp. 270–305.
13 Rapoport and Savage-Smith, ed. and trans., *The Book of Curiosities*, p. 457.
14 Quoted from Adam Mez, *The Renaissance of Islam: History, Culture and Society in the 10th Century Muslim World* (Patna, 1937), p. 46, based on the *Chronicle* of Michael the Syrian (d. 1199).
15 Ibn Ridwan, *On the Prevention of Bodily Ills in Egypt*, p. 115.
16 Most of this section on Fatimid Alexandria is based on Miriam Frenkel, 'Medieval Alexandria – Life in a Port City', *Al-Masaq: Journal of the Medieval Mediterranean*, XXVI/1 (2014), pp. 5–35.
17 Gary Leiser, 'Muslims from al-Andalus in the Madrasas of the Late Fāṭimid and Aiyūbid Egypt', *Al-Qantara*, XX/1 (1999), pp. 137–59 (pp. 143–7).
18 On Sunni scholarship in Alexandria see Delia Cortese, 'Transmitting Sunnī Learning in Fāṭimī Egypt: The Female Voices', in *The Fatimid Caliphate: Diversity of Traditions*, ed. Farhad Daftary and Shainool Jiwa (London and New York, 2018), pp. 164–91.
19 On the Nile during the Fatimid period see Delia Cortese, 'The Nile: Its Role in the Fortunes and Misfortunes of the Fatimid Dynasty during Its Rule of Egypt (969–1171)', *History Compass*, XIII/1 (2015), pp. 20–29.
20 Marlis J. Saleh, 'Government Intervention in the Coptic Church in Egypt during the Fatimid Period', *Muslim World*, XCI/3–4 (2001), pp. 381–98 (pp. 381–4).
21 On Tripoli caught in Fatimid–Byzantine politics between 1032 and 1057 see 'Umar 'Abd al-Salam Tadmuri, *Tarikh Tarabulus al-siyasi wa al-hadari abara al-usur*, 2 vols (Tripoli, 1978), vol. I, pp. 228–33.
22 Yossef Rapoport, '1068 in the Fayyum: A Micro History of an Environmental Crisis', in *Living with Nature and Things: Contributions to a New Social History of the Middle Islamic Periods*, ed. Bethany J. Walker and Abdelkader Al Ghouz (Bonn, 2020), pp. 185–93.
23 Nasir-i Khusraw, *Book of Travels*, p. 65.
24 Ibn Ridwan, *On the Prevention of Bodily Ills in Egypt*, pp. 113–14.
25 See Stéphane Pradines, 'Madagascar, the Source of the Abbasid and Fatimid Rock Crystals: New Evidence from Archaeological Investigations in East Africa', in *Seeking Transparency: Rock Crystals Across the Medieval Mediterranean*, ed. Cynthia Hahn and Avinoam Shalem (Berlin, 2020), pp. 35–50.

26 Majid 'Abd al-Mu'nim, *Zuhur khilafat al-fatimiyya wa suqutiha fi Misr: al-tarikh al-siyasi* (Alexandria, 1968), p. 495.
27 Taqi al-Din al-Maqrizi, *Al-Bayan wa'l-i'rab 'amma bi ard Misr min al-a'rab* (Cairo, 2006), pp. 32, 34, 40, 159.
28 Ugo Monneret de Villard, *La necropoli musulmana di Aswan* (Cairo, 1930), p. 6.
29 Fatma Keshk et al., 'Pilot Documentation on the Arabic Graffiti from the Fatimid Cemetery in Aswan', in *Die Nekropole der Fatimiden in Assuan*, ed. Philipp Speiser and Giorgio Nogara (Wiesbaden, 2021), pp. 183–96 (p. 186).
30 See Delia Cortese, 'Upper Egypt: A "Shi'a" Powerhouse in the Fatimid Period?', *Studi Magrebini*, XII–XIII (2014–15), vol. I, pp. 153–68.
31 Jonathan M. Bloom, *Arts of the City Victorious: Islamic Art and Architecture in Fatimid North Africa and Egypt* (New Haven, CT, and London, 2007), p. 81.

7 From Propaganda Ideals to Managing the State Administration

1 On al-Qadi al-Nu'man's role in providing the theological and legal rationale for the establishment of the Fatimid state see Sumaiya Hamdani, *Between Revolution and State: The Path to Fatimid Statehood* (London, 2006), pp. 33–92.
2 A tradition of the Prophet ranked as authentic in the corpus known as *Sunan* by Abu Dawud (d. 889), no. 4604.
3 Andrew J. Newman, *The Formative Period of Twelver Shī'ism: Hadīth as Discourse Between Qum and Baghdad* (London and New York, 2000), p. 74.
4 Farhad Daftary, 'The Ismaili Da'wa outside the Fatimid Dawla', in *L'Egypte Fatimide, son art et son histoire*, ed. Marianne Barrucand (Paris, 1999), pp. 29–43.
5 Jenny Oesterle, 'Missionaries as Cultural Brokers at the Fatimid Court in Cairo', in *Cultural Brokers at Mediterranean Courts in the Middle Ages*, ed. Marc von der Höh et al. (Paderborn, 2013), pp. 63–72.
6 *A Code of Conduct: A Treatise on the Etiquette of the Fatimid Ismaili Mission. A critical edition of the Arabic text and English translation of Aḥmad b. Ibrāhīm al-Naysābūrī's al-Risāla al-mūjaza al-kāfiya fī ādāb al-du'āt*, ed. and trans. Verena Klemm and Paul E. Walker (London, 2012), pp. 66–75 (English text); and Wladimir Ivanow, 'The Organization of the Fatimid Propaganda', *Journal of the Bombay Branch of the Royal Asiatic Society*, new series, XV (1939), pp. 1–35 (pp. 34–5).
7 The organization outlined here is based on a work by the eleventh-century *da'i* Ahmad al-Nishaburi. On Isma'ili sources reflecting the shifting roles of the *da'i* see Simonetta Calderini, 'The Portrayal of the Ismaili Dā'ī and of His Roles According to Some Ismaili and Early Fatimid Authors', in *Egypt and Syria in the Fatimid, Ayyubid and Mamluk Eras*, ed. Urbain Vermeulen and Kristoff D'Hulster, vol. V (Leuven, Paris and Dudley, MA, 2007), pp. 37–62.
8 Taqi al-Din al-Maqrizi, *al-Mawa'iz wa'l-i'tibar bi-dhikr al-khitat wa'l-athar*, 2 vols (Beirut, rep. [197?]), vol. I, p. 391.

9 Nasir-i Khusraw, *Nāṣer-e Khosraw's Book of Travels* (*Safarnama*), ed. and trans. Wheeler M. Thackston Jr (Albany, NY, *c.* 1986), p. 75.

10 Yaacov Lev, *State and Society in Fatimid Egypt* (Leiden, 1991), pp. 160–61. I thank Prof. Lev for his comments and suggestions on this chapter. I am solely responsible for any mistakes or shortcomings.

11 Ahmad Ghabin, *Hisba, Arts and Crafts in Islam* (Wiesbaden, 2009), p. 223; on the *hisba* in the Fatimid period, pp. 67–9.

12 Boaz Shoshan, 'Fatimid Grain Policy and the Post of the Muhtasib', *International Journal of Middle East Studies*, XIII/2 (1981), pp. 181–9 (pp. 184–6).

13 On the organization of Fatimid-era justice administration see Amin Haji, 'Institutions of Justice in Fatimid Egypt', in *Islamic Law: Social and Historical Contexts*, ed. Aziz al-Azmeh (London and New York, 1988), pp. 198–214. See also Yaacov Lev, *The Administration of Justice in Medieval Egypt: From the 7th to the 12th Century* (Edinburgh, 2020), ch. 3.

14 Thierry Bianquis, 'Le Fonctionnement des dīwān financiers d'après Al-Musabbiḥī', *Annales Islamologiques*, XXVI (1992), pp. 47–61.

15 Jeremy Johns, *Arabic Administration in Norman Sicily: The Royal Diwan* (Cambridge, 2002), pp. 3–5.

16 On the organization and administration of the Fatimid army see Yaacov Lev, 'Army, Regime and Society in Fāṭimid Egypt 358–487/968–1094', *International Journal of Middle East Studies*, XIX/3 (1987), pp. 337–66 and Lev, *State and Society*, pp. 81–122.

17 Nasir-i Khusraw, *Book of Travels*, p. 76.

18 On the binding rules of patronage and their implication in Islamic courts see Roy Mottahedeh, *Loyalty and Leadership in Early Islamic Society* (Princeton, NJ, 1980), pp. 73–93.

19 On the *jawwala* see Lev, 'Army, Regime and Society', p. 341.

20 Muhammad al-Musabbihi, *Akhbar Misr fi sanatay 414–415 H.*, ed. William G. Millward (Cairo, 1980), pp. 40, 57, 169, 171, 180, 194, 240, and ed. Ayman Fu'ad Sayyid and Thierry Bianquis, *Tome quarantième de la chronique d'Egypte de Musabbiḥī, 366–420/977–1029* (Cairo, 1978), vol. I, pp. 43, 96.

21 As well as Lev's contributions, on Black elements in the Fatimid army see also Jere Bacharach, 'African Military Slaves in the Medieval Middle East: The Cases of Iraq (869–955) and Egypt (868–1171)', *International Journal of Middle East Studies*, XIII/4 (1981), pp. 471–95, and Abbès Zouache, 'Remarks on the Blacks in the Fatimid Army, Tenth–Twelfth Century CE', *Northeast African Studies*, XIX/1 (2019), pp. 23–60.

22 On the principle of *istina'*, the paternal-like favour of the master towards his protégés, see Mottahedeh, *Loyalty and Leadership*, p. 77, and Marina Rustow, 'Formal and Informal Patronage among Jews in the Islamic East: Evidence from the Geniza Documents', *al-Qanṭara*, XXIX/2 (2008), pp. 341–82 (pp. 366–75).

23 On the '*utufiyya* see Bacharach, 'African Military Slaves in the Medieval Middle East', p. 482, and Lev, 'Army, Regime and Society', pp. 340–42.

24 On the ascendancy and roles of the Armenians in the service of the Fatimid regime, see Seta Dadoyan, *The Fatimid Armenians: Cultural and Political Interaction in the Near East* (Leiden, 1997), pp. 81–178.

25 [Muhammad al-Jawdhari], *Sirat al-ustadh Jawdhar*, ed. and trans. Hamid Haji, *Inside the Immaculate Portal: A History from Early Fatimid Archives. A New Edition and English Translation of Manṣūr al-ʿAzīzī al-Jawdharī's Biography of al-Ustādh Jawdhar, the Sīrat al-Ustādh Jawdhar* (London and New York, 2012), pp. 108–9, 126, 132.
26 Simonetta Calderini, 'Women and Trade during the Fatimids', *Atti del Convegno: I Fatimidi e il Mediterraneo. Il sistema di relazioni nel mondo dell'Islam e l'area del Mediterraneo nel priodo della daʿwa fatimide (sec. x–xi): istituzioni, società, cultura* (Palermo, 2008), pp. 71–80 (pp. 71–4).
27 Michael Brett, *The Rise of the Fatimids: The World of the Mediterranean and the Middle East in the Tenth Century CE* (London, Boston, MA, and Cologne, 2001), p. 235.
28 For a comprehensive history of the Fatimids at sea, see David Bramoullé, *Les Fatimides et la mer (909–1171)* (Leiden, 2020).
29 Ibn Butlan's treatise is *Risala fi shiraʿa al-raqib wa taqilb al-ʿabid*. See Delia Cortese and Simonetta Calderini, *Women and the Fatimids in the World of Islam* (Edinburgh, 2006), p. 204.
30 Jennifer A. Pruitt, *Building the Caliphate: Construction, Destruction and Sectarian Identity in Early Fatimid Architecture* (New Haven, CT, and London, 2020), pp. 66–7.
31 On this figure see Elinoar Bareket, 'The Head of the Jews (*ra'is al-yahud*) in Fatimid Egypt: A Re-Evaluation', *Bulletin of the School of Oriental and African Studies*, LXII/2 (2004), pp. 185–97.
32 Marlis J. Saleh, 'Government Intervention in the Coptic Church in Egypt during the Fatimid Period', *Muslim World*, XCI/3–4 (2001), pp. 381–98 (pp. 385–7).

8 The Making of a Golden Age: The Cultural Life and Its Industry

1 Translated from al-Maqrizi's *Khitat* in Heinz Halm, *The Fatimids and Their Traditions of Learning* (London, 2001), pp. 73–4.
2 Charles Pellat et al., eds, *Etudes arabes et islamiques. Actes du xxixe congres international des orientalistes. Etudes arabes et islamiques*, 3 vols (Paris, 1975), vol. I, pp. 39–47; and Delia Cortese, 'Voices of the Silent Majority: The Transmission of Sunni Learning in Fatimid Egypt', *Jerusalem Studies in Arabic and Islam*, XXXIX (2012), pp. 345–66 (pp. 353–6).
3 Gérard Troupeau, 'La Description de la Nubie d'al-Aswani', *Arabica*, I (1954), pp. 276–88 (pp. 278–9).
4 François Viré, 'Le Traité de l'art de volerie (Kitāb al-Bayzara). Rédigé vers 385/995 par le Grand-Fauconnier du calife fāṭimide al-ʿAzīz bi-llāh', *Arabica*, XII (1965), pp. 1–26.
5 The extent of al-Mubashshir's popularity is mapped in David J. Wrisley, 'Modelling the Transmission of al-Mubashshir Ibn Fātik's *Mukhtār al-Ḥikam* in Medieval Europe: Some Initial Data-Driven Explorations', *Journal of Religion, Media and Digital Culture*, V/1 (2016), pp. 228–57.
6 See Daphna Ephrat, *A Learned Society in a Period of Transition: The Sunnī Ulamāʾ of Eleventh-Century Baghdad* (Albany, NY, 2000), in particular pp. 35–6, 58–68; Hayyim J. Cohen, 'The Economic Background and the

Secular Occupations of Muslim Jurisprudents', *Journal of the Economic and Social History of the Orient*, XIII/1 (1970), pp. 16–61; and Abraham L. Udovitch, 'Merchants and Amırs: Government and Trade in Eleventh-Century Egypt', *Asian and African Studies*, XXII (1988), pp. 53–72.

7 Nasir-i Khusraw, *Nāṣer-e Khosraw's Book of Travels (Safarnama)*, ed. and trans. Wheeler M. Thackston Jr (Albany, NY, 1986), pp. 75–6.

8 Nathan Hofer, 'Sufism in Fatimid Egypt and the Problem of Historiographical Inertia', *Journal of Islamic Studies*, XXVIII/1 (2017), pp. 28–67 (pp. 35–55).

9 On the mechanisms of book exchange in the Fatimid period and the major personalities involved see Delia Cortese, 'Beyond Space and Time: The Itinerant Life of Books in the Fatimid Market Place', in *Intellectual Interactions in the Islamic World: The Ismaili Thread*, ed. Orkhan Mir-Kasimov (London, 2019), pp. 407–26. See also Paul E. Walker, 'Libraries, Book Collection and the Production of Texts by the Fatimids', *Intellectual History of the Islamicate World*, IV/1–2 (2016), pp. 7–21.

10 Shelomo D. Goitein, *A Mediterranean Society: The Jewish Communities of the World as Portrayed in the Documents of the Cairo Geniza*, vol. I: *Economic Foundations* (Berkeley, CA, 1999), p. 196.

11 On Ibn Sura see Ibn Khallikan, *Biographical Dictionary*, trans. William Mac Guckin De Slane, 4 vols (Paris, 1842–71), vol. I, pp. 178–9. See also Zaki al-Din Abu Aḥmad al-Mundhiri, *al-Takmila li-wafayat al-naqala*, ed. Bashshar 'A. Ma'ruf, 4 vols (Najaf, 1981), vol. III, pp. 323–4.

12 The vicissitudes of the Fatimid royal libraries are narrated by al-Maqrizi in *Itti'az* and *Khitat*. For a summarized version see Halm, *The Fatimids and Their Traditions of Learning*, pp. 81, 91–3. For an alternative view on the fate of the Fatimid royal libraries following the advent of the Ayyubids see Fozia Bora, 'Did Ṣalāḥ al-Dīn Destroy the Fatimid Books? A Historiographical Enquiry', *Journal of the Royal Asiatic Society*, XXV (2015), pp. 21–39.

13 Miriam Frenkel, 'Book Lists from the Cairo Genizah: A Window on the Production of Texts in the Middle Ages', *Bulletin of the School of Oriental and African Studies*, LXXX/2 (2017), pp. 233–52. On book production and the circulation of books among Jews in Medieval Egypt see also Judith Olszowy-Schlanger, 'Cheap Books in Medieval Egypt: Rotuli from the Cairo Geniza', *Intellectual History of the Islamicate World*, IV (2016), pp. 82–101.

14 The social life of books among Jews in the Fatimid period is extensively commented on by Goitein in *A Mediterranean Society*. For Jewish book culture in tenth-century Egypt see also Marina Rustow, *Heresy and the Politics of Community: The Jews of the Fatimid Caliphate* (Ithaca, NY, 2008), pp. 35–66; and Paula Sanders, 'Jewish Books in Fatimid Egypt', in *The World of the Fatimids*, ed. Assadullah Souren Melikian-Chirvani, exh. cat., Aga Khan Museum (Toronto, 2018), pp. 218–29 (pp. 218–27).

15 Matti Friedman, *The Aleppo Codex: A True Story of Obsession, Faith, and the Pursuit of an Ancient Bible* (Chapel Hill, NC, 2013).

16 Michael S. Fulton, *Contest for Egypt: The Collapse of the Fatimid Caliphate, the Ebb of Crusader Influence and the Rise of Saladin* (Leiden, 2022), p. 15.

17 Johannes den Heijer, 'Coptic Historiography in the Fatimid, Ayyubid and Early Mamluk Periods', in *Medieval Encounters. Special Issue. Non-Muslim Communities in Fatimid Egypt (Tenth–Twelfth Centuries CE)*, ed. Maryann M. Shenoda et al., XXI/4–5 (2015), pp. 67–98.
18 Johannes Pahlitzsch, 'The Melkites in Fatimid Egypt and Syria (1021–1171)', in *Medieval Encounters*, pp. 485–515 (pp. 510–12).
19 For an overview of Fatimid rock crystals see Anna Contadini, 'Facets of Lights: The Case of Rock Crystals', in *God Is the Light of the Heavens and the Earth: Light in Islamic Art and Culture*, ed. Jonathan M. Bloom and Sheila Blair (New Haven, CT, and London, 2015), pp. 125–55.
20 Nasir-i Khusraw, *Book of Travels*, p. 69.
21 Ibid., p. 72.
22 Yedida K. Stillman, *Arab Dress, A Short History: From the Dawn of Islam to Modern Times* (Leiden and Boston, MA, 2003) – on the *tiraz* in general see pp. 120–37 and as a Fatimid institution pp. 128–33.
23 Shelomo Goitein, *A Mediterranean Society*, vol. III: *The Family*, p. 132.
24 On policing transactions between male vendors and female customers in early and medieval Islam see Ahmad Ghabin, *Ḥisba, Arts and Crafts in Islam* (Wiesbaden, 2009), pp. 223–4. On medieval negative attitudes to female workers see Maya Shatzmiller, *Labour in the Medieval Islamic World* (Leiden, 1994), pp. 350, 359.
25 Ghabin, *Hisba*, p. 235.
26 Nasir-i Khusraw, *Book of Travels*, pp. 61–2.
27 On this form of investiture see Stillman, *Arab Dress*, pp. 70–71, 120–37.
28 Nasir-i Khusraw, *Book of Travels*, pp. 64–5.
29 Goitein, *A Mediterranean Society*, vol. I: *Economic Foundations*, p. 150.
30 On the decorative scheme inside Durzan's mosque see Jonathan M. Bloom, *Arts of the City Victorious: Islamic Art and Architecture in Fatimid North Africa and Egypt* (New Haven, CT, and London, 2007), p. 113. On the ceiling of the Cappella Palatina see Richard Ettinghausen, 'Painting in the Fatimid Period: A Reconstruction', *Ars Islamica*, IX (1942), pp. 112–24 (pp. 113–18); and Ugo Monneret de Villard, *Le pitture musulmane al soffitto della Cappella Palatina in Palermo* (Rome, 1950).
31 Sheila S. Blair and Jonathan M. Bloom, *The Art and Architecture of Islam, 1250–1800* (New Haven, CT, 1994), p. 117.
32 Bloom, *Arts of the City Victorious*, pp. 111–13. On the Keir Collection drawing see Ernst J. Grube, 'A Coloured Drawing of the Fatimid Period in the Keir Collection', *Rivista degli studi orientali*, LIX (1985), pp. 147–74.
33 On textual and material evidence of the high quantity of Chinese ceramics in the Fatimid palaces see Paul Kahle, 'Die Schätze der Fatimiden', *Zeitschrift der Deutschen Morgenländischen Gesellschaft*, LXXXIX/14 (1935), pp. 329–62 (pp. 330–31), based on al-Maqrizi.
34 Ernst J. Grube, 'Realism or Formalism: Notes on Some Fatimid Lustre Painted Ceramic Vessels', in *Studi in onore di Francesco Gabrieli nel suo ottantesimo compleanno*, ed. Renato Traini (Rome, 1984), pp. 423–32.
35 See, for example, Elias Khamis, *The Fatimid Metalwork Hoard from Tiberias: Excavations in the House of the Bronzes. Final Report, Volume II* (Jerusalem, 2013).

36 Taqi al-Din al-Maqrizi, *Le traité des famines de Maqrīzī*, trans. Gaston Wiet (Leiden, 1962), pp. 15–17.
37 Irene Bierman, *Writing Signs: The Fatimid Public Text* (Berkeley, CA, 1998), p. 112.
38 On this object see Avinoam Shalem, 'The Rock-Crystal Lionhead in the Badisches Landesmuseum in Karlsruhe', in *L'Égypte fatimide, son art et son histoire*, ed. Marianne Barrucand (Paris, 1999), pp. 359–66.

9 Being a Woman in the Age of the Fatimids

1 Simonetta Calderini and Delia Cortese, 'The Architectural Patronage of the Fatimid Queen-Mother Durzan (d. 385/995): An Interdisciplinary Analysis of Literary Sources, Material Evidence and Historical Context', in *Material Evidence and Narrative Sources: Interdisciplinary Studies of the History of the Muslim Middle East*, ed. Daniella Talmon Heller and K. Catia Cytryn-Silverman (Leiden, 2015), pp. 87–112.
2 It is possible that this description refers to a later interior. See Jonathan M. Bloom, *Arts of the City Victorious: Islamic Art and Architecture in Fatimid North Africa and Egypt* (New Haven, CT, and London, 2007), p. 113.
3 Yaacov Lev, 'The Fāṭimid Vizier Ya'qūb ibn Killis and the Beginning of the Fāṭimid Administration in Egypt', *Der Islam*, LVIII (1981), pp. 237–49.
4 Paul E. Walker, 'The Fatimid Caliph al-'Azīz and His Daughter Sitt al-Mulk: A Case of Delayed but Eventual Succession to Rule by a Woman', *Journal of Persianate Studies*, IV (2011), pp. 30–44.
5 Delia Cortese, 'A Patron of Men: Sitt al-Mulk and the Military at the Fatimid Court', in *Guerre et paix dans le Proche-Orient Medieval (Xe-XVe siècle)*, ed. Mathieu Eychenne, Stéphane Pradines and Abbès Zouache (Cairo, 2019), pp. 217–34.
6 Marina Rustow, 'A Petition to a Woman at the Fatimid Court (413–414 A.H./1022–23 C.E.)', *Bulletin of the School of Oriental and African Studies*, LXXIII/1 (2010), pp. 1–27.
7 Johannes Pahlitzsch, 'The Melkites in Fatimid Egypt and Syria (1021–1171)', in *Medieval Encounters. Special Issue. Non-Muslim Communities in Fatimid Egypt (Tenth–Twelfth Centuries CE)*, ed. Maryann M. Shenoda et al., XXI/4–5 (2015), pp. 485–515 (pp. 488–9).
8 Cited by the eleventh-century Fatimid chronicler Muhammad al-Musabbihi, quoted in Delia Cortese and Simonetta Calderini, *Women and the Fatimids in the World of Islam* (Edinburgh, 2006), p. 126.
9 Simonetta Calderini, 'Sayyida Rasad: A Royal Woman as "Gateway to Power" during the Fatimid Era', in *Egypt and Syria in the Fatimid, Ayyubid and Mamluk Eras*, ed. Urbain Vermeulen and Kristoff D'Hulster, vol. V (Leuven, Paris and Dudley, MA, 2007), pp. 27–36.
10 Daniel De Smet, 'Une Femme Musulmane Ministre de Dieu Sur Terre? La réponse du dâ'î ismaélien al-Hattâb (ob 1138)', *Acta Orientalia Belgica*, XV (2001), pp. 155–64.
11 R. Ravagnan and M. Merlo, eds, *The Great Mosque of San'a' (2005–2015)* (Venice, 2022), pp. 155–7.

12 Taef El-Azhari, *Queens, Eunuchs and Concubines in Islamic History (661–1257)* (Edinburgh, 2019), pp. 196–252; Shahla Haeri, *The Unforgettable Queens of Islam* (Cambridge, 2020), pp. 79–105.
13 El-Azhari, *Queens, Eunuchs and Concubines*, pp. 253–84.
14 There are many such figures in circulation, varying in quality and craftmanship but standardized in format. The practice of using bone or ivory naked figurines by female patients to communicate their ailments to male doctors was widespread in medieval Europe. In Islamic context their use has been interpreted in various ways from being amulets to being used as musical instruments.
15 For an overview see Avner Giladi's 'Liminal Craft, Exceptional Law: Preliminary Notes on Midwives in Medieval Islamic Writings', *International Journal of Middle East Studies*, XLII /2 (2010), pp. 185–202, and *Muslim Midwives: The Craft of Birthing in the Premodern Middle East* (Cambridge, 2015).
16 Cortese and Calderini, *Women and the Fatimids*, p. 202.
17 Shelomo D. Goitein, 'A Jewish Business Woman of the Eleventh Century', *Jewish Quarterly Review*, LVII (1967), pp. 225–42.
18 Yaacov Lev, *State and Society in Fatimid Egypt* (Leiden, 1991), p. 158.
19 On the female contribution to Sunni scholarship in Fatimid Egypt see Delia Cortese, 'Transmitting Sunni Learning in Fatimid Egypt: The Female Voices', in *The Fatimid Caliphate: Diversity of Traditions*, ed. Farhad Daftary and Shainool Jiwa (London, 2018), pp. 164–91.
20 Bernard Roy and Paule Poinssot, *Inscriptions Arabes de Kairawan*, 2 vols (Paris, 1950), vol. II, pp. 27–32; Hady Roger Idris, *La Berbérie orientale sous les Zīrīdes*, 2 vols (Paris, 1962), vol. I, p. 141 and vol. II, pp. 417, 771; Lucien Golovin, *Le Magrib central a l'époque des Zirides* (Paris, 1957), pp. 159–61.
21 On Jewish female education in this period see Shelomo D. Goitein, *A Mediterranean Society: The Jewish Communities of the World as Portrayed in the Documents of the Cairo Geniza*, vol. II: *The Community* (Berkeley, CA, 1999), pp. 183–5.
22 Angie Heo, *The Political Lives of Saints: Christian-Muslim Mediation in Egypt* (Berkeley, CA, 2018), p. 72.

10 High Drama: The Long Reign of al-Mustansir

1 Assadullah Souren Melikian-Chirvani, 'Fatimid Art and Its Unresolved Enigmas: From Ceramics to Rock Crystal to Its Vanished Silverware', in *The World of the Fatimids*, ed. Assadullah Souren Melikian-Chirvani, exh. cat., Aga Khan Museum (Toronto, 2018), pp. 70–141 (p. 125).
2 Shelomo D. Goitein, *A Mediterranean Society: The Jewish Communities of the World as Portrayed in the Documents of the Cairo Geniza*, vol. II: *The Community* (Berkeley, CA, 1999), p. 377.
3 Quoted in Mark R. Cohen, *Under Crescent and Cross: The Jews in the Middle Ages* (Princeton, NJ, 1994), p. 67.
4 Nasir-i Khusraw, *Nāṣer-e Khosraw's Book of Travels* (*Safarnama*), ed. and trans. Wheeler M. Thackston Jr (Albany, NY, *c.* 1986), pp. 74–5.
5 Ibid., p. 58.
6 Ibid., p. 73.

7 [Qadi b. al-Zubayr] *Book of Gifts and Rarities: Kitāb al-Hadāyā wa al-tuḥaf*, trans. Ghāda al-Hijjāwī al-Qaddūmī (Cambridge, MA, 1996), pp. 108–9.
8 On his burial shrine see Marcus Schadl, 'The Shrine of Nasir Khusraw: Imprisoned Deep in the Valley of Yumgan', *Muqarnas*, XXVI (2009), pp. 63–94.
9 Yaacov Lev, *State and Society in Fatimid Egypt* (Leiden, 1991), pp. 42–3.
10 Taqi al-Din al-Maqrizi, *Le traité des famines de Maqrīzī*, trans. Gaston Wiet (Leiden, 1962), pp. 18–21. On al-Yazuri's bread policies see also Lev, *State and Society*, pp. 164–6.
11 Hady Roger Idris, 'L'invasion hilālienne et ses conséquences', *Cahiers de civilization médiévale*, XLIII (1968), pp. 353–69.
12 On these Italian campaigns see Herbert Edward John Cowdrey, 'The Mahdia Campaign of 1087', *English Historical Review*, XCII (1977), pp. 1–29; and Alasdair C. Grant, 'Pisan Perspectives: The *Carmen in victoriam* and Holy War, *c.* 1000–1150', *English Historical Review*, CXXXI/552 (2016), pp. 983–1009.
13 Richard Ettinghausen, Oleg Grabar and Marilyn Jenkins-Madina, eds, *Islamic Art and Architecture, 650–1250* (New Haven, CT, 2001), p. 302.
14 Timothy Smit, 'Weaving Connections: Sicilian Silk in the Medieval Mediterranean', *Textile History*, LII (2021), pp. 5–22 (p. 15).
15 Qadi b. al-Zubayr, *Kitāb al-Hadāyā wa al-tuḥaf*, pp. 109–10.
16 See Rafael Azuar Ruiz, 'La Taifa de Dénia en el comercio mediterráneo del siglo XI', *Anales de la Universidad de Alicante. Historia Medieval*, 9 (1992–3), pp. 39–52 (p. 43).
17 In recent years this story has attracted extensive attention in the West, covered by a range of media from documentaries and newspaper articles to academic literature, either disputing or supporting the link between the León chalice and al-Mustansir.
18 Delia Cortese and Simonetta Calderini, *Women and the Fatimids in the World of Islam* (Edinburgh, 2006), p. 102.
19 Michael Brett, *The Fatimid Empire* (Edinburgh, 2017), pp. 192–3.
20 Tayeb El-Hibri, *The Abbasid Caliphate: A History* (Cambridge, 2021), p. 205.
21 Brett, *The Fatimid Empire*, pp. 194–7.
22 Based on al-Maqrizi's *Khitat*, see Jonathan M. Bloom, *Arts of the City Victorious: Islamic Art and Architecture in Fatimid North Africa and Egypt* (New Haven, CT, and London, 2007), p. 114.
23 Arie Schippers, 'Arabic and Hebrew Love Poetry in Sicily in the Middle Ages and Their Contacts with Early Romance and German Poets in Sicily: Suffering of Love in Sicilian Poetry', *Quaderni di Studi Arabi*, nuova serie, X (2015), pp. 87–102 (p. 88).
24 See Thelma K. Thomas, '"Ornaments of excellence" from "the miserable gains of commerce": Luxury Art and Byzantine Culture', in *Byzantium and Islam: Age of Transition, 7th–9th Century*, ed. Helen C. Evans and Brandie Ratliff (New York, 2012), pp. 124–33, n.96.
25 Owen Wright, 'Music at the Fatimid Court: The Evidence of the Ibn al-Tahhan Manuscript', in *L'Egypte Fatimide, son art et son histoire*, ed. Marianne Barrucand (Paris, 1999), pp. 537–45 (p. 538).
26 Lev, *State and Society*, p. 73.

27 On al-Yazuri and a critical review of the possible circumstances leading to his demise see Michael Brett, 'The Execution of al-Yāzūrī', in Michael Brett, *The Fatimids and Egypt* (Abingdon, 2019), pp. 83–93.

28 al-Maqrizi's vivid account of the events that took place during this crisis can be found in *Le traité des famines*, pp. 24–7.

29 Yaacov Lev, 'The Fatimid Caliphs, the Copts and the Coptic Church', in *Medieval Encounters. Special Issue. Non-Muslim Communities in Fatimid Egypt (Tenth–Twelfth Centuries CE)*, ed. Maryann M. Shenoda et al., XXI/4–5 (2015), pp. 390–410 (pp. 406–7).

30 The inventory of the objects taken, based on al-Maqrizi, is discussed and translated in Paul Kahle, 'Die Schätze der Fatimiden', *Zeitschrift der Deutschen Morgenländischen Gesellschaft*, LXXXIX/14, nos 3/4 (1935), pp. 329–62 (pp. 338–61).

31 Respectively in the Chester Beatty Library, Dublin, the Victoria and Albert Museum, London, and Dar al-Kutub Library, Cairo.

32 Taqi al-Din al-Maqrizi, *Le traité des famines*, p. 26.

33 Bloom, *Arts of the City Victorious*, p. 101.

34 Farhad Daftary, *The Ismāʿīlīs: Their History and Doctrines*, 2nd edn (Cambridge, 2007), p. 198.

35 On Badr al-Jamali's background, career and activities see Seta Dadoyan, *The Fatimid Armenians: Cultural and Political Interaction in the Near East* (Leiden, 1997), pp. 106–27; and Brett, *The Fatimid Empire*, pp. 205–76.

36 Marlis J. Saleh, 'Government Intervention in the Coptic Church in Egypt during the Fatimid Period', *Muslim World*, XCI/3–4 (2001), pp. 381–98 (p. 392).

37 Michael Brett, 'Badr al-Jamālī and the Fatimid Renascence', in Brett, *The Fatimids and Egypt*, pp. 137–51.

38 Samuli Schielke, *The Perils of Joy: Contesting Mulid Festivals in Contemporary Egypt* (Syracuse, NY, 2012), p. 22.

39 On the commemoration of al-Husayn in Fatimid 'Asqalan see Daniella Talmon-Heller, *Sacred Place and Sacred Time in the Medieval Islamic Middle East* (Edinburgh, 2020), ch. 4; and Brett, *The Fatimid Empire*, p. 218. I am grateful to Prof. Talmon-Heller for her comments and clarifications regarding the vicissitudes of the relic of al-Husayn.

40 Daniella Talmon-Heller et al., 'Vicissitudes of a Holy Place: Construction, Destruction and Commemoration of Mashhad Ḥusayn in Ascalon', *Der Islam*, XCIII/1 (2016), pp. 211–14. My thanks to Prof. Talmon-Heller for pointing out this Da'udi Bohra expression of faith and sharing her paper on the topic with me.

41 Stephennie Mulder, 'The Mausoleum of Imam al-Shafiʿi', *Muqarnas*, XXIII (2006), pp. 15–46 (p. 20).

42 Bernard Lewis, 'The Fatimids and the Route to India', *Revue de la faculté des sciences économiques de l'Université d'Istanbul*, I (1949–50), pp. 50–54. On the influence of Fatimid style on Gujarati religious architecture see Mehrdad Shokoohy, *Bhadreśvar: The Oldest Islamic Monuments in India* (Leiden, 1988), pp. 22, 39, 54–9.

43 On Badr's dynastic successors see Seta Dadoyan, *The Fatimid Armenians*, pp. 127–38.

11 The Darkest Hours of the Fatimids

1 Shihab al-Din al-Nuwayri, *Nihayat al-arab fi funun al-adab* (Cairo, 2002), pp. 243–4; Paul E. Walker, 'Succession to Rule in the Shiite Caliphate', *Journal of the American Research Center in Egypt*, XXXII (1995), pp. 239–64 (pp. 248, 253).
2 Delia Cortese and Simonetta Calderini, *Women and the Fatimids in the World of Islam* (Edinburgh, 2006), p. 37.
3 Delia Cortese, 'Lost and Found: The Sargudhasht-i Sayyid-nā. Facts and Fiction of Ḥasan-i Ṣabbāḥ's Travel to Egypt vis-à-vis the Political and Intellectual Life of 5th/11th Century Fatimid Cairo', in *Science in the City of Fortune: The Dustūr al-munajjimīn and Its World*, ed. Eva Orthman and Petra Schmidl (Berlin, 2017), pp. 199–222 (p. 207).
4 Nasr Allah Falsafi, *Chand maqale-yi tarikhī wa adabi* (Tehran, 1963), p. 418. In the letter, allegedly sent by Hasan-i Sabbah to the Seljuq Sultan Malik Shah, it is stated that Badr al-Jamali eventually sent Hasan out of Egypt to conduct the Ismaili *da'wa* among the Byzantines and – anachronistically – the Franks.
5 Caroline Williams, *Islamic Monuments in Cairo: A Practical Guide* (Cairo, 2002), p. 48.
6 Michael S. Fulton, *Contest for Egypt: The Collapse of the Fatimid Caliphate, the Ebb of Crusader Influence and the Rise of Saladin* (Leiden, 2022), pp. 19–34.
7 Irene Bierman, 'Art and Politics: The Impact of Fatimid Uses of *Ṭirāz* Fabrics', PhD thesis, University of Chicago, 1980, p. 111.
8 Sumaiya Hamdani, 'Worlds Apart? An Andalusi in Fāṭimid Egypt', *Journal of North African Studies*, XIX/1 (2014), pp. 56–67.
9 Cortese and Calderini, *Women and the Fatimids*, pp. 77, 81.
10 Nico J. C. Kaptein, *Muḥammad's Birthday Festival: Early History in the Central Muslim Lands and Development in the Muslim West Until the Tenth/Sixteenth Century* (Leiden, 1993), pp. 20–25.
11 Cortese and Calderini, *Women and the Fatimids*, pp. 84–5.
12 Michael Brett, *The Fatimid Empire* (Edinburgh, 2017), pp. 262–7.
13 Farhad Daftary, *The Ismā'īlis: Their History and Doctrines*, 2nd edn (Cambridge, 2007), p. 269.
14 Brett, *The Fatimid Empire*, p. 264.
15 For a comphrehensive comparative stylistic analysis of Fatimid and Norman *tiraz* see Isabelle Dolezalek, *Arabic Script on Christian Kings' Textile Inscriptions on Royal Garments from Norman Sicily* (Berlin, 2017), pp. 74–120.
16 Taqi al-Din al-Maqrizi, *al-Mawa'iz wa'l-i'tibar bi-dhikr al-khitat wa'l-athar*, 2 vols (Beirut, rep. [197?]), vol. II, p. 449.
17 Jonathan M. Bloom, *Arts of the City Victorious: Islamic Art and Architecture in Fatimid North Africa and Egypt* (New Haven, CT, and London, 2007), pp. 146–9.
18 Caroline Williams, 'The Cult of 'Alid Saints in the Fatimid Monuments of Cairo Part II: The Mausolea', *Muqarnas*, III (1985), pp. 39–60 (pp. 44–52).
19 Samuel M. Stern, *Fāṭimid Decrees: Original Documents from the Fāṭmid Chancery* (London, 1964), pp. 46–64.
20 Cortese and Calderini, *Women and the Fatimids*, p. 175.

21 For Usama b. Munqidh as primary informant on the events of his time see *An Arab–Syrian Gentleman and Warrior in the Period of the Crusades: Memoirs of Usāmah Ibn-Munqidh*, trans. Philip K. Hitti (New York, 2000). For a biography of this figure see Paul M. Cobb, *Usama ibn Munqidh: Warrior Poet of the Age of Crusades* (London, 2005).
22 For the convoluted history of the relic and its shrines see part 1 of Daniella Talmon-Heller's *Sacred Place and Sacred Time in the Medieval Islamic Middle East* (Edinburgh, 2020).
23 Simonetta Calderini, 'Two Radical Hair-Cuts in Medieval Egypt: Gendering Politics in Times of Trouble', *Al-Masaq: Journal of the Medieval Mediterranean*, XX/1 (2008), pp. 17–28 (pp. 19, 21).
24 Helene Wieruszowski, *Politics and Culture in Medieval Spain and Italy* (Rome, 1971), pp. 34–5.
25 Hartwig Derenbourg, *Oumâra du Ymen: sa vie et son oeuvre*, 2 vols (Paris, 1897–1909), vol. II, pp. 120–21.
26 Brett, *The Fatimid Empire*, p. 286.
27 Ibid., pp. 286–8.
28 Fulton, *Contest for Egypt*, pp. 31–2.
29 Simonetta Calderini, 'Two Radical Hair-Cuts', pp. 19–20, 23.
30 Niall Christie, 'Cosmopolitan Trade Centre or Bone of Contention? Alexandria and the Crusades, 487–857/1095–1453', *Al-Masaq: Journal of the Medieval Mediterranean*, XXXI (2014), pp. 49–61 (p. 50).
31 Muhammad b. 'Ali al-Tiqtaqa, *Al Fakhri; on the systems of government and the Moslem dynasties, composed by Mohammad son of 'Ali son of Tabataba, known as the rapid talker, may God have mercy on him*, trans. C. E. Whitting (London, 1990), pp. 257–9.

12 The Legacy of a Golden Age

1 Delia Cortese, 'Beyond Space and Time: The Itinerant Life of Books in the Fatimid Market Place', in *Intellectual Interactions in the Islamic World*, ed. Orkhan Mir-Kasimov (London, 2019), pp. 413–25.
2 See Alphonse Delort de Gléon, *L'Architecture arabe des khalifes d'Egypte à l'Exposition universelle de Paris en 1889: la rue du Caire* (Paris, 1889), p. 5.
3 Ministry of Culture of the Arab Republic of Egypt, *Colloque international sur l'histoire du Caire* (Cairo, [1972]), pp. 15–18.
4 Bernard Lewis, 'An Interpretation of Fatimid History', *Colloque international* [1972], pp. 287–95.
5 Ministry of Culture of the Arab Republic of Egypt, *Cairo: The Life-Story of 1,000 years* (Leipzig, 1969), pp. 17–20.
6 On the Fatimids' re-inscription into Cairo's landscape via the Bohra-led restoration programme see Paula Sanders, 'Bohra Architecture and the Restoration of Fatimid Culture', in *L'Égypte Fatimide, son art et son histoire*, ed. Marianne Barrucand (Paris, 1999), pp. 115–42.
7 Paula Sanders, *Creating Medieval Cairo* (Cairo and New York, 2008), pp. 115–42.
8 On the Alawis' understanding of the Fatimid age as a 'Faatemi' way of life see Olly Akkerman, *A Neo-Fatimid Treasury of Books: Arabic Manuscripts among the Alawi Bohras of South Asia* (Edinburgh, 2022), pp. 60–61.

9 See Robert Harry van Gent, Mathematical Institute, Utrecht University, 'Online Calendar Converters Based on the Tabular Islamic Calendar', https://webspace.science.uu.nl, accessed 5 January 2023.

10 On AKDN's al-Azhar park project see Daryoush Mohammad Poor, *Authority without Territory: The Aga Khan Development Network and the Ismaili Imamate* (London, 2014), pp. 180–81.

11 Jennifer A. Pruitt, *Building the Caliphate: Construction, Destruction, and Sectarian Identity in Early Fatimid Architecture* (New Haven, CT, and London, 2020), p. 93.

12 Many media reports include Andrew Hammond, 'Arab History Spat Highlights Sunni-Shi'ite Rift', *Reuters*, 14 May 2007; 'Gaddafi Sees Muslims as Shiites "by default"', *al-Arabiyya News*, https://english.alarabiya.net, 11 October 2007; Mshari Al-Zaydi, 'The Return of the Fatimids', *Asharq al-awsat*, https://eng-archive.aawsat.com, 26 March 2009. An extract from one of al-Qadhdhafi's speeches extolling the Fatimids is featured in 'Qaddafi's Views on Fatimid State', April 2019, www.youtube.com, accessed 20 June 2023.

13 Cited in Hammond, 'Arab History'.

14 On the Sulaymanis' plight see Robert F. Worth, 'Muslim Sect Sees Struggle Through Christian Lens', *New York Times*, www.nytimes.com, 20 October 2010. The text of the HRW report is accessible at www.hrw.org.

15 See Delia Cortese, 'Common Threads: Women and the Making of Fāṭimid and Norman Textiles', in *Muslim Sicily: Encounters and Legacy*, ed. Nuha Alshaar (Edinburgh, 2024), pp. 161–77.

16 [Qadi b. al-Zubayr] *Book of Gifts and Rarities: Kitāb al-Hadāyā wa al-tuḥaf*, trans. Ghāda al-Hijjāwī al-Qaddūmī (Cambridge, MA, 1996), pp. 30–31.

17 See Anna Contadini, 'Le arti del periodo fatimide', in *Il Mediterraneo e l'arte nel Medioevo*, ed. Roberto Cassanelli and Maria Andaloro (Milan, 2000), pp. 118–37 (p. 124).

18 Georgette Cornu, 'Les tissus d'apparait fatimides, parmi les plus somptueux le "voile de Sainte Anne" d'Apt', *L'Égypte Fatimide, son art et son histoire*, ed. Marianne Barrucand (Paris, 1999), pp. 331–7.

19 See Cortese, 'Common Threads', pp. 174–6.

20 Karen Rose Mathews, 'Other Peoples' Dishes: Islamic *Bacini* on Eleventh-Century Churches in Pisa', *Gesta*, LIII/1 (2014), pp. 5–23.

21 Jonathan M. Bloom, 'Fatimid Gifts', in *Gifts of the Sultan: The Arts of Giving at the Islamic Courts*, ed. Linda Komaroff with contributions by Sheila Blair et al. (New Haven, CT, 2011), pp. 94–109 (p. 96).

22 Anna Contadini, *Fatimid Art at the Victoria and Albert Museum* (London, 1998), pp. 30–32. See also Jeremy Johns, '"The Magnificent Seven": The Great Fāṭimid Rock Crystal Ewers', *The Ravi and Seran Trehan Lectures in Islamic Art and Material Culture*, www.youtube.com, 5 March 2015.

23 The inscription on this jug refers to a commander identified by some scholars as al-Husayn, the son of General Jawhar, conqueror of Egypt in 969. This identification is disputed by Paul E. Walker, 'The Pitti Palace Rock Crystal Ewer and the Sordid Story of How and Why It Came to Exist', *Journal of Near Eastern Studies*, LXXVII/1 (2018), pp. 41–6.

24 Museo Diocesano Agrigento. My thanks to Ms Annachiara Oliva for pointing out this object to me.
25 This section deals with an area of cultural history that is in constant flux, with the ongoing addition of new productions and technologies. The content here is intended as a survey of examples and trends in a large and diverse field.
26 First published in the pulp magazine *Golden Fleece* in January 1939. It is also known by the title *The Road of the Mountain Lion.*
27 First published by MacMillan in 1981, this is the fifth novel of *The Cadfael Chronicles* by the same author, a series of historical murder mysteries published between 1977 and 1994.
28 Bensalem Himmich, *The Theocrat*, trans. Roger Allen (Cairo, 2005).
29 The project was led by artist Gabriella Ciancimino, https://m12.manifesta.org, accessed 30 January 2023.
30 Released by IQRA Cartoon (2019).
31 Angie Heo, *The Political Lives of Saints: Christian-Muslim Mediation in Egypt* (Berkeley, CA, 2018), pp. 96–7.
32 The account of the miracle was made into a short docu-film, *The Miracle of the Muqattam Mountain*, produced by the YouTube channel Coptic Bulgaria in 2018, see www.youtube.com, accessed 8 November 2024.
33 See also Pruitt, *Building the Caliphate*, pp. 59–63.

SELECT BIBLIOGRAPHY

Akkerman, Olly, *A Neo-Fatimid Treasury of Books: Arabic Manuscripts among the Alawi Bohras of South Asia* (Edinburgh, 2022)

Baffioni, Carmela, 'Gli Iḫwān al-Ṣafā' e la loro enciclopedia', in *Storia della filosofia nell'Islam medievale*, ed. Cristina D'Ancona, 2 vols (Turin, 2005), vol. I, pp. 449–89

Bareket, Elinoar, *Fustat on the Nile: The Jewish Elite in Medieval Egypt* (Leiden, 1999)

Barrucand, Marianne, ed., *L'Égypte Fatimide, son art et son histoire* (Paris, 1999)

Bianquis, Thierry, *Damas et la Syrie sous la domination Fatimide (359–468/969–1076. Essay d'interprétation des chroniques Arabes médiévales*, 2 vols (Damascus, 1986–9)

Bloom, Jonathan M., *Arts of the City Victorious: Islamic Art and Architecture in Fatimid North Africa and Egypt* (New Haven, CT, and London, 2007)

Bramoullé, David, *Les Fatimides et la mer (909–1171)* (Leiden, 2020)

Brett, Michael, *The Fatimids and Egypt* (Abingdon, 2019)

—, *The Fatimid Empire* (Edinburgh, 2017)

—, *The Rise of the Fatimids: The World of the Mediterranean and the Middle East in the Tenth Century CE* (London, Boston, MA, and Cologne, 2001)

Calderini, Simonetta, 'Women and Trade during the Fatimids', *Atti del Convegno: I Fatimidi e il Mediterraneo. Il sistema di relazioni nel mondo dell'Islam e l'area del Mediterraneo nel priodo della da'wa fatimide (sec X–XI): istituzioni, società, cultura* (Palermo, 2008), pp. 71–80

—, and Cortese, Delia, 'The Architectural Patronage of the Fatimid Queen-Mother Durzan (d. 385/995): An Interdisciplinary Analysis of Literary Sources, Material Evidence and Historical Context', in *Material Evidence and Narrative Sources: Interdisciplinary Studies of the History of the Muslim Middle East*, ed. Daniella Talmon-Heller and K. Catia Cytryn-Silverman (Leiden, 2015), pp. 87–112

de Callatay, Godefroid, *Ikhwan al-Safa': A Brotherhood of Idealists on the Fringe of Orthodox Islam* (London, 2005)

Contadini, Anna, *Fatimid Art at the Victoria and Albert Museum* (London, 1998)

Cortese, Delia, 'Beyond Space and Time: The Itinerant Life of Books in the Fatimid Market Place', in *Intellectual Interactions in the Islamic World*, ed. Orkhan Mir-Kasimov (London, 2019), pp. 407–26

—, 'The Nile: Its Role in the Fortunes and Misfortunes of the Fatimid Dynasty during Its Rule of Egypt (969–1171)', *History Compass*, XIII/1 (2015), pp. 20–29

—, 'A Patron of Men: Sitt al-Mulk and the Military at the Fatimid Court', in *Guerre et paix dans le Proche-Orient medieval (xe–xve siècle)*, ed. Mathieu

Eychenne, Stéphane Pradines and Abbès Zouache (Cairo, 2019), pp. 217–34
—, 'Voices of the Silent Majority: The Transmission of Sunni Learning in Fatimid Egypt', *Jerusalem Studies in Arabic and Islam*, XXXIX (2012), pp. 345–66
—, and Simonetta Calderini, *Women and the Fatimids in the World of Islam* (Edinburgh, 2006)
Dadoyan, Seta, *The Fatimid Armenians: Cultural and Political Interaction in the Near East* (Leiden, 1997)
Daftary, Farhad, *The Ismāʿīlīs. Their History and Doctrines*, 2nd edn (Cambridge, 2007)
—, and Shainool Jiwa, eds, *The Fatimid Caliphate: Diversity of Traditions* (London, 2018)
Fierro, Maribel, 'On Fāṭimī and Fāṭimiyyūn', *Jerusalem Studies in Arabic and Islam*, XX (1996), pp. 130–61
Frenkel, Miriam, 'Medieval Alexandria – Life in a Port City', *Al-Masaq: Journal of the Medieval Mediterranean*, XXVI/1 (2014), pp. 5–35
Goitein, Shelomo D., *A Mediterranean Society: The Jewish Communities of the World as Portrayed in the Documents of the Cairo Geniza*, 6 vols (Berkeley, CA, 1999)
Haji, Amin, 'Institutions of Justice in Fatimid Egypt', in *Islamic Law: Social and Historical Contexts*, ed. 'Aziz al-Azmeh (London and New York, 1988), pp. 198–214
Halm, Heinz, *The Empire of the Mahdi: The Rise of the Fatimids*, trans. Michael Bonner (Leiden, 1996)
—, *The Fatimids and Their Traditions of Learning* (London, 2001)
—, 'The Isma'ili Oath of Allegiance and the "Sessions of Wisdom"', in *Mediaeval Isma'ili History and Thought*, ed. Farhad Daftary (Cambridge, 2001), pp. 91–116
—, *Die Kalifen von Kairo. Die Fatimiden in Ägypten, 973–1074* (Munich, 2003)
—, *Kalifen und Assassinen: Ägypten und der vordere Orient zur Zeit der ersten Kreuzzüge, 1074–1171* (Munich, 2014)
Hamdani, Abbas, and François de Blois, 'A Re-Examination of al-Mahdī's Letter to the Yemenites on the Genealogy of the Fatimid Caliphs', *Journal of the Royal Asiatic Society of Great Britain and Ireland*, CXV/2 (1983), pp. 173–207
Hamdani, Sumaiya, *Between Revolution and State: The Path to Fatimid Statehood* (London, 2006)
Hunsberger, Alice C., *Nasir Khusraw, The Ruby of Badakhshan: A Portrait of the Persian Poet, Traveller and Philosopher* (London, 2000)
[Ibn al-Haytham, Abu 'Abd Allah Ja'far, *Kitab al-Munazarat*], *The Advent of the Fatimids: A Contemporary Shi'i Witness Account of Politics in the Early Islamic World*, ed. and trans. Wilfred Madelung and Paul E. Walker (London, 2000)
[Ibn Ridwan], *Medieval Islamic Medicine: Ibn Riḍwān's Treatise 'On the Prevention of Bodily Ills in Egypt'*, ed. and trans. Michael W. Dols (Berkeley, CA, 1984)
[Idris 'Imad al-Din], *The Fatimids and Their Successors in Yaman: The History of an Islamic Community*, Arabic edition and English summary of *Idrīs*

'Imād al-Dīn's 'Uyūn al-akhbār, vol. VII, ed. Ayman Fu'ād Sayyid in collaboration with Paul E. Walker and Maurice A. Pomerantz (London and New York, 2002)
Ivanow, Wladimir, 'The Organization of the Fatimid Propaganda', *Journal of the Bombay Branch of the Royal Asiatic Society*, new series, XV (1939), pp. 1–35
[Ja'far b. 'Ali] *Sīrat Ja'far al-ḥājib* (full original title *Sirat Ja'far al-hajib: sirat al-hajib Ja'far b. 'Ali wa khuruj al-imam al-Mahdi min Salamiyya wa wusuluhu ila Sijilmasa wa khurujuhu minha ila Raqqada)*, comp. Muhammad b. Muhammadal-Yamani, trans. Wladimir Ivanow, *Ismaili Tradition Concerning the Rise of the Fatimids* (London, 1942), pp. 184–223
Jiwa, Shainool, *The Fatimids*, vol. I: *The Rise of a Muslim Empire* (London, 2018)
—, *The Fatimids*, vol. II: *The Rule from Egypt* (London, 2023)
—, 'Governance and Pluralism under the Fatimids (909–996 CE)', in *The Shi'i World: Pathways in Tradition and Modernity*, ed. Farhad Daftary, Amin Sajoo and Shainool Jiwa (London and New York, 2015), pp. 111–30
—, 'Kinship, Camaraderie and Contestation Fatimid Relations with the Ashraf in the Fourth AH/Tenth CE Century', *Al-Masaq: Journal of the Medieval Mediterranean*, XXVIII/3 (2016), pp. 242–64
Kahle, Paul, 'Die Schätze der Fatimiden', *Zeitschrift der Deutschen Morgenländischen Gesellschaft*, LXXXIX/14, nos 3/4 (1935), pp. 329–62
Klemm, Verena, *Memoirs of a Mission: The Ismaili Scholar, Statesman and Poet al-Mu'ayyad fi'l-Dīn al-Shīrāzī* (London, 2003)
Lev, Yaacov, *The Administration of Justice in Medieval Egypt: From the 7th to the 12th Century* (Edinburgh, 2020)
—, 'Army, Regime and Society in Fāṭimid Egypt 358–487/968–1094', *International Journal of Middle East Studies*, XIX/3 (1987), pp. 337–66
—, 'The Fāṭimid Vizier Ya'qūb ibn Killis and the Beginning of the Fāṭimid Administration in Egypt', *Der Islam*, LVIII (1981), pp. 237–49
—, *State and Society in Fatimid Egypt* (Leiden, 1991)
Lewis, Bernard, *The Origins of Ismā'īlism: A Study of the Historical Background of the Fāṭimid Caliphate* (Cambridge, 1940)
Madelung, Wilfred, and Paul E. Walker, eds and trans., *Affirming the Imamate: Early Fatimid Teachings in the Islamic West: An Arabic Critical Edition and English Translation of Works Attributed to Abū 'Abd Allāh al-Shī'ī and His Brother Abu'l-'Abbās* (London, 2021)
Majid, 'Abd al-Mu'nim, *Zuhur khilafat al-fatimiyya wa suqutiha fi Misr: al-tarikh al-siyasi* (Alexandria, 1968)
[Mansur al-'Azizi al-Jawdhari] ed. and trans. Hamid Haji, *Inside the Immaculate Portal: A History from Early Fatimid Archives. A New Edition and English Translation of Manṣūr al-'Azīzī al-Jawdharī's Biography of al-Ustādh Jawdhar, the Sīrat al-Ustādh Jawdhar* (London and New York, 2012)
al-Maqrizi, Taqi al-Din, *Al-Bayan wa'l-i'rab 'amma bi ard Misr min al-a'rab* (Cairo, 2006)
—, *al-Mawa'iz wa'l-i'tibar bi-dhikr al-khitat wa'l-athar*, 2 vols (Beirut, rep. [197?]); ed. Ayman Fu'ad Sayyid, 4 vols (London, 2002–3)

—, *Itti'az al-hunafa' bi-akhbar al-a'imma al-fatimiyyin al-khulafa'*, ed. Jamal al-Din al-Shayyal and Muhammad Hilmi M. Ahmad, 3 vols (Cairo, 1967–73); ed. Ayman Fu'ad Sayyid, 4 vols (London, 2012)

—, *Kitab al-Muqaffa al-kabir*, ed. M. al-Ya'lawi, 8 vols (Beirut, 1987)

—, *Le traité des famines de Maqrīzī*, trans. Gaston Wiet (Leiden, 1962)

Melikian-Chirvani, Assadullah Souren, ed., *The World of the Fatimids*, exh. cat., Aga Khan Museum (Toronto, 2018)

al-Musabbihi, Muhammad, *Akhbar Misr fi sanatay 414–415 H.*, ed. William G. Millward (Cairo, 1980); ed. Ayman Fu'ad Sayyid and Thierry Bianquis, *Tome quarantieme de la chronique d'Egypte de Musabbiḥī*, 366–420/977–1029 (Cairo, 1978)

Nasir-i Khusraw, *Nāṣer-e Khosraw's Book of Travels* (*Safarnama*), ed. and trans. Wheeler M. Thackston Jr (Albany, NY, 1986)

al-Nishaburi, Ahmad, *Istitārul'-Imām* (full original title *Istitar al-imam wa tafarruq al-du'at*), trans. Wladimir Ivanow, *Ismaili Tradition Concerning the Rise of the Fatimids* (London, 1942), pp. 157–84

—, *A Code of Conduct: A Treatise on the Etiquette of the Fatimid Ismaili Mission. A critical edition of the Arabic text and English translation of Aḥmad b. Ibrāhīm al-Naysābūrī's al-Risāla al-mūjaza al-kāfiya fī ādāb al-du'āt*, ed. and trans. Verena Klemm and Paul E. Walker (London, 2012)

Pradines, Stéphane, and Sher R. Khan, 'Fatimid Gardens: Archaeological and Historical Perspectives', *Bulletin of the School of Oriental and African Studies*, LXXIX/3 (2016), pp. 1–30

Pruitt, Jennifer A., *Building the Caliphate: Construction, Destruction, and Sectarian Identity in Early Fatimid Architecture* (New Haven, CT, and London, 2020)

al-Qadi al-Nu'man, *Da'a'im al-Islam wa dhikr al-halal wa'l-haram wa'l-qadaya wa'l-ahkam*, ed. Asaf A. A. Fyzee, 2 vols (Cairo, 1969)

—, *Iftitah al-da'wa*, trans. Hamid Haji, *Founding the Fatimid State. The Rise of an Early Islamic Empire. An Annotated English Translation of al-Qāḍī al-Nu'mān's Iftitāḥ al-Da'wa* (London and New York, 2006)

—, *Kitab al-Majalis wa'l-musayarat*, ed. Habib al-Faqi, I. Shabbuh and M. al-Ya'lawi (Tunis, 1978)

[Qadi b. al-Zubayr] trans. Ghāda al-Hijjāwī al-Qaddūmī, *Book of Gifts and Rarities: Kitāb al-Hadāyā wa al-tuḥaf* (Cambridge, MA, 1996)

Rapoport, Yossef, and Emilie Savage-Smith, eds and trans., *An Eleventh-Century Egyptian Guide to the Universe: The Book of Curiosities* (Leiden and Boston, MA, 2014)

—, and —, *Lost Maps of the Caliphs: Drawing the World in Eleventh-Century Cairo* (Chicago, IL, 2018)

Raymond, André, *Cairo*, trans. Willard Wood (Cambridge, MA, and London, 2000)

Rustow, Marina, 'Formal and Informal Patronage among Jews in the Islamic East: Evidence from the Geniza Documents', *al-Qanṭara*, XXIX/2 (2008), pp. 341–82

—, 'A Petition to a Woman at the Fatimid Court (413–414 A.H./1022–23 C.E.)', *Bulletin of the School of Oriental and African Studies*, LXXIII/1 (2010), pp. 1–27

Sanders, Paula, *Creating Medieval Cairo* (Cairo and New York, 2008)
—, *Ritual, Politics, and the City in Fatimid Cairo* (Albany, NY, 1994)
Sayyid, Ayman F., *La capitale de l'Égypte jusqu'a l'époque Fatimide: al-Qāhira et al-Fusṭāṭ. Essay de reconstruction topographique* (Beirut, 1998)
Shenoda, Maryann M., et al., eds, *Medieval Encounters. Special Issue: Non-Muslim Communities in Fatimid Egypt (Tenth–Twelfth Centuries* CE), XXI/4–5 (2015)
Stern, Samuel M., *Fāṭimid Decrees: Original Documents from the Fāṭmid Chancery* (London, 1964)
[Usama b. Munqidh], *An Arab-Syrian Gentleman and Warrior in the Period of the Crusades*, trans. Philip K. Hitti (New York, 2000)
Straface, Antonella, *Gli Ismailiti: storia e dottrina* (Rome, 2019)
Vatikiotis, Panayiotis J., *The Fatimid Theory of State* (Lahore, 1981)
Vermeulen, Urbain, and Kristoff D'Hulster, eds, *Egypt and Syria in the Fatimid, Ayyubid and Mamluk Eras*, vol. V (Leuven, Paris and Dudley, MA, 2007)
Walker, Paul E., *Caliph of Cairo: Al-Hakim bi-'Amr Allah, 996–1021* (Cairo and New York, 2012)
—, 'The Fatimid Caliph al-'Azīz and His Daughter Sitt al-Mulk: A Case of Delayed but Eventual Succession to Rule by a Woman', *Journal of Persianate Studies*, IV/1 (2011), pp. 30–44
—, *The Fatimids* (Leiden, 2023)
—, *Ḥamīd al-Dīn al-Kirmānī: Ismaili Thought in the Age of al-Ḥākim* (London, 1999)
—, 'Libraries, Book Collection and the Production of Texts by the Fatimids', *Intellectual History of the Islamicate World*, IV/1–2 (2016), pp. 9–21
—, 'Succession to Rule in the Shiite Caliphate', *Journal of the American Research Center in Egypt*, XXXII (1995), pp. 239–64

ACKNOWLEDGEMENTS

In the same way a portrait artist works alone in the studio while facing the sitter, so has the writing of this portrait of the Fatimids been for me a solitary journey. A solo endeavour, but an animated one nonetheless. As I worked my way through capturing the smiles and the wrinkles, the beauty spots and the warts, the glint in the eye but also the looks of horror of my sitter – the Fatimid dynasty and its age – unsolicited cups of tea and assortments of treats appeared on my desk courtesy of Chris. After a lifetime together, he knows what I need even before I do. Over time friends and family, near and far, have provided most welcome doses of distraction, interruption and entertainment opportunities, thus forcing me out of spending my days locked in a tenth- or twelfth-century court in the company of some crafty vizier or astute princess. You know who you are: I thank you all.

As with everything else in the world, the COVID-19 pandemic and the lockdowns that followed impacted on the research process involved in the writing of this book. With sudden limited access to sources and resources, scholars in this field came to the rescue by sending me their papers or making themselves available for consultation in writing or via cloud-based video conferencing. Thank you for your cooperation. The closure of libraries made us even more aware of how precious these institutions are. In London I have benefited immensely from having access to the resources of the Aga Khan Library and the Ismaili Special Collections Unit, at the Aga Khan Centre, London, the British Library and the library of the School of Oriental and African Studies, University of London. I take this opportunity to express my gratitude to their respective librarians and staff for facilitating my research and for all the help I have received.

I salute my former colleagues at Middlesex University, London, for creating the friendly and collaborative work environment that provided me with the space to focus on this project. As an amateur portrait artist, I was inspired in the conceptual framing of this book as a portrait by drawing sessions I have been attending at the Royal Drawing School, London. Many thanks to my tutor and fellow artists at my regular group for their support in honing my ability to look rather than see, to sharpen my pencil in crafting lines into written narratives.

Last but not least I am grateful for the trust that Reaktion Books has placed in me in writing this book. The support I have received from the editorial team, especially Alex Ciobanu and Amy Salter, has been tremendous.

Looking back, it has not been a solitary journey after all.

PHOTO ACKNOWLEDGEMENTS

The author and publishers wish to express their thanks to the sources listed below for illustrative material and/or permission to reproduce it. Some locations of artworks are also given below, in the interest of brevity:

akg-images: 9 (Hervé Champollion), 41 (Erich Lessing/Museum of Islamic Art, Cairo); © The al-Sabah Collection, Dar al-Athar al-Islamiyyah, Kuwait: 38 (Inv. no. LNS 48 I), 49 (Inv. no. LNS 55 W); Alamy Stock Photo/Album: 10 (Museu de Lleida); Art Institute of Chicago: 30; The Ben-Zvi Institute, Jerusalem: 35; Biblioteca Nacional de España, Madrid (VITR/26/2, fol. 148r), photo World Digital Library: 18; Bodleian Library, University of Oxford (MS Arab. c. 90): 23 (fols. 23b–24a), 24 (fols. 32b–33a), 32 (fol. 34a); Cambridge University Library (T-S 18J3.9): 28; Cathédrale Sainte-Anne d'Apt: 40; The Cleveland Museum of Art, OH: 21; photos Delia Cortese: 7 (Museo Arqueológico Nacional, Madrid), 31 (Palazzo Abatellis, Palermo), 51; The Dallas Museum of Art, TX (Keir Collection of Islamic Art on loan to the Dallas Museum of Art, K.1.2014.1.A–B): 39; © Germanisches Nationalmuseum, Nuremberg/Bridgeman Images: 22; The Getty Research Institute, Los Angeles, photo courtesy of the Getty's Open Content Program: 48 (Duomo di Sant'Andrea Apostolo, Veroli); courtesy of Russell Harris, The Institute of Ismaili Studies, London: 1; © Ismaili Special Collections Unit, The Institute of Ismaili Studies, London (photos Nourmamadcho Nourmamadchoev): 5 and 6 (CWM C 301), 11 and 12 (CWM C 399), 17 (Zahid Ali Collection, MS 1003, p. 46), 52 and 53 (CWM C); © The Israel Museum, Jerusalem: 25 (Gift of Mr and Mrs Ralph Harari, London, B65.04.0165, photo Nahum Slapak), 50 (Israel Antiquities Authority, photo Meidad Suchowolski); iStock.com: 54 (sharrocks); photo Dennis Jarvis/Flickr, CC BY-SA 2.0: 55 (Kunsthistorisches Museum, Vienna); photo Nizhat Khaddam, Studio Tareq for Photography, Salamiyya, courtesy of Nuha Al-Sha'ar: 3; Los Angeles County Museum of Art (LACMA): 19; The Metropolitan Museum of Art, New York: 26; Museo Nazionale del Bargello, Florence (Inv. no. 8000/16), photo Gabinetto Fotografico delle Gallerie degli Uffizi, Florence: 8; Museum of Islamic Art, Cairo: 34; Museum für Islamische Kunst, Staatliche Museen zu Berlin: 20 and 29 (photos Johannes Kramer, CC BY-SA 4.0), 36 (photo Christian Krug, CC BY-SA 4.0); photos © Bernard O'Kane: 14 (Museum of Islamic Art, Cairo), 42, 43 and 44 (Museum of Islamic Art, Cairo), 46, 47 (Museum of Islamic Art, Cairo); from Paradox Interactive AB's award-winning game *Crusader Kings® II*, © 2012–2021 Paradox Interactive AB: 45; courtesy of Protomonastero di Santa Chiara, Assisi, through the kind intercession of Franco Alunno Rossetti and Mauro Botti: 56; courtesy of Science History Institute, Philadelphia, PA: 2; Shutterstock.com: 15 (Mohamed Barboura), 16 (SyahmiJamil), 27 (Andreas Zerndl), 33 (PRILL); SuperStock/Interfoto: 37; © Tareq Rajab Museum, Kuwait (MET-76-TSR): 4; Topkapı Sarayı Müzesi Kütüphanesi, Istanbul (MS Revan 1638, fol. 254b): 13.

INDEX

Illustration numbers are indicated by *italics*